PAUL NEWMAN
A Life

PAUL NEWMAN

A Life

SHAWN LEVY

Harmony Books New York

Title page photo credit: © Bettmann/Corbis
Part title photo credits: Parts One and Three are courtesy of Photofest; Part
Two is courtesy of Special Collections, Cleveland State University Library;
Parts Four, Five, and Six are from the author's collection.

Library of Congress Cataloging-in-Publication Data
Levy, Shawn.
Paul Newman: a life/Shawn Levy.
p.   cm.
1. Newman, Paul, 1925–2008.   2. Motion picture actors and
actresses—United States—Biography.   I. Title.
PN2287.N44L48   2009
791.4302'8092—dc22
[B]   2009011220

ISBN 978-0-307-35375-7

Printed in the United States of America

Design by Lauren Dong

10 9 8 7 6 5 4 3 2 1

First Edition

Part One

AMERICA DOESN'T HAVE A NATIONAL EPIC, BUT *Our Town* MIGHT do in a pinch. The cracker-barrel homilies; the good-natured ironies; the snapshots of bygone ways; the razor-sharp observations couched in polite language; the hints of pain; the hesitance toward joy; the sneaky surges of emotion; the climax that brings a welling to your eyes despite yourself. It contains us, Thornton Wilder's chestnut.

That's why it can sometimes feel that if you've seen one production of it, you've seen 'em all.

Or maybe not.

Take this one—in particular, take the male leads.

The Stage Manager is a hawkish fellow: slender, purposeful, knowing, vigilant. He dresses for comfort and doesn't care if his collar is straight or if his tie is askew. Disheveled, with his spectacles perched on the tip of his nose and a vaguely distracted air, he's still rakishly handsome; clearly he was a corker in his time. He appears to have lived every vicissitude of life, and while experience hasn't entirely softened him, it has provided him a store of indulgence to mete out, judiciously but amiably, as he sees fit. There's no doubt that he can size a body up in a few piercing measures, and there's no doubt, either, that his arithmetic is sure. But such is his air of decency and authority that you find yourself hoping he deems you worthy.

George Gibbs, the youthful hero, is another matter: an all-American boy with muscles in his shoulders and, you can't help but suspect, in his head. His heart is in the right place, heaven knows, even if he must occasionally be reminded of just where that place is. He's a handsome thing, and enthusiasms burble out of him infectiously. His gaze is open, and his springy mien belies a real zest for life. But when he takes the time to notice smaller things or surprises himself by stumbling upon a sincere emotion, he turns puppyish. He even, caught up in the swell of love, croons; you wouldn't tune a piano to it, but it's sincere.

Their interactions are brief but memorable. At one moment the Stage Manager assumes the aspect of a biddy and lashes out at poor, dim George for tossing a ball to himself in the middle of the road. "You got no business playing baseball on Main Street," he cackles in an old lady's voice, cowing the boy, and you reckon he's getting a kick out of his charade as the lad dutifully scampers off.

Later, when George escorts his sweetheart, Emily, to the drugstore for an ice cream soda, the Stage Manager takes on the persona of Mr. Morgan, proprietor and counterman. Precisely and warmly, he crafts the fountain treats for the youngsters, and when it turns out that George has forgotten his pocket money at home, he refuses to accept the boy's gold watch as collateral for the debt: "I'll trust you ten years, George—not a day over."

You sense affection in the older man and, equally, respect in the younger; the mutuality is warming. And as is so often the case, the warmth arises not only from the material but from the actors themselves—a real coup of casting, in fact.

The old man has acted for Leo McCarey, who directed the Marx Brothers, and Michael Curtiz, who made *Casablanca*, and he appeared many times on live television during that medium's golden age. The kid has worked with the Coen Brothers and Martin Scorsese and Sam Mendes and lent his voice to a big-budget Pixar movie *and* the video game version of it.

The old man is world famous: you can't go to the supermarket, the video store, or the Indianapolis Motor Speedway without encountering his image or his legacy. You think of Henry Fonda, Humphrey Bogart, and James Stewart as his equals. The kid is making a big name for himself, but he keeps getting compared to other actors, often as a way of dismissing him or counting him short: Marlon Brando, most often, and James Dean.

One has just turned thirty, has been married for six years, and has three children, the oldest not quite five. The other is seventy-eight, with his forty-fifth anniversary coming up and five grown daughters and a pair of grandkids with whom to celebrate it.

Physically, they share some traits: wavy hair, icy blue eyes, a classical handsomeness that looks patrician on the old fellow and preppy on the kid, and a springy grace that makes the young man seem coltish and the old man seem spry.

But their personalities are pretty distinct. The old guy is serious, a World War II vet who attended Kenyon College and the Yale School of Drama on the GI Bill and dreamed of becoming a teacher and takes an active part in politics; he's raised hundreds of millions of dollars for charity and served as president of the Actors Studio. The young guy is famous for his beer drinking and his practical jokes and his goofball sense of humor and his love of fast cars and motorcycles and his roles as antiauthoritarian rebels; he's already created a couple of parts on Broadway that have maintained a place in the national repertoire and made a few indelible TV dramas.

The older man you know: Paul Newman, playing the Stage Manager in the Westport County Playhouse production of *Our Town* as filmed at the Booth Theater on Broadway in early 2003.

And the younger man, well, you know him too: Paul Newman, playing George Gibbs in the same play, adapted as a musical for NBC television's *Producers' Showcase* in September 1955.

Between those two performances sits an entire career and, indeed, an entire life—not only of one man but of the culture in which he thrived.

THE BLIND, impetuous vigor of youth; the wry, still acceptance of maturity; the progress of an artist in his craft; the maturation of a soul, a mind, a body; the life of a man and the half-century of history he lived and echoed and symbolized and even shaped: Paul Newman's story is all of it.

From a burgeoning Jazz Age suburb to a torpedo bomber in the Pacific, from the womb of academia to the free-for-all of Broadway and live TV, from the gilded cage of a Hollywood studio contract to the wild freedom of directing films for his own production company, from the filth and noise and danger of professional auto racing to the staid and venerable confines of the Philanthropy Hall of Fame, Paul Newman's life is a blazon of the American century, incorporating the very best national traits in a compact and comely package.

For fifty years, on-screen and off, Newman vividly embodied certain tendencies in the American male character: active and roguish and earnest and sly and determined and vulnerable and brave and humble and reliable and compassionate and fair. He was a man of his time, and that time ranged from World War II to the contemporary era of digitally animated feature films. He was equally at home on Hollywood soundstages, in theatrical workshops, in the pits of racetracks, and especially on the blessedly raucous fields and in the log cabins and swimming holes of the camps he built and maintained for seriously ill children. The world was his for the claiming—and he claimed only the bit that he felt was reasonably due him, and he gave back more, by far, than he ever took.

He was ridiculously handsome and trim, with a face that belonged on an ancient coin, eyes that stunned and dazed even cynics, and an athlete's compact, lithe, and peppy body. Having fallen into acting as a profession, he would have been guaranteed at least minimal success by sheer virtue of his physical charms. If he'd had no talent or tenacity or intellect or drive, he might still have enjoyed fame and riches. Put him in a dinner jacket, and he could sit confidently at table with presidents or poets or kings. He looked the part—in fact, he looked *any* part, virtually, that he was asked to play.

But he was smart and cagey and suspicious of fortune too easily won, and he was scrupulous in distinguishing the things that came to him through luck from those he felt he'd earned. He opted to live as far as reasonable from Hollywood, preferred barn coats and blue jeans to tuxedos, and chose the company of troupers and mechanics and beer-swillers over that of celebrities and swells and hobnobbers every time. There was crust and vinegar to him, and he relished the opportunity that his position in life afforded him to startle big shots with his sometimes downmarket tastes and preferences. And vice versa: he loved to sprinkle unexpected stardust in the humblest of contexts, just when he was taken for an ordinary joe.

He was, as he always insisted, a private man whose profession gave him a public face. And he grappled with the incongruity of that for a long time. If he was a cautious and shy fellow raised to a painfully puritanical ethos, he would learn to espouse his inner wildness by adapting personae—in life and in art—that camouflaged his insecurity and reticence in the cloth of exuberance and levity. If he was treated as a freak because of the inescapable fact that he was born beautiful, he would learn to turn that beauty into a tool of subterfuge, creating characters whose allure hid complex and painful depths. If his looks would make him a star, he would redirect that stardom into a benefit for others, slapping his face on labels for food products and creating staggering wealth—then giving all the money away. If he was, regardless of his age, a sex symbol, he would work hard at being a good husband and father. If his personal wealth meant that he could take up motor sports at a high level, he would work as tenaciously at racing as he did at acting and earn acceptance in that world through sheer application and diligently acquired skill. If things came easily to him, he determined to share the benefit he accrued.

FEW HAVE lived fuller or richer lives than Paul Newman, and at the time of his death, the world seemed to take stock for the first time of all the Paul Newmans it had known: the actor, the driver, the public citizen, the entrepreneur, the philanthropist, the family man. But as Newman always knew, it all began with luck—the genetics, upbringing, education, and career fortunes that uniquely enabled him to become a movie star. And it was as a movie star that he made his most obvious mark on the world.

In ways, he did it through the back door. Rarely appearing in obvious blockbusters, striving to reinvent himself by shedding his skin every few years, he compiled a cinematic résumé over five decades that was studded regularly with milestone films and performances: *Somebody Up There Likes Me; The Long, Hot Summer; The Left Handed Gun; Cat on a Hot Tin Roof; Exodus; The Hustler; Paris Blues; Hud; Harper;*

Hombre; Cool Hand Luke; Butch Cassidy and the Sundance Kid; The Life and Times of Judge Roy Bean; The Sting; The Towering Inferno; Buffalo Bill and the Indians; Slap Shot; Fort Apache the Bronx; Absence of Malice; The Verdict; The Color of Money; Blaze; Mr. & Mrs. Bridge; The Hudsucker Proxy; Nobody's Fool; Road to Perdition; Empire Falls; Cars. This is more than just a litany of estimable (and in some cases commercially gigantic) film titles. It's the trajectory of an actor determined to squirm away from preconceptions and to sharpen his artistic abilities at the same time. It stands against the very few similar lists of films ever compiled, and it spans eras, styles, generations. He wasn't the greatest American actor, and he was not even the greatest actor of his own vintage. But he was arguably the *most* American actor, the fellow whose roles and accumulated persona best captured the tenor of his times and his people.

Newman arrived in movies with the Method actor invaders of the 1950s and rode out their splashy heyday, becoming a commercial superstar while insistently pushing forward the boundaries of his craft. If you approached him initially only at the superficial level—the level of beauty, as it were—you might have mistaken him for Rock Hudson or Tony Curtis or Robert Wagner, handsome and capable, sure, but movie stars principally rather than craftsmen. Newman, though, had an internal discipline that demanded he make more of himself, and he earned, through sheer perseverance, a place alongside—and in ways, above—the Method gods Marlon Brando, Montgomery Clift, and James Dean. He was ultimately the one true superstar to emerge from the original Actors Studio generation, the most popular and enduring Stanislavskyan actor in American screen history, the only one who could sit comfortably alongside big-time Golden Era movie stars and newfangled subversive interlopers.

And he was able to bridge the space between those two brands of actors for decades. In a half-century of movies, the characteristic Newman role morphed from almost-too-pretty to dangerously sleek to deliberately wily to weathered and weary-wise. At his best he played against his looks—which may be why he is widely regarded as improving as an actor as he aged. And his instinct to cut against himself meant that he couldn't personify scions of wealth and privilege as well as he could ordinary men struggling with quotidian issues—particularly the struggles of fathers and sons who couldn't communicate adequately or, indeed, love each other enough. Even though he was a partner in a famed half-century marriage, he rarely played a romantic lead and, truly, never all that well. Rather, he played broken athletes, half-crazed outlaws, cocky scam artists, insouciant iconoclasts, and a long skein of rascally and unreliable private eyes, liquor salesmen, cops, spies, lawyers, loggers, and construction workers. Very occasionally—and perhaps only to satisfy a seemingly visceral need to avoid repeating himself—he played men of ramrod morality and authority whose positions as social leaders belied their failures as human beings; predictably, as with so many other types he essayed, he nailed them.

Taken as a whole, Newman's body of work nicely encapsulated the history of an in-between generation of American men who helped their fathers and uncles conquer the world in war and commerce but who could only watch—likely with some jealousy—as their younger siblings and their own children acted out on the native rebellious impulse to overturn everything. He fit in precisely with neither the Greatest Generation nor the Baby Boomers but represented instead a vital link in the American century—a band of men who were meant to inherit a system that was no longer reliably in place by the time their fathers willed it to them. Torn by the conflicting impulses to rule and rebel, his was arguably the pivotal generation of the twentieth century, and Newman, almost unconsciously, was its actor laureate.

NEWMAN WAS proud of his profession, eternally grateful to his teachers and peers and colleagues and to the writers and directors who created the roles and the projects he appeared in. But like other men's men who take up acting, he could find himself embarrassed by the fussiness of his craft, and he had a need to assert himself in other, more physical areas of life in order to pass muster with himself. And so auto racing, as alien a pastime to the arts as could be imagined, became a second world for him. Picking it up in his mid-forties, he was seen at first as a dilettante. But his bulldog tenacity (and, too, his native athleticisim and his uncommon financial means) took him to remarkable levels of accomplishment: four national amateur titles, two professional race victories, a second-place finish at the famed twenty-four-hour race in Le Mans, and, at age seventy, a victory in his team's class in the 24 Hours of Daytona—making him the oldest person to win a sanctioned auto race ever, anywhere. As a team owner in even higher classes of competition, his success was greater still: 8 national titles and 107 individual race victories—a massive haul.

And he was nearly as accomplished an entrepreneur as he was a race-car driver and owner. As a purveyor of food products, a business that he didn't enter until his mid-fifties, he created new standards for the elimination of preservatives and the use of fresh ingredients in salad dressings, spaghetti sauces, salsas, and snack foods. And when he expanded into organic foods, his became one of the nation's most recognized and trusted brands. Those businesses led to another area of achievement: philanthropy. Aside from the millions of dollars and thousands of hours he donated privately over the years, his Newman's Own Foundation, which gave away all posttax profits from the food businesses, doled out more than $250 million in its first twenty-five years of existence. And in the final years before his death, Newman bequeathed his share of the company—valued at nearly $120 million—for similar distribution.

It's a staggering list of achievements—the acting, the racing, the earnings, the giving away—and he could sometimes seem uneasy about it all and, especially, about the image that the rest of the world had of him as a result. The great sportswriter Jim Murray, who met him on a racetrack, opined, "He's probably the only guy in America who doesn't want to be Paul Newman." And William Goldman, who wrote *Harper* and *Butch Cassidy and the Sundance Kid*, remarked similarly, "I don't think Paul Newman really thinks he is Paul Newman in his head."

In rare unguarded moments, he admitted as much. "The toughest role is playing Paul Newman," he told a reporter. "My own personality is so vapid and bland, I have to go steal the personalities of other people to be effective."

He wasn't blowing smoke. He was a man of great gifts, but he was genuinely humble, believing in work and family and luck and community and the greater good—and if a surfeit of that good slopped up onto his plate over the years, he would be sure to share it, and he would do so in the best humor he could. Somehow he had turned the gifts life and luck had granted him into things he could multiply and give back. Occasionally along the way he would misstep or be discourteous or make a wrong aesthetic choice or drive ill-advisedly or whatnot, but what he never did was hole up, retreat, give in, surrender, or fail to engage.

"What I would really like to put on my tombstone," he once said, "is that I was part of my time."

And he was.

Part Two

One

SHAKER HEIGHTS WAS A DREAM WITHIN A DREAM, PART GARden of Eden, part Camelot, part World of Tomorrow.

It had lawns and trees and winding roads and handsome homes and golf courses and some of the nation's best schools and rapid transit into the heart of a major city. Its parks were slices of raw wilderness left unspoiled and right at hand to enjoy. Its commercial heart, Shaker Square, was a modern, well-appointed shopping district built to recall a New England village green. The town was among the crests of that great energetic wave of American expansion known as the Roaring Twenties. A man who brought his family to live there could count himself a true success. And children born there could count themselves truly lucky.

Or so it would seem.

"Shaker Heights was a cloister," said Paul Newman, who grew up there from the age of two.

It happens that he was a restless sort. But it also happens to be an apt description: the town had, in fact, been built on hallowed ground.

Shaker Heights stood about ten miles from Public Square, the traditional heart of Cleveland, Ohio. Originally known as North Union, the area had first been settled in the 1820s by a colony of Shakers, one of those Protestant sects that thrived in young America and that took its name from the physically vigorous style of prayer practiced by its adherents. They called their new home "the Valley of God's Pleasure," but it didn't please God for them to thrive there for long: Shakers are, by doctrine, celibate, increasing their numbers only through adoption and conversion; by 1889 a lack of newcomers meant that the once-thriving community of hundreds had dwindled to twenty-nine aging folks who could no longer maintain their homes or work their land. They sold their bit of heaven—1,366 acres, including mills and other buildings—to a consortium of Cleveland investors for $316,000. The land was platted and renamed Shaker Heights, but it lay undeveloped for more than a decade. In 1905 Mantis and Oris Van Sweringen, a truly eccentric pair of Cleveland developers, acquired and built on a few of the unused lots, creating a small village. Within two years the brothers had arranged for a streetcar line to come out to their parcels, acquired the rest of the undeveloped land, and unveiled their scheme for the town.

What they had in mind was an exacting utopian plan, an idyll far enough from the center of Cleveland to be free of smoke and noise and tumult but sufficiently close that commuting would be but a comfortable morning's and evening's ride. They imagined a genteel garden of a suburb governed by strict housing codes and covenants, a paradise for prosperous families built along the English bourgeois ideal of the village.

Anyone from Cleveland could appreciate the desire for such a retreat. The city from which Shaker Heights residents would be migrating was one of the chief cauldrons of the American industrial epoch, young and brawny and composed of equal parts New England propriety, frontier rascality, and immigrant vitality. And it was constantly growing: a century earlier it had been a wilderness outpost with a population of literally one, and by the end of the First World War it was a crucial hub of oil refining, iron and steel manufacturing, retail commerce, and transit—the sixth largest city in the United States.

As a city, Cleveland was a stripling: grimy, raucous, and rude, its Lake Erie waterfront choked with shipping traffic, its Cuyahoga River slow and fetid, its railyards and factories belching smoke and bleeding noise, its inner core a patchwork of immigrant neighborhoods teeming with imported sights, sounds, and smells. There was always a portion of the city dedicated to civic enrichment, organization, culture, the finer things; it had gentility. But it was far more impressed with its industry than with its soul. Anyone with a head to make a business for himself could create wonders in such a freewheeling environment; local boy John D. Rockefeller had already risen from dubious roots to become a metaphor for unimaginable wealth created out of thin air. But anyone with a head to make a life for himself would seek more easeful and commodious surroundings. And on the anticipation of fulfilling that urge the Van Sweringens' plan was realized.

BY 1920, when the Shaker Heights Rapid Transit line was inaugurated to speed riders to and from Cleveland, Shaker Heights had more than 1,600 residents; ten years later, it had swelled to more than 17,000, all living in single-family homes, none of which, per the Van Sweringens' plan, were exactly alike. Among the newcomers were Arthur S. Newman and his wife, Theresa, who invested in the dream of Shaker Heights in 1927, moving with their two sons, three-year-old Arthur and two-year-old Paul, into a big but not ostentatious $35,000 house at 2983 Brighton Road.

That was a lot of money for the time—nearly a half-million dollars in contemporary terms—but it was a remarkably flush moment for the national economy, and Art, as he was commonly known, wouldn't have spent it if he couldn't afford it. As secretary and treasurer of Newman-Stern, Cleveland's largest and best-liked sporting goods and consumer electronics store, he was a man who had created out of whole cloth a business built on a nation's increased devotion to entertainment and leisure time. The 1920s were a golden age of sports heroes—Babe Ruth, Red Grange, Bobby Jones, Bill Tilden, Jack Dempsey—and Newman-Stern could sell you not only all the gear and accoutrements that you'd require to emulate those greats but also a radio on which to listen to accounts of their achievements. As long as Clevelanders had money in their pockets and free time in which to spend it, the sporting goods and electronics business was sure to thrive.

So why not buy a nicer home? Previously the Newmans had lived in Cleveland Heights at 2100 Renrock Road, a small, trim, undistinguished single-family dwelling in a neighborhood close by a pair of busy streets—not the nicest part of Cleveland Heights but conveniently near the home of Arthur's older brother Joseph, who also happened to be his business partner and, probably, best friend in the world.

Brighton Road was an obvious step up. An English Tudor house with a peaked roof, it was a pleasant stroll away from Shaker Boulevard, the town's main artery, and it was set back from the curling street on which it stood by two rectangles of lawn and a handful of oak and maple trees. A fireplace dominated the front room, and big windows looked out over the front and back yards. There were more imposing homes on the street—indeed, there were outright mansions nearby. But the Newmans' home would certainly satisfy anyone's idea of comfort, modest luxury, and good taste.

For Arthur and Theresa, the house was a physical realization of the dreams of all those immigrants who had left Europe for America and a chance to make something of themselves. Arthur's parents were both born in the old country, as was Theresa herself. Their ability to rise from those roots to the prosperity of Shaker Heights was an instance of what many would call the American dream, and it was also a crucial element in what would become the character of their younger son.

CLEVELAND WAS a city of three genetic threads: the New England gentility of its founders, who hailed from Connecticut and tried to build a city according to their sense of propriety; the frontier wildness of its first inhabitants, who were drawn to a settlement on the edge of civilization, where the laws of nature and the frontier trumped those of governments; and the immigrant waves who filled and fueled the factories that came to define the city when industrialization supersized it from a town to a metropolis. In 1800 the hamlet had a single resident; eighty years later there were more than 260,000 Clevelanders, at least a third of whom were foreign-born.

Those immigrants are a crucial part of the city's story. They came from all the predictable places: England and Ireland and Germany at first, then Italy, Poland, Austria, Hungary, Bohemia, Russia, the Slavic states, Greece. They brought with them languages, customs, foods, social modes, and ways of worship never before seen in the region. Before 1836, for instance, there is no record of a Jewish resident in the place named for a man called Moses Cleaveland. By 1850, though, there were enough Jews in the city for them to have a theological falling-out: a pair of rival synagogues existed in an uneasy truce. By 1880 more than three thousand Jews were living in the booming city, mostly German, with more on the way from farther east.

Among that small but highly visible group of Jewish immigrants were Simon Newman, who had been born in 1853 in Hungary, and Hannah Cohn, who was born four years later in what was variously described as Hungary and Poland in legal documents throughout her life. Simon had arrived in the United States as a young, footloose man and found work as a dry goods peddler. Hannah had emigrated as a seventeen-year-old in 1870, along with her parents and some older siblings who moved on to settle in Arkansas.

Hannah and Simon were married in Cleveland on October 10, 1876, and they started a family almost immediately. In the 1880 census the Newmans listed two girls in their household: Minnie, not quite two, and an infant, Lillian. At nearly regular intervals they added to the family: a son, Aaron, born in 1881, followed by another pair of girls, Ottile (1884) and Gertrude (1886). By then Simon had graduated from peddler to manufacturer-merchant, with his own hat-making workshop and store, Newman's Millinery. Perhaps that accounts for the pause in births in the family. It wasn't until 1891 that Joseph, the second son, was born, followed by the last of the bunch, Arthur, in 1893.

The Newmans lived in the Jewish neighborhoods of Cleveland that resembled the Jewish enclaves of other big American cities, with push-carts and small family businesses and tenements pouring out old-world noises and aromas—cauldrons from which bright young men and women strove toward integration into American society through education and entry into social and cultural institutions. As in New York and Chicago, the Cleveland Jews established themselves relatively rapidly in professional, academic, and public pursuits throughout the city. They may even have made a quicker ascent there than in other places because of the youth of the city and its lightning rise and its sprawl.

Consider the Newmans. There were grander birthrights, even among recent immigrant families, than the Newmans' tiny family hat-making business. But Hannah and Simon were raising a remarkably creative and successful group of offspring. Their hat shop, for instance, would one day be immortalized in 1943 in *Polly Poppingay, Milliner,* a popular chapter book for children written by Gertrude Newman, who by then had already published another children's book, *The Story of Delicia, a Rag Doll.* Lillian, too, was a writer, producing verse in Yiddish. Ottile would become a schoolteacher and go on to head the drama group at the Euclid Avenue Temple, probably the most prominent synagogue in Cleveland; one of her sons, Richard Newman Campen, would graduate from Dartmouth College and forge a career as a noted historian of midwestern art and architecture.

The Newman boys were also to make marks on the world. Aaron attended some college and then became a reporter for the *Cleveland World* and, in 1906, the cofounder and business manager of the *Jewish Independent,* one of several Jewish papers in town. In 1927, that incredibly flush year, he inaugurated two enterprises: the Little Theater of the Movies, the first cinema in Cleveland devoted exclusively to foreign films, and the Cleveland Sportsman's and Outdoors Show, a trade fair at which manufacturers and retailers exhibited the latest recreational gear. During the Depression he wrote several satirical pamphlets about the fear of Communist strains in the New Deal.*

Quite a character. And yet his brother Joseph made even more of a splash in the world. No history of twentieth-century Cleveland is truly complete without mentioning, at least in passing, the ingenious, loquacious, mercurial, professorial, practical, affable, quixotic sprite born Joseph Simon Newman. Poet, inventor, orator, journalist, gadabout, boulevardier, and mensch, Joe Newman published science columns and light verse in newspapers, held patents on electronic communications gizmos, wrote the annual musical comedy revue for the City Club for more than three decades, taught at Cleveland College, served as a

---

* And he produced an accomplished son in William S. Newman, a classical pianist and music scholar who taught at the University of North Carolina for more than thirty years. (A concert series there still bears his name.) His three-volume *History of the Sonata,* first published in 1963, is considered a landmark, and he was also something of an eccentric, once crossing the United States on a motorcycle in a barnstorming concert tour.

trustee of the Cleveland Play House, published four books of poetry, and built with his kid brother, Arthur, the most successful sporting and recreational goods store between Chicago and New York.

Joe was always good with both words and numbers. After high school he spent a year at college and then worked for six months in an electrical lab. Then he went into retail, working for the big Stearn and Co. department store in the electrical, camera, and mechanical toy departments. All the while he fussed with electrical equipment and with words. Under the name Dr. Si. N. Tiffic, he wrote a kids' science column for the *Plain Dealer*, as well as a stream of light verse on public issues of the day. And he invented things—small radio and telegraph components, remote-controlled switches for toys and lights, a telephone system for children—some of which he took out patents for.

By 1913 he was married to the daughter of Maurice Weidenthal, who had cofounded the *Jewish Independent* with Aaron Newman. The following year he was on his own in business, using $500 to establish the Electro-Set Company, which built and sold lines of radio gear, telegraph equipment, electrical experiment kits, telescopes, and microscopes. The business took off, especially with kids, and moved from what was essentially a warehouse to a proper retail space. Joe had all kinds of schemes to grow the trade, such as a daily telegraph message to all customers to announce sales or new equipment: e-commerce in 1915! And because he knew his way around the insides of the equipment he sold, the shop became Cleveland's first supplier of radio parts; soon it was involved in a thriving national mail-order enterprise.

Unfortunately, World War I put an end to the sale of wireless equipment to civilians, and Electro-Set was suddenly deprived of a large part of its business. In 1917 it morphed, changing its name to Newman-Stern and mixing in sporting goods with the remaining lines of scientific and electrical equipment. Joe would serve as president of the company, and he had two partners: Arnold L. Stern, who was strictly an investor, and as secretary and treasurer his own younger brother, Art, a bachelor and failed journalist then twenty-three years old.

ARTHUR SIGMUND NEWMAN was born on August 29, 1893, and soon afterward the family was altered forever; by the time of his second birthday, his father had died. Art, as he was always known, would be raised by his sisters and brothers, all still living at home as late as 1900. Hannah ran Newman's Millinery in the bustling Jewish commercial district on Cleveland's West Twenty-sixth Street. Like Joe, who was only two years older, Art attended Central High School; like Aaron, he was drawn into newspaper work. Not long after high school he founded, published, wrote, and solicited ads for a local business circular, the *Home Advertiser.* He parlayed that into a job in the advertising and news departments of the *Cleveland Press,* where he proved unlucky: in 1915, phoning into the newsroom to report a scoop regarding a contentious strike at the Mechanical Rubber Company, he was inadvertently connected to the rival *Cleveland News,* which published his story while his own paper got nothing; they canned him.

And so Art went straight to work at Electro-Set, finding in Joe not only a surrogate parent (Hannah had died in 1913 when Art was seventeen) but a perfectly complementary partner as well. A few years later, interviewed in a Cleveland business journal, Joe said: "Art and I are as alike as sunup and sundown. I am the maniac of the business— the long-haired dreamer. At least that's Art's diagnosis. He is the hard-shelled, brass-tacks man. Every business needs both types. One counteracts the other." The brothers would work together side by side for decades: Joe a wise and wacky jester filled with unpredictable energies, Art balding and sad-eyed and diligent and upright and exact. (Even in his twenties he looked older than his older brother.)

The Newman-Stern Company they built would break all sorts of new ground: it was the first entity in Cleveland to broadcast election results by radio and the first to offer steel fishing rods and steel-shafted golf clubs; its sale of microscopes for children virtually invented the field. In 1921 the business relocated to a large downtown storefront, where it would expand again after just seven years and then again after World War II, by which time it had become the premier destination in the region for sporting equipment: baseball, camping and fishing gear, skis, small boats, tents, as well as radios, even television sets. And it always had a hand in gizmos: in 1946 Art stumbled upon a sweet deal on army surplus bombsight parts and gyroscopes and did a rampaging business liquidating it.*

In all that time the brothers remained extremely close. Joe Newman filed away his personal correspondence for decades, including letters written by Art while Joe was off on business trips or family vacations with his wife and two sons. Dutifully, Art would tell him which shipments had arrived, which sales items were moving or not, what the next round of advertising would promote, and other mundane matters. There was fluency and energy in Art's prose but rarely anything very personal or revelatory. On the odd occasion when Art would encounter Joe's family during the latter's absence, he would note it, but never sentimentally. In comparison, Joe's letters to his brother, some of which he kept carbon copies of, were filled with levity—he would often insist that Art actually enjoy a vacation and not worry about business while on holiday—and Joe's letters back and forth with his wife and sons were extremely tender, playful, open, and rich. Art was the worker ant, Joe the butterfly: together they were a natural team.

Before he built this empire, though, Art Newman had to emerge as his own man. On December 7, 1917, he enlisted in the army reserve corps; he was called up to active duty three weeks later and lasted in the service until he was honorably discharged in February 1919. He never went overseas but rather spent his time with the Quartermaster Corps in Johnston, Florida, and later in Maryland and Virginia. He attained the rank of corporal and served mainly in motor pools, a dreary existence that he described in letters to Joe and in accounts of military life in the *Plain Dealer*. By 1920 he was back in Cleveland and living on East Ninetieth Street, the core of one of the city's old Jewish communities. And sometime between then and 1925, he got married.

IF THE marriage of Arthur and Theresa Newman is clouded in a mist of half-facts, that may be because Theresa Newman herself came from

---

* A version of this coup is credited to a character in the 1984 film *Harry & Son*, which Paul Newman cowrote and directed.

a more imprecisely chronicled background than did her husband. She was of either Hungarian or Bohemian stock and seems to have been born overseas sometime in the 1890s or maybe even earlier. She came to America at perhaps age four, perhaps in 1901. In one of the earliest official documents associated with her life—the birth certificate of her second son—she claimed to have been born in 1897 in Homona, Austria, citing the Hungarian name for the modern-day Slovakian town of Humenne. But that was only one version of her story.

How she arrived in America and with whom is a mystery. Her father bore the Christian name Stephen, but in legal documents over the years his surname was variously rendered as Fetzer (which Theresa and her sons used most commonly), Fetsko (favored by most of Theresa's siblings), Fetzko, Felsko, and, once, Fecke. Stephen was born in 1854 or 1855; by one account, he arrived in America in 1890 at the port of Philadelphia; by another, he came through New York in 1889. (Both dates, crucially, predate Theresa's year of birth, as she identified it.) On August 11, 1902, he married Mary Polinak (or Polenak), who was born in either Hungary or Bohemia and was about twenty years his junior. Together they raised seven children; in Stephen's 1946 obituary, they were listed as "Theresa Newman, Mae Eskowsi, Jewell and Andrew, Steve Polenak, Anna Kurma and Michael (deceased)."

Over the years Stephen worked at various manual trades: laborer, shipbuilder, bricklayer. When her house was empty, Mary took work in a mill. Their contradictory, inconsistent, and seemingly hesitant attitude toward official record keeping may just be part of the family heritage as unschooled immigrants who came to America to fuel the industrial expansion of towns like Cleveland. They had neither the intellectual bent of the Newmans nor that family's capacity for invention and self-fulfillment. If the Newmans were archetypical incarnations of the clever, successful Jewish immigrants who refashioned themselves in America, the Fetsko-Polenaks were among the imported labor force that did the thankless, muscular work of the great American industrial expansion. They stayed out of the papers for all the right reasons and formed large, hearty families throughout the Midwest that replaced Eastern Europe as their home.

Stephen and Mary's blended family moved around every few years, and they either were overlooked by census takers or got hinky when they came around: only in 1920 were they fully polled in the national head count. And Theresa was even more elusive. Indeed, for much of her early life, surmise is all that's possible. In 1910 a seventeen-year-old Theresa Fetzer was working as a domestic at the home of Meyer E. Loeb of Cleveland. If it was she, it meant that she was a little older than she later claimed. (Perhaps she and/or the Loebs lied about her age in order to acquire or legitimize her working situation.) She didn't appear in the 1920 census, but she showed up in 1930, by which point the received impression of her life story has begun to gel. There she's a thirty-two-year-old woman of Czech heritage, naturalized in 1902 and living in Shaker Heights with her husband, Arthur (described as a shoe store merchant), and their two boys, Arthur Jr., age six, and Paul, five. But even then there's a snag: Arthur, then thirty-six, asserted that he was married for the first time seven years before, in 1923, at age twenty-nine; Theresa, though, revealed that she was first married at age nineteen—thirteen years earlier, in 1917, when she may have been as old as twenty-four.

Decades later the murkiness of her early life outlived her. Just ask her son: "My mother, on her deathbed, said, 'Paul, you have to excuse me, I've been lying all these years. I'm not eighty-three, I'm eighty-seven.' And when we took her back to Cleveland to be buried next to my father, her sister was there. And I said, 'You know, Mother said that she had been lying all these years, and that she wasn't eighty-three, she was eighty-seven.' And her sister said, 'Baloney! She was ninety-three!' "

THE WEDDING of this rootless, pretty woman and her owlish, responsible husband would also provide a mystery: unique among their parents and siblings, they weren't issued a marriage license in Cuyahoga County. Wherever the ceremony was held, it was almost certainly a civil one. Through his life Art belonged to the synagogue known as the Temple in the old Woodland Avenue Jewish enclave of west Cleveland, but his son Paul remembered, "[He] was not a religious man in the sense of going to synagogue or thrusting religion down our throats." And Theresa would soon leave her native Catholicism for

Christian Science—the modern American spiritualist belief popular in the 1920s. She wasn't so ardent as to deny her sons the benefits of medical care, as strict Christian Scientists would, and she seemed not to mind that her boys didn't follow her faith. "That didn't really take on me," Paul would say of the religion (although he did declare himself a Christian Scientist on college applications, probably reckoning that claiming Jewish heritage would have put him at a disadvantage).*

The prevailing religion of the household seemed, in fact, to be Americanism. The Newmans set about creating a tidy little family and situating it in increasingly comfortable houses. In January 1924 Arthur Jr. joined the family in the small, neat house on Renrock Road in Cleveland Heights. On January 26 of the following year, in snow and ice so daunting that Art and Theresa dared not venture out, Paul Leonard joined the family. Within two years he was tumbling and stumbling on the floors of the Newmans' dream house in Shaker Heights—the only childhood home he would ever remember.

---

* The Newman boys received no formal religious instruction after grade school, and later on Paul would come more or less to see himself as an areligious Jew. He was so out of touch with the faith, though, that he was once caught by a journalist declaring frustration at not being able to reach anybody in the movie business on the phone—only to learn to his surprise that it was, in fact, Yom Kippur.

Two

IN THE SUMMER OF 1946, TWENTY-ONE-YEAR-OLD NAVY VETERAN Paul Newman handwrote an application to Kenyon College in Gambier, Ohio. Asked to provide a short autobiography, he began, "My life from the beginning has been uneventful and sheltered, my environment always clean and pleasant. My father is a self-made man with a remarkable fund of knowledge at his disposal, my mother is understanding and intelligent."

And indeed he had no reason not to be satisfied with his situation. The success of Newman-Stern meant that the family had all they could want in the way of clothes, furniture, food. Theresa didn't have to work outside the home, and she had live-in domestic help in the person of Ruth Bush, a teenage housemaid originally from Pennsylvania. There was a membership at the Oakwood Club in Cleveland Heights, and Theresa eagerly attended the road-show plays staged at the Hanna Theater in downtown Cleveland. The mailman regularly delivered *Fortune, Time, Life,* and *Reader's Digest.* In the summertime the boys attended a camp in Michigan. The family traveled to Colorado, Florida, Quebec, and Chicago, where they dined in the famed Pump Room. ("This was *the* place then," Paul remembered on a later visit, "one of the legends.")

The house, the money, the luxuries, the travel, the security, the ease: all of it would have been heavenly to Theresa Newman. Why shouldn't it have been? She had been brought across the world on the outside chance of what might come true, and here she was, still youthful, living a dream, with a family of her own to share it. Still, the idea that she may have been interested overly in the things that money can buy caused discomfort for her son. "She was raised in a very poor family," Paul explained decades later, "and had a sense of values that we pooh-pooh right now—you know, materialistic things, trying to get two cars in the garage."

Perhaps that's why his favorite memories of his boyhood would so often be set out of doors. Shaker Heights was genteel and grand, yes, but it was still in Ohio, and it provided an Eden for a knockabout pair like Paul and his brother, Art. "We would explore lakes and forests," Paul recalled. "You could almost see the Indians hunting there and fishing." The Newman boys and their dog, Cleo, were outside all the time, even in the coldest weather that the winds of Lake Erie could dish out. Paul especially recalled tobogganing and skating on frozen ponds and scaring neighborhood girls with jack-o'-lanterns on Halloween nights.

And when it wasn't wintertime activities, it was organized team sports. Surely the sons of *the* Newman of Newman-Stern would be drawn into team games, in an era when American manly vitality expressed itself so sensationally in athletics. But there was a problem. "My brother and I," Paul would say, "we both went in for every single sport you could think of. And *I* was terrible at all of them. Really— notoriously ungifted." He played baseball, football, and basketball, but in none did he ever feel fluent or graceful or even able. It had partly to do with youthful klutziness: "Boy, was I accident-prone. If there was a tree with a creaky limb, you could be sure that was the one I would pick to climb, and snap!" But it was partly due to self-consciousness too. He had developed into a critic of himself, seeing flaws where others might have seen mere ordinariness.

It made him reticent, cautious, a little introverted. Hugh Leslie, who grew up five houses away from the Newmans on Brighton Road and was in Paul's grade through high school, remembered, "He wasn't shy, but I think he was more on the quiet side, the humble side. He participated in school activities, but he wasn't gregarious or real outgoing." The Newmans, he said, "were good people, good neighbors," but Paul never particularly stood out.

Worse, he grew late. He was a more or less average-size boy, but as a young teen he leveled off, causing him genuine agony in the thing he most loved. "I wanted to play football so bad," he remembered. "And I played in junior high school." Don Mitchell, the captain of that junior high team, had strong memories of Newman's ability. "He played center for us, and he wasn't afraid of anybody," Mitchell recalled. "He could really hit people. He was built. He could have wrestled." But he stayed small, and it cost him. "In high school, in the ninth grade," Paul remembered, "I still weighed ninety-eight pounds and was about five foot three. So I had to get a special dispensation so I wouldn't have to play with the lightweights, because the lightweights were all sixth graders. And I was fucked if I was going to play with those guys." The dispensation didn't come: he never did play organized sports in high school.

But he had started to blossom in other ways, ways less interesting to a rollicking boy, perhaps, but readily noticed by a mother. "He was such a beautiful little boy," Theresa Newman told a reporter in 1959. "In a way it was a shame to waste so much beauty on a boy." He also became one of those people who struggled against a native reticence by overcompensating, in certain situations, as a gadabout or a show-off. He wasn't comfortable in his own skin, but in the right circumstance he could don another and let himself go. "Paul was the neighborhood clown," Theresa remembered. "He yodeled and sang and acted in all sorts of little neighborhood stunts."

His youthful exhibitionism spilled onto the stage. At Malvern Elementary School he performed as an organ grinder in a class play, bouncing about and singing mock-Italian. ("I made up in volume what I lacked in tone," he recalled.) When he was seven, he appeared as a court jester in a play entitled *The Travails of Robin Hood*, singing a song written especially for the occasion by his uncle Joe. "I didn't like it," Paul later said. "I felt as uncomfortable and disturbed then as I do now when I'm onstage. I had one entrance and one exit. I was a big hit. My family was hysterical with pride and admiration."

Surely Theresa was the proudest and most admiring. "She was a frustrated actress, I guess," Paul said, and she saw in him a channel for her blunted ambitions. When he was eleven, she enrolled him in the

Curtain Pullers, a newly organized program in which children studied and performed at the renowned Cleveland Play House. "The Play House was a first-rate regional theater, and everybody who was in those classes felt they were lucky," remembered Joel Katz, who joined the Curtain Pullers about five years after Paul and later adopted the stage name Joel Grey.* "We went to class on Saturday mornings, and then we had productions on Saturdays, and some of us had roles in the grown-up productions that the Play House put on."

On Halloween morning 1936 Paul made his debut as the human lead in *St. George and the Dragon* by Alice Buchan. He wore a florid costume and poured salt on the Dragon's tail. "I wanted to play the Dragon," he moaned mockingly years later. "It was a meatier part. But I was too big for the costume." (Even then, a preteen, he considered himself a character actor in a leading man's body.) Bill DeMora, who played the Dragon in that production, didn't recall being able to fit the costume any better than Paul, whom he remembered as "just a little guy, a couple of years behind me." But he did recall that the death of the Dragon was a highlight of the show. "I was this bad guy kind of taking over, and he slew me." Paul too remembered it as a success: "I was a big hit." But again he had reservations: "I didn't enjoy it, and I wouldn't enjoy it now."

It's clear that even at a young age he had an acute self-awareness and a sense of what behavior was and wasn't appropriate in front of other people. By all accounts, people enjoyed watching him perform. But somehow he seems to have acquired the idea that doing it at all, even well, was inappropriate or unbecoming. Maybe it was because he was the pretty younger brother who took more than just the usual ribbing from his older sibling; describing Art Jr. years later, Paul called him "belligerent" and a "fierce son of a bitch." Too, Art Jr. wasn't the student his younger brother was. "Art was always in trouble in school," remembered a classmate. "A fun guy, but as sharp as Paul was, Art was

---

* Other Curtain Pullers who would go on to fame included Eleanor Parker and Jack Weston. Two other famed actors born in Cleveland within months of Newman, Ruby Dee and Hal Holbrook, never joined the group as they were largely raised elsewhere.

not." In all likelihood a regular diet of teasing and torment was on the menu.

But Paul's self-consciousness might also have stemmed from the different attitudes his parents held toward the very idea of acting. As his youthful passion for performing turned into a young man's intention to be involved with the theater, Theresa, her son remembered, was "supportive," but Art considered it all to be nothing more than "star-gazing." And that would be the opinion that mattered, because, as Paul himself put it, "I'm my father's boy."

FOR ALL the encouragement his mother gave him to think well of himself and to express himself in front of others, Paul Newman's memories of childhood and youth would always be dominated by the figure of Art Newman Sr. For the rest of his life, Paul would speak admiringly of Art's bookish intelligence, his high moral standards, his discreetly but firmly held convictions, his gentle sense of humor, his diligence, and especially his impeccable reputation for honesty and integrity. And he would speak too of the distance between them. "I don't know that we ever connected as father and son," he reflected years later, and he would always be haunted by that failure.

Sometimes he seemed to put the blame on Art, depicting him as "a very shy, very uncommunicative man." But Art Jr. disagreed with that characterization. "Dad was undemonstrative, not uncommunicative," he observed. More tellingly, Art Jr. said of his dad, "Like Paul, he was quiet." So maybe the gulf between Paul and his dad was just a simple case of two taciturn types who were unable to tell each other what they really thought or felt. Whatever the reason, Paul saw in his father's cool attitude a stamp of disapproval. He was painfully aware of his own flaws and shortcomings, and he felt that Art too saw them plainly. So he came to blame himself for the tone of dismissiveness he felt emanating from his father. "He worked six days a week in those days," he remembered, "and I didn't know what was going on, either with myself or with the outside world. I don't think he had the patience to deal with things in a superfluous way—which, again, isn't a criticism of him. It's a criticism of myself." Indeed, along with an ardent work ethic, Art Newman's lesson to keep one's head down and not crow over triumphs or good fortune became ingrained in his boys. Paul's deep-seated lifelong humility about his achievements was no act but rather a significant inheritance from his father.

Both Paul and his brother enjoyed visits from their uncle Joe, who was always a light spirit, a grown-up genuinely interested in whatever kids thought or imagined. He was an especially keen tour guide to books, Paul recalled: "He had an informal way of talking about the great writers that brought them alive to us. He gave me insights into literature that I didn't get from any of the teachers at school." Young Paul was a great one for reading: "When I was a kid," he later re-flected, "I used to go up into the attic with a good book, a glass of iced tea, and a bowl of popcorn."*

Art Newman's lessons to his boys, on the other hand, would be re-membered not for playfulness or the sense of wonder they imparted but for their moral dimension. "He was still suffering from the old Judeo-Christian guilts and the feeling that for anything to be meritori-ous it would have to be painful," Paul recalled. ("I certainly have lived up to that," he added ruefully.) Art was a quiet, determined, and up-right man, and in his deep-set eyes his sons took measure of their worth. He made sure they learned to live his example, regardless of the family's economic advantages. "I didn't get my first baseball glove until I was ten," Paul remembered. "This was intended as a lesson. Just be-cause your father's shop was crammed with sporting gear, it didn't mean that baseball mitts grew on trees." Art worked his sons on Satur-days at Newman-Stern, starting them earlier in the day, keeping them later, and paying them less than other employees. And Paul would keep other jobs during his school years: a paper route, a job selling Fuller brushes, and a stint as counterman at Danny Budin's Jewish deli in Shaker Heights, the first recorded instance of his famous love of food. ("It was a toss-up whether he drew in pay as much as he ate," his old

---

* Is it too much to surmise that among the things he read up in that attic were comic books, perhaps even a few detailing the adventures of Superman, the blue-eyed Amer-ican hero of foreign origins who had been invented not three miles from the New-mans' house by a couple of Jewish sons of Cleveland, Jerry Siegel and Joe Shuster?

boss would say.) "I was always working, a lot of heavy work on bicycles," Paul said. "That's what I remember about my childhood."

The emphasis on hard work would take on new meaning before the Newmans had spent even three years in Shaker Heights. The stock market crash of 1929 and the downward economic spiral that followed hit the blossoming suburb very hard. The school system shrank by 25 percent, and those employees who remained were paid partly in scrip. Improvements to the rapid train line ceased. Homes were lost. Plans to expand the city were scrapped.

Art Newman must have been mortified. He hadn't all that long ago spent his life's savings on an upscale home for his young family—how was he to maintain his situation at a time when people were worrying about buying bread and milk, let alone catchers' mitts and crystal radio sets? But Newman-Stern, to Paul's unending admiration and appreciation, survived, and the Newmans remained in their "clean and pleasant" home. "I never came home and found there was no food on the table," Paul remembered, "but we felt the pinch." He added, "I saw my father going to work and knew what a struggle it was for him."

Indeed, it was a near thing for Newman-Stern. In the first years of the Depression, upward of 80 percent of the nation's sporting goods retailers went bust. Newman-Stern, however, had Art's good business sense and sterling reputation to rely upon. In 1931, on what Paul remembered as "a messy winter day," Art, "looking as gray as the day itself," left home for Chicago to negotiate a unique deal with Spalding and Wilson, the two enormous sporting goods manufacturers. When he returned, it was in triumph. Both companies had agreed to consign goods to Newman-Stern—to give the store a line of credit, in effect, for more than $150,000 worth of goods. For the rest of his life Paul would recollect this as a moment of great triumph for his father. Yes, Spalding and Wilson had fewer customers than ever and surely were thus more willing to extend themselves in order to hold on to them. But in Paul's eyes the deal proved not the dire straits of the recreational gear business but the depth and renown of Art Newman's character: "Spalding and Wilson knew that if he sold a glove for $3.95, they'd get their $2.50."

During this period, Paul caught glimpses of Art's politics; he would recall that his father was "Rooseveltian" and more: "I never heard my father discuss politics in the home, but I know he was a liberal, perhaps even a socialist." What impressed him most, though, was Art's tenacity and integrity and the fact that those two combined to keep Newman-Stern in business when so many like operations went under. Over the years Paul would speak fondly of the shop—"one of the greatest sporting goods stores in the country," he would brag, and "it was a marvelous shop and sold all kinds of things"—but Art's success in securing those letters of agreement particularly stood out, and his son would relate it with pride for the rest of his life.*

PAUL, OF course, had no such laudable achievements to his credit. He hadn't done anything in sports. He was merely an adequate scholar: "I was always one of those students of whom it was said, 'He is very promising,' " he said, suggesting, in typically self-effacing fashion, that the promise was rarely fulfilled. Girls around Shaker Heights knew who he was but not necessarily in a way that led to romance. According to Peggy Behrens, a high school classmate, "Nobody really noticed him at that time. You heard talk later about his blue eyes, but none of the girls ever talked about them back then. And he didn't look like a football player with broad shoulders or anything." Jane Connolly, another classmate, remembered him distantly: "There was something dangerous about him. You felt he was not really tamed, that just beneath the surface there was a streak of violence. He was very popular—there were a lot of girls who wanted to date him—but he wasn't a chaser." Don Mitchell remembered him as one of the unattached clutch of boys at high school socials. "He was no Beau Brummel," he said. "He used to come to all the dances like every other guy, and he'd be in the stag line with the rest of us."

---

* More than seventy years later a grown Paul Newman would contribute a sketch of Art's big consignment coup to the book *My Hero*, a publication of My Hero Project, a charitable endeavor aimed at providing role models for underprivileged children.

Paul noticed the girls but felt hopelessly outclassed by them: "Most of them towered over me." So rather than suffer the rejections of girls, he found other ways to be popular and get noticed. He turned his job at Danny Budin's deli into a showcase. "He would bow deeply to the customers and smile constantly as though he knew he was always on display," remembered his boss.

In fact, the idea of being on display appealed to him—so long as he was on display in the persona of somebody else. In time the theatrical impulse that led his mother to steer him toward the stage took hold in his own heart. By his teens the worst of the Depression was over, and Shaker Heights High School had reinstituted its fine programs of the 1920s, in particular its drama program. Denied football as an outlet but itchy to do something big, Paul became part of that little world of kids, found at every high school, who put on shows. "I stage-managed and acted in plays in the usual extracurricular routine," he would recall, "and I remember that one of my big disappointments was not getting the role of the First Gravedigger in *Hamlet.*" He watched on, rather, as Jack Foley, the young Barrymore of the Shaker High drama club, played the lead; he did, however, land a role in the play *Black Flamingo* meaty enough for him to be photographed for the school newspaper while rehearsing for it.

Whether or not they cast him in plum roles, his teachers thought well of him. "Paul's outstanding quality was the seriousness with which he worked," recalled William Walton, who taught drama at Shaker Heights High. "He was extremely intelligent and, unusual for a high school boy, was interested in serious drama." But, Walton continued, he stood out in other ways, ways that made it clearer, perhaps, why he was drawn to acting: "He loved his fun. During rehearsal breaks he used to head for the piano and pound out boogie-woogie. A flock always gathered around."*

---

* Decades later, in the first filmed episode of the TV series *Inside the Actors Studio*, he would sit down spontaneously at a piano and pound out some quite creditable boogie-woogie, to the delight of the audience.

ON JANUARY 22, 1943, four days shy of turning eighteen, Paul got in the car with Art and drove to Athens, Ohio, where he'd been accepted into Ohio University. Anticipating his birthday, Paul had enlisted that morning in the navy—his brother, Art Jr., then a freshman in college, was just days away from joining the army—and he had decided to attend school while awaiting the call-up.

Ohio U was a big school in a little town, one of the largest universities in Ohio, a state full of colleges, and the oldest college in the midwestern region originally known as the Northwest Territory. It had been graduating students since 1815 and was known for its well-balanced liberal arts curriculum and the blossoming E. W. Scripps School of Journalism—a trade that might've drawn a young man with so many writers and newspapermen in his family.

But academics seemed not to matter to Paul, who by his own confession "majored in beer drinking" at such OU student haunts as the Sportsman Tavern in Athens. "Paul liked to quaff a few beers," remembered Wanda Quest, an Athens girl he dated. Yes, during wartime, in college, there were girls—or more precisely, according to Newman's version of the times, there were girls *around.* "A date back then was sitting around with a bunch of students, drinking beer or going to a film or [on] a hayride, or singing songs by the river," he remembered. "Nice girls didn't fool around, and nice guys didn't try to fool around with nice girls. Them was the bylaws."

He rushed a fraternity, Phi Kappa Tau, one of only three pledges in a time when so many young men were off at war. Wayne Blodgette, a fellow pledge, remembered him as a young rascal who liked to call himself Gus: "Gus was a good jazz pianist and played at our parties. He improvised, never read music, and liked boogie-woogie . . . Gus wasn't a wild student—just the usual amount of drinking parties—and he had no problem with his studies."

The piano playing was a running theme. Edith Quest, Wanda's mom, remembered how the young man would come over to the house for dinners and "used to make our old upright piano jump." Wanda would recollect him as "a good dancer," adding, "He had a very care-free attitude, wonderful personality and a laugh that was infectious."

Away from home, beyond Art's disapproving gaze and Theresa's uncomfortable materialism, he was blossoming, even if he had to invent an alter ego—Gus—in which to do so. He was technically a business major, but as in high school he was drawn to the theater. Though only a freshman, he auditioned for a play, *The Milky Way*, a comedy about the boxing world by Lynn Root and Harry Clork, and he was given a lead role: Speed McFarland, the middleweight champ. College seemed to be bringing his native talents to the surface.

And then, on June 6, 1943, almost immediately after the term ended, he was called up to the navy.

Just eighteen, he was off to war.

Three

"I COULDN'T WAIT TO BE A PILOT," NEWMAN REMEMBERED. "I loved to fly."

Having volunteered for the Navy Air Corps, the eager recruit found himself sent to Yale University in Connecticut, marking his very first visit to the state from which so many of the original settlers of Cleveland had migrated. He had gone there hoping to advance to flight school, but his dreams of becoming a flyboy died a quick and ironic death. A routine eye test revealed that the blue eyes that would someday become world famous were, in fact, color-blind: he was booted from the flight school portion of the training and into the more general V-12 Officer Candidate School, a sort of fast-track operation for college boys who were prospective officer material, also based at Yale.

It wasn't a good fit. "They didn't know what to do with me," he recalled. For starters, he was still the scrawny kid who was too small to play football back in Shaker Heights; he cut a comic figure as a military man. "The first time I got in my uniform," he continued, "I was walking down to get a peanut butter and jelly sandwich. A guy looked over at me, and I thought he was gay or something. I had my sailor outfit, my hat on. He looked at me and said, 'Aren't you a little old to be in the Sea Scouts?' "

Soon enough it was determined that he wouldn't make a proper officer, so he was sent to a traditional navy boot camp in Newport, Rhode Island (it's said that one of his instructors there was a stern-

jawed fellow by the name of Robert Stack), and then on to more specific training as a rear-seat radioman and gunner in torpedo bombers.
In all, his training took him to Newport, Jacksonville, Miami, Norfolk,
and San Diego. Qualified as an aviation radioman third class, Newman
was shipped out to Barber's Point, Hawaii, and assigned to a series of
Pacific-based torpedo squadrons; he and his crewmates were responsible chiefly for training replacement pilots and air crewmen in a variety
of skills, including carrier landings. The various units in which he
served moved west with the progress of the war: Eniwetok, Guam,
Okinawa, and finally Saipan, where they arrived in January 1945 and
would remain until the Japanese surrender.

So it was probably a good thing that he and his crewmates didn't see
Throughout the war, Newman was assigned to routine patrols in
torpedo bombers, aircraft intended to seek out and sink enemy ships
and submarines: the sort of hairy business that could make a young
man's blood race. Unfortunately, he rarely rose to the tasks set before
him. "I was a pretty good radio man but a terrible gunner," he remembered years later. And he wasn't much help to his crewmates when it
came to the puzzle of reading their instruments, either: "I made errors
in altimeters. When I thought we were at the moment of contact, the
altimeter read that we were two or three hundred feet under water, in
the sea! And the pilot is sitting up there chortling to himself and having a great time."

So it was probably a good thing that he and his crewmates didn't see
any significant action. "I think we took some potshots at submarines
that we saw," he recalled. "A couple of times, flying over Saipan, we saw
some Japanese guys and we strafed them. I had a .30-caliber machine
gun in the tail, which, of course, was like a peashooter. It was the same
as pissing into a propeller."

He would later sum it all up as "mostly years of frustration." But
the sentiment wasn't shared back in Shaker Heights, where Art and
Theresa Newman were cross with him for signing up for a genuinely
dangerous job. "I don't think they ever forgave me for volunteering for
torpedo duty," Newman remembered much later. "That was not fair
to either of them. That worried them and pissed them off."

And they likely couldn't imagine the other sorts of peril he faced.
Years later Newman related to Gore Vidal the story of a particular

encounter he had at sea. "I went up on deck with a copy of Nietzsche to improve my mind," he said; once there he was approached by a chaplain who sat beside him to speak about the book and then made a sexual advance.

"Now *that* really put me off," Newman said.

"Off Christianity or homosexuality?" Vidal asked.

"Neither," Newman replied. *"Nietzsche."*

When the *Enola Gay* dropped its famous payload on Hiroshima on August 7, 1945, Newman and his squad mates were aboard the aircraft carrier *Hollandia,* cruising about five hundred miles off the coast of Japan. A photograph taken of the celebration belowdecks shows a cohort of big, strapping sailors with mustaches and sideburns and old-fashioned anchor tattoos and, among them, a kid with arms like pipe cleaners and a wide, goofy grin on his face: Newman might have been the orphan they'd taken on board as a mascot during their journeys, possibly the youngest guy on the ship.*

When his squadron broke up, Newman was assigned to a Carrier Aircraft Service Unit operating out of Seattle. There he took on the dreary shipyard tasks of servicing, repairing, and rearming various vessels; on the side, he ran a little business smuggling whiskey onto the base, as he confessed years later. On January 21, 1946, he was honorably discharged at Bremerton, Washington, with five fairly ordinary citations to his name: a Navy Combat Action Ribbon, the American Area Campaign Medal, the Asian Pacific Campaign Medal, the Good Conduct Medal, and the World War II Victory Medal. He headed back home, intending to resume his schooling.

IF HIS service record was relatively undistinguished and his experience of the war dull, his three-year tour of duty had its effect. For starters, he grew. He liked to joke that he was so undersize and under-

---

* The idea that he was so close to the atomic bomb blasts didn't bother him at the time—"I was twenty years old and I had no idea of the consequences of it. No one even discussed the morality of it or the alternatives." Years later he would become an outspoken opponent of nuclear proliferation.

developed that he "got through the whole war on only two razor blades." But in fact he shot up five or six inches and bulked up accordingly. (His Ohio U pal Wayne Blodgette saw him on-screen a few years later and immediately thought, "The navy must have really developed him.") From the time he left Washington and for the rest of his life, he would reckon himself to be five foot ten or eleven and to weigh in the neighborhood of 160 pounds. (Decades later he claimed his navy uniform still fit him.)

And he learned a brief and slightly painful lesson about matters of the heart. He'd been involved with a girl back in Ohio—"very attached" is how he put it—and about midway through his service he got sucker-punched. "There I was," he remembered, "in the middle of the Pacific, and I opened this *letter* that went something like 'Dear Paul, I don't know how to break this to you, but I have met someone who loves me very much and wishes to marry me.' I went and had a few drinks, and when I woke up the next morning I was feeling no pain at all. It was over, just like that." (Here's hoping the choice that this mysterious lass made turned out to be a happy one.)

That wasn't the only letter he would recall. Just as he would write to his brother Joe to keep him abreast of developments at Newman-Stern whenever the latter was away on business or pleasure trips, Art Newman wrote to his two boys in the service regularly. "My father wrote us every single day," Newman said. "Every day for three years he wrote us a letter. If you go back and look at the letters, they were distant. There was no familial kind of sense to them. But there was an obligation to somehow remind us that there was somebody back home that was thinking about us." That sense of diligence and duty—even if it was cool in its emotions—struck a deep chord, another lesson Art Newman taught his youngest son through deeds and not words: the sheer duty of a thing needed to be seen to, whether or not it was heartfelt or even heartening.

He learned something else, not exactly a lesson: during his time in the navy Newman came to consider himself lucky. For the rest of his life he would tell the story of the day in May 1945 when he and his crewmates were assigned, along with the rest of their squadron, to practice landings on the aircraft carrier *Bunker Hill*. That morning, the pilot of Newman's plane woke up with an earache, and their plane was grounded. Just a few days later two kamikaze planes attacked the *Bunker Hill* and killed nearly four hundred sailors, including the entire contingent from Newman's squadron—one of the worst kamikaze attacks in the entire war. As he reflected upon one telling, "When you miss something like that because your pilot happened to have an earache . . . *wow!*"

The incident marked perhaps the most dramatic example of what he would come to call Newman's Luck, a lifetime of fortunate turns that started with his very genes—the eyes, the lean frame—and came to include various incidents that led to specific circumstances that defined him. He didn't read anything more than happenstance into it. "I'm not a religious person," he would explain. "You can't say God is looking after *you* because He gave your pilot an earache but put the fifteen other guys in coffins." But he was certain that serendipity seemed to favor him; for what purpose or reason he could not say.

It wasn't Newman's Luck that brought him to apply to Kenyon College in the summer of 1946. It was, rather, the simple fact that the school had no female students. As he considered the possibility of returning to Ohio University, he reflected that he had "become much more interested in the ladies than I was in my studies." Kenyon, a much smaller, all-male school in the hamlet of Gambier, would, he hoped, be more free from female temptation. It was a strange claim—why wouldn't a twenty-one-year-old navy veteran want to be around women?—but he unswervingly swore it was the case.

It was certainly the way Kenyon intended its students to live. The school had been founded in 1824 by an Episcopalian clergyman from New England named Philander Chase who sought to establish a "Theological Seminary of the Protestant Episcopal Church in the Diocese of Ohio." With money raised from English subscribers (including a generous donation from one Lord Kenyon), Chase built a small and beautiful campus on a hill in the Kokosing River Valley, roughly midway between Cleveland and the state capital at Columbus. Over time the school shed most of its religious trappings, although chapel attendance was required until the 1960s, and it was always linked with other nearby colleges—Antioch, Denison, Oberlin, Ohio Wesleyan, and Wooster—in what was known as "the Ohio six," a group of small liberal arts schools with religious origins.

Kenyon was an absolutely idyllic place, a cluster of stone buildings that looked like they'd been there for centuries and bled seamlessly into Gambier, where horses still pulled carts up and down the modest main street, often with Amish or Mennonite riders holding the reins. At the school's gates the quaint town road turned into Middle Path, the spine of the campus, which was plotted around it in a subtle grid. Perched high on a hill and miles from the nearest thing you would call a town, the college was dominated by Old Kenyon, a large and imposing gothic structure that contained classrooms, dormitories, and common spaces. Beside the campus chapel lay a pioneer cemetery, its headstones decayed into stubs by the passing decades.

By the time Newman wrote out his application, Kenyon had grown in size and developed fine programs in business, divinity, and, especially, English: the famed *Kenyon Review* was first published there in 1939, and the faculty boasted such impressive icons of American letters as John Crowe Ransom, Randall Jarrell, Robert Lowell, and Allen Tate. The New Criticism, the chief American school of literary thought of the postwar period, was virtually invented at Kenyon and thrived in a summer institute, the Kenyon School of English, which brought to campus such notables as Robert Frost, Alfred Kazin, Lionel Trilling, and Robert Penn Warren.

Most all of those names probably meant nothing to Newman, although he was an avid reader while in the navy and claimed, in his Kenyon application, to have recently read, among other books, *Crime and Punishment; The Brothers Karamazov; Native Son; I, Claudius; Of Human Bondage; Fathers and Sons;* and *The Decameron.* He acknowledged an interest in the theater—"my main extracurricular activity has always been dramatics"—but he declared that his purpose for attending college was more practical: "After absorbing a broad education I intend to take a postgraduate course in Business Administration, [to] enter the retail merchandising field, and later, perhaps, to hold an executive position with a large department store." In short, he'd go into the family business, just as had always been intended. Before that time came, though, Newman would enjoy what he would later describe as the happiest days of his life.

As YOUNG men like Newman returned from the war with GI Bill benefits that could be used toward tuition, Kenyon's enrollment had exploded, so the school had knocked together some makeshift dorms—barracks, essentially—to house not only single students but also some married young men with their families. Newman was assigned to live in one of these, the building known as T-Barracks because of its shape.* Very quickly he reclaimed his Ohio U reputation as a bon vivant, a joker, and a stirrer of high spirits—literally and figuratively. Once again he recollected college as a fine place to indulge in beer drinking. (He was inordinately fond of saying that he graduated Kenyon "Magna Cum Lager" or alternately "Magna Cum Kindness-of-Their-Hearts.") But this time his antics led to a paper trail and, indeed, a change in life.

That growth spurt in the navy meant that Newman could finally do at Kenyon what he couldn't at Shaker Heights High School: play football—albeit only on the practice squad. As it happened, the extra size he'd gained didn't come with a commensurate increase in ability. "I was one of the *worst* football players in the history of Kenyon," he remembered later. "I was a defensive linebacker, and I weighed 152 pounds. *Crunch!* Oh man, I used to get *hit!*"

But being on the team meant being one of the boys, and that ultimately may have been his true goal. From the start of the 1946–47 academic year, he could hang his identity on the fact that he was a football player, even if only on the reserve team. It wasn't an earth-shaking status, but being an athlete may have been even more important to him because he didn't join a fraternity at Kenyon, as he had at

---

* Among Newman's dorm mates in T-Barracks was a Swedish student, Olaf Palme, who would go on to become president of his country and die at the hands of an assassin in an Oslo metro station. Comedian Jonathan Winters was also a Kenyon student in 1946, but it's not clear where he lived.

Ohio U. He was in his glory, but barely two months into his first term at the school, the bill for the booze and rambunctiousness came due.

The police got the first word: at approximately midnight on Wednesday, October 23, 1946, somebody at the Sunset Club in Mount Vernon, Ohio—the nearest town to Kenyon—summoned the cops to help break up a fight between some local boys and a band of Kenyon football players who'd come into town to slug back beers and chat up girls. Two plainclothes deputies, one a veteran of the Navy Shore Patrol, wandered into the melee and separated Kenyon football star Bert Fulton from the fracas. As they headed toward the door with him, somebody tripped one of the cops (remember, they weren't in uniform), and then a small posse of students jumped the duo, intent on freeing Fulton. The officers managed to get out the door and were pursued by the rowdy mob. They bundled Fulton and another Kenyon student, Richard Paisley, into a car and took them to the station. A small contingent followed, four of whom wound up getting arrested along with their friends. One of those four was Newman.

On Thursday afternoon all six were charged with "willfully resisting and obstructing" police officers and were released on $200 bond apiece; more than one hundred Kenyonites were in the courtroom to witness the arraignment. Four of the six arrestees were first-team players, and they were immediately dismissed from the Kenyon team, even with a game scheduled for the very next day. Newman and another player were kicked off the reserve team. On Friday the *Cleveland News* ran a front-page account of the incident and named all the boys involved, specifically mentioning not only Art Newman but the Newman-Stern Company. About ten days later Fulton and Paisley were sentenced: $200 in fines and thirty days in jail, the latter penalty suspended. Newman and the three others had the charges against them dismissed because, according to the prosecutor, they were "a part of the resistance only as they were a part of the crowd." Fulton and Paisley were expelled from Kenyon; Newman and the others were put on probation.

Those are the facts as the newspapers reported them. Newman, who dined out on this tale of youthful miscreance for years, had his own version, which usually went something like this:

A bunch of us got rowdy in a bar and got thrown in the slammer overnight. And all the kids in the courtyard were coming by singing Kenyon songs. It was just gorgeous. Very touching. What happened was all of these college guys were trying to pick up town girls, 'cause Kenyon wasn't coed then. We were always getting in fights with the town guys—a bloody nose, a black eye, a chipped tooth—but the next day you'd see the guy in the street and say "Hi." So anyway one night somebody called the cops. And two plainclothesmen came through the door. Our quarterback didn't have any idea who they were, and he decked one of them. The cops dragged him and another guy off. And he flipped me his keys and said, "Bring my car into town if you can." I said, "Sure." So I walked into the police station and said, "I would like to give these keys to my friend." He said, "Let me take a look at your knuckles." So the door slammed behind me and they went out and got the other two guys in the car and threw them in the slammer too.

Fair enough. But if he found a way to burnish the memory and make it easy to brush off decades later, the episode must have occasioned some intense soul-searching at the time. Newman was of legal age and paying for college through the GI Bill, so there wasn't anything his parents could do to punish him beyond the discipline that the court and the school dished out. And he absolutely loved donning the image of a brawling no-goodnik. But he had shamed Art—a sin he couldn't bear—and had gotten himself separated from the one thing that he most loved at school: football. As it stood after the fact, he was an economics major uninterested in business and deprived of the camaraderie that came with being on the team.

AND so he turned to the stage—eventually.

In most of his accounts of the fight at the Sunset Club and its aftermath, Newman explains that finding himself a man without a football team, he wandered over to the speech department, where auditions were being held for a production of *The Front Page*. Within ten days, he would claim, he was immersed in a new activity.

But memory played tricks on him. Newman did, in fact, make his debut on the Kenyon stage in the role of Hildy Johnson in *The Front Page*. But that production took place something like one year and ten days after the Sunset Club brawl: a program dates the performances as being held on November 6, 7, and 8, 1947.

In the time between the fight and his stage debut, he continued to struggle along as an unwilling economics student who hadn't yet discovered a channel for his talents. "He was a C student," recalled James Michael, who taught drama at Kenyon, "but it wasn't because he wasn't bright." Indeed, certain aspects of his intelligence and effervescence shone right on the surface. He had a positive genius, in fact, for partying, for enterprise, and for cutting a singular figure on campus.

"Almost everybody knew Paul," recalled a classmate, Lewis Weingard. "We had Saturday night parties in every fraternity, and I don't think Paul ever missed making the total rounds . . . He had a coonskin coat that he always wore around the campus on party night, and you would know Paul was coming when people would say, 'Here comes the coonskin coat!' " When there wasn't a party, he was a regular at the Gambier tavern known as Dorothy's Lunch. "I lived there," he recalled fondly. "It had a certain grubbiness about it." Another classmate, Robert G. Davis, remembered him as a fixture at the tavern: "He gave the impression that drinking and carousing were his primary priorities."

But he was also an entrepreneur of some repute. When Kenyon held dance weekends and women were allowed on campus, Newman would make runs to Cleveland and load up on corsages and bouquets to sell to his classmates at a premium. Soon after getting thrown off the football team, Newman became the operator of a student laundry on Gambier's quaint little main street, renting a storefront and some washing machines and cleaning his classmates' clothes and linens over the weekend. ("I washed so many socks: that's why I hate 'em today," he'd later claim.) A light went on in his head one day, and he modified the business in a way Tom Sawyer would've admired: he created a do-your-own-laundry policy, luring customers by bringing in kegs of beer that they could partake of gratis while they scrubbed, dried, and folded their things. It was an inspired bit of promotion: "The beer cost me eleven dollars," he recalled, "and I was getting 25 percent from the gross of the laundry. Those guys used to bring $250 of laundry each week, and sometimes they got so drunk we put them in the bins with the clothes!"

And it gave rise to another example of Newman's Luck—another near-escape of the sort that seemed to bless him regularly. Toward the end of his senior year Newman sold the laundry to a fellow who followed the same business model but was less charmed than his predecessor. "One day a stallion had the misfortune of standing in front of the laundry," he said. "It wasn't long after the Saturday beer had been delivered. One of the college customers had put on a pair of boxing gloves and was seen performing an unnatural act on the stallion. Suffice it to say that they shut the laundry down the next day."

He escaped blame for that one, but he was still notorious for cutting up. In his senior year Newman took a major part in an invasion of the women's dorms at nearby Denison College. As a witness put it, "Various groups of men dispersed themselves throughout the buildings, serenading the occupants and at the same time securing dates for Saturday. Meanwhile, Mr. Newman, who had arrived somewhat earlier than the rest, was entertaining the crowd outside. In the tradition of a gentleman from Kenyon, Paul graciously offered to burn his car to amuse the people. This is representative of the chivalry that Kenyon offers."* On another occasion he convinced a Kenyon policeman to handcuff him to his date during a dance weekend, one of the few times all year when women were permitted on campus; the joke backfired when the young woman needed to use a restroom and she and Newman had to race around the grounds to find the fellow with the key.

Both of those events occurred in his senior year, by which time it was an even bet whether Newman was better known on campus for his antics or for his acting. From the start of his junior year until he graduated in May 1949, he appeared in or helped stage nine plays: *The*

---

* Decades later, recalling the first cars in his life, Newman remembered that, "exuberant at winning a football game," he had once set a Model A Ford on fire.

Front Page, Antigone, The Alchemist, R.U.R., Charley's Aunt, Ghosts, The Taming of the Shrew, Heartbreak House, and *Rude Awakening,* which was written by his professor James Michael, who directed every one of the productions in which Newman appeared.*

Later, when asked to discuss the early work of his most famous student actor, Michael would recall "having trouble not casting Paul as the lead in every play." (To his credit, he forced his star to paint flats, work the lights, and carry out other glamour-free duties.) He recognized a spark in the young man: "He showed all kinds of talent." But he recognized too that Newman tended to lapse into lethargy and bad habits if not pushed. "I pride myself on the fact I called the turn on Newman. I told him if he learned discipline he would go far." The result was a kind of determination, inherited perhaps from Art Newman, to turn acting into a job that could be mastered through application and sheer dogged effort. "He was not a faddist," Michael remembered, "but a good technician and a no-nonsense actor. He had great intelligence, physical stamina, and the ability to work hard."

Later on Newman would dismiss his own collegiate ability. "I was probably one of the worst college actors in history," he'd declare. "I didn't know anything about acting. I had no idea what I was doing. I learned my lines by rote and simply said them, without spontaneity, without any idea of dealing with the forces around me onstage, without knowing what it meant to act and to react." But that was an experienced veteran of the Actors Studio talking. At the time he was rather delighted with his success. "I got some measure of local recognition," he admitted. "I took several bows and had my first, heady taste of acting."

Kenyon student Ira Eliasoph saw some of Newman's first performances, and as he remembered, "He took that stage. He had a wonderful voice that projected through the auditorium with style and grace. It was quite apparent that he had the presence and the charm and the vocal ability. He certainly was more capable than most of the people around."

---

* It wasn't only the stage that Newman dominated. As a senior, he cofounded a campus movie society that was inaugurated with a screening of *The Cabinet of Dr. Caligari.*

But he had his limits. "In college once," Newman confessed, "I took five or six bottles of beer before doing a play. I thought I was brilliant. Without exception, everybody said, 'What the hell was wrong with you?'" That misstep aside, he really did become a standout through his theatrical efforts, developing a kind of grace that made his peers respond to him with more than the ordinary acknowledgment one grants a chum who sticks his neck out to perform in public. He had magnetism, charisma, and a kind of glow that inspired affection and admiration in audiences. This latter quality came to the surface in his final term at Kenyon, the spring semester of 1949, by all accounts one of the most wrenching ever to hit the tiny school.

On a February night Old Kenyon, the gothic edifice that stood as the traditional heart of the campus, was engulfed in fire. Seven students died. Five others were hospitalized. It was a staggering loss, even for a campus filled with World War II veterans. Barely a week later, the drama department was set to put on its production of *Charley's Aunt*, the classic farce by Brandon Thomas about randy students who connive to get a friend to pose as a spinster and serve as their chaperone while they enjoy a pair of hot dates. Naturally, given the devastating fire, it wasn't obvious that staging such a lighthearted entertainment was appropriate. After some debate, though, the school decided that the show should in fact go on. Newman was singled out in the campus newspaper, the *Kenyon Collegian*, for his contribution: "Paul Newman starred as Lord Fancourt Babberley, the impersonator of Charley Wykeham's real aunt, Donna d'Alvadorez. Dressed in demure black, he looked and acted convincingly enough to convince almost all that he might be the real aunt. However, he could have been more careful when he was pouring tea." "His hilariously broad interpretation," another review noted, "will long be remembered."

Two months later Newman further cemented his reputation as a fellow of unusual gifts with *The Kenyon Revue*, a comic musical that he coauthored with classmate Doug Downey and in which he took the role of Dean Frank E. Bailey, the actual name of the dean of the school. As Downey recalled, they put the thing together during the spring break: "Paul wrote most of the lyrics, I wrote most of the dialogue, and we shamelessly stole all of the music." Burlesque or pastiche or what have you, with some of its all-male cast dressed as chorus girls, it took the form of a freshman's introductory tour of an unnamed college that had many not-so-coincidental resemblances to Kenyon. Coming near the end of such a traumatic semester, it was a tonic and a hit. The real Dean Bailey declared of Newman's performance, "He played me better than I could have played myself," and the president of the college, Dr. Gordon Keith Chalmers, was seen in the audience on all three nights of the production.

To COMMEMORATE this triumph, and the many other vivid impressions he made on Kenyon in his three years there, Newman was granted by the editors of the *Collegian* the rare privilege of writing what was dubbed "A Brief Autobiographical Encomium," a comic sketch about himself published on the front page of the paper as a farewell to the school. Written in a mock-heroic style and filled with references to boozing and fisticuffs and womanizing and his famed escapades as a laundryman and an actor, it was at once a throwaway and an unintentional confession. Making reference to the brawl at the Sunset Club, he half-joked, "The people at home began to wonder what kind of company I was keeping. And people who were keeping company with me began to wonder what kind of company *they* were keeping." He spoke of his turn to the theater—"I modestly nicknamed myself 'Barrymore' "—and ended by bragging about the most unlikely achievement in his entire Kenyon career: being named to the Merit List as a first-semester senior for maintaining an average grade above B. " 'Merit list!' My dream come true."

Later, when the ninety-fourth edition of *Reveille*, the school's yearbook, was published, the editors ran two pictures of him beside a drawing of a hand mixing a cocktail and bade him adieu thus:

"Paul L. Newman, Perennial T-Barracks master of ceremonies, itinerant laundryman, antagonist of roommates and proctors alike, author of musical review, leading actor in dramatic productions, host to innumerable parties and never one to miss the opportunity for a fast buck are just a few of Paul's endearing charms. Prone to getting out of hand on long and trying evenings."

Over the years he would say of Kenyon, "My days there were the happiest of my life," and he would maintain strong ties to the school. He had entered as a confused young navy vet trudging thoughtlessly toward a career selling sporting goods and had transformed, accidentally but purposefully, into someone with an increasing set of skills and a genuine aim in life.

He wasn't going back to Cleveland to sell golf clubs and microscopes at Newman-Stern.

He was going off to summer stock theater in Wisconsin.

He was going to try to become an actor.

Four

H E WAS TWENTY-FOUR YEARS OLD, AND HE SHOULD HAVE BEEN preparing for whatever life it was that was lined up for the heirs to Newman-Stern. Instead, he was on a train headed to Williams Bay, Wisconsin, where he'd received a room-and-board scholarship for a season of summer stock at the Belfry Theater.

All of Art Newman's lessons about responsibility and dedication seemed, apparently, to have been in vain. The boy who was never quite able to do the right thing was now throwing his upbringing and education away on a chimera, a quixotic pursuit of art and self-identity more suited to a bohemian or a bum than a college graduate from Shaker Heights. Art's response, as his son recalled, was "consternation."

But it may not have been so severe as all that. For one thing, this wasn't Newman's first stab at semiprofessional acting, and his father may have indulged his decision to pursue his chosen path. In the summer after his junior year, he had performed in stock at the Priscilla Beach Theater in Plymouth, Massachusetts. There, according to fellow trouper Terry Lewis, "he told us that he had made a deal with his family. They would support him for a year while he was trying to be an actor, but after the year he either had to go back and work at the store, like his brother, Art, or he was on his own."

Certainly the idea that Newman's future lay either in acting or in the aisles of Newman-Stern rings true. He would forever explain his choice of a potential career not as a calling to thespianism but as a flight from the path that had been lying in wait for him his entire life. "I grew up with the idea that I was going into the sporting goods store," he confessed. "My whole family, including a couple of uncles, took it for granted." But that seemed like a trap, and he was too squirrelly by nature to accept that he should simply walk into it. Acting had brought him success at Kenyon; maybe he could keep riding that unlikely streak of good results.

"I wasn't 'searching for my identity,' " he'd later say. "I didn't have greasepaint in my blood. I was just running away from the family retail business and from merchandising. I just couldn't find any romance in it. Acting was a happy alternative to a way of life that meant nothing to me." He confessed that the taste of his college triumphs lingered: "I was instinctively pursuing the only thing I'd ever done really well." But mainly, he would admit, "I didn't quite know what to do."

So he wound up in Williams Bay, a lakeside vacation spot for well-to-do Chicagoans, and right away they put him to work. His first role was as a soldier in Norman Krasna's *John Loves Mary*. Next he was cast as the Gentleman Caller in Tennessee Williams's *The Glass Menagerie*. In all he stayed nine weeks in Wisconsin and probably appeared in as many plays, and directed a little bit, and came to develop a dislike for the hectic routine of stock acting. Years later, when he was appearing on Broadway, he reflected, "I think the only thing you can do with those, in such a short time to prepare, is to develop your bad mannerisms, or discover possibly successful mannerisms—but mannerisms nevertheless. Sure, what can you do in four days of rehearsal? You can hope to Christ that you can remember your lines, and that's about as far as it goes."

But when the season closed, he decided to stick with the hectic schedule of repertory acting. He moved on to Woodstock, Illinois, an outerlying city of northwest Chicagoland, the longtime home of *Dick Tracy* creator Chester Gould and the fictional birthplace of the famed comic strip lawman. There, in an old-fashioned town center that would someday be the location for the film *Groundhog Day*, stood the Opera House, built in 1889 and home for decades to the Woodstock Players, a troupe that had included among its ranks Tom Bosley, Shelley Berman, and just the previous season a promising young actress named Geraldine Page.*

And he wouldn't make the trip to Illinois alone. He brought with him a tall, dark-eyed blonde he'd met in Williams Bay, an aspiring actress named Jacqueline Emily Witte who would, on December 27, 1949, become the first Mrs. Paul Newman.

They married at an anomalous moment in his life, to say the very least. By all accounts, they were both attractive, and they both claimed theatrical professions on their marriage license, so they were matched in some ways. But Jackie, as she was known, had only turned nineteen at the end of that summer, and she hadn't yet graduated Lawrence College, the liberal arts school from which she was on vacation when she went off to Williams Bay. She was born in Illinois and raised in Beloit, Wisconsin, the oldest child of Frank T. Witte and the former Irene Elizabeth Telgman. Frank was one of five sons of Theopolis and Emma Witte and had joined his father in the family business, Witte and Son, a Beloit butcher shop. Frank and Irene weren't young parents; when Jacqueline was born in September 1929, he was forty-one and she was thirty-five, and they had been married for ten years. Surely they shared some apprehensions as they watched, along with best man Art Newman Jr., as this handsome but unsettled couple exchanged rings and vows at the family church, St. Paul's Episcopal.

Even with Kenyon and the navy behind him, even with his good looks and athletic build, Newman still wasn't what folks would have called a ladies' man. During vacations from college, his high school chum Don Mitchell remembered running into him regularly at Louie's, a restaurant-tavern-dance hall on the eastern edge of Shaker Heights. "The rule there was that you couldn't go into the dance hall if you were a guy without a girl," said Mitchell. "And he'd always be in the bar with the other guys who didn't have a date." Given that, there have been various surmises over the years as to just what led Newman

---

* The precocious Orson Welles attended prep school in Woodstock and performed Shakespeare at the Opera House with his classmates.

to marry so quickly and to someone so young. Pregnancy is a popular first guess, given the era and the midwestern morality that was in place. But no child was imminent. Newman accrued no advantage professionally or as a veteran for being married. One of his snarkier biographers has suggested that Newman wed Jackie out of homosexual panic, having gotten a sense of how many gay men there were in the theatrical world and how they would treat a handsome, fit young newcomer whom they suspected might be available. But the simplest explanation, if also the most conventional, is best: they were in love, and they could imagine staying together and being in love together for the rest of their lives. There's no record of whether Art and Theresa Newman attended the wedding, but Art might very well have been pleased to think that his younger son was now responsible for somebody else's welfare. It might straighten the boy out.

SOMETHING MIGHT have to, because acting in stock companies wasn't exactly the path to stability and security. What's more, even in the context of the Woodstock Players, Newman didn't make a stunning impression. "There wasn't much to set him apart from the rest of them that were here at the time," recalled W. H. "Bill" Tammeus, in whose house the newlywed Newmans rented a pair of rooms for $10 a month during their time in Illinois. "He was one of about twenty here during that period . . . and about fifteen were pretty equal in their accomplishments."

Karin, the oldest Tammeus child, remembered that the Newmans "were both very beautiful people in all ways. She was lovely and quiet, and he and my dad were real comfortable with each other." The Tammeus family lived just a couple of blocks from the Opera House, and they supported the institution with membership in the Theater Guild and by regularly housing actors in their rambling thirteen-room Civil War–era house. The young Newmans slept in an upstairs bedroom, had access to a second kitchen in the basement, and shared the house's one bathroom with the Tammeuses and their four children.

Shared it, as in literally. Barbara, the Tammeuses' second oldest, remembered, "When I about seven years old, on a warm, sunny afternoon, I was taking one of my monthly baths and was scrunched down in the water enjoying what I hated to do, take a bath. The door to the bathroom off the kitchen opened, then closed, and Paul, reading a *Time* magazine, dressed in his usual blue jeans and white undershirt and [with] bare feet, walked to the john and sat down. Moments later when I rose up out of the water, he said, obviously not having seen me on his way in, 'Oh, hi. Well, I'm going to finish.' And he did. He then got up, walked out while still reading *Time*, and didn't say another word."

The Players' shows were poorly attended. Kurt Wanieck managed the theater, and he had hired Newman, who, he remembered, "was just a good-lookin' blue-eyed guy." According to Wanieck, the bugaboo wasn't the quality of the productions or the choice of material but rather TV. By 1948 more than one million television sets were in use in the United States, with four national networks broadcasting programs featuring such overnight stars as Milton Berle and Ed Sullivan. "People just started to stay home to get their entertainment," Wanieck said.

The movie business took a hit—1948 would be the year in which it sold fewer tickets than any other since, even with the American population increasing annually. And live theaters got hit even worse. "If twenty or thirty people came out, that was a good showing," Bill Tammeus remembered. But like Newman, he blamed not Uncle Miltie for the poor turnout but rather the pace of the Opera House production schedule: sixteen shows in sixteen weeks. He depicted a company "trying to learn the stuff by heart in a hurry . . . They put on too many plays in too short a period of time. It was a different play every week." Among the quickly revolving slate of shows was *Our Town*, in which Newman played the Stage Manager (and in which Karin Tammeus had a role), and *Cyrano de Bergerac*, in which Newman was cast rather uncomfortably to type as the attractive but dim-witted would-be courtier Christian. "Paul was not a leading man," Tammeus stated bluntly.

But he was a trouper: Newman was keen on sitting up nights and talking about the latest production with Jackie and the other actors. "The best thing he could do while he was here was eat popcorn," Tammeus said. "That guy would eat a dishpan full of popcorn at least once a day. When they came home about midnight after the play, he would make the popcorn and go up to his room to talk about the play, eat popcorn, and have a beer." As the winter season came to a close, New-man found that he needed to supplement his diminishing earnings as an actor, and so he took work at Bill Tittle's farm just outside town. "He shocked grain like any other farmer would," Tammeus recalled.*

The image of him out in those fields in early 1950 doing the work of a laborer seems unlikely, but at some level the quiet of the outdoors and the dulling routine of farm work must have come as welcome dis-tractions. Sometime that winter he learned that Jackie was pregnant. And in the spring, just as he was looking for another summer theatri-cal job, he got a terrible phone call at the Tammeus house: Art New-man had died.

"I remember it really clearly," Karin said. "It was five or six in the evening, and he was speaking on the phone in the kitchen, and then he sat at the table to talk with my parents. He realized that might be the end of his career. He felt that he would have to go back and take over the family business, and that horrified him."

The next day, with his pregnant wife and his empty sack of prospects, he drove home to Cleveland in a 1937 Packard he'd bought for $150. "They just left," Karin remembered. "It was just a very sad day for all of us."

ART NEWMAN had fallen ill suddenly about six weeks prior, his stom-ach swelling and his complexion taking on a jaundiced cast. Doctors at St. Luke's Hospital, admitting to being puzzled by his symptoms, sus-pected fibrosis of the pancreas and/or the liver and/or colitis and/or cancer. A number of steps were followed: blood transfusions, intra-venous feeding, a shunt for the bile that was accumulating in his ab-domen. Joe Newman was alarmed by his brother's worsening condition and the doctors' failure to identify the causes. In mid-April he wrote to specialists in other cities and was considering taking Art to Boston for care.

---

* Yes, he *shocked* corn—that is, piled stalks of it in a field with the butt ends down—as opposed to *shucking* it, which is to remove the husks. (Who knew?)

But Art's disease was moving too quickly. On May 1 he was back in St. Luke's. At 9:20 A.M. on May 11, he died. In the coming days, obituaries appeared in the *Plain Dealer,* the *News,* and the *Press,* as well as in the city's Jewish papers, the *Independent* and the *Review and Observer.* Alongside most ran a recent picture of a man looking older and more shrunken than his age would indicate. But the *Plain Dealer* ran an archival photo from a decade or two earlier that showed him as a balding but still vital man with his jaw and gaze set firmly.

The funeral service was held on a warm, showery morning. It was a Sunday—Mother's Day—and the Newman-Stern Company was advertising sales on everything you'd need for summer fun: fishing and camping and golf gear, baseball cleats, tennis rackets. After a service at the Deutsch Funeral Home, Art was interred in the mausoleum at Mayfield Cemetery in Cleveland Heights, not far from the graves of his parents. In the coming days Joe Newman wrote poignantly of his pain to a business acquaintance, "Art was not only my brother but my business partner for thirty-five years. His loss in both services will be difficult to make up, if, indeed, it can ever be made up. In all these years we never had a quarrel."

For Art's younger son, undoubtedly shocked by the suddenness of his father's passing, there was a disturbing hangover. He had never shown his father that he was a capable young man. Without a career and without prospects, with a pregnant wife and no sure purpose or direction, he felt an acute pang of shame.

"He treated me like he was disappointed in me a lot of the time," Newman recalled later of his father, "and he had every right to be. I wanted desperately to show him that somehow, somewhere along the line I could cut the mustard. And I never got a chance." The sense that he'd failed his father haunted him for years: "One of the great anguishes of my life is that he didn't see my success. He thought I was a ne'er-do-well."

And so, perhaps in a mood of penance, he set about doing what it always seemed he would: working at Newman-Stern alongside his brother, Art, and his uncle Joe and Joe's son, Jim, selling canoes and binoculars and basketballs and whatnot to recreation-minded Clevelanders—and desperately yearning for a way out. "I was a pretty good salesman," he later admitted, quickly pointing out that he had no innate love of business. "I couldn't relate to the romance of retailing," he'd say in a common plaint. "It just wasn't a good match."

He rented a house for himself and Jackie and their soon-to-arrive child in Bedford, a blue-collar community just southwest of Shaker Heights on the outskirts of Cleveland. A son, Alan Scott, was born to Jackie on September 23. (The boy would always be known as Scott; the Alan portion of his name may have been in honor of Art Newman, following the Ashkenazi tradition of naming newborns after recently deceased relations, if only with an initial.)

Newman was twenty-five, a college graduate, a navy veteran, a failed actor, a dad, an inheritor of a dependable business—in short, a young man staring squarely at a future that, surely, struck him as miserable. "I was very successful at being something I was not," he remembered in pain, "and that's the worst thing that can happen to a person." It was evident to those close to him that he wasn't happy. "Paul worked hard," Joe Newman remembered, "but his heart just wasn't in the business."

As it happened, Joe also felt that the Newman-Stern portion of his life was over. Throughout the summer of 1950 he sought buyers for the store, and by Labor Day he'd found them: Nat Marcus of Marcus Department Stores; Allan Kramer, a salesman and executive in a number of midwestern firms; and Nate Schultz, a movie theater owner and speculative investor, bought what the newspapers called "a substantial interest" in the business and began managing it on October 1. Joe retained a percentage and stayed on as an adviser and a living link to the store's history and renown.*

Joe's role became slighter and slighter, though, and by 1952 he was

---

* The new owners would themselves sell Newman-Stern to a Kansas City concern in 1963. That company would merge the store with a couple of suburban outlets operating under the Gateway Sporting Goods name. In 1968 the big downtown store was demolished in an urban renewal project and replaced by a smaller space, which in turn was shut down, along with its suburban satellites, in 1973. A spin-off of the family business run by Jim Newman, Joe's son, formed as Newman-Adler and continues to sell camping and outdoor equipment in the Cleveland suburbs under various names to this day.

able to devote himself fully to writing. In the years remaining to him he continued to write columns for Cleveland newspapers and published his second and third volumes of verse.* When he died in 1960, felled by a bad heart, he was eulogized in editorials in both of Cleveland's then-surviving daily papers. They recalled his round glasses, his pipe, his lanky physique, and his thatch of stiff hair. The *Cleveland Press*, for which he'd written regularly for nearly a decade, spoke of his sense of justice, his mischievousness, his agreeable temper, his collegiality, his wisdom. "Joe Newman came pretty close to being a ray of sunshine in a too drab world," said the *Cleveland Plain Dealer.* "The city will miss him."

AFTER THE sale of Newman-Stern, Jim Newman stayed on at the store, Art Newman went off and became a Cadillac salesman, and Paul spent the autumn of 1950 managing a driving range that the new Newman-Stern owners were operating just outside of town. But the urge that had vexed his final months at Kenyon was still eating at him throughout a winter that was brutal even by Cleveland standards. (Two feet of snow hit the city the day after Thanksgiving.) He pined for the theater. "I remember going to the Play House and watching the actors taking their curtain calls," he said. "It nearly drove me out of my mind." He auditioned for acting work at local radio and TV stations, landing a couple of spots in ads for the Ohio Bell Telephone Company and National City Bank and for some clients of the McCann Erickson ad agency. ("How the hell they chose me I don't know," he later declared.) He made the trek to the nearby town of Brecksville and its Little Theater, where he directed *Here Today*, a society comedy written by George Oppenheimer. And all the while he was, no doubt, putting his head to the task of coming up with a way to be gone tomorrow.

---

* Before his death Joe Newman had the singular honor of having three of his poems recorded by the beatnik poet and performance artist Lord Buckley. One of those works, "Black Cross," a frightening dialect poem about a lynching, was performed in the early 1960s by a young Bob Dylan when he was still on the folk club circuit.

It hit him: with what he had saved over the year, plus a bit of the proceeds from Art's estate, he had nearly $2,000. Add the college aid remaining to him on the GI Bill, and he could go to graduate school and get a sheepskin—a master's degree in theater that would allow him to teach, maybe even at Kenyon. "My ambition had always been greater than my talent," he would later say of his young self. "But the best of whatever I did was in the theater, and that wasn't very good, but it was still the best that I had." He even had the perfect graduate school in mind. He'd already been there, in fact: Yale.

AND WHY not Yale?

At the time he applied to it, the department of drama at the venerable university hadn't yet become its own school, but it had been awarding master of fine arts degrees for more than two decades, and there could be no more secure credential than a Yale diploma. There was a natural progress from Shaker Heights to Kenyon to the Ivy League, even if the fellow making it was something of a rake. And the sheer practical nature of his intent must have impressed the faculty who admitted him to the program. "I had no stars in my eyes or aspirations to be a Broadway actor," he recalled, "but I did want to be in some part of the theater, and a master's degree always protects you. You can teach at Kenyon, which I would have loved to have done." So for the second time in a little more than a year, he loaded his possessions and his wife—and now a baby boy—into the car and headed off into uncertainty.

It wasn't a popular decision in the family. Theresa Newman was so worried about the young family that she gave them her '46 Chevy rather than watch them pull away in the old Packard. Art took his brother aside and asked him flat out, "Why would you want to do this? You're married and have a baby."

But he was determined. In New Haven they rented the top floor of what Newman described as "an old wooden three-family house." Jackie commuted occasionally into New York City to seek modeling assignments, and Newman augmented his savings with work as a door-to-door encyclopedia salesman. He loved to tell the story of his successes: "I went out and in ten days sold $1,200 worth of the *Encyclopaedia Britannica*."*

His academic triumphs were less obvious and less forthcoming. He had chosen to specialize in directing but was required to act as part of the degree program. The very first assignment nearly did him in. He was given a few pages from George Bernard Shaw's *Saint Joan*, and he felt a sick-making jolt when he saw the initial stage directions for his character, who was to enter the scene after being heard sobbing and howling offstage. As Newman recalled, "The machinery started going almost immediately—how can I duck this? How can I find some intellectual way of playing this? Because I had never been able to break through that sound barrier, the emotional barrier." Lightheartedness he could feign, but not real depth of feeling.

It seems odd that a war veteran with a family and some professional acting experience should be so threatened by the requirement to show a bit of his inner self, but perhaps the atmosphere of Yale, far more sober than the antic days at Kenyon or the hurried merry-go-round of stock acting, made him realize just what acting entailed. As he said, "The muscles contracted in my stomach, and immediately I tried to figure out some way to play the whole thing facing upstage. And then I thought, 'What an ass! I drag my family with only nine hundred dollars in the bank all the way to Connecticut and then think of all the ways I can to cop out.' "

A sense of responsibility, then, rather than an impulse to artistic expression, drove him to craft a solution. "I took that script downstairs to the boiler room and I said, 'Okay, buddy, you are going to sit here until you find out where it is going to come from, or you get out of this business right now.' "

He cracked the scene, and he wound up performing more often than directing, taking classes in acting from Constance Welch, a mainstay of Yale's programs for four decades. Welch had been exposed to

---

* It is impossible to imagine New Haven housewives answering the doorbell to find the young Paul Newman peddling encyclopedias and think that sex never entered into the picture. Impossible.

the famed system of acting developed by the great director Konstantin Stanislavsky through lessons from one of his acolytes, the actress Maria Ouspenskaya. But the technique she came to teach Yale students diverged importantly from the Stanislavsky system or, as it came to be known in America, the Method. As Elia Kazan, who studied with her at Yale in the early 1930s, at the very beginning of her tenure there, recalled, "She believed that imitating the exterior would produce the interior feeling in the actor and the audience"—the opposite, in many key ways, of what such mavericks as Kazan and Stella Adler and Lee Strasberg would come to teach their acting students.

Welch's emphasis on external technique may not have been strictly Method, but it suited the repressed young Newman. "I was terrorized by the emotional requirements of being an actor," he confessed. "Acting is like letting your pants down: you're exposed." Having a series of concrete physical exercises to follow—voice, breathing, anger, jealousy, laughing, crying—appealed to his practical, problem-solving side and allowed him to create at least a simulation of letting himself go emotionally. In a raw actor such as Newman, Welch's teaching allowed not for genuine psychological exploration but rather for an old-fashioned declamatory style. As a result, even though he was earnest and looked great, he lacked poetry, and he knew it. "If you talk with the people I worked with in school," he confessed later on, "they will say I had a great deal of promise. Two years of drama and undergraduate school, a year at Yale for my master's, two years of summer stock, and a year of winter stock—but *I really didn't know anything!*"

Still, he cut a good figure at Yale. Decades after the fact, Frank McMullan, one of his teachers, recalled that "he proved to be a very good student . . . He was in my first-year directing class, and he was interested in acting as much as directing and, indeed, showed talent in both of those fields." He appeared in three or four full-length plays and perhaps a dozen one-acts. And he progressed well enough to get a role in one of the major productions of the academic year, an original student play about Ludwig van Beethoven. "I like to think I gave him a chance," McMullan said, "when I cast him in the role of Beethoven's nephew, Karl . . . It was apparent to me that his was a magnetic presence on the stage."

It may have been apparent to McMullan, but Newman was still un-comfortable: stiff and repressed on the inside, even if he could harness the confidence to make it seem otherwise to an audience. He remembered Karl without much affection as "a very formal guy"—but it simply may have been that he was still far enough from mastering his craft to make the character into anything else.

BESIDES THE education and the teaching credential, Newman had another reason to be at Yale: New York was a mere train ride away. That allowed Jackie to pursue her sputtering modeling career, and it also meant that New York theatrical agents would occasionally attend Yale's plays to scout for new talent. And thus it was that the stiff but handsome young actor playing Beethoven's nephew in the spring of 1952 got noticed by Audrey Wood and William Liebling, a pair of New York agents who were married to each other and who represented a number of important theatrical and cinematic figures, including Tennessee Williams, William Inge, Carson McCullers, Marlon Brando, Montgomery Clift, Elizabeth Taylor, Elia Kazan, and Joshua Logan. After a performance of the Beethoven play, Liebling came backstage, Newman remembered, "and suggested that if I ever came to New York I should look him up."

Summer was fast approaching, as was the unpleasant prospect of looking for a gig in stock somewhere. So why not take a flyer on the big city, the big time, a real career? Newman and Jackie thought hard about it, and he consulted with the faculty at Yale. Eventually he came to a decision. "I was prepared to try it for a year," he later said, "and if I got nowhere, to go back to Yale and get my degree. I had a family, I had responsibilities. Things were a little crowded in New Haven financially, but I was making out fairly well with the encyclopedias."

It was a calculated gamble. This wasn't Williams Bay or Plymouth or Woodstock. This was an international center of art and business with the potential for paying work in several media: theater, television, advertising, and, as location shoots were becoming more common, film. Jackie had an aunt there who could watch little Scott; Paul had connections at the McCann Erickson advertising agency from his Cleveland days. If he was leaping from a height, he was doing it with a parachute and a plan. "I wasn't going to subject my family to the hanging-out-at-Schwab's-drugstore-in-Hollywood routine," he remembered. "I had no intention of waiting around till I was bruised and bitter." A reasonable stance.

New York in the summer of 1952, then: the sort of place where anything could happen.

Part Three

Five

IT'S ONE OF THE MOST EXCITING FIVE-WORD PHRASES IN THE language: *New York in the '50s.*

The anxiety and privation of World War II were memories. The economy was bounding. There was money; there was promise; there was robust vitality and opportunity. But there was a layer, too, of contentment in the air. To be a white American male of twenty-something years of age and some education in that city at that time was to be a king, or at least a prince. New York was the gilded metropolis where the elite met at their most feverish, a home of champions in commerce, in geopolitics, in sports, and, perhaps most of all, in the arts.

Name a field of creative activity, and the New York of the 1950s was its font or its center or was striving mightily to overtake any other city in the world at excelling in it. Revolutions in painting, jazz, pop music, and poetry spilled out of nightclubs and lofts and walk-up flats and dingy rented offices and rubbed up against one another in the streets. Beatniks, abstract expressionists, be-boppers, Method actors, folkies, comics, critics, tunesmiths, hoofers, longhairs, ad men: a fantastical stew of creative humanity.

The prewar culture of symphonic music and quality publishing and international dance and opera had fully revived, and bracing waves of modern architecture and fashion and decorative art buoyed alongside. And the dramatic arts were particularly vital. Broadway thrived with delightful musicals and titanic dramatic voices: Williams, Miller, Inge. On any given night of the summer of '52 you could see *The King and I, I Am a Camera, Pal Joey, Top Banana, Guys and Dolls, Stalag 17.* Movie theaters were bursting almost literally with wide-screen spectacles like *The Greatest Show on Earth, This Is Cinerama,* and *Quo Vadis,* while such stalwart exemplars of the Hollywood system as *The Quiet Man, High Noon,* and *The African Queen* vied with them for attention. TV studios around town ravenously ate up every script and performance and gimmick that the sharpest new minds could produce and poured out live dramas and variety shows and experiments in bringing movie and radio dramas to the new small screen.

Hit the street, and giants of painting, acting, poetry, theater, journalism, architecture, photography, jazz, fashion, classical music, and a dozen other fields might walk right by you on Broadway or in Greenwich Village. It was arguably the greatest heyday in a city that's had more than its share of them.

Imagine Augustan Rome or Elizabethan London with V-8 engines and an upwardly mobile middle class; imagine fin-de-siècle Vienna or Paris of the 1920s without old-world prejudices or class divisions and with air-conditioning and reliable plumbing. Can you talk about a center of the world? New York in the summer of 1952 might well have been it.

ALAS, THE young Newman family wasn't quite capable of pulling up a chair to Manhattan, the grown-up table at this remarkable feast of affluence and artistry. Rather, they rented a furnished room in the Art Deco–style Ambassador Apartments at 30 Daniel Low Terrace in the New Brighton section of Staten Island. It was a building popular with theatrical types; some years later another Ohio actor, Martin Sheen, would be living there with his wife when their son Emilio Estevez was born. The place was cheap: the Newmans paid $60 a month in rent, and they availed themselves of the babysitting services of Jackie's nearby aunt. And it was conveniently close to the Staten Island Ferry and quick commutes into Manhattan, which glistened across the harbor with promises of work, pay, and advancement.*

Being Art Newman's son, Newman worried about money, especially in these circumstances. Even more than going to Yale, moving to New York was a leap of faith—and before very long Jackie told him that she was expecting another child. If New York was truly the El Dorado it seemed to be, he had better figure out how to get some of its riches for his family.

So he developed a routine. "I had one decent suit in those days," he remembered, "an old seersucker. And I'd put it on every morning. I'd start out at eight every morning, take the ferry to Manhattan, make the rounds of the casting agents, follow up all the tips in the trade papers, and then get back to Staten Island in time to peddle encyclopedias." (Ah, the encyclopedias . . .) "It was one of the hottest summers I can remember in New York," he said, but he persevered, making a regular if genial pest of himself at all the casting agents' offices ("The guy in the white seersucker is here again," he recalled secretaries saying) and then ringing doorbells around Staten Island until suppertime.

Before long, little bits of fortune started to fall to him. He got small roles on television, some quite well-paying. He earned, he claimed, $75 for dressing as an old man applauding at the inauguration of President McKinley on *The March of Time*. In August he got his first credited part, playing an air force sergeant in an episode of the TV science fiction series *Tales of Tomorrow*, a ludicrous little potboiler called "Ice from Space." Performing half his lines off camera and another half with understandably strained seriousness, he certainly couldn't be said to have transcended the laughable material, which concerned a chunk of extraterrestrial ice that was slowly turning the Earth into a frozen wasteland. To his credit, he knew how silly it was. "For the strange

---

* Living in Staten Island got Newman some publicity of a sort, actually. In September 1952 he was stopped by the Inquiring Photographer of the *Staten Island Advance* and asked, "Are good-looking candidates likelier to garner the votes of women?" He reckoned they were: "I guess I haven't much faith in the ability of women to make up their minds who to vote for."

block of alien ice," he recalled, "they had built a huge plastic cube filled with pulsating lights. So here we are, standing around and supposedly freezing, when a fly buzzes onto the set. And for the big close-up you see this little fly hopping around on the giant ice cube. I could barely get out my lines, I was trying so hard not to laugh."

These were wildcatting days in the television business, though, so working on such a trifle didn't count as a black mark. Indeed, as Newman began to make the rounds, he landed a number of gigs. He got the gigantic MCA talent agency to represent him, and they helped him secure a sporadically recurring role on *The Aldrich Family*, the TV version of the popular radio drama about the life and times of Henry Aldrich, Normal Teen. Typecast as the College Hero, Newman made $50 a week—enough that he could give up the encyclopedias and tell his professors at Yale that he was staying in New York.

He liked the odds. "Boy, there was work," he recalled. "You got a week off and you could be right back in a film or on television or in a play." By September, Cleveland newspapers, no doubt tipped off by Joe Newman, were writing about his minor successes, as was *The Kenyon Alumni Bulletin*, which referred to him fondly as "one of the finest actors we've ever had."

BEING ONE of Kenyon's finest actors may have constituted high praise in Gambier, but in New York it was hardly a calling card of distinction. Regardless of Newman's success in getting small roles on the strength of his telegenic looks, he knew that his appearance alone wasn't going to get him far. Yale had shown him just how much he lacked as an actor, and he determined to apply what resources he had to continuing his education and honing his craft. And he knew exactly where he wanted to do it. At Yale, he remembered, "I heard a lot of reverent talk—and rightly so—about the Actors Studio." So he thought he'd give it a try.

In some ways this was like a weekend hiker declaring himself interested in an assault on Everest. Only five years old, the Actors Studio had been, virtually from its opening day, the high temple of the new American acting style, the Method. The most exciting actor of the moment—Marlon Brando—was the talismanic figure of the Studio, and he and the techniques he practiced there were spoken about in tones of awe and mystery wherever people chattered about acting.

The Actors Studio was founded by Cheryl Crawford, Elia Kazan, and Robert Lewis, who had spent the 1920s and 1930s with the Group Theater developing the acting techniques pioneered by Konstantin Stanislavsky and staging plays that promoted their liberal (indeed, radical) political ideals. The Group was a volatile band—incestuous, cliquish, rabid, blessed with a surfeit of geniuses, given to internecine quarrels. It gave the theater some truly extraordinary productions— most notably Clifford Odets's *Golden Boy*, *Awake and Sing!*, and *Waiting for Lefty*—and its ranks included a veritable pantheon of theatrical gurus and demigods: Stella Adler, Harold Clurman, Sanford Meisner, and Lee Strasberg.

The Group dissolved in 1941, and six years later Crawford and Kazan initiated the Actors Studio as a place where actors could practice their craft independently of specific stage or film projects. The idea was to teach Stanislavskyan principals—or, at least, the sundry versions of them that had evolved in America—in workshop settings. Actors would prepare scenes and then present them to an audience of actors and teachers, and they would get feedback right on the spot about, say, a specific interpretive problem or whether a new approach was working. There were exercises, improvisations, and lectures, but mostly there were short performances and the ensuing critiques— which could be ten times as long as the scenes that occasioned them: "the work," as Studio regulars called it.

Within weeks of the founding of the Actors Studio, Kazan and his star pupil, Marlon Brando, stunned the world with their stage production of Tennessee Williams's *A Streetcar Named Desire*, which boasted in its cast two other charter members of the fledgling Studio, Kim Hunter and Karl Malden. Their peers in that first class represented a phalanx of young talent that ensured the Studio would be taken seriously: among them Montgomery Clift, Julie Harris, Anne Jackson, Cloris Leachman, Sidney Lumet, E. G. Marshall, Patricia Neal, Maureen Stapleton, and Eli Wallach. In the next few years Richard Boone, Lee Grant, Eva Marie Saint, Kim Stanley, and Rod Steiger would join as well. At any random workshop you might find yourself among a crop of young talents who would literally define the face of American acting for the next half-century.

This pantheon of acting giants met in a series of rented halls and dance studios, finally settling down in 1955 in a former Greek Orthodox church at 432 West Forty-fourth Street. As they moved about in those early years, the rules for selecting and granting membership also evolved. At first admission was by invitation. By 1952 a more or less permanent system was in place: applicants to the Actors Studio needed to perform two auditions for the selectors, and membership, once granted, was for life.

Newman came to the Studio in sidelong fashion. He was savvy enough about his own limitations that he didn't consider himself adequate Actors Studio material. But he was always game, if nothing else, so when an acquaintance asked him to stand in for the actor with whom she had already performed at her first audition, he agreed. The text she'd selected was a scene from *Battle of Angels,* Tennessee Williams's first Broadway play. Even though it wasn't his own head on the chopping block, Newman was deeply anxious. He was acting in front of the most respected teachers in the world. Or maybe he wasn't acting at all. "They must have misunderstood sheer terror for honest emotion," he recalled.

He survived, and somehow in the aftermath of the audition, there was a foul-up. The actress who was auditioning wasn't admitted. But Newman—who technically hadn't auditioned at all—received notice in the mail that he, in fact, had been. It was a perfect instance of Newman's Luck—and the most important influence on what would become his life's work. "The Actors Studio, whether they like it or not, has either credit or blame for what I've become as an actor," he said throughout his life. "I learned everything I've learned about acting at the Actors Studio."

What he learned was the specific flavor of Stanislavskyan practice developed and propagated by Lee Strasberg, a feisty Ukrainian Jew with a professorial bent who had become the most visible proponent of the Method. Following the Russian model, Strasberg insisted that an actor's chief responsibility was to ferret the emotional truth out of each work, each scene, each line. Specifically, he demanded that his students use their own life histories as reservoirs of emotions that could be used to express the sentiments their roles demanded. Acting became, in his model, a process of self-discovery and even self-analysis.

He encouraged the use of specific techniques to assist his students. In one, "sense memory," they learned to recall and even relive specific emotional events from their lives by thinking of the physical sensations that accompanied the initial experience: how things sounded, smelled, felt to the touch, and so on. Actors could then use these recollected sensory experiences as paths to recovering the emotions that their work called on them to reproduce.

Coupled with this deeply psychological work, Strasberg encouraged a naturalistic acting style that scraped away at the layers of glamour and artifice that were common in older styles of acting and that, he believed, impeded an actor's ability to share emotional truths with the audience. Stereotypically, this combination of unwelled emotion and raw technique could produce overemoting and mumbling; at its finest, though, it gave rise to the Stanley Kowalski and Terry Malloy of Marlon Brando and to the Cal Trask and Jim Stark of James Dean, characters ripped apart by powerful emotional struggles in a way that seemed more real than anything that had ever been filmed before.

Given the frankness and unabashedness that Strasberg's techniques called for, Newman was predictably cautious about diving into work at the Studio. Indeed, as he soon learned to his great pain, he had reason to be. "When I did my first scene for them," he confessed, "there must have been some agonizing reappraisal." The piece he chose was from Pirandello's *Tonight We Improvise*, and as he remembered, Strasberg ripped into his performance. "Lee can be destructive," Newman remembered, "as any teacher can be. That sort of set me back, and from that time on I went mostly as an observer." (Years later Broadway director Gene Saks also recalled Newman's Studio debut as forgettable: "I said, 'He'll never make it. Good-looking kid, but . . .' ")

But Newman was canny enough to understand that simply being in the room—head down, determined—was a blessing. "It gave me a chance to see how the most gifted American actors worked and to see the nature of their exploration," he recalled. And despite the crankiness and pain connected with it, he came to recognize and even revere Strasberg's genius: "Doesn't he get to the heart of the matter beautifully?" he asked a reporter who accompanied him to the Studio a few years later. For at least a decade he would make a regular habit of attending the Tuesday and Friday sessions at the Studio whenever he was in New York, no matter how busy he might be onstage or with a film shoot.

In 1953 photographer Eve Arnold was assigned to shoot a day at the Actors Studio. In the most famous image she created, Newman is right in the center, staring with fierce determination at the work going on in front of him. Around him virtually every man is in a suit and tie, but he's wearing chinos, a white T-shirt, white socks, and deck shoes. He sits astride a chair backward, with one leg up on the seat and the other dangling. His left hand (with wedding band on his pinky) worries an unlit cigarette. His right arm, muscled, sports a chain bracelet. Surely he knows the camera is there, but the look of concentration and attentiveness on his face is deep and genuine; he's there to learn (and yeah, maybe a little bit to be noticed).

At the Actors Studio Newman emerged from his collegiate acting habits into something more fluent, realistic, and professional. "I watched those people," he said, "and realized where my style was sort of oratorical, something out of the 1920s, really, and phony." If, as he later admitted, "I don't think I came to bat frequently: a matter of courage," he nevertheless absorbed everything he saw and heard. "It was monkey see, monkey do," he remembered. "I just sat back there and watched how people did things and had enough sense not to open my big mouth."

He did a few more scenes, seeking help from his teachers and peers in conquering the emotional blockage that he had first encountered at Yale. Some of the instruction he received was technical: "My body movements were all wrong. I was an untuned piano." But some of it went deeper, into the sort of psychological probing that Strasberg considered essential to the acting process. "I discovered that I was primarily a cerebral actor," Newman recalled. "I had a lot to overcome." He would have to learn to access his emotions and incorporate them in performances through sheer application and hard work, and he found that he enjoyed the challenge of it. He was no longer a kid larking about on a stage at Kenyon or a young dad looking for a Yale degree that could get him a job. He had discovered his profession. He was an actor.

WHAT'S MORE, he was a working actor—and not just on TV. In late 1952, at around the time when he was becoming acquainted with the Actors Studio, Newman found himself involved with a new play that, it was hoped, would open on Broadway in the winter.

It was Bill Liebling, one of the agents who'd found him in New Haven, who thought of him for the cast of the latest project by one of his wife's literary clients, William Inge—the follow-up to his debut hit, *Come Back, Little Sheba*. Liebling got Newman a chance to audition for the playwright. "I read for him and thought I'd read very badly," Newman recalled. And he had. But Liebling was tenacious—"Bill always had someone he was pushing," remembered the play's director, Josh Logan—and Newman got a second chance. This time, after reading for Logan, he found himself cast in the small role of a wise-cracking paperboy.

The show was originally called *Front Porch*, but it would soon be retitled *Picnic*. It was the story of a Kansas town seemingly populated primarily by lonely women and dominated by a wealthy family. In the course of a steamy summer day, it is turned upside down by the arrival of a sexually magnetic vagrant named Hal who has come to visit a friend he'd made in college and perhaps cadge a job or at least a few weeks' respite from the road. Rather than money or work, though, Hal winds up helping himself to his old chum's sweetheart, the prettiest girl in town, and running off with her.

The role of Hal was already cast with Ralph Meeker, then an unknown Broadway understudy with a few minor film credits; Janice Rule, another newcomer with a handful of stage and film roles, would play Madge, the female lead. Alan Seymour, the wealthy guy who loses the girl, was written by Inge as someone older and less virile than Hal—which meant, as rehearsals began to reveal, that the character didn't add much spark to the romantic triangle. Worse, as Logan later recalled, the actor who was originally cast as Alan wasn't helping to sell the role: "He was kind of dull." Logan had a brainstorm—why not rewrite the role so that Alan was *younger* than Hal and put Newman in the part? He approached the playwright with this suggestion and received approval. ("Bill Inge, who liked young boys very much, said, 'Oh, sure.'") The role was rewritten specifically for Newman. Suddenly he had gone from a bit part to a featured role.

But he found himself struggling to make the part his own. As he remembered:

> I had it for about four days of rehearsal, and then they said it didn't work this way either, and they engaged somebody older again. He lasted about a week, and then they put me back in it for two days. And Josh Logan said, "There are going to be a few people here to watch the rehearsal tonight, and if you pass with them you can have the part." Well, I saw Elia Kazan walk in, and Tennessee Williams and Dorothy McGuire and a lot of people from the Theatre Guild. I thought it was a wrap. My knees were literally shaking very badly when I got on to the stage. But afterwards Logan came to the footlights and motioned me over and told me I'd got the part.

Indeed, he got more than the part. He would also understudy Meeker in the lead. That meant that he would have two entire rehearsal schedules to deal with. With the main cast he would be Alan Seymour, collegiate and privileged and just a slight bit full of himself, yet too blinded by his own rosy situation to see that he's losing the girl; with the rehearsal cast he would be Hal, a renegade with a checkered past, an animal sensuality, and a willingness to risk his neck for something he wanted. Obviously Alan Seymour was well within the grasp of Paul Newman of Shaker Heights, Kenyon, and Yale. But he would need Logan's help in turning himself into a credible Hal. In particular, he was having trouble with the scene in which Hal seduces Madge while twirling her at the picnic dance.

"He was such a clean-cut, well-put-together boy," Logan said of Newman, "that I said, 'Now, you've got to learn how to be a little *dirtier* to play the part of Hal.' And he said, 'How do you mean?' I said,

'Well, wiggle your ass a little bit when you're dancing.' And he said, 'Do you think I really should?' And I said, 'Sure, go ahead.' And he did, and was just as physical, quickly, as Meeker. He changed from all of his nice-boy upbringing in order to aim for this kind of a dirty Hal, and I think it did Paul a lot of good."

If nothing else, the transformation was definitely noticed by the girl with whom he was dancing throughout all those rehearsals, the young actress who had been cast as the understudy to the role of Madge.

Her name was Joanne Woodward.

Six

ACTUALLY, THEY HAD MET BEFORE.

Earlier in the summer, when he was still in his "guy in the seersucker" phase, Newman had been visiting Maynard Morris, the MCA agent who got him the "Ice from Space" job, and the meeting went on a little long. The agent's next appointment was already waiting for him in the reception area, a young actress with credits and experience no more impressive than Newman's. Morris introduced the two by way of apologizing to her for running late.

As Woodward later remembered it, "I had been making the rounds, and I was hot, sweaty, and my hair was all stringy around my neck. [Morris] brought out a pretty-looking young man in a seersucker suit, all pretty like an Arrow collar ad, and said, 'This is Paul Newman,' and I hated him on sight, but he was so funny and pretty and neat."

Newman too took away an instantaneous reaction: "Jeez, what an extraordinarily pretty girl."

IF THAT neat young man had come to be in the MCA offices that day as a result of a roundabout flight from the sporting goods business, that extraordinarily pretty girl was there because she had always wanted to be. She had been born twenty-two years earlier in the Georgia town of Thomasville and was given a name that bespoke old-time southern origins: Joanne Gignilliat Trimmier Woodward. Gignilliat and Trimmier were family names on her mother's side, the latter indicating a Huguenot lineage. The name Joanne was actually a tribute to her mother's favorite actress, Joan Crawford, altered to accommodate a southern drawl.

Like Theresa Newman, Joanne's mother, the former Elinor Trimmier, had stars in her eyes, and she shared her enthusiasm for the theater and movies with her only girl, the younger of her two children. The zeal took. "My mother tells a marvelous tale of my getting up to do the pledge of allegiance to the flag when I was two," Joanne remembered. "My brother had the measles. He was supposed to do it. I said the pledge of allegiance to the flag, and they applauded, and I said it again, and they applauded again, and I was well into my third rendition when she finally dragged me off the stage."

Elinor Woodward took this irrepressible girl to movies, and the child demonstrated a precocity of taste by naming Laurence Olivier her favorite star. In 1939, when *Gone with the Wind* had its premiere in Atlanta—just fifteen or so miles from Marietta, where the Woodwards were then living—Elinor took nine-year-old Joanne to the big gala; the girl not only scooted away from her mom, she popped up in a car carrying Olivier and his wife, Vivien Leigh, and sat in her idol's lap. She'd go far.

Joanne's father, Wade Woodward, was a public school official, a job that offered neither great security nor great remuneration during the Depression. "He started off being a teacher," Joanne recalled, "and then became a principal in another school, and a superintendent in another, which is one of the main reasons we moved around." He was a cultured man, who eventually left the schooling profession for a position in book publishing, and he was shaping his older child, Wade Jr., into an upright citizen. But he was remote from his daughter and, indeed, had a strained relationship with his wife.

By the end of World War II, when Joanne was in high school, the Woodwards were living in Greenville, South Carolina, and her parents divorced—in part, it has been hinted, because of Elinor's stage-motherly encouragement of Joanne's charm and talent. Always a strong student, Joanne was prompted by her mother to enter beauty pageants and throw herself into the theater program at her high school. Upon graduating in 1947, Joanne wanted to go to Hollywood or New York and become a professional actress, and she had encouragement from one of her teachers. But her father believed in education, and in a compromise Joanne enrolled at Louisiana State University in Baton Rouge, which boasted one of the best drama departments in the region.

After two years of college, though, she returned to Greenville, where she did some secretarial work and acted in some local productions. She appeared in the role of Laura Wingfield, the physically and emotionally hobbled girl in Tennessee Williams's *The Glass Menagerie*, and her performance was strong enough to convince Wade to let her go to New York to take a stab at a career onstage. What was more, he agreed to fund her with a stipend of $60 a month. By 1951 she was on her own—and exactly where she wanted to be.

In New York she lived in the stereotypical starving-actress flat, breakfasting on hot dogs, spending days trudging to modeling agencies and casting offices, buying standing-room tickets to Broadway shows, and nursing coffees and beers in the luncheonettes and bars that young actors favored. She was admitted to the Neighborhood Playhouse, an acting school run by Sanford Meisner, practitioner of a Stanislavskyan acting theory and system distinct from Lee Strasberg's. Meisner saw talent in Joanne, but he also heard a Georgia drawl that had to go, and he forced her to speak differently and to adopt his techniques and strategies for acting. It was a tough education: two acting classes a day, dance classes (taught by Martha Graham), and classes in speech, singing, and theater history. Meisner was a demanding mentor: "Sandy Meisner discovered at an early stage of my career in the Playhouse that I was a character actress, which was a shock to me," Joanne recalled. "I'd always thought I was an ingénue. So he refused to give me anything but character roles, which I hated at the time." The stern education bred a kind of competitive spirit in her. "For two years I was slapped down, torn apart, and taught to act by Sandy Meisner," she said. "One of my ambitions has always been to 'show' Sandy Meisner."

All her effort paid off. Joanne was spotted by a scout for MCA in a Neighborhood Playhouse showcase and brought into the agency as a client of a young agent named John Foreman, who was handling the

television careers of new actors. He got her a series of roles on TV—
in episodes of *Robert Montgomery Presents, Philco Television Playhouse,*
and *Goodyear Television Playhouse*; she played Ann Rutledge in a five-
part series about Abraham Lincoln on *Omnibus*; she even got TV roles
that required that she travel to Hollywood, where she worked regularly, she claimed, because she had nothing else to do with her time. "I
didn't have enough money to rent a car," she later boasted. "Can you
imagine being in California with no car?"

The steady stream of TV jobs was a bracing education, a true trial
by fire: "I remember playing a twelve-year-old girl," Joanne said, "and
two weeks later I played a butcher-knife murderess . . . Those were
marvelous days!" When she made her way back to New York, her
agents got her into the understudy cast of *Picnic*, which was how she
wound up spending afternoons dancing with the newly wiggly-assed
Newman.

THOSE REHEARSALS were only part of what Newman was up to in December 1952. *Picnic* was paying him $200 a week for the twin work of
playing Alan Seymour and understudying Ralph Meeker's Hal.
He and Jackie and little Scott and the baby-on-the-way moved from
Staten Island to a two-bedroom, $88.50-a-month unit in an airy com-
plex of garden apartments in Queens Village, a semisuburban development within a commute of Manhattan yet with some of the feel of a
village—a little like Shaker Heights, in fact. But he would be on the
road before long with the touring tryouts of the show—right after
Christmas.

The plan was to take the play to Columbus, Ohio; then to William
Inge's hometown of Saint Louis; and then of all places to Cleveland,
where Jackie and Scott would join Newman for a brief family reunion.
After that it was on to Boston, where, as so many shows routinely did,
it would apply a final coat of polish under the gaze of Elliot Norton of
the *Boston Post*, the genteel dean of theater critics. If all went to plan,
the show would debut on Broadway in February.

Picnic premiered at the Hartman Theater in Columbus and was well received in *Variety* ("a generous, moving slice of life") and the *Columbus Dispatch* ("a play of wide-dimensional quality, of immediate theatrical effectiveness"). Quite naturally, the bulk of critical attention centered on Inge's script, the acting of Meeker and Janice Rule, the electric support of Eileen Heckart, the stage design by Jo Mielziner, and Josh Logan's directorial hand. But Newman—not identified as a local boy, despite being a hundred miles from Kenyon—also got a couple of nice nods. *Variety* lumped him in with other supporting players in adding "strong assists"; but the *Dispatch* took the time to note, "Mr. Newman plays Alan with sensitively precise understatement"—his first professional review.

From Saint Louis, Newman wrote to his uncle Joe to thank him for sending along a copy of his latest book of poems and to let him know about the upcoming engagement in Cleveland. "A pretty damn good part, too," he bragged. By the time the play arrived onstage at the Hanna Theater, where Theresa Newman used to watch the touring stars perform, it was still a bit wobbly. The daily papers were divided on the play, and even its admirers expressed confusion as to whether certain moments were meant as drama or comedy. Nightlife columnist Windsor French in the *Cleveland Press* called it "an evening to remember forever," and Omar Ranney, drama critic for the same paper, praised it as "a drama of vigorous contents." But W. Ward Marsh in the *Plain Dealer* confessed that it "made me unhappy most of the time," and Arthur Spaeth in the *News* called it "rambling, uneven, thin and minor." All three critics mentioned Newman favorably, but none pointed out that he was a native son of their city, and the show left Cleveland without anyone's writing anything about Newman's connection to his famed newspaperman uncle or the iconic downtown sporting goods store that bore their name.

In Boston, Norton declared *Picnic* "a terrific, driving drama which fills the stage with lusty life and the harsh clamor of passion." He wrote two feature stories about the show, including a lengthy one describing the fixes that Logan and Inge had instituted during the tryouts, but he never once mentioned Newman, not even in his review.

That would change on Broadway. The show opened at the Music

Box Theatre on West Forty-fifth Street on February 19, 1953, and was immediately (although not unanimously) recognized both for its artistic quality and for its commercial appeal. In the *New York Times* Brooks Atkinson called it "an original, honest play with an awareness of people"; in the *Journal-American*, John McClain said "it succeeds wonderfully well in bringing a small theme to a high level." Most of the reviews focused, rightly, on Inge's sophomore effort, the debuts of Meeker and Rule, and the work of reliable pro Josh Logan. But Newman was noticed by the *New York Post* ("excellent work"), the *New York Daily News* ("well played"), the *New York Mirror* ("excellent"), and the *New York World-Telegram* ("does well"). The initial run, a subscribers-only sale to members of the Theatre Guild, was completely sold out. By summer the production was running a profit, and it would pay off the entire $90,000 invested in it before Labor Day. In all it would play 477 performances in its initial production before becoming a standard of the American stage.

Being in a hit play must have been nice, but it's hard to imagine that Newman had much time to appreciate it. While he performed on opening night, Jackie was nigh bursting with their second child; on February 21, less than forty-eight hours after the first Broadway performance of *Picnic*, Newman was a father once again, this time to a daughter, Susan Kendall Newman. Looking at his situation, all Newman saw was luck: "I could just as easily have landed in a flop which closed in a few days. But instead, there I was with no financial responsibilities for over a year, able to continue my studies at the Actors Studio and appear on Broadway at the same time." For the next fourteen months he could reliably bank his *Picnic* checks, attend sessions at the Actors Studio, oversee his growing family, bask in a little bit of glory (*Theater World* named him one of the most promising new stars of the year), and maybe look ahead to bigger things.

HE HAD an additional reason to think positively about his situation. Television series kept scooping him up, for instance. MCA had assigned a young agent named John Foreman to find him work, and

Foreman remembered it as one of the easiest jobs he ever had. "He looked like a Greek god," Foreman later said. "Paul was cast for nearly every part he tried out for."*

In 1953, while he was still performing in *Picnic*, Newman appeared at least five times on TV. On the episodic dramatic showcase *The Web* he played the spoiled, gambling, womanizing son of an immigrant scrap metal magnate (in "Scrap") and a Korean War veteran en route to prison on a murder charge who manages to escape, only to fall in love with a blind girl he meets in his flight (in "One for the Road"). The scripts were awful—he admitted as much in a letter to his uncle Joe—but the parts were juicy, and his approach to them was wisely utilitarian: it sometimes seemed as if he was working out problems of technique in an Actors Studio session.

He had better luck with material and collaborators in a trio of performances on *You Are There*, the famed CBS series in which Walter Cronkite and other actual newsmen pretended to offer live coverage of historical events. In the show's initial season he portrayed Brutus in "The Assassination of Julius Caesar" and Plato in "The Death of Socrates." ("Not right now, please," he says to a reporter sticking a microphone in his face outside the prison where the doomed philosopher is being held.) When the series debuted its second season, in September 1953, he played the title role in "The Fate of Nathan Hale." All three shows were directed by Sidney Lumet, and the casts included the likes of E. G. Marshall, James Gregory, Joseph Wiseman, Robert Culp, and Richard Kiley. It was top-shelf stuff, and Newman played it well, imparting some modern vitality and convincing passion into characters and situations that might otherwise have tended toward the formal, stiff, and declamatory. The freedom from financial concerns, the stability of the play, the careful, silent observation of powerful players at the Actors Studio—it was all turning him into a capable performer.

But he still had his limits. In January 1953 Ralph Meeker needed

---

* He wasn't alone in this impression. Among Newman's neighbors in Queens Village was a comic book artist named Gil Kane who saw in Newman's face the makings of an iconic American hero and actually designed his most famous character, Hal Jordan, aka the Green Lantern, after Newman.

some time away from *Picnic*, and Newman filled in as Hal for eight performances. Suddenly he seemed to understand why Josh Logan had deemed him insufficient in the role during the understudy rehearsals. "Ralph [was] a big, beefy, muscular, sexual, physical kind of guy," Newman remembered. And he tried hard to project the same animal qualities that had made Meeker's performance a success. But he didn't quite make it. After Meeker returned, Newman asked Logan if he could play Hal in the touring company of the show. "Well," Logan responded, "it was a very interesting performance, but you don't carry *any* sexual threat at all." Newman reeled: "I worried that bone around for a long time," he confessed later on. "I've been chewing on that one for twenty years."

AT LEAST one member of the understudy cast of *Picnic* would have disagreed strongly with Logan's assessment. Joanne Woodward didn't reckon too much of Newman's craft off the bat. "When I first saw him act," she remembered, "I thought he was terrible. And he was. Just a pretty face." But the face, nevertheless, was pretty enough to remind her of a Botticelli angel.

In New York she had been dating a lot of young men, even if she wasn't exactly the type that was in vogue. "The fashion," she recalled, "was for little, dark neurotic girls from the wrong side of the tracks. The boys wouldn't date anybody else. I tried to turn myself into that type, but it didn't work."

She needn't have bothered, though, for the sake of catching Newman's eye. As he'd said, she'd struck him with her looks at their first meeting, and as they got to know each other during the rehearsals and downtime on *Picnic*, she came to seem to him an ideal girl. "She was modern and independent," he remembered. "I was shy, a bit conservative. It took me a long time to persuade her that I wasn't as dull as I looked."

Too, there was the impediment that he was married, with two kids—forbidden fruit, at least in theory. Some observers saw clearly that something was brewing between Joanne and Newman. "We all suspected," said Eileen Heckart, who was in the cast of *Picnic*. "In her little assertive way there was quite a lot of steel in that lady." But she wasn't so stuck on Newman that she denied herself romantic entangle-ments. She dated Marlon Brando for a time in 1953 and for a period was engaged to James Costigan, a playwright and actor who was a member of the Actors Studio. Newman, in fact, introduced them, telling Costigan that he could get him a date with "a wonderful girl."

For his part, Newman was caught in a household that seemed more and more like a trap. Scott, not yet three, was a real discipline prob-lem, prone to temper tantrums and refusing to be consoled. "I can re-member going to Paul and Jackie's apartment," recalled a friend, "and being unable to carry on a conversation because he was yelling and screaming. He was uncontrollable." Jackie, initially supportive of her husband's career choices—she'd already followed him to Woodstock, Cleveland, New Haven, and New York, after all—began to feel like a satellite. She was stuck at home with two small children while he spent days and often nights in Manhattan working, looking for work, schmoozing, and drinking with his acting buddies.

There were real tensions between them. "Jackie lost her interest in acting and the world that meant everything to Paul when she had her children," remarked a friend. "Her nature is shy and retiring, while Paul's is gregarious and blossoms when he's with people interested in the same things he is. He likes late gatherings of writers and actors, as did Joanne. But you seldom saw Jackie. Paul and Joanne were simply two highly attractive people with a deep mutual interest and an obvi-ous feeling of companionship."

Jackie had good reason to be suspicious. Of all the time that her husband spent in Manhattan, a considerable portion was in Joanne's company. Mutually attracted but staying at a remove from each other out of respect for Newman's marriage, the two were bonding. As Joanne remembered, "From the beginning, Paul and I had an advan-tage: we were good friends before we were lovers. I mean, we really liked each other. We could talk to each other, we could tell each other anything without fear of ridicule or rejection. There was trust."

As THIS taboo romance kindled, Newman held on to a semblance of familial normalcy in part by striking up a semiregular correspondence with his uncle Joe. In July 1953 Minnie, the eldest of Simon and Hannah Newman's children, died, and Paul wrote in part to offer condolences and in part to claim entitlement to a portion of her estate. Joe must have agreed, because in November Newman wrote to thank him for a check and to explain that "Jackie and I have been toying with the idea of getting away from apartment house living and buying a small house in Connecticut."

In lively, literate letters, some written between cues at the theater during performances of *Picnic*, Newman told his uncle of the various cousins who passed through New York—Dick and George Campen, Ed Newman—and the dinners, drinking bouts, and free theater tickets he bestowed upon them. He asked Joe several times to come to New York himself (often jokingly calling it "New Yorick") and enjoy similar hospitality. He sent pictures of "Mad Scott" and news of baby Susan and of "Jackson," as he occasionally referred to his wife. He spoke excitedly of taking a getaway trip to Key West when his vacation from the play came due in February.

And he revealed that he still harbored anxieties about his chosen profession: "The old addage [*sic*] about actors goes something to the effect that for every dollar earned, fifty cents should be saved, because an actor does well if he works an average of every other day. This quaint phrase has stuck in my memory, tho [*sic*] I confess a certain inability to conform to it." By the end of 1953 he was wondering if the continued popularity of the play that had made his name, such as it was, wasn't hurting him: "Some offers . . . are coming my way, which are difficult to even think about, because I'm tied to *Picnic* until June. After that I'll probably be a nice cold property."

But then in January 1954, in the last of the letters that his uncle saved, a note of cautious optimism entered in a guarded and slightly remote phrase: "There are some movie offers."

Seven

THERE THEY STAND, ELBOW TO ELBOW, ICONS OF MALE BEAUTY as perfect as classical sculptures or paintings of Renaissance boys, but living and breathing.

The one on the left is shorter and thicker of brow, with a slit of a smile and an open-necked shirt and a pocketknife that he tosses in his hand, blade bared. The one on the right is longer of face, and his hair is wavier, and his polka-dot bow tie and the pencil wedged behind his left ear give him the air of a shopkeeper.

They're delicious, both of them, with slender bodies, finely cut faces, thick heads of hair, killer smiles. Energized and chummy and young and burgeoning with the heady promise of themselves, they take your breath away: you simply can't decide which is the more perfect.

The taller seems more nervous, quicker to joke and snicker and touch a finger to his nose and, as well, to drop the pretense of play and get serious when asked to; he even gives direction to the other fellow. The little guy seems genuinely edgy: not just because of the knife play, which introduces a random threat into a mundane moment, but also in the insouciant mumbling of his words and in the unfettered way impulses burst out of him.

For instance, somebody off camera starts talking about girls and asks the little guy if he thinks the girls go for the tall fellow. Before an answer can come, the tall guy anxiously interrupts: "It's a point of whether I go for the girls, you know." So the off-camera voice changes tack and asks the tall guy if he thinks the girls would go for the other fellow. He can barely find words: "Ooooh . . . great . . ."

And then they turn and face each other and the smaller guy blurts out, just like that, "Kiss me." "Can't here," the tall guy snaps back, and they both laugh, but he's been rocked on his heels a bit; you can see it.

If you were scoring it as a prizefight, the little guy would have won on points. In fact, it's something rather like a prizefight: a screen test, conducted sometime in early 1954. Newman is the taller guy, trying to convince the director of his aptness for a big new movie with two meaty roles for young leading-man types.

Surviving details are scant, but the sense is that the two weren't auditioning for the same role. The other guy was probably already cast and Newman was fishing for a chance to play his brother. He didn't get it. Instead a third actor, who like these two was clawing his way up from TV to the movies, played the part—a fellow by the name of Richard Davalos, who would never again get near anything like this part, the morally upright but emotionally hollow son of a successful California farmer in Elia Kazan's adaptation of John Steinbeck's *East of Eden*.

Playing his brother, Cal, the headstrong and yearning black sheep of a fractured family was, of course, the guy with the knife from Newman's screen test: James Dean.

NEWMAN ARRIVED in Hollywood in 1954 on the strength of one of those offers he wrote his uncle Joe about. The movie studios were signing talent from the Actors Studio, and Newman, like Dean, was among the lucky cohort they chose.

During the run of *Picnic*, despite his fears that he would become a cold property, Newman's MCA agents had pricked Hollywood's interest in signing him to a contract. Anyone could see that he had the looks to make it in movies. And if his performance as Alan Seymour wasn't exactly a sizzler, his increasingly confident and competent work on television showed that he could, potentially, muster whatever a film role might require of him.

It was still potential, though. In 1953 he was one of three Actors Studio members to audition for a production of *Oklahoma!* that was being planned by Fred Zinnemann. The big dog in the trio of hopefuls was Rod Steiger, who remembered testing in color and in black and white with James Dean and said, "None of us knew Newman at the time." Zinnemann didn't like what he saw in any of them, however, particularly not Newman. "Paul Newman is a handsome boy, but quite stiff, to my disappointment," he wrote in his casting notes. "He lacks experience and would need a great deal of work. Still, in the long run he may be the right boy for us. He certainly has a most winning personality, although I wish he had a little more cockiness and bravado."

Later that year, with the end of his commitment to the Broadway production of *Picnic* in sight and no interest in playing the role of Alan Seymour in the upcoming road production, Newman took a hard look at other movie offers his agents at MCA were bringing him. "I had a lot of people inquire—Metro, Columbia, Paramount, Hal Wallis. All of them were sort of sniffing around, and I kept saying no," he recalled. But, he said, "There's that horrible moment when people say, 'You know, you are hot and cold in this business, and there comes a time when opportunity knocks, and if you pass up the last one, then all of a sudden, for no reason . . .' "

As with other major decisions he'd made about his career, he acted out of practical necessity: "I was starting to get a little worried, and I had a family to support and everything, so I went into this thing." He was flown out to Los Angeles for screen tests, and on April 8 Warner Bros. signed him to the sort of contract that it had been presenting to fledgling actors for decades: two movies a year, with an option on a third, for five years, plus the right to loan him out to other studios; in exchange, he got $1,000 a week, with a guarantee of ten weeks of work annually, a promise of a $250-per-week raise each year, and the opportunity to appear in a "first-class" stage show in New York for up to nine months.

Three weeks after he signed the deal, the *New York Times* reported that he had been cast in a feature role as Basil, the hero of the biblical drama *The Silver Chalice*, a $3 million adaptation of a popular novel by

Thomas B. Costain about the creation of a drinking cup commemorating the last supper of Jesus Christ. The veteran (if not especially distinguished) English director Victor Saville had been assigned the material, and he dutifully—if dubiously—pronounced of his star, "I saw Paul Newman on Broadway and I knew here was the ideal man for the role of the Greek silversmith who fashioned the chalice."

The cast would include Virginia Mayo, Jack Palance, and the Italian starlet Pier Angeli, and it was intended to be a big Christmastime CinemaScope release in an age when movie theaters that had lost customers to television were being filled once again by such classical spectacles as *Quo Vadis*, *The Robe*, and *The Egyptian*. It was a plum, in fact—and it might well have been the last film Newman ever made.

In May Newman packed up Jackie, Scott, and Susan and, stopping en route to pay a visit to Shaker Heights, dropped them off in Wisconsin and headed out to Hollywood. He rented a furnished apartment— little more than a glorified motel room—and the family would visit him during the production. But most of the time he was on his own.

He didn't embrace the lifestyle. He felt an immediate kinship with the handful of New York actors then working in Hollywood, and he spent a little time socializing with Dean, whom he introduced to Angeli on the set of *Chalice*, kindling what would become a brief, intense affair. But he found himself by and large deprived of the camaraderie of actors that so enthralled him on Broadway and around the New York TV studios. And he developed a reputation as an uncooperative smart-ass.

There was the time he met the producer Sam Spiegel, who had just made *The African Queen* and was now casting *On the Waterfront*. Spiegel had only recently begun to work under his own obviously Jewish name rather than billing himself as S. P. Eagle, as he had done previously. Newman was screen-tested, among scores of other actors, for the role of ex-boxer Terry Malloy. And when he met the producer, he recalled, he was offered what was no doubt meant to be sage advice.

" 'Have you ever thought of changing your name, from Paul Newman to something else?'

"I said, 'Why?'

"He said, 'Well, it doesn't sound very phonetic.'

"I said, 'You mean it sounds Jewish.'

"He said, 'All right, if you want to put it like that—it sounds Jewish.'

"So I said, 'Yes, as a matter of fact, I have thought about changing my name.'

"He said, 'To what?'

"I said, 'To S. P. Newman.' "

("That was the last conversation I ever had with him," Newman later confessed. "I could have destroyed my career.")

He wasn't doing much better on the film set. As soon as the shoot began, trouble started. Newman had been attending classes at the Actors Studio for nearly eighteen months and was accustomed to talking about the intricacies of performances in ways that didn't necessarily fit into Hollywood's clock-punching production schedules. It was still the early days in the history of American Method acting, and the style of performer that the Studio produced hadn't yet been absorbed comfortably into an industry interested in stars and not artists. Right away Newman gave the studio just the sort of fits they'd come to expect from New York Method actors, questioning the script and the direction in a way that his bosses and colleagues saw as confrontational and insubordinate.

One day a *Variety* reporter showed up during the production and found Newman at loggerheads with Saville over a speech Basil was supposed to deliver after having a divine revelation that would inspire the crafting of the chalice. "If you had just seen a vision, what would you do?" he asked the reporter. "Wouldn't you want to be completely quiet and go off by yourself for a while? They had some words for me to say, but I don't want to say any—I just want to show what I feel. Maybe it won't work out. Maybe I won't be able to show it at all, and we'll have to go back to the words. But I think this man is so worked up that when the vision comes he's—well, he's limp. It would take an hour for him even to touch his hand to the chalice to try to reproduce what he has seen."

Jack Warner, notoriously boorish and bullheaded even for a Hollywood studio boss, didn't take to such fussiness, and he made it clear to

Newman that he should shut up and work. "I was flailing around and got a reputation in Hollywood as a very difficult actor," Newman admitted. "Every time I asked a question there was trouble." He couldn't do the smallest thing that was asked of him without causing an incident. "I had to ride a camel," he remembered years later. "Have you ever tried to ride a camel? The gait is very uneven. Just try to hit a mark on a camel." What was worse was that he knew in his heart that he was doing a poor job: "I couldn't handle the language I was supposed to speak. My acting was terrible, and I knew it was terrible."

This wasn't the sort of nervous fear he had felt about exposing himself at Yale. This was an honest professional assessment of himself and the production: he was doing a lousy job and he was making a lousy picture, and if nothing else, he was smart enough to recognize it and come up with a plan. "Three weeks after we started shooting," he said, "I called my agent in New York screaming desperately for him to get me a play. I figured the picture would kill me. I wasn't really convinced that I would survive as an actor."

He made it back to New York at the end of the summer with his tail between his legs, eager to get as much work under his belt as he could and strengthen his reputation prophylactically for the big hit it was about to take when *Chalice* saw the light of day. Again he got lucky: Robert Montgomery, the actor who'd become a successful television producer and film director, had planned to bring a new drama, entitled *The Desperate Hours*, to Broadway at the end of the year, but he had pushed the opening back a few months so that he could act as an adviser on Dwight Eisenhower's presidential election campaign. As a result of the delay Cliff Robertson, who'd been set to play one of the leads, had to back out of the show. By October, Newman had been cast in his role, with rehearsals planned for the holiday season and an opening on Broadway scheduled for February.*

In the interim, Newman's agents landed him some solid television roles. In "Guilty Is the Stranger," an episode of *Goodyear Television*

---

* Robertson would, ironically, appear in the 1955 film of *Picnic* in the role Newman had originated onstage.

Playhouse directed by Arthur Penn and written by Tad Mosel, he played a Korean War veteran who visits the wealthy, widowed mother (Fay Bainter) of a slain comrade. The young man speaks of his great affection for the dead boy, and he knows all kinds of details about the house, the family, and the fellow's sweetheart (Pat Crowley). He's embraced by the older woman, but the younger one remains suspicious of him, eventually tricking him into revealing that not only wasn't he a friend of her fallen beau but that he may have accidentally caused his death. His confession is so wrenching, heartfelt, and tragic that he is taken in by the women despite his awful deed.

Newman is strong in the role, believable first as an overeager gladhander, then as a conniving huckster with a surfeit of charm (he absolutely preens in the ugly suit of clothes—the "Dapper Dan"—he buys himself with the widow's money), and finally as a young man riddled with guilt and shame. It was the first time he ever displayed the combination of brashness, fragility, impulsiveness, and struggle toward decency that would become his screen skin. "I felt comfortable in the part," he recalled. "It was the first part I'd ever played that I found the character for."

The performance caught the eye of a young screenwriter named Stewart Stern who was finishing a similar script, "Thunder of Silence," for the same TV series. He wound up convincing the producers to cast Newman in the role of a soldier who comes home from World War II to the family farm to find a pair of displaced European immigrants who've been sent by the U.S. government to live and work alongside his parents. Until his arrival, the arrangement is going poorly, but the young man, despite being haunted by his wartime experiences, is able to help the immigrants adapt to their surroundings and turn the situation around.

Both productions were well received, within the business and by audiences. And it would just be a matter of weeks between their airing and the start of rehearsals on *The Desperate Hours*. But in that time, during the week before Christmas, *The Silver Chalice* was released, and Newman reaped just the whirlwind he had feared.

THE PICTURE was ponderous, wooden, static, contrived, and unintentionally funny—and not often enough to transform it into campy fun. Saville and his producers had decided to make a kind of experimental film set on stark, expressionistic stages with hints of modernism in the design and color; nothing was realistic and all the decor was geared for an effect that was more puzzling than dramatic. It begins with a prologue set in A.D. 20, when the gifted boy silversmith Basil (played by Peter Reynolds) and the slave girl Helena (a sixteen-year-old Natalie Wood) share their dreams before having them dashed by the death of their kindly master. Helena becomes a courtesan (and Virginia Mayo); Basil (now Newman), who had been promised both liberty and an inheritance by the kindly master, finds himself enslaved to the man who stole his fortune.

Eventually he runs off and is taken in by a group of Christians, who ask him to fashion a chalice commemorating their lord, Jesus, and his disciples. Basil actually meets Jesus and has a religious awakening, and so he agrees to craft the cup, which becomes the most wanted object in all the world: the Roman government feels that capturing and melting it would help them quell the Christian fervor sweeping the provinces, while the Christians venerate it as an object bearing the exact likeness of their god. Basil, who is presumed to know where the chalice is hidden, becomes a hunted man. At the same time, he is caught in a love triangle between the wanton Helena and Deborra (Pier Angeli), the Christian girl he has married and whose faith he has adopted.

It's awful. One scene, one calculated effect, is worse than the next— or maybe they're equally bad; it's hard to say. As a sexpot, Mayo is absolutely curdling: matronly at thirty-four despite her garish seraglio costumes and floozy's makeup. ("Be neither slave nor Christian but an artist . . . and my love," she implores Basil as she peers up from beneath silver-painted eyelids, and never has slavery held such visceral appeal.) Angeli is a pleasingly waiflike presence, and Jack Palance has meaty, eye-rolling fun as a charlatan named Simon the Magician who proposes to perform miracles even more astonishing than those attributed to Jesus. Newman, wearing a short costume that barely reaches his lower thighs (he castigated it as a "cocktail dress"), often bears a pained, puzzled look in his eyes; he's handsome enough, and he seems earnest, but he's also hopelessly out of place, and to be fair, there would have been no apparent advantage in harmonizing with such a garish, stilted, and vacuous film. Words dribble from him in agonizing rote. Your heart goes out.

Alas, critics don't work from the heart, and the reviews were more or less savage. *Variety* called the picture "episodic and overblown"; "cumbersome and sometimes creaking" hissed the *New York Times*. And Newman himself came in for the worst of it: the *New York Daily News* called his "static performance . . . disappointing"; the *New York World* called him "Jack Newman" and found him "excessively sullen"; and *The New Yorker*, in a comment that he would commit to memory and recite back to interviewers for years, declared, "[He] delivers his lines with the emotional fervor of a Putnam Division conductor announcing local stops."

Newman caught up with the film in January, when he was in Philadelphia for the trial run of *The Desperate Hours*. At the time—and for some years yet to come—it was his habit to sneak cans of beer and bags of homemade popcorn into theaters to enjoy during the show. As he recalled, on this particular night,

> About 10 of us went to this little all-night movie house to see my screen debut. We must have smuggled four cases of beer into that place. And we finished them all. This friend of mine, who had just recovered from hepatitis, couldn't drink. They had a musical going on afterward and he wanted to see it, so he stayed. We got halfway down the block when another guy realized he had left his gloves in the theater. So we went back. The usher shoved his light underneath the seats. There was this one guy sitting in the middle of four cases of empty beer cans. He looked like the guy who passes gas at a party.

In fact, his actual reaction to the film and its reception was deeper and more disturbing. "I was horrified and traumatized when I saw the film," he confessed. "I was sure my acting career had begun and ended in the same picture." For years he would groan at the mention of the thing. "It was god-awful," he said in a typical assessment. "It's kind of a distinction to say I was in the worst film to be made in the entirety of the 1950s."

In 1963, when *The Silver Chalice* was scheduled to play several nights on a local Los Angeles television station, Newman spent $1,200 on ads in the city's two daily newspapers attempting to dissuade people from watching it: Bordered in black like funeral announcements, they read "Paul Newman apologizes every night this week—Channel 9." (The ads backfired: people tuned in to see what sort of train wreck had occasioned this gesture, and the ratings were strong. Newman laughed off the stunt as "a classic example of the arrogance of the affluent.")

Eventually, he saw some good, not in the film itself, but in having made it at all and, in time, in transcending it: "Everyone thinks it was a disaster just because it was terrible, but I say it wasn't. It's like juvenile delinquency: if you can be the worst kid on your block, you can make a name for yourself." But he never quite forgot the sting. When it was proposed to him a few years later that he read the script for *Ben-Hur* with an eye toward starring in it, he declared, "I wore a cocktail dress once. Never again!" And more than four decades later, when he costarred with the rising young actor Liev Schreiber, he offered this advice: "When they ask you to do *The Silver Chalice 2*, don't do it!"

THERE WAS one bit of fallout from *The Silver Chalice* that lingered in a way that stung as badly as the negative reviews—virtually everybody who wrote about it parroted the strange claim that Newman looked like somebody else: "a tall, blue-eyed young man named Paul Newman who will inevitably be compared to Marlon Brando because of his striking resemblance to the actor" *(Los Angeles Examiner);* "bears an astonishing resemblance to Marlon Brando" *(New York World);* "looks like Marlon Brando" *(Hollywood Reporter);* "a lad who resembles Marlon Brando" *(The New Yorker);* "a poor man's Marlon Brando" *(The Saturday Review);* and on and on.

It was a damning and, frankly, dunderheaded claim. The two looked almost nothing alike: Brando, even the fit and youthful Brando, was wide-faced, with a bigger nose, thicker lips, and heavily lidded eyes; his vaguely simian air looked sensual and subversive even when, as in his debut film, *The Men*, he was playing an ordinary fellow. Newman's features were always more angular and delicate, and Warner Bros. had gone to some lengths to soften his appearance for the role of Basil, even experimenting with dying his hair a lighter shade. He was pretty, preppy, and decent: Alan Seymour, the rich boy who didn't win the girl. The two did share a similar brow line—dark and strong and often furrowed to connote emotion—but for the most part it was an absurd comparison.

And that wasn't what was worst. What embarrassed Newman most, as can be imagined, was the comparison of their acting. Brando, the colossal Method actor of the moment, had already amassed a body of screen work that would be the envy of any actor of any school: *A Streetcar Named Desire, Viva Zapata!, The Wild One*, and, most recently, *On the Waterfront*. As a regular at the Actors Studio, Newman knew exactly where he stood in relation to Brando as a talent; at his most self-satisfied, which wasn't often, he wouldn't ever have dreamed of putting himself in the same league. To be fair, in a couple of his television roles he played punks and drifters and confused kids who had more than a bit of a Brandoish vibe about them. But there was nothing of that in *Chalice*.

If anybody knew what the real gap was between the two—in looks and actorly skill—it would have been Newman, and he writhed when he read these dismissive comparisons. "First they said I looked like Brando," he complained to a reporter. "Then it was agreed that we had the same 'quality.' All I want to know is what quality? I have yet to have anyone come up with the answer to that."

In fact, he himself had the answer, as he revealed some years later: "I like to nail those guys, and it's very simple to do. You ask them, 'What is Marlon's basic quality? What does he carry within himself?' Well, they're absolutely stumped, and they flop around a lot, and I ask, 'Well, what do you think *my* basic quality is?' And they wouldn't know that either. They didn't have the vaguest idea of what Marlon's focus is, which is eruptability. Eruptability is always in the potential of the masses-type hero. And the quality that I carry is Ivy League—Shaker Heights and like that."

So he could explain it: Brando was volatility, explosiveness, danger, excitement, sex, risk, passion; he, on the other hand, was a nice-looking young man from a respectable family and good schools. If he was going to get anywhere as an actor, he knew, he would have to find a way to break out of himself.

Eight

TAUT AND ITCHY, WITH HIS COARSE DENIM CLOTHING AND brush-cut hair, he roams about the room spilling unfocused energy, somehow imparting at once a sense of ownership and the appearance of having never been in so fine a place before: a wild beast brought in from the outdoors without being housebroken. He waves a pistol around with a frightening lack of caution and speaks from behind the mean slits of his eyes in an insinuating, guttural tone: "You don't gotta do nothin' but keep your trap shut," he tells the people around him, and, "I could kill you just for kicks."

His name is Glenn Griffin, and he's famous—or, more correctly, infamous: not even twenty-five years old and on the front pages of all the newspapers. ("They always gotta use the same lousy picture," he whines.) With his kid brother, Hank, and a muscle-bound goon named Robish, Griffin has busted out of prison and found a suburban Indianapolis house in which to hide and wait for money and a ride to freedom. Gun in hand, oozing with angry contempt for a typical household run by a dad with a white-collar pedigree, he's the nightmare lurking just beyond the hedgerows protecting the postwar American dream from the interlopers who would shatter it.

The situation—three fugitives taking a random family hostage—had actually occurred in Pennsylvania in 1952, and it had inspired the author and playwright Joseph Hayes to fictionalize the scenario as a novel entitled *The Desperate Hours*. The book was a best seller, and Hayes was called upon, uniquely, to develop it as a play and a film at nearly the same time. While Robert Montgomery was working in New York rehearsal spaces with a cast that included Newman as Griffin, newcomer George Grizzard as his brother, and Karl Malden as the man of the house, William Wyler was doing the same in Hollywood with Humphrey Bogart, Dewey Martin, and Fredric March, respectively. The play would debut in Philadelphia in January 1955, move to Broadway in February, and run through August; two months later the film, rewritten to recast Griffin as a man of Bogart's age, would have its own premiere.

The success of *The Desperate Hours* was hardly guaranteed. Montgomery hadn't wanted Newman, who turned thirty before the show came to New York, but rather someone older; only when he went down to a police station and saw how many hardened juvenile offenders came through the doors did he see the sense of casting someone with a youthful air. (Montgomery was quite fond of authority; an outspoken proponent of the anti-Communist blacklists in the entertainment business, he had the FBI vet every member of the play's cast for subversive affiliations.) As he had with Victor Saville, Newman peppered Montgomery with inquiries about his character's motivations; questioning the logic of a stage direction to move around a table, he was told testily, "Damn it! Because there's no place else to go!"

"Mr. Montgomery and I never saw eye to eye on any particular thing," Newman confessed. "He's a very bright guy, but we had personality clashes." More deeply, he declared that he never had a handle on the character of Glenn Griffin and that the entire enterprise was melodramatic. "We got it up on its feet too fast," he opined. "There was no foundation underneath it—we blocked the first three acts the first three days of rehearsal—I never had any exploratory period." Later he added, "I had played the whole thing at a terrible pitch of panic." There was some truth to this: the scene that the original Broadway cast played for a March salute-to-Broadway show on NBC certainly bore traces of a potboiler. But *The Desperate Hours* was a sensation wherever it played, and Newman was especially lauded, even by those critics who agreed with him that his performance was too wound up from the start.

In Philadelphia the reviews from the local papers and the showbiz trades were uniformly positive, and Newman—still on-screen in *The Silver Chalice*—was cited as a standout. In New York the notices were even better: "Paul Newman plays the boss thug with a wildness that one is inclined to respect," wrote Brooks Atkinson in the *New York Times;* "an effective performance on a fairly splashy level," said Walter Kerr in the *New York Herald-Tribune;* and John Chapman in the *New York Daily News* called the performance "evil, neurotic and vibrant—a first-class piece of work." Most gratifying, perhaps, was an item from the Louisville *Courier-Journal,* of all places: "Newman is so thoroughly contemptible as Griffin that it is hard to believe he is playing a part. One knows he is after seeing him in *The Chalice* [*sic*] in which he in no way resembled the role he has in *The Desperate Hours*"—precisely what he had hoped for when he sought the role. The play was almost unanimously cited as a crackerjack bit of tension, several critics compared it to *The Petrified Forest,* and it wound up winning Tony Awards for best play and best direction.*

It wasn't a complete triumph. Newman was paid $700 a week for the show—$300 less than he would have earned in a film at Warner Bros. And by the end of the run audiences had dwindled despite the rave reviews; the cast, who took pay cuts as a result of the poor financial condition of the production, blamed the producers for not sustaining the advertising campaign; investors, who included Stephen Sondheim, Dominick Dunne, John Forsythe, and Montgomery himself, didn't make nearly what they should have. The show was finally forced to close in August after 212 performances when Malden, its biggest star, left.**

Despite that disappointment, Newman had to be happy: twice he'd been on Broadway, and twice he'd come away with his professional

---

* At the time the Tonys did not name the nominees who didn't win, so it's impossible to know where Newman stood.
** There was a strange footnote to the play's success: *Life* magazine sent a camera crew to photograph the actual house where the invasion took place and wound up being sued by the very family who had been taken hostage there, who felt their privacy was being violated by the publicity. Their suit went all the way to the U.S. Supreme Court where, in 1966, it was unsuccessfully argued by Richard M. Nixon, then working as a Wall Street lawyer.

standing and personal confidence enhanced. Warner Bros. still held his leash, but he had demonstrated a flexibility that surely they would notice. He had also demonstrated a collegiality uncommon in the profession. George Grizzard was even less known than Newman when he auditioned for *The Desperate Hours*, and he was so out of his element in New York that he showed up to read for the role of a juvenile criminal in a jacket and tie. Newman felt comfortable with him in the role, though, and lobbied Montgomery to give him the part. Through the run of the show, the two palled around a bit. "He treated me like a little brother," Grizzard recalled. "He introduced me to movie stars."

At home things were peaceful. Newman had rented a large apartment in the Fresh Meadows section of Queens, a former golf course that had been transformed into a postwar suburban paradise—a place even more like Shaker Heights than Queens Village. Theresa Newman had come to New York for the opening night of *Desperate Hours* and stayed on to help after Jackie gave birth to another daughter, Stephanie, that spring. Newman's neighbors recognized him as a celebrity, but they also appreciated him as a down-to-earth sort. Recalled Bob Lardine, later a writer at the *New York Daily News*, "It didn't annoy him in the least when fellow residents called out, 'Hi, Paul' as he walked around outside his duplex with his shirt off, taking in the sun. He was always cheerful, always ready to talk with anyone." In August the growing Newman family was photographed, along with other members of *The Desperate Hours* cast, cavorting at a newly opened amusement park. Happy times.

While the play was still running, Newman took television engagements. In July he appeared in *The Death of Billy the Kid*, a teleplay by Gore Vidal, to whom Newman had recently been introduced by Tennessee Williams. The script that Vidal had produced at once celebrated the independence and individuality of the famed western outlaw, revealed the violence and possible madness at his heart, and critiqued the culture that turned a troubled young man with such cruel tendencies into a folk hero. Robert Mulligan was selected to direct, and the cast included Jason Robards and Harold J. Stone. The intense psychological nature of the depiction was something of a novelty, and Newman's performance was received well—better, generally, than the film itself. He tried to interest Warner Bros. in a feature film version as a follow-up to *The Silver Chalice*, and they nibbled, but they felt the property needed to be altered for the screen.*

In fact, Newman and the studio couldn't agree on much of anything, even though his contract called for him to get back to work. Absent a firm assignment, he stayed on in New York. His next TV job was his strangest yet: the role of teenage George Gibbs in a musical production of *Our Town*. The show was an odd mix of talent. Frank Sinatra, still surging after having his career and personal life bottom out in the early 1950s, would play the role of the Stage Manager and have songs written especially for the production by his in-house composing team of Sammy Cahn and Jimmy Van Heusen. (One bona fide standard, "Love and Marriage," would come out of their work.) Sinatra's favorite arranger, Nelson Riddle, would lead the orchestra. Emily Webb, George's neighbor, classmate, and eventual wife, would be played by Eva Marie Saint, fresh off her Oscar-nominated performance in *On the Waterfront*. And Delbert Mann, whose film *Marty* was currently in release and would dominate the next round of Oscars, would direct.

Sinatra was the big dog at the party, and he didn't do a lot of television, and he hadn't much enjoyed working with Method actors. (He'd just completed *Guys and Dolls* with Marlon Brando, and had made his famous comeback in *From Here to Eternity* alongside Montgomery Clift, and he had bonded with neither.) So there was ample opportunity for friction when Newman, with his love of rehearsal and breaking things down and his habit of asking about motives, turned up for not one or two or three but *four* weeks of rehearsals. Newman, of course, loved all the tinkering and speculation this allowed, and he used the time to ease his way into the skin of the young George Gibbs. "Every day he comes in for rehearsal he's a year younger," said a witness on the set. Sinatra, an infamous one-take-and-I'm-outta-

---

* At least one critic complained that Vidal and Newman's Billy "traipsed about" too much, a thinly veiled innuendo about the homosexual implications in the script, which might explain Warner Bros.' trepidation.

here actor, griped predictably about the very same process: "It takes only four weeks to do some good *movies.*" But then, the two were very different talents. As Newman admitted to a reporter, "I'm not much of a singer . . . They wanted me to harmonize, and somewhere I lost the harmony and never found it again."

But the production wound up a success. Sinatra is cool and jaunty, and yet with his pipe and his knowing air, he seems curiously at home in Thornton Wilder's bit of old-time New Hampshire. Newman is filled with coltish energy, breathy awkwardness, and when George needs to get serious, an applied sobriety that feels genuinely adolescent. He does, indeed, struggle with the one song he's asked to perform—a duet with Saint. He recovers nicely, though, in a wedding dance, where his physical coordination shines through. The play isn't George's, though, and Newman's being billed third is entirely appropriate since Emily and the Stage Manager dominate the final act. Anyone associated with the production could have been pleased; of all the many versions of *Our Town* that Americans would see, this experimental musical adaptation, aired live, could still charm and entertain a half-century later.

Our Town aired on September 19, 1955, and yet another nice TV gig lay ahead of Newman the following month: he would play Nick Adams, Ernest Hemingway's picaresque autobiographical hero, in *The Battler,* an account of Adams's encounter with a broken-down prizefighter named Ad Francis. As scripted by A. E. Hotchner, who had befriended Hemingway during World War II and would write a memoir of him entitled *Papa Hemingway,* the film would tell Francis's story in reverse and involve a series of dramatic makeup changes that turned the character from an old, cauliflower-eared pug into, finally, a handsome young champion of the ring; the actor in the title role would be required to begin the live broadcast in heavy old-man makeup and then have it removed in stages until he finally appeared as, more or less, himself. Newman didn't have to worry about any of that, though: he would be playing Adams, the passive observer and chronicler; playing Francis would be his old screen-test buddy, James Dean.

Or rather that was the plan. On September 30, a little more than two weeks before *The Battler* was to air, Dean was killed in his Porsche near San Luis Obispo, California. That should have scuttled the show, but its creators—Fred Coe, who had produced *Our Town*, and Arthur Penn, who had directed "Guilty Is the Stranger"—both believed Newman capable of playing the title role and implored him to save the project by stepping into it. "I was rocked by Dean's death," Penn remembered, "but Paul was a very interesting young actor, and he was already involved. He knew the project." Offered the role, though, Newman hesitated. "I can't do that, emotionally," he said flatly. But he was ultimately convinced that it was appropriate, literally, for the show to go on; in another bit of rush casting, Dewey Martin, who had just appeared as Glenn Griffin's kid brother in the film version of *The Desperate Hours*, filled in as Nick Adams.

There were other obstacles to the production. NBC's censors were concerned with some of the language in the script, and they hovered around the set until Coe blasted them with words stronger even than Hemingway's. Newman continued to be anxious about the requirements of the role and the appropriateness of stepping into Dean's shoes; Hotchner took him out to lunch to reassure him, and they were joined, at Newman's request, by Joanne Woodward, who was back from Hollywood and her own benighted film debut, the western *Count Three and Pray*. As Hotchner later remembered, Newman spent the lunch explaining how inadequate he felt in the role (it didn't help that he'd been told that Hemingway would be watching from Cuba); Joanne spent the meal reassuring him, "You'll be fine."

The Battler aired on October 18, and it wasn't very well received. *Life* published a photo essay revealing the transformation Newman underwent at the hands of the makeup artists, and some reviewers made a point of praising his performance ("quite effective" said the *New York Times*). But it seemed to Newman as much a detour as singing alongside Eva Marie Saint. To other eyes, though, it was a revelation.

ONE OF the surprise best sellers of 1955 was *Somebody Up There Likes Me: The Story of My Life So Far,* in which boxer Rocky Graziano related, with the aid of journalist Rowland Barber, details of his life: tough times, comic misadventures, philosophies, proclivities, and triumphs. MGM had acquired the film rights early on, and an adaptation by Ernest Lehman was set to be directed by Robert Wise, who already had one top-notch boxing film, *The Set-Up*, behind him. The part of the title character—comic and feral, sensual and gritty, explosive and athletic—had been considered a prize by young Hollywood actors; among those vying for it was James Dean, who came to be seen as the favorite. Now, with Dean gone, Newman was the prime choice for the part.

Coincidentally, Newman was already being spoken about in connection with another MGM project, a film version of Rod Serling's televised courtroom drama *The Rack*, which concerned an army captain, son of a distinguished colonel, who comes home from a Korean War POW camp to be tried on charges of colluding with the enemy. Producer Arthur M. Loew Jr. had acquired the property and asked his cousin, screenwriter Stewart Stern, to turn it into a film. Stern did fresh research on the subject of brainwashing and psychological torture and did some rewriting to accommodate the concerns of military censors. But he'd finally completed a satisfactory script, and the studio sent it to Newman so that he could consider playing the lead; after he'd read it, he replied with a three-page letter in which he asked questions about the character's emotions and state of mind and suggested changes that he felt would punch up the tensions in the relationship of father and son.

Stern was impressed with what Newman had written. "He is the most aware and the most disciplined story-mind that I have ever come across in terms of being able to space, measure and orchestrate a script from an actor's point of view," he said years later. He insisted to Loew that they'd found their man. MGM boss Dore Schary agreed, and he reckoned that he could strike a better deal for Newman's services with Warner Bros. if he got him for two pictures, so he had Robert Wise test Newman for the role of Graziano. Meanwhile he assumed Newman's salary from Warner Bros. and, on October 29, announced that he had cast him in *The Rack*.

The six weeks of filming began almost at once; Newman would be home with Jackie and the children for only a few days during the holidays. But that would change: almost as soon as he got to Hollywood, he landed the lead in *Somebody Up There Likes Me*, and come springtime he would be working back east in one of MGM's first location shoots in New York.

It was a windfall, but it was bittersweet. "I'm still convinced that if Jimmy had done *The Battler*, he'd have gotten the role in *Somebody Up There Likes Me*," Newman confessed. But rather than credit his lucky streak, he found a more palpable outlet for his gratitude: "Although I'd lost most of my self-confidence, Dore Schary did more than anyone else to help me regain it."

He determined to prove to Schary that he hadn't made a mistake, by giving his all to the roles. In *The Rack*, most of which consisted of strained tête-à-têtes with his father (played by Walter Pidgeon) and anguished courtroom testimony, he had the biggest part of his career to date. Fortunately, the script resembled a play sufficiently for him to apply his version of Actors Studio praxis to it. The night before shooting a scene, he would record his lines in a strict monotone—just to get the words right—and then work on various interpretations and strategies for performing them. Now and again he would call Stern to test a theory he had or to ask whether it would be okay to "restate it or find a different way," as the writer recalled. He worked like this for more or less the length of the production, and then he segued into *Somebody Up There* and the difficult job of transforming himself credibly into an Italian-American juvenile delinquent who became middleweight champion of the world.

A couple of years earlier Josh Logan had told him that he carried no sexual threat, and so Newman had applied his habitual doggedness to the problem: "The way I translated that was six hours in the gym every day," he remembered. For *Somebody Up There*, it would pay off. He trained at Manhattan's famed midtown boxing mecca, Stillman's Gym, where Graziano himself had learned the sport. The routine transformed his body from slender to muscular, so much so that he began to overestimate his athletic prowess. He was given a chance to spar with former champion Tony Zale, against whom Graziano fought in an epic trilogy of title bouts in the span of two years; when Newman started coming on a little strong, Zale stopped toying with the actor and hit him good. As a result Zale lost the chance to play himself in the film, which had been the studio's original plan. Zale didn't care: "I don't mind waltzing a little bit, but you gotta show who the boss is."

Newman had more—and more pleasurable—contact with Graziano himself, a wily character who'd grown up as a Lower East Side truant and a reluctant soldier (he changed his name from Barbella to Graziano in order to avoid detection for deserting the army) before discovering that he could put his temper, his fierceness, and his ability to take a punch to some professional purpose. The actor and the former fighter, who had become a kind of public comedian playing a tongue-in-cheek version of a punch-drunk palooka, palled around for a couple of weeks so that Newman could observe and absorb some of his personality.

"I tried to find universal physical things that he did," Newman recalled, "or emotional responses that he had to certain things, that would allow me to create not *the* Rocky Graziano but *a* Graziano." They visited several key locations from the boxer's life, and Newman cagily sized up his target.

"There were two things that I discovered about him," he revealed. "One was that there was very little thought connected with his responses; they were immediate and emotional. Another was that there was a terrific restlessness about him, a kind of urgency and a thrust." They hit pool halls and bars and such, and Newman found him good company and an agreeable research subject, to a point: "He didn't want to talk about his family. So one night at the Embers, Bob Wise, the director, and I tried to get Rocky stoned so that he'd loosen up and talk about himself. The fact is that Rocky loosened *us* up. We told him *our* life stories. He poured us into two taxicabs." If he didn't get deep into Graziano's soul, he picked up his vocal and physical mannerisms almost a little too well. "He spits a lot, which I do to this day," Newman confessed a few years later. "In the middle of Fifth Avenue, walking down the street . . . a particular kind of hangover."

Newman didn't know it at the time, but he would be the second actor, in a sense, to play Graziano. A few years earlier another Method actor had hung around Stillman's for a few weeks and watched Graziano move and talk and fight and laugh. Sometime later the actor returned and offered the boxer a pair of tickets to a show he was appearing in on Broadway. Graziano and his wife went to the theater, and as he sat watching the performance, he had the most amazing revelation: "That kid is playin' *me!*" The actor was—and it would have to be, wouldn't it?—Marlon Brando, and the play was *A Streetcar Named Desire*. Later, with his role as Terry Malloy in *On the Waterfront*, Brando cemented the cinematic image of the punchy boxer from the rough-and-tumble northeastern city for the rest of time. This again would haunt Newman: playing Graziano was guaranteed to garner even more of the "poor-man's Brando" notices he'd gotten for *The Silver Chalice*.

Robert Wise proved an ideal director for Newman, allowing for a couple of weeks' rehearsal and giving him a chance to make suggestions. "Paul would get an idea for something," Wise later said, "a little switch or a change, something he wanted to do—and on the surface I would say, 'No, I don't think that's right, Paul. Forget it.' And we'd go on. But I learned very quickly that he couldn't forget it—it was stuck in his craw. So I found it was simpler with him to let him try it and then prove to himself that it was not good."

The film shot in New York locations throughout the beginning of March 1956: Stillman's, Riker's Island, the Lower East Side, the Brooklyn Bridge, and various other sites with scenic resonance or a particular connection to Graziano's life. Then they went to Hollywood, where the bulk of the film was made, including the vivid fight scenes. It was a comfortable set: Wise had cast a couple of young up-and-comers, Sal Mineo and Steven McQueen (as the future star was billed at the time), as members of Rocky's gang; Pier Angeli, who had also survived *The Silver Chalice*, as Rocky's sweetheart and eventual wife, Norma; and Eileen Heckart, from the Broadway cast of *Picnic*, as Rocky's mother.

Like *The Rack*, *Somebody* has a strong subtext of father-son conflict, but there was broad humor, too, and a kind of knockabout quality to the plotting and—Warner Bros. was pleased to notice—a handsome young star who looked like a million bucks shirtless in the boxing ring. They liked what they saw so much that they decided to finish and release *Somebody* before *The Rack*, even though the latter was already completed, just to let the small psychological thriller enjoy some of the publicity spillover from the boxing picture that they were sure would be a big hit. As a result, *Somebody* would come out almost immediately after being shot—just after the Fourth of July.

It's an evocative and truly pleasurable picture, redolent of the great Warner Bros. urban dramas of the 1930s, with an ethnic slum setting, an antiheroic hero, and a surprising amount of honest edge for a film about a living celebrity. Newman is *definitely* (to quote Graziano's catchphrase) channeling another persona, a garrulous pug with marbles in his mouth; a shuffling, jittery walk; and a certain slowness to absorb good advice or to read the subtext of a situation. He's believably explosive when he needs to be, but he plays Rocky the swain and family man and loyal old friend with real pathos and a light comic touch. There's plausible ferocity in the fight scenes (both in and out of the ring) and genuine tenderness in his dealings with Angeli. Wise sets the performances in a peppy and sometimes dark melodrama, giving it hints of neorealism and film noir when appropriate.

The reviews were good, although filled with the inevitable Brando references. "Let it be said of Mr. Newman that he plays the role of Graziano well," said Bosley Crowther in the *New York Times*, adding with the left hand, "making the pug and Marlon Brando almost indistinguishable." In the *Los Angeles Times* Philip K. Scheuer similarly intoned, "Newman's personal triumph is that of an actor who redeems the character he is portraying," quickly undercutting this praise by declaring that Newman was "inescapably, in anything, a 'Brando type.' " These sorts of things drove Newman to complain to an interviewer, "See how the guy haunts me? I wonder if anyone ever mistakes him for Paul Newman. I'd like to see that." But that was a minor issue; most important, he had managed, with the one-two of *The Desperate Hours* and *Somebody Up There*, along with all his good TV work, to erase the awful impression of *The Silver Chalice*.

IT WAS time to celebrate, then, and celebrate he did. On the night of July 6, the day Crowther's positive review ran, Newman and Jackie left the kids with a sitter at the home they were newly renting in Lake Success, a small, affluent town in Long Island's Nassau County, and headed out to meet a party of friends at the Jolly Fisherman Restaurant in nearby Roslyn. A bit past midnight on what was turning into a toot of an evening, Newman left Jackie and the others in the restaurant and went roaring off in his Volkswagen. He drove through some shrubs at the Jolly Fisherman, knocked over a fire hydrant on Roslyn's Main Street, and then ran a red light on Northern Boulevard, after which he was chased by police cars for a mile or so before being pulled over by Nassau County patrolman Rocco "Rocky" Caggiano and his partner.

Obviously drunk, Newman stepped out of his car and approached Caggiano defiantly. "I'm acting for Rocky Graziano. What do you want?" he barked.

"I'm Rocky too," said the cop, "and you're under arrest."

Newman was handcuffed, put into a patrol car, and taken to the Mineola police station, where a band of reporters had been camped out waiting for news of a local boy who'd been kidnapped the day before.

When he was pulled from the car and led to the station, Newman caught sight of the crowd of pressmen and said to the cops, "This is a big deal! How did they know I'd been pinched?" Told why the reporters and photographers were actually there, he barked, "If they want a kidnapper, I'll give them a kidnapper!" And he went into a little theatrical bit, stomping his feet and posing menacingly.

He was duly photographed by the bored press (as was Jackie a few hours later when she came to check on him) and then hustled into a jail cell, where he seemed to discover his contrition. "Don't lock the door on me," he asked. "I don't like locked doors." (They locked the door.)

The papers, including the *New York Times*, all ran stories about the incident in the next day's editions. (Honors for best headline would go to the *New York Journal-American:* "Star of Film Rams Hydrant and Now Nobody Likes Him.") The next day Newman paid the Jolly Fisherman for the damages and pleaded innocent to the charge of running a red light.

THIS UNINTENTIONALLY comic arrest had deeper causes and repercussions. In part it was an instance of high spirits, yes, but in part too it was symptomatic of an ambivalence that was welling up inside of him. In California, while making *Somebody Up There*, and now again in New York, he had spent a lot of time with Joanne Woodward. And the growing sense of pain, confusion, and guilt that he had brought upon himself for threatening his marriage was driving him toward an alcoholic release valve.

As his escapades at Ohio U and Kenyon indicated, Newman did like to take a drink—beer mostly. But he could slip into a bottle of whiskey quite comfortably too. "They say you can take the kid out of Shaker Heights, but you can't take Shaker Heights out of the kid," he confessed years later. "Well, *oh yes you can*! You can do that very simply with a fifth of good scotch. Because then you can never tell what the kid's likely to do . . . hanging from chandeliers was not beyond the realm of possibility. A lot of bad stuff with cars. Generally boorish behavior."

In this case, the outré behavior began before the heavy boozing. In the spring while in California making films, Newman and Joanne both stayed at the Chateau Marmont, the gothic folly on the Sunset Strip favored by slumming East Coast actors, jaded European bohemians, and anyone else looking to do something considered untoward in the relatively starchy moral arithmetic of a company town like Hollywood. Gore Vidal was also in residence, and the three spent a good deal of time together, lounging at the pool or in conversations, during which Newman and Vidal schemed about reviving *The Death of Billy the Kid* as a feature film. Nobody at the Chateau questioned their behavior; the whole point of the place was quiet, discretion, and worldliness. Newman and Joanne could be as open as they wished with each other, and their romance took deeper root.

Since he'd come back from Hollywood and moved the family out to Long Island, Newman had begun once again, inevitably, seeing a lot of Joanne in the course of his actor's-days-out: in casting offices, at Actors Studio sessions, at coffee klatches at theater district drugstores and luncheonettes, at late-night drinking parties at hangouts like Downey's on Eighth Avenue ("the poor actor's Sardi's," as Newman called it), and in the homes of fellow performers. Their mutual attraction was common knowledge among their circle, and so too was the strain that it created. A friend commented soon afterward that the romance was "more of an ordeal than a courtship. Paul was torn between his loyalty to his children and honesty with his feelings for Joanne. And Joanne, who was friendly with Jackie, suffered torments at finding herself in the role of a homewrecker. But being what they were, neither could help what was happening to them."

The drunk-driving incident seemed to bring matters to a boil. Despite the genuine anguish it caused him to break up his home, Newman acknowledged first to friends and then to Jackie that he was in love with Joanne. All that was left of that surprise marriage in Wisconsin was the dissolution of it, and in the way these things could happen back then, Jackie wasn't letting go easily. She had a right to her family, even if her husband was disloyal, and she had a right, too, to a fair portion of what seemed to be a blossoming career. She determined to hang on. But Newman wasn't cheating so much as he was recognizing that he'd found his ideal partner. And so he made up his mind to leave, regardless of how Jackie took it, regardless even of what it meant to the kids.

"They were so young when they married," a friend said of Newman and Jackie. "They just grew up to be two different people." And now they would be separated into two different households. Before the end of the summer, Newman moved out of Lake Success and into a rented apartment in Manhattan.

Nine

O N THE STRENGTH OF *SOMEBODY UP THERE LIKES ME* AND *THE Rack*, Newman was a rising star. There was talk of an Academy Award nomination for his versatile work in *Somebody*, Warner Bros. was peppering him with scripts for his next picture, and he was doing some tremendous work on television.

In August 1956 he appeared in a psychological drama that had echoes of *The Rack*. "The Army Game," the inaugural episode of TV's *Kaiser Aluminum Hour*, was written by Loring Mandel and Mayo Simon and directed by Franklin Schaffner. It focused on Danny Scott (Newman), a wealthy, athletic army recruit of superior intelligence who, with the encouragement of his overbearing widowed mother, tries to obtain a medical discharge by feigning cowardice and madness. He is ostracized, berated, and even beaten by his peers, he is imprisoned and punished, and yet he continues his ruse. (We know he's faking because he speaks his thoughts in a voice-over.) Eventually he's forced to visit a psychiatrist, who's clever enough to figure out the scheme but who detects genuine instability in the very fact of the soldier's determined efforts to be perceived as unstable: Joseph Heller's *Catch-22* in reverse. In an effort to crack the fellow's facade—or perhaps to determine if he really is unwell—the psychiatrist calls in the soldier's mother. A ghastly moment of oedipal anger ensues, and the soldier breaks down in a heap, truly psychologically damaged by his efforts only to seem that way.

The role gave Newman a lot to play in a brief time, and he handled it very well, from the cocksureness of the opening sequences, in which he finesses people with cool preppy aplomb, to the defiant selfishness with which he brings trouble down on his barracks mates, to the tango with the psychiatrist, to the very convincing scenes of mental break-down and fierce anger. His "sound and sensitive portrayal" was singled out for praise by the *New York Times*.

In his next major TV role he fared equally well. *Bang the Drum Slowly* was a successful novel by Mark Harris, the second of four books centered on Henry Wiggen, a talented pitcher who narrates baseball stories in a homespun vernacular that wins him the nickname "Author" from his teammates. *Drum* traces two narratives: Wiggen's tussles with management over his contracts, and his friendship with Bruce Pearson, a simpleminded, countrified second-string catcher who's been assigned to Wiggen as a roommate. Wiggen is part of the crowd that teases Pearson and hopes for a more talented player to take his place, but Pearson is dog-loyal to Wiggen, which dampens the pitcher's enthusi-asm for the hazing. The turn comes when Pearson reveals to Wiggen that he is dying of Hodgkin's disease and wishes to hide it from man-agement and the rest of the team so that he can play in the majors as long as possible. Wiggen keeps the secret, and when Pearson finally dies, he declares that he is through, both as a player and as a man, with belittling others: "From here on in," he declares in the novel's famous last line, "I rag nobody."

Arnold Schulman adapted the book, and Daniel Petrie directed a cast that included Newman as Wiggen, Albert Salmi (another Actors Studio member) as Pearson, and Clu Galager, Bert Remsen, and George Peppard (making his professional debut) as various teammates and associates. Schulman handled the book's first-person narrative by having Wiggen speak directly to the camera. ("We don't have too much room in the studio here," he apologizes, "so once in a while you're going to have to use your imagination.") Newman looks the role of the star athlete, of course, and is quite convincing as a guy who (wrongly) thinks he can bamboozle the big bosses out of some extra money. But he's especially affecting as someone who has to give up his love of horseplay for a more earnest aspect when he learns of his friend's illness—the news hits him and takes over his whole being. There are a couple of little live-TV glitches, but it's genuinely mesmerizing: a truly original and heartfelt sports story executed with polish and sincere emotion.*

Just one week later Newman was on TV in another baseball-related role—of a sort. He appeared as the Special Guest on the popular quiz show *I've Got a Secret,* where he stumped a panel consisting of Bill Cullen, Ann Sheridan, Jayne Meadows, and Henry Morgan with the revelation that he'd posed as a hot dog vendor earlier in the day during the first game of the World Series at Ebbets Field and sold a hot dog to Morgan. Animated and clearly enjoying himself, he went offstage to don his vendor's gear and returned with this tale:

> I got the tray full of hot dogs ["haht dawgs," he said, Ohio-like], and I got into the outfit, and I started to walk into the area where you were. And I just got into the aisle and I was surrounded by a pack of hungry rats. This one guy kicked me and said, "Six, please." So I turned around and I started handing out hot dogs. I sold one whole tray of these things and had to go back for a second one. And by this time someone had given you a hot dog already, and I didn't know what to do. So I went back for a beer, and it was very nerve-wracking. I was terribly nervous. It's survival of the fittest, and you discover that you've gotta have a system. First you take the wax paper out and you put the thing in the bun. And this one time I was so nervous that I put this wiener in the wax paper and handed it to some guy—no bun. One time I got some mustard on my finger and I went like this [he put the tip of a finger in his mouth and then acted like he was handing someone something], and he gave me a dirty look. I was asked by several people where the bathroom was. And I didn't know anything. I didn't see any of the game. And incidentally I sold $26 worth of merchandise in half an hour. And my cut was $2.60!

---

* A few years later Josh Logan announced that he was planning a film version and that Newman was in his mind to play Wiggen, but a big-screen adaptation of *Drum* didn't appear until 1973, with Michael Moriarty in the lead and Robert De Niro as Pearson.

His sense of humor and delight in pranks would have to sustain him professionally, for a while, at least. Warner Bros. kept throwing him scripts and he kept refusing them, deeming the material substandard. It was an awful relationship: not only could the studio demand his services for films of its own, no matter what he thought of the projects, but it had the final authority to decree which pictures he could do for other studios when they loaned him out. And if he refused a certain number of the opportunities they presented him, they could put him on suspension and keep him from working anywhere in any medium at all. He was playing with fire, and he knew it. "One time I remembered they reneged on an outside film they had promised me," Newman recalled, "so I told Jack Warner to go fuck himself—and this was very early in the game, when I really couldn't afford to tell him to go fuck himself. But I didn't give a damn."

Finally, just after the New Year, he was assigned a role in *The Helen Morgan Story*, a biopic of the popular Prohibition-era torch singer who died of alcoholism in 1941 and had more or less slipped into obscurity. Morgan's sad life, with such highs as appearing in *The Ziegfeld Follies* and the original Broadway cast of *Showboat* (she introduced the song "Bill"), was the stuff of a gritty tearjerker, and Warner Bros. had been eager to shoot it for more than a decade.* No fewer than four writers contrived a script, the veteran Michael Curtiz (*Casablanca, Yankee Doodle Dandy*, and dozens more) was assigned to direct, and Ann Blyth, most famous for her role as the daughter in Curtiz's *Mildred Pierce*, was cast in the lead. Among the supporting players, in an essentially straight role, was Alan King—to give an idea of the quality of the thing.

Newman was to play bootlegger and conman Larry Maddux, a fictionalized composite of all the opportunistic heels who sucked blood

---

* But they weren't foresighted enough: they didn't secure the TV rights, and another version of the story ran on CBS while the feature film was still in production. Coincidentally, it was written by Paul Monash and directed by George Roy Hill—who, in a dozen or so years, would, respectively, produce and direct Newman in *Butch Cassidy and the Sundance Kid.*

from Morgan while the sucking was good. And he hated every minute of it. "That was a painful experience," he said a couple of years later. "But there comes a time, after you've turned down fifteen or twenty scripts, when you suddenly feel, you know, you have to work."

He amused himself with pranks. At the start of production, he had a photograph taken of himself emerging from a restaurant freezer and sent it to Jack Warner with the caption "Paul Newman, who was kept in the deep freeze for two years because of *The Silver Chalice*, has at last been thawed out by Warner Bros. to play the coldhearted gangster in *The Helen Morgan Story.*" He presented Curtiz with a bullwhip and a gift card reading "To be used on me—in case I get difficult." He didn't exactly bond with Curtiz, complaining that the director would tell him "Go faster" rather than give specific counsel as to the emotions that were required in a scene. But he admired Blyth's work ethic (she had just had a baby), and he got out of the picture more or less unscathed.

And he would have to: he was granted but a single day off before the start of his next picture, *Until They Sail*, a wartime romance based on a James Michener story. Newman was cast as an American officer stationed in New Zealand during World War II and assigned to assure that marriages between the local girls and the U.S. troops were on the up-and-up; that he has received a Dear John letter from his wife and developed a cynical hide makes him especially effective in his work. But then he meets a character played by Jean Simmons, one of four local sisters looking for love in a country with virtually no men left in it (her siblings were played by Joan Fontaine, Piper Laurie, and Sandra Dee—go figure), and some of his toughness is scraped away.

"I had grave misgivings about the script and about the character and about my usefulness in it," he admitted. But he took the role because the film's director, Robert Wise, and the producer, Charles Schnee, had taken a gamble with him on *Somebody Up There Likes Me:* "[They] went out on a limb to allow a newcomer to do something as important as Graziano. I felt that the least I could do would be to return the favor . . . I'm not sorry I did the picture for that one reason, a very personal reason."

MAKING BACK-TO-BACK Hollywood pictures meant that he would be away from New York for months. And as when he was shooting *Somebody Up There*, that meant spending an extended period of time with Joanne Woodward, who was in California working on her third film, a psychologically daring work written, directed, and produced by veteran screenwriter Nunnally Johnson. Taking its name from the book that was its source, *The Three Faces of Eve* was a reality-based drama about an ordinary housewife who suffered from dizzy spells and blackouts and sought help from a psychiatrist, who diagnosed her as having what is now termed dissociative identity disorder—more commonly, multiple personalities. Johnson had hoped to cast Judy Garland in the role, and June Allyson was also said to have been in the running for the part. But when Garland failed to follow through on the overtures he made, Johnson opted for a controversial but compelling choice in Joanne, who conveniently was already under contract to 20th Century–Fox, where the film was being made. The bosses wanted to reach for a bigger name, but Johnson got his way. And Joanne spent the spring under his direction working at portraying three distinct women connected tenuously by a single psyche.

If that was hard work, the context in which she was doing it was certainly pleasurable. She and Newman had taken a house in Malibu with Gore Vidal and his longtime companion, Howard Austen—a particularly odd arrangement since it had once been hinted in the gossip pages that Joanne and Vidal were engaged. ("That was at her insistence," Vidal later recollected, "and based entirely on her passion not for me but Paul"—that is, she thought that a fake engagement might force Newman to leave Jackie for once and for all.) Life on the beach was idyllic—"a marvelous time," according to Vidal, "like a delayed adolescence for Paul and me." He teased the couple, calling them "Miss Georgia and Mr. Shaker Heights," nicknames he would use for them all their lives.

In the mornings Newman would drive off to Warner Bros., Joanne would take off for Fox, and Vidal would, if so moved, drive to MGM, where he was working on scripts, including *Ben-Hur*. On the weekends, parties. "The house was full of people that, often, none of us knew," Vidal said. "I would think they were friends of Paul's or

Joanne's, and they thought that they were friends of mine." (Among the guests they did know were Theresa Newman and Arthur Jr., who visited from Ohio and whose visit might also explain the fiction of a Woodward-Vidal engagement.)

By springtime, though, Vidal and Newman had developed a hiccup in their cheery relationship. One of their mutual interests had been turning *The Death of Billy the Kid* into a feature film. They'd talked Fred Coe, the producer of the TV version, into shepherding the project at Warner Bros., and he intended to make his film debut with it. In the fall of 1956 Vidal told the *New York Times* that he would be writing a new version of the script for Arthur Penn to direct, and he promised that his take on the western outlaw's story wouldn't "be like the others." But when winter came and went, Coe and the studio still weren't satisfied with what they had. "They've been stalling," Newman said of Warner Bros. "They think it ought to end happily. That's like filming the life of Lincoln and having it end happily; like having his wife come in and say, 'Abe dear, I forgot the tickets for the theater tonight. We'll have to stay home.'"

But the studio heads weren't the only ones unhappy with Vidal's work. "The Gore Vidal script didn't sit particularly well with me," Penn remembered. "It seemed too specialized and too narrow." In the spring of 1957 Coe hired a new writer, Leslie Stevens, who had no previous film credits, and the studio gave the green light to his modified version of Vidal's script—without Vidal's knowledge or consent; they even changed the name, from *The Legend of Billy the Kid*, which had been the working title, to *The Left Handed Gun*. Vidal understood why Coe did it: "He sees what he thinks is a stupid movie star in Paul Newman and a scatterbrained playwright who's all over the place in me, and he has an opening to get in and take it over and [he] did." And Newman, who had gone off to a ranch in Tucson to absorb some atmosphere for the role, wasn't able to lobby for his friend's interests. "Maybe I should have pushed a little more," he later admitted, "but I didn't know much about the politics of Hollywood." Too, he had fought hard with the studio just to shoot the material at all; unless he wanted to keep appearing in the likes of *The Helen Morgan Story*, he would have to give a little bit. Vidal understood Newman's situation—

their friendship would thrive for decades—but he never forgave Coe and cut himself out of the film entirely. ("It was an *auteur film*," Vidal sneered years later. "I say no more.")

In Arizona Newman practiced his riding—a useless effort, he admitted: "The horse and I have been a continuing disaster. I had to learn to ride Western saddle when we started, and I had never ridden at all. I can still see that horse looking up at me and wondering what the hell was going on." He was only slightly more successful at finding someone whose manner he could imitate as a basis for his performance. "I lived in a bunkhouse for about a week, chased cows," he remembered. "There was a young kid there who I really wanted to get on tape. He was so shy, he wouldn't do anything. Finally, after about a half a bottle of Jack Daniel's, he loosened up, and I set the tape recorder down in front of him. He started to say a sentence, but then stopped right in the middle and said, 'I cain't talk to nothin' that don't talk back.' And that was the end of it. Those were the only words I ever got out of him."

Back in Hollywood, where the film would be shot, he was appalled at what had happened to the script. "Somewhere along the line that whole thing fell apart," he remembered. "I never saw a script until two weeks before we started shooting, at which time I flipped my wig." Leslie, who he'd originally thought would simply smooth over some problems the studio had with Vidal's script, had completely rewritten it. "There were good scenes in it," Newman admitted, "but all of a sudden there would be a visual jar, or a story jar, and you'd sort of shake your head, and it would take you ten minutes to get with it again."

Warner Bros. had stood firm against allowing Penn and the actors a rehearsal period, but they had managed to work around it. "My wife and I had rented a house," Penn remembered, "and Paul and Hurd Hatfield and some others came by, and we rehearsed in the house. Paul began wearing his gun belt at those sessions, with the holster on the left side, and he kept drawing it and practicing and practicing. And Joanne came along to those rehearsals, too."

At the same time he was gearing up to play his psychologically scarred Billy the Kid, Newman was seeing a psychiatrist—not for re-

search into his character but to address the genuine pain that was ac-
companying the dissolution of his marriage. "It helped me in some
ways to have a more realistic appraisal of myself, to get in touch with
my emotions. Some of it was effective and some of it was helpful," he
would reflect. But helpful only to a point: "He taught me to like myself
better, which I don't. He taught me to recognize the level of my
achievements, which I don't. He taught me not to 'should' myself,
which I still do." Inevitably, given his training and the sort of work that
attracted him, he gleaned insights for acting: "I was very surprised at
how little I knew about myself."

Throughout the summer, as he made *Left Handed* in the great outdoors of Burbank and learned about himself in a more intimate setting
with his therapist, Newman and Joanne became more honest about
their relationship; photos of them dining and attending premieres in
Hollywood had been published, and writers were openly asking him if
they were a couple. ("There's been too much talk," he told one, bringing that particular set of questions to an end.) Newman worked up the
gumption to ask Jackie for a divorce, but despite the ongoing humiliation, which wasn't always subtle, she wasn't willing to just give in. She
had three children under seven years of age; they didn't own their own
home; Newman hadn't yet started to make significant money; they had
been married in church less than eight years earlier; and it was *he* who
was cheating on *her:* why should she budge? They had, in effect,
reached a miserable standoff.

THEN ANOTHER movie role forced all their hands. Newman had been
loaned out once again, this time to 20th Century–Fox, for a film called
The Long, Hot Summer, which had been loosely adapted by the screenwriters Irving Ravetch and Harriet Frank Jr. from William Faulkner's
novel *The Hamlet* as well as a couple of his short stories. Martin Ritt,
who worked in New York theater and taught at the Actors Studio and
had recently begun making films in Hollywood, would direct. Anthony Franciosa, another Actors Studio member, would costar, as
would Orson Welles. Newman was cast as Ben Quick, a sharp and
scheming ne'er-do-well who wanders into a small southern town

presided over by a rich, domineering man (Welles) and ingratiates himself to the patriarch at the expense of the man's son (Franciosa); at the same time, and with her father's blessing, he courts the rich man's daughter, Clara, who is calcifying into a spinster while waiting on a proposal from a childhood sweetheart, who everyone but she can see is an inveterate mama's boy.

Ritt had originally wanted Eva Marie Saint for Clara, but he knew that Joanne, whom he had worked with at the Actors Studio and had just directed in *No Down Payment*, a drama about the intertwined lives of four suburban couples, was capable of the role too. At first he faced some resistance from the studio: "She was tougher to cast [than Newman] because she was just a very good actress," he later said. But word about *The Three Faces of Eve*, which hadn't yet been released, was very strong around the Fox lot. And so Joanne got the part—and a chance to spend a couple of months working with Newman on location in Louisiana, where the entire film would be shot.

Newman went down south first, hanging around the film's projected locations in Baton Rouge and nearby Clinton for a few weeks. "The newspaper editor of Clinton knew what I was down there for," Newman remembered. "He got me with a bunch of guys." As Newman described it, "[I] sort of latched on to a guy who was working on an oil pipeline—a big guy, six four. We sat around drinking beer and playing pool. He name was Brother Fochee. I got a tremendous sense of physical solidity from him. He'd walk into a room and talk, and his feet would stay in exactly the same position, no shuffling. He had a tremendous kind of physical presence." And he wasn't the only one. There were lots of fellas in Clinton who would be handy to have around if you were a married man working with your girlfriend and trying to keep that fact out of the papers. When a big-city journalist visited the set later on to pry into the Newman-Woodward romance, it was made clear to him that it wasn't a healthful line of inquiry; the reporter presently left town.

Had he stayed, he would have seen the two stars behaving quite openly in front of everyone like a couple in love with each other. "We thought they were already married," Tony Franciosa joked years later. "They were so obviously together, so beautifully close." They even allowed the set photographer to take candid photos of them hanging around Clinton's town center, reading the newspaper and eating picnic lunches between takes.

Ritt and his cast (which also included Lee Remick as Franciosa's randy young wife and Richard Anderson as Clara's prim almost-suitor) were given what they felt was a proper amount of rehearsal time, which is to say more than most films allowed for, and they seemed truly to enjoy working together. "We understood each other," Ritt said. "That was the advantage—like the orchestra players knowing the taste of a conductor." The odd man out, though, was also the biggest fish in the pond: Welles. The onetime wunderkind who had conquered Hollywood with his first film and then been systematically rebuffed and broken by the town, he had come into the project with the promise of turning in one of his patented scenery-chewing turns as a mean old lusty drunk who used his power to crush everyone around him. He found, instead, that he was expected to take part in the sort of collaborative exploration that the Actors Studio members around him thrived upon. He understood theater, of course, but he couldn't catch on with the techniques, and he would become easily irritated during rehearsals and even during takes.

Ritt would later admit that he had considered Lee J. Cobb, another Actors Studio vet, for the role, but that Welles had the stronger persona. Ritt had to fight the studio to get the notoriously difficult Welles onto the film, and then he had to fight Welles himself, who challenged his directorial skills and, among other discourtesies, chose not to reveal until they were on location that he couldn't drive a car as the script called for him to do.

"I took a lot of crap from him," Ritt admitted, "because I knew that that extraordinary figure would be there on the screen." And he knew too that Welles was exceedingly anxious about the state of his own most recent project as a director, *Touch of Evil*, which was being taken away from him and recut by the studio. So he tolerated the great man's outbursts—although he did warn him away from certain others in the cast who mightn't have been so indulgent. As Ritt recalled, "I said to him one day, 'Don't fuck around like that with Tony Franciosa, because he doesn't understand you, and he's going to knock you on your ass.'"

Newman admitted that he didn't especially care for Welles until he realized that something painful was at the root of his behavior:

> Orson and I didn't see eye to eye about a great many things, and I had no truck with his temperamentality . . . I was terribly aware of the fact that he thought he was surrounded by a bunch of New School and Method actors, which is not true because I don't consider myself a Method actor. If an old-time actor had suddenly been confronted with four Orson Welleses, he probably would have felt a little uncomfortable. But he said a very touching thing. By this time Marty had started to get to him, and I think he'd begun to trust him a little bit, and he said, "I didn't play that scene very good, did I?" And Marty said, "No, I think you could have done better in it, but, you know, the light's gone and we can't—" And he said, "I don't know; I feel like I'm riding a tricycle in a barrel of molasses." Up until that time I'd been terribly resentful of him, but I saw something in a statement like that, so that all of his belligerency came out of a terrible insecurity. That sort of sank in, and after that, whatever flagrant temperamental kind of thing he went through with me, I just ignored him, or tried to understand him, as much as I could . . . I finally wound up liking him very much and being able to talk to him without being uncomfortable. We weren't at all close, but I had tremendous admiration for him.

Despite Welles's obstreperousness, the shoot wrapped before winter. And aside from their work on it, Newman and Joanne took from Louisiana a most unusual memento: a gigantic brass bed that they'd discovered while antique shopping in New Orleans. Newman loved to speculate as to its origins. "Three could sleep in it very comfortably," he told a reporter. "We figure it must once have stood in a cathouse; there'd be no other reason to make a bed that big." Tennessee Williams, he once bragged, had tried to buy the bed from them: "He considers it the most perfect example of Southern decadence he has ever seen." But he couldn't have it. Pretty soon Newman and Joanne would be able to sleep together in their big brazen folly for the rest of their lives.

THEY WERE a hot couple. The press and public had finally seen *The Three Faces of Eve* and were celebrating Joanne's tour-de-force performance in the lead(s). At virtually the same time, despite the rather tepid one-two of *The Helen Morgan Story* and *Until They Sail*, Newman was a rising commodity, and he was connected in both trade and mainstream papers with a number of roles: the male lead in *Marjorie Morningstar*; an adaptation of Erich Maria Remarque's *A Time to Love and a Time to Die*; and an adaptation of Nelson Algren's *A Walk on the Wild Side*. As it happened, none would pan out (the roles went to Gene Kelly, John Gavin, and Laurence Harvey, respectively), but the increasing frequency of his name in the press evinced his gathering stardom.

His next film would prove it. He won the role of Brick Pollitt, the alcoholic, bisexual scion of a powerful southern family in *Cat on a Hot Tin Roof*, which writer-director Richard Brooks was adapting from the scandalous and successful Broadway version of Tennessee Williams's play. Elizabeth Taylor would play the heroine, Brick's wife, Maggie the Cat, with a far more cinematic brand of sensuality than Barbara Bel Geddes, the original stage Maggie, could bring to the screen. That was obvious recasting. But Brick was a tricky part. Ben Gazzara had created the role on Broadway, and he had tremendous theatrical credentials. But he had no value as a name; there was no way he'd get the movie role. A lengthy search for a screen Brick had ensued, and Newman was selected only when Brooks and Taylor's husband, impresario Mike Todd, warned MGM that she would walk from the project if a Brick wasn't found soon. "For Christ's sake," Todd told the studio brass, "we're gonna blow this thing." His threats worked: Newman, Brooks's favorite for the role, was to be paid $17,000, his highest fee yet, for his work.

The shoot was scheduled for Hollywood in March, which would allow both Newman and Taylor to work on their southern accents with dialect coaches and generally to take the holidays for themselves.

For Taylor, this meant a Christmas with Todd, whom she'd married in February (at age twenty-four, it was her third wedding), and their baby daughter, Liza. For Newman, it meant arduously working out the terms of a divorce from Jackie, who had finally agreed to give up her claim on him.

The gossip press scented something in the air—the *New York Post* ran a photo of Newman and Joanne in December with a caption implying a wedding was impending. But nothing concrete was revealed. On January 16 they appeared on television together in "The 80 Yard Run," a *Playhouse 90* production of Irwin Shaw's story about a college football hero's unlikely romance with a sophisticated rich girl and the troubled marriage that results. It was their first filmed work to appear anywhere, and it proved what all the directors and fellow actors and Actors Studio colleagues had always said about them: Newman had indelible star power, but Joanne was by a good measure the more accomplished actor. There's a vivid naturalness to almost everything she does—tapping concert tickets on her chin anxiously as she waits for a date, nibbling her lower lip and grinning broadly as she picks up the star halfback, joking with her dad (she calls him "Sam"), giving the cold eye to her husband's secretary. She's alive in an indeterminate number of ways, all fresh and exciting. In comparison, Newman is game and ardent and a bit stiff; you sense him planning and staging his emotions and reactions. He's stunning to look at—it's one of the first times a job calls for him to take his shirt off simply for the beefcake effect, a trope that will appear regularly in his screen work—but he's not her equal, not nearly.

Funnily enough, the differences between their levels of skill add credibility to the script. Joanne's character is meant to be the sophisticate, and she winds up dumping her simple Adonis for a pipe-smoking New York magazine editor (a Hugh Hefner type played, ironically, by Richard Anderson, the mama's boy from *Long, Hot Summer*). Newman's character, on the other hand, needs to develop a sense of himself and discover, if not build, a reservoir of self-respect and self-reliance. Dramatically, he needs to be less effective than she; credit the producers and director Franklin Schaffner with recognizing this—and Newman too, for not letting ego get in the way of an effective collaboration. Which isn't to say he didn't do a nice job: it would be his final appearance on live television and a thoroughly creditable one: lively and knowing and with a broad swath of blue-collar decency and plausible streaks of insecurity and shame.

FOR A fact he was acting. In real life he was surely caught up in drama and emotion that had little to do with what he played in the film. Chief was the knowledge that Joanne was carrying his baby. Sometime during the shoot of *Long, Hot Summer*, perhaps on that voluptuous brass bed, they had conceived a child—the reality of which may have been the final straw in Jackie's agreeing to let him go. And now that there was to be an end to his marriage, he and Joanne could make wedding plans of their own: she'd take the train (she hated flying) to Las Vegas, and he'd meet her there after a side trip to Mexico to obtain his divorce.

Divorce. It was one of the strangest things about his entire life: he would come to be celebrated for decades for his long and lasting marriage, yet it had been built on the foundation of a previous—and fecund—marriage that had failed. At first he would dance gingerly around questions about his time with Jackie: "It wouldn't be fair either to Jackie or to Joanne. But I was probably too immature to make a success of my first marriage." But in time he became bolder in his refusal. "What happened to us during that period is not gonna help anybody live a happy life," he said to a reporter. "It's not going to help people's marriages, it's not going to destroy their marriages. And it's simply nobody's business." He did, however, confess to one emotion: "Guilty as hell" was how he described himself, adding "And I'll carry it with me for the rest of my life."

On January 29, 1958, Joanne arrived on the Las Vegas Strip with a small coterie of friends, including her manager, Ina Bernstein, who was to serve as maid of honor, and Judy Balaban, the wife of Joanne's agent, Jay Kantor (and not two years earlier a bridesmaid in Grace Kelly's fabled royal wedding). At around suppertime Newman arrived from Mexico via plane along with his best man, Stewart Stern. A marriage license was acquired, and then a vital ritual was performed: the couple rang Hedda Hopper with the news that they would be wed. (In

Hollywood in the 1950s this was a mandatory rite disguised as a courtesy, like a young Sicilian couple seeking the matrimonial blessing of the local Mafia don before heading to the altar. Joanne actually apologized to Hopper for keeping her in the dark until the last minute, explaining that she didn't know when Newman would arrive: "I didn't want it to appear that I was left waiting at the church.")

In a bungalow at the El Rancho Vegas casino resort, owner Beldon Katleman, who regularly made his private quarters available for just these sorts of occasions, stood by as District Judge Frank McNamee united the couple. Among the celebrants were singers Eydie Gorme and Steve Lawrence, who were next in line to be married, and the members of their own wedding party, including Sophie Tucker and Joe E. Lewis. Katleman gave Newman a pair of gold cuff links in the form of roulette wheels, and Newman gave Joanne a sherry glass (she collected them) inscribed *So you wound up with Apollo / If he's sometimes hard to swallow / Use this.* The following morning they flew to New York and, after a few quiet days, flew off once again for a honeymoon in England.

Ten

THEY MADE PLANS TO VISIT PARIS, AS HONEYMOONERS WOULD, but London, in that moderately mild winter of 1958, would stand as the real starting point of their marriage. "There were no tourists to speak of," Newman remembered later, "and we would get a car and head off into the country till we were literally lost. Hundreds of miles from London and checking into country inns at nightfall—there's a lot to be said for a winter honeymoon." After all the anxiety and secrecy surrounding the romance and the divorce, the ability to walk around freely as man and wife was intoxicating, he said: "It felt good, being married."

On their first days in London they stayed in quiet luxury at the Connaught; after side trips around England and a little bit of time in France and Switzerland, they returned and bunked with Gore Vidal and Howard Austen at their dark and drafty flat on Chesham Place. They went to the theater and toured historical sites. Newman, who had never been to Europe, was especially dazzled, as Austen remembered. "I've never seen anything like this before," he repeatedly blurted out with enthusiasm on a visit to Hampton Court. They socialized with Vidal's London friends and with luminaries from the theater—Claire Bloom, John Gielgud, Ralph Richardson, Kenneth Tynan.

It was a dream, but it ended with a sting. Newman had to be back in Hollywood by early March to begin work on *Cat on a Hot Tin Roof*; Joanne would, of course, join him there in his tiny rented home—"a glorified shanty," as Hedda Hopper described it—so that she could take part in the Oscar campaign for *The Three Faces of Eve*. But he left without her when, without warning, she had a miscarriage. She was admitted to St. George's Hospital, where Claire Bloom visited her, as Joanne recalled, daily. And then she returned to the States on her own. "That very nice doctor then put me on a plane and sent me home," she said. "It was a terrible end to a lovely honeymoon."

In Hollywood, *Cat on a Hot Tin Roof*, which was teeming with even more drama than Newman's own life, was proving difficult to translate to the screen. The homosexual themes had to be washed out of the film; Brooks had attempted to rewrite the play so that the gist of the original remained beguilingly close beneath the surface but never explicit.

Shooting began in March with several members of the original stage cast—including Burl Ives, who'd originated the role of Big Daddy, and Madeleine Sherwood—joined by the likes of Judith Anderson and Jack Carson. At first Newman had trouble with Taylor because their styles of acting were so different. "He needed to rehearse and explore," remembered Stewart Stern, who heard all of Newman's complaints. "She would just be doing nothing in rehearsals except saying the lines and walking along. He'd go to Richard Brooks and say, 'What's going to happen when we get to a shot? She's not doing anything.' Brooks said, 'Just wait a minute.' He'd say 'Action,' and Paul's eyes fell out because she'd be there with a full performance, and he never knew where she found it."

A couple of weeks passed with good progress made amid an atmosphere of great seriousness—as Newman learned when a joke he pulled on the set backfired. He was playing a scene in which the drunken Brick, who has been filled with guilt at the apparent suicide of his schoolmate (and, it is implied, lover) Skipper, brushes up against one of Maggie's nightgowns. "I'm in my pajamas," Newman remembered, "and I'm supposed to slam out of a door, and when I do, my wife's nightgown, hanging on the door, brushes against my face. So anyway, during the rehearsal, when we got to that point, I suddenly tore off my pajama top and started trying to climb into my wife's nightgown crying, 'Skipper! Skipper!' There were twenty people on that set, and do you know, not one of them laughed. To them, this was the Method in action, and they stood in respectful silence."

If Newman's penchant for awkward jokes didn't impair the flow of work, the events of March 22 did, awfully. That day Mike Todd was killed in the crash of his private plane, the *Lucky Liz;* Taylor herself was to have been on the flight with him but had a cold and chose not to travel. She was, naturally, hysterical, and Brooks went to her house to see if she could continue making the picture. Unfortunately, he had been preceded by various agents and producers asking the same thing. "You son of a bitch," she greeted him. "I guess you're here like all the rest of those bastards who've been here all day long!" Brooks tried to assure her that she, and not the film, was his chief concern. "It's a movie, that's all it is," he said. "If you never want to come back, that's fine." "Well, I'm not," she replied. "I'm never coming back. Fuck you and the movie and everyone else."

The studio was, indeed, ready to pull the plug, but Brooks was able to mollify them temporarily by changing his shooting schedule and rewriting some scenes so that he could shoot without her for a couple of weeks. And then he got a call from Taylor's secretary saying that the actress wanted to visit the set. "I think I'd like to come back to work," she told him. "I don't know how long I'll be able to work. Maybe I'll start and something will happen." Brooks eased her back into the production with short bursts—an hour, then two. "By the end of the week," he remembered, "she was working four or five hours. Never missed a day and was never late." As impressed as he was with the transformation in Taylor between rehearsals and the actual shoot, Newman was even more awestruck by her work in completing the film. "She was extraordinary," he recalled. "Her determination was stunning."

CURIOUSLY, THE same could not be said for Joanne. As award season dawned, she was frequently cited as a contender for an Academy Award for *The Three Faces of Eve.* She won a couple of prizes in the run-up to the Oscar season, including a Golden Globe. But she was reluctant to get all goggle-eyed about any of it. "If I had an infinite amount of respect for the people who think I gave the greatest performance, then it would matter," she said when asked about her prospects for the big prize. When the nominations were announced, she had in fact made the final cut, along with the formidable quartet of Deborah Kerr *(Heaven Knows, Mr. Allison)*, Anna Magnani *(Wild Is the Wind)*, Elizabeth Taylor *(Raintree County)*, and Lana Turner *(Peyton Place)*.

Whether out of nerves, perversity, or hardheaded independence, Joanne did all she could to talk down her chances. "Deborah Kerr will win," she announced on the red carpet of the Pantages Theater on Oscar night. And that wasn't her most self-deprecating gesture. She revealed that the green taffeta gown she was wearing at the big show had been made not by a famed designer but rather by *her:* "I spent a hundred dollars on the material, designed the dress, and worked on it for two weeks." The gesture stunned the old movieland cohort, no one more than Joan Crawford, for whom Joanne had been named. "Joanne Woodward is setting the cause of Hollywood glamour back twenty years by making her own clothes," she fumed.*

It was Joanne's night, though, despite her crimes against fashion. John Wayne opened the envelope and called out her name, and she stood at the podium breathlessly, saying, "I've been daydreaming about this since I was nine years old. I'd like to thank my parents for having more faith in me than anyone could."

But she was still chary of the whole thing. "Acclaim is the false aspect of the job, which screws you up," she later said. "You start to need it, like a drug, and in the final analysis, what does it all mean? I won my Academy Award when I was very young. Sitting in bed afterward and drinking my Ovaltine, I said to Paul, 'Is that it?' "

In fact, she wasn't very persistent in stoking her career. She followed *Eve* with two films without her husband—adaptations of works

---

* "I'm almost as proud of that dress as I am of my Oscar," Joanne replied when she was told about the comments. Eight years later she presented the screenwriting Oscars while dressed in an expensive gown designed by William Travilla and declared, "I hope that it makes Joan Crawford happy."

by William Faulkner *(The Sound and the Fury)* and Tennessee Williams *(The Fugitive Kind)*—and then settled into a pattern of working only with him for the next several years as their family grew and his career rocketed. In the wake of her Oscar win, she soured on the movie business. "In Hollywood the big producers, big directors, big stars band together, the lesser ones band together, and the strugglers band together," she reflected. By dint of her New York connections, she explained, she was always relegated to a lower tier. But when she won her Academy Award, that changed: "Suddenly I became 'acceptable,' and I felt that I was being 'acceptable' on a very false level which had nothing to do with me per se, or whether someone liked me, but only because I became an asset, in a certain respect, that I hadn't been previously. A property."

Her ambivalence about her career was entangled with her feelings about her marriage, she revealed: "I was raised forties style to believe that a woman should be both wife and mistress to her husband, and only in that could she find her true fulfillment. I bought into that philosophy, and it caused me grief . . . Although I loved being wife and mistress to my husband, I was bothered. I had always acted and had always wanted to be a star, but because of my upbringing, I thought there must be something wrong with me for wanting to be more than a wife and mistress."

Still, she had advantages over him: that Oscar, for instance, which he posed with in a gag photo, eyeing it enviously,* and in February 1960 the very first star on the newly established Hollywood Walk of Fame. (Newman would have to wait until 1980, unbelievably, to get his.) In certain respects, even as she shunned the sort of stardom that was falling to him, she would always have his respect as the superior—and more acclaimed—actor.

---

* He wasn't the only one with eyes for it: in September 1976 burglars broke into the Newmans' home in Connecticut and took her Oscar, among other items. Police recovered the statuette in a matter of a week or so.

IN THE spring of 1958, both *The Left Handed Gun* and *The Long, Hot Summer* were released. Arthur Penn claimed he never saw *Left Handed* between the day he finished shooting it and the day the studio dumped it as a second-tier feature into the sorts of grindhouses that specialized in B westerns. "Warner Bros. brought in an editor," he recalled. "In television we were essentially editing our shows on the air. I thought that's what I would be doing." Those critics who did manage to catch it in its limited release, like Howard Thompson of the *New York Times*, weren't impressed: "Poor Mr. Newman seems to be auditioning alternately for the Moscow Art Players and the Grand Ole Opry," he hissed. And given the mishmash of the script and the jerky structural rhythm, it was a fair, if cutting, comment. But the film would go on to find appreciative audiences overseas, especially in France, where, Newman bragged later, it was almost always playing in some small Parisian theater.

The Long, Hot Summer was treated with far more care by the studio and got more respect from critics. It wasn't universally admired: *Variety* summed up the consensus by declaring "It may be preposterous but it is never dull." And Newman, blossoming into a sexual confidence and a willingness to dance with, if not marry himself to, immoral behavior, was particularly cited, even in dismissive reviews, as a highlight. In the spring his performance won the first important award of his career—a best actor prize from the Cannes Film Festival.

With so much new product on-screen and a marriage to an actress with an Oscar, he seemed on the verge of becoming a major star himself. But he was at constant loggerheads with Warner Bros., which was determined to work him in what he considered substandard material and at a salary that was, given his rising profile, ridiculously low. He griped about his situation in the press, courting the wrath of the studio. "Major studios have a way of taking care of their contract players in even the most minute respects," he told columnist Joe Hyams. "For example, Warner Bros. has done everything possible to keep me from getting into a high income tax bracket." He complained that the studio was making money by loaning him out—they'd used him only on three films in five years, compared to the five that he'd done for MGM and Fox combined. And he even called them out for boorish manners:

"When Joanne and I went on our honeymoon to Europe, Warner's was so tactful. The studios I did pictures for on loan-out—Fox and MGM—sent flowers, arranged a car for us, took care of theater tickets. But Warner's left us completely alone, ignored us."

Hyams made light of these complaints, but they were genuine, and they were part of a plan that Newman had begun to discuss with his agent, Lew Wasserman, to separate himself from his contract. Wasserman, another Jewish son of Cleveland, was a cutthroat operator who had risen from selling candy in burlesque houses to doing promotions for big bands to running MCA, the largest talent agency in the business, by the time he was in his mid-thirties. He was an absolute shark who prided himself on impeccable manners and ruthless partisanship. Acquiring Wasserman as his agent certified Newman as a top talent; it was just a matter of prying him loose from Jack Warner's greasy-thumbed clutches for his career to truly take off. "Wasserman was a master charlatan," Newman recalled, "and I say that in the best sense. And he had a better idea of what I was worth on the open market than I did. He said, 'What if you could buy your way out of your contract for half a million dollars?' I said, 'Are you kidding? I'll be working for twenty years to pay that off!' He said, 'Let me do it.' "

There was another thing Wasserman had to convince him of. Above all else in his work, Newman relished the challenge of playing men very different from himself: Rocky Graziano, Ben Quick, Brick Pollitt, Billy the Kid, Glenn Griffin. Even though those were leading roles, Newman saw them as character parts, as chances to build personae from the raw materials of a script and his own analytic process and present them in wholly realized performances. But for Wasserman's plan to work, Newman would have to assent to being restyled as a movie star, to submit himself more frequently to leading man roles that would, in the prevailing sense of the term in Hollywood, lack the subtle definition he enjoyed teasing out of roles. He would be cast as a function of his looks and his ability to sell tickets more than on the strength of his craft. If he was to become the sort of money-maker that Wasserman assured him he could be, he would have to allow himself to be refashioned as a traditional matinee idol. It was a devil's bargain for an actor of his temperament and preferences, but he could see the practicality of it and agreed to let Wasserman explore the chance further.

First, though, he would have to be patient and compliant as Warner Bros. put him out on loan yet again for *Rally 'Round the Flag, Boys!*, a comedy about the opposition of suburban Connecticut housewives to military plans to build a nuclear missile base in their town. Newman was cast as a low-level corporate executive whose marriage is failing because his wife ignores him in favor of community work. Joanne would play his missus, who can't say no to any worthy cause but constantly puts off her husband and his manly urges; Joan Collins was to appear as a local femme fatale intent on making time with Newman's character so as to make her *own* husband jealous enough to take interest in her.

The film shot through the summer in Hollywood, with some location work in Connecticut, and Newman and Joanne found themselves immediately disenchanted. Leo McCarey, the old-timer who had directed the likes of *Duck Soup*, *The Awful Truth*, and *Going My Way*, had taken much of the darkest cynicism out of the script and ladled on some corny gags such as a drunken Newman swinging from a chandelier. "This was my first crack at comedy," Newman remembered. "I wasn't comfortable enough so that I could relax in it. As a result, I overplayed a lot of things."

And prospects for his next picture weren't much better. Warner Bros. was angling to get him into an adaptation of a novel by Richard Powell called *The Philadelphian*, a melodrama about a young man from an ordinary background who callously works his way up in Philadelphia society and the legal profession. "It's just a glorified cosmopolitan soap opera," Newman complained even as he was making it. Prior to that, he had met with the director Vincent Sherman, a veteran Warner Bros. hand whose career was just recovering from a spell on the anti-Communist blacklist, and expressed the gravest reservations. "The property was just not worth doing," he insisted. "It got to the point where in talking with him I said, 'Don't do the movie. Forget about whether I do it or not. Just don't do the movie.' " But Sherman was going to proceed and so, in pain and chagrin, would Newman.

First, though, he would treat himself to another project in compensation. He had angled for an opportunity to star in the original Broadway production of Tennessee Williams's latest play, *Sweet Bird of Youth*, which would start rehearsals as early as the fall under the direction of Elia Kazan. This was a truly plum role, and Newman wanted it badly enough that he agreed to make *The Philadelphian* just so he could be given leave by the studio to appear onstage. The play's producers, for their part, were so keen on having Newman in the lead that they agreed to push the show into the winter of 1959, when he would finally become available.

Through the fall Newman reported doggedly to the set of *The Young Philadelphians*, as the film had been retitled, often after staying up late working with a writer whom he'd insisted be recruited to punch up the script. He was wretched. "The mistake that you make is, it's bad, and then you work on it like hell, and you walk in, and this scene maybe plays," he explained. "And because things get better, so much better, you almost mistakenly feel that it's good—until, of course, you see it, and then it comes back on you with terrible force."

But he did acknowledge a certain sympathy for his scruple-free character. He was, he said, "much closer to me as a human being" than most roles he'd played, and he went so far as to buy his wardrobe from the studio, keeping three of the six suits he obtained in a closet on each coast. He didn't take out his frustrations on the director or his costars. Robert Vaughn, who was counting on it as his first big picture (he would be nominated for an Oscar in the part), knew that Newman "just wasn't crazy about doing it" but added, "he was very conscientious . . . I had to test for it, and Paul was there to read lines opposite me. It's very unusual for someone to do that, and I think it helped put me over." Vaughn took part in many of the rewrite sessions, during which the two would stay up, rehearse new lines, and "put away a bottle of scotch."

As NEWMAN slogged through this dreary nightmare—his third film in five years for his home studio, each as bad as the last—he was given the treat of the dazzling and far more rewarding process of preparing for *Sweet Bird*. Kazan was a director after his very heart, given to talking at great length about motivations, contradictions, and nuances of character, providing copious notes, taking plenty of time to rehearse and to analyze each scene and exchange and line and pause. "I was so amazed with the amount of preparation he put into this play," Newman enthused. "There would be long pads of paper, on which he had gone into the exploration of certain character dualities and certain other concerns and attitudes, in writing. It just involved a tremendous amount of work—the dramatic development of the play."

Newman hadn't been Tennessee Williams's first choice for the role. The writer had, naturally, hoped for Marlon Brando; moreover his preferred leading lady, Anna Magnani, had looked at pictures of Newman and declared that his face lacked "poetry." But it turned out that neither of those stars would be available; Geraldine Page would ultimately land the lead, and Kazan shrewdly recognized in casting Newman that he had on his hands an actor whom he could manipulate into the various contradictory colors required to play the role of Chance Wayne, a gigolo who has attached himself to an aging movie star and hopes to use her influence to launch a movie career for himself and return in glory to the southern hometown he fled a few years before.

Chance is an enormous heel—a social-climbing charmer who has won the heart of the daughter of the town's big boss and given her a venereal disease, rendering her barren, then gone on to bed rich ladies at a Florida resort using an arsenal of seductive techniques including drugs: a noteworthy creep even amid the gallery of Williams's malignant characters. Kazan's task, as he saw it, was to take the gorgeous rising star Paul Newman and turn him into a believably desperate and sweaty schemer, and he had some tricks to help him pull it off. One was to force Newman to cut his hair close and dye it red, giving him an unappealing and slightly Luciferian sheen. Then he made sure that the cast didn't get too friendly with Newman but rather treated him as a pariah, much as the townspeople would treat Chance upon his homecoming. "From now on, until the play opens," he told the rest of the players in secrecy when they were engaged in rehearsals for the Philadelphia tryout run, "I don't want any of you to socialize with Paul.

Let him feel that you don't like him and that he's alienated from you. Right now you're too chummy with him, and it shows up in the play."

Finally Kazan used Newman's obvious deference to him to put doubts into the actor's mind about whether he understood anything about his performance or Page's or indeed acting or drama at all. As Newman recalled,

Whenever he would give me a piece of direction, or whenever I would come over with an idea, he would say, "Paul, try this." And I would say okay. Or he'd come over to Geraldine Page and she'd say, "What if I tried this?" And he'd say, "Try it." And so we would play the scene, and then we would separate, and I would hear him go over to Geraldine and say, "Ah, right on!" I'd say, "God, I thought she was really off a little bit, that's not what I expected her to do." Then he would walk over to me and say, "Ah, try it again." He was chopping me down. By opening night it was marvelous. I didn't have any security in the part at all. And that's precisely what he wanted.

Newman wasn't entirely isolated during the early phases of the play. Bruce Dern, playing an old friend of Chance's, became a pal. When they had a break from rehearsals in Philadelphia, the two took the train up to New York together, one time sharing the club car with comedian Jonathan Winters (a Kenyon College dropout), with whom they drank and laughed heartily. Later Kazan too softened, taking the opportunity of the Broadway opening to reveal to Newman what he had done behind the scenes to help craft his performance. The director soon came to regard the confession as a mistake. "Kazan said that from that point on, the play was never the same," Dern remembered. "After that all the electricity was gone."

Philadelphia had certainly been an unusual choice for the debut of such risqué material. On opening night Joanne quietly seethed as a Main Line society family tsked and tutted at each of Williams's outlandish ideas. "It's the dirtiest thing I ever saw," one of them finally pronounced. "If you don't like it, why the hell don't you leave?" Joanne hissed back. "And they did!" Newman boasted. But New York wasn't nearly so easily shocked, and when the play premiered on Broadway on March 10, 1959, the critics were impressed. In the *New York Times* Brooks Atkinson called it one of Williams's "finest dramas" and declared that it was "brilliantly acted." Walter Kerr in the *New York Herald-Tribune* called it "a succession of fuses deliberately—and for the most part magnificently—lighted." The *New York Daily News* said, "It cannot be ignored," and the *New York Mirror* took special notice of Newman's intensity when it noted, "His disintegration, when he finally faces up to reality, has genuine emotional impact. Newman, as well as the audience, was moved by the concluding passages of the play. There were tears in his eyes as well as in those of the audience."

They might have been tears of exhaustion as much as genuine emotion. "I wanted to come back to Broadway," he told a columnist, "and I'm glad I did. But it's a lot of work, boy. I forgot." And to another he confided, "It takes at least three hours to unwind after each performance." But he may have been especially skittish because he and Joanne were expecting once again, and this time things were going well. It had been a little over a year since her miscarriage in London, and in the interim she had worked on a film, Martin Ritt's awkwardly realized version of Faulkner's *The Sound and the Fury* (in which a bewigged Yul Brynner played the lead). But now she was ensconced at their New York apartment on West Eleventh Street waiting for the baby to come.

The apartment was the first one they shared that wasn't a temporary rental or a vestige of their unmarried lives. As Newman told Hedda Hopper, "It was remodeled by a young man for his bride, but the marriage broke up almost immediately and it was thrown on the market. There's a small garden with a fish pond and trees, a room we'll convert into a nursery—we'll need that by April. All the furniture from Joanne's old apartment is already there. We've shipped our books, paintings, four lamps, and most of our clothes by express." Joanne seemed perfectly happy spending her days with her two Chihuahua dogs and her books and a baby on the way. "I'm into a correspondence course in algebra, anthropology, and the history of philosophy," she said. "I think I'll enroll in Columbia when the play is on its Broadway run. I've always regretted not having a college degree."

She seemed deliberately to be avoiding capitalizing on her Oscar and was inclined to express her dismissive attitude toward her own career with jokes. "A baby was always a possibility," she said, "but it wasn't as scheduled time-wise as other details of our life . . . I cleverly arranged to be pregnant when Paul was starring in *Sweet Bird of Youth*. I wanted Paul to be close when the baby was born, and I kept praying I would have it during the day or after midnight when Paul wouldn't be on stage." On the morning of Wednesday, April 8, she was fortunate enough to get her wish. Elinor Theresa Newman—named for her grandmothers—was born in time for her dad to welcome her into the world and then race over to the Martin Beck Theatre to play the matinee.*

In the summer he let off steam by playing first base for the *Sweet Bird* team in the Central Park softball league. "I'm pretty good," he boasted to a columnist, and Bruce Dern concurred: "He could hit." He took care to make his visits with his three older kids meaningful. "One of my dad's favorite pastimes," Scott remembered years later, "was to take me and my two sisters out in a little wobbly rowboat and fish off Long Island Sound. He'd sit at one end with his hat pushed back on his head and swig a bottle of Budweiser."

And he prepared to dabble in a new pursuit: film directing. As part of an initiative to have film and stage personalities make short movies to be shown at charitable fund-raisers in the New York area, Newman and a team of ten or twelve shot Anton Chekhov's monologue "On the Harmfulness of Tobacco" as a one-man film starring Michael Strong, whom Newman had admired deeply in a performance of the same material at an Actors Studio session. He had real Hollywood pros on the set, including cinematographer Arthur Ornitz and production designer Richard Sylbert. But he harbored no great illusions about what he was doing. "We've had some distributional encouragement," he told a reporter, "but we'll talk distribution only if we find we've made

---

* For those keeping count of such things, this was the third time Newman had become a father while appearing onstage in a Broadway play.

a good picture. Otherwise we'll burn it. This picture is an emotional commitment, not a binding, legal one."*

No, for binding, legal ones he had other strategies and other plans. His contract for *Sweet Bird* stipulated that he would play Chance for less than a year, and he had to consider what to do when that period came to a close. This was just the opportunity Lew Wasserman had been looking for, to prize him free of Warner Bros. and turn him into a more valuable commodity. As Newman recalled, "He waited until Jack Warner was in a terrible humor about something, and Warner said, 'Now this moron Newman is coming back, and he's going to be a pain in the butt.' And Wasserman said, 'Why do you have to put up with that stuff? Let the guy buy his way out. He's not going to amount to anything.' Warner bought it, and that was the end of that." At the end of August Newman paid Warner Bros. a flat half-million of blood money and bought his freedom.

For the son of Arthur Newman, this was a terrifying leap. He was supporting four children, a wife, an ex-wife, and, with his brother, a widowed mother, and now he was without guaranteed work. He acknowledged that parting from Warner Bros. was a risk that kept him "poor for several years"; he spoke of lying awake thinking about the possibility of everything's caving in on him, of having to start from scratch without anything. "I have a recurring nightmare," he admitted, "in which I always dream that the bottom is going to fall out of my career . . . I worry so much that I'm lucky if I get five hours of sleep." But he knew too that the decision was justified on artistic grounds and even sheer principle: "I was free at last to make my own decisions. If I failed in anything it would be *my* failure, no one else's."

Still, the money worries dominated his thoughts sufficiently that he took the exceedingly rash step of shooting a movie while still onstage in *Sweet Bird*. In November 1959 he started appearing in the mornings on various soundstages and locations in New York for the shoot of

---

* He wound up pouring, by his own estimation, $22,000 into the project and showing it for two days at a New York theater. "It was the best creative experience I've ever had," he said. "I was just absolutely alive. My wife must have thought I was on dope."

From the Terrace, another potboiler about a young man on the make, this time from a John O'Hara novel. Joanne starred opposite him as the society girl he marries and can't hold on to; Ina Balin played the sweet girl he meets too late and decides to love anyhow. Never missing a single one of the three-hundred-plus performances of *Sweet Bird* during his run with the play, he kept on schedule with the movie. Sol Jacobson, the press agent for *Sweet Bird,* recalled of this grueling routine, "Eight times a week he created the part as if it were opening night. And what is even more astonishing, by day he got up before dawn and commuted to the [film] set."

Newman admitted to being shattered by the workload. "We've been under pressure from the start," he told an interviewer. "I worked day and night . . . I guess I was greedy." But having Joanne on the set with him was a balm against his worst impulses. "When I get home," he explained, "I can't bluster around growling that the director fouled me up on this or that scene, because Joanne was there." And he joked too about her love scenes with Patrick O'Neal: "When she finished, I let her have it across her behind—just in case she got any romantic notions."

Making time for silliness came naturally to them, such as the November afternoon when they appeared on the panel quiz show *What's My Line* in the "mystery celebrity guest" slot. Before a blindfolded panel consisting of Bennett Cerf, Arlene Francis, Dorothy Kilgallen, and Art Linkletter, Newman grunted yesses and nos to questions and Joanne answered them in a variety of accents before they were recognized by Francis, who knew all about their work, including what they were up to next; she even asked about baby Nell. ("She ate a cigarette yesterday," Joanne revealed, drawing a big laugh from the audience.)

All this activity seemed to be taking a toll on Newman's stage work, at least in the eyes of Sidney Blackmer, the veteran stage and screen actor who played the tyrannical town boss in *Sweet Bird.* "Paul hasn't had a great deal of experience," he told an interviewer near the end of the year. "He needs great coaching in timing; his instinct is off in timing . . . I think he's getting things that he has added—as a Method actor, or even not as a Method actor you try to improve the performance—but he's changing his reactions. He's putting in an interpretation." And Newman admitted that the hard work of appearing in the play and making a film had gotten to him; Joanne attended a performance late in the run and chastised him for putting in a half-effort. "That hurt," Newman admitted, "but Joanne was right. I had been doing the part so long that I was rushing through it. After her chewing out, my last ten performances were just great."

He finally let it go. In February, Newman was replaced in *Sweet Bird* by Rip Torn, who had played the sadistic son of the town boss, and he and Joanne decamped to Hollywood to finish *From the Terrace*. He admitted that he missed the play. "It's hard to describe the sense of loss," he said. "It was like watching a wonderful barrel of brandy being thrown over the side of a ship . . . I've been in two New York plays, but I never felt the same way about them. On closing night, after the final curtain came down, we had a champagne party backstage. I told Rip Torn that I wished him all success and a long run. Then I added that I hoped he would never be better than I was in the role."

But truly, how competitive could he have been feeling? Wasserman was shopping him around at $200,000 a picture—more than ten times what he would expect to earn as a Warner Bros. contract player—and his first job under these rich new terms would be *Exodus*, Otto Preminger's epic adaptation of Leon Uris's novel about the Israeli struggle for independence. When Oscar nominations came out for the previous year's films, he was cited for his performance as leading actor in *Cat on a Hot Tin Roof*, rectifying the slight he'd felt when he was overlooked for *Somebody Up There*.

He was thirty-four years old, and he had a new wife, a new baby, new confidence in his abilities as an actor, and a new and potentially very lucrative lease on his own career. He had made eleven movies, several of which had been well received, and had premiered three memorable roles on Broadway. His picture was on magazine covers, and he was featured in newsreels just for showing up at restaurant openings or theatrical premieres.

It was 1960, and he could justifiably feel that he had a hell of a future ahead of him.

Eleven

"I'M TWO PEOPLE," HE WOULD TELL THE PRESS. "I'M ME, PAUL Newman. And I'm Paul Newman the actor. The first one is not for sale. When they hire the second one, I do the best job I can, but nobody has the right to tell me how to live, how to dress, or how to think."

Of course he was right: there was a public Newman and a private one. But each was, in fact, a mosaic of other, smaller identities, some potent and patent, some obscure and oblique.

He was an actor and a husband and a father—each for at least a decade. He had directed a short film and had begun to take an active interest in the operations of the Actors Studio. As a performer, he had created a persona of his own—neither the new Marlon Brando nor the guy who got lucky when Jimmy Dean cracked up, but a man whose talent, commitment, and, yes, looks, set him apart even in the company of his Hollywood peers. He was a sex symbol whose allure spanned generations, possessed of a kind of relaxed, intelligent manliness with an ageless style. And he was half of an enormously famous showbiz couple, a modernish pair whose frank and footloose manner made them an emblem of a new all-American domestic cool.

He was a burgeoning superstar, a trouper of stage and screen, a stud who could act, dishy, inquisitive, romantic, a blue-blooded shapeshifter who could project chilly and hot and broken and cruel and chatty and tetchy and decent and shameless and stifled and unsheathed, quite often in combinations and quite often very well—a real talent of shades and depths and taste.

And he was well liked, and by a variety of people and audiences. Like Brando and Dean and Steve McQueen, he was a rebel who dressed like a slob (but with taste), hung out in déclassé joints, got around on motor scooters or in sports cars, stayed out of L.A. as much as he could, played brassy scoundrels and real heels and the occasionally arty part, and seemed the whole while to be having a blast. Young audiences loved all that about him, even though he was in his thirties. At the same time, he was a pragmatic businessman's son and a war veteran, he'd attended two prestigious colleges, and he had children to support, and he took all that seriously enough to win the approval of a generation who'd grown up with Henry Fonda, James Stewart, and Clark Gable. He was easy on the eyes and a man's man. He was charming, if never exactly comic, and determined, if never quite heroic. He always got the girl (hell, every leading man always got the girl), but you sensed that he might have been just as content not to. His victories were satisfying, but sometimes only he and the audience knew the truth of them. And oddly, even his defeats somehow pleased; in failing in their quests, his characters seemed to find greater personal victories than those they'd intentionally pursued—the very archetype of the modern antihero.

He signed on to make *Exodus* in September 1959, and in the span of the next decade he would become the biggest movie star in the world and tailor a public image for himself that would suit him the rest of his life. He would make some very good films (*The Hustler, Paris Blues, Hud, Harper, Hombre, Cool Hand Luke*) and some absolutely awful ones (*The Prize, Lady L, Torn Curtain, The Secret War of Harry Frigg*). He had as representatives Hollywood's most powerful agent (first Lew Wasserman, then, after Wasserman left the agenting business, Freddie Fields) and its most respected publicist, Warren Cowan. He formed a production company with Martin Ritt (at first it was named Jodell, as if by a pair of Jewish partners in the garment district paying homage to their wives, Joanne and Adele; eventually they called it Salem Pictures) and then another with a powerful agent, John Foreman. He would be written and spoken about, inaccurately, as being on the verge of taking parts in dozens of films, some of which would never be made, and he often, with no fanfare, passed on films that became career-making hits for other actors. By 1968 he would be nominated for four best actor Oscars; he would top the likes of John Wayne, Clint Eastwood, and Sean Connery in annual polls naming Hollywood's most popular star; he would command more than $1 million a film (and more still for those he produced); and he would direct a theatrical feature.

In virtually every picture he made as an actor, he took the effort to create a credible personality out of his role, extending his art the way his schooling and his work at the Actors Studio had taught him: hard application, thorough analysis, emotional exploration, and the exact construction of a character so that it seemed organic and spontaneous when presented. He was one of those rare Hollywood icons who cared about the actual craft of acting: he distracted directors and probed screenwriters and bored interviewers with his discussions of motivation, structure, and technique. And although he could be caught out working his machinery deliberately in a number of films—stiffness and calculation somewhat limited even the best performances of his first decade or so in movies—he always managed to seem normal or matter-of-fact or familiar in a way that made it easy to forgive his occasionally misguided forays, such as playing a Mexican bandit *(The Outrage)*, or a French anarchist *(Lady L)*, or a goofball GI with a knack for going AWOL *(Harry Frigg)*. He was hardworking enough to put the bad ones behind him and had sufficient taste and talent to turn out good ones regularly, enabling audiences to forget his fumbles as well. And he was good enough from the start that watching him evolve into a real master was not an ordeal.

He was expert in a lot of things but never really figured out how to play a romantic lead. That may have been because he was so well and publicly married. His life with Joanne was the stuff of Hollywood legend: two talented and brassy and attractive people with an admirably collegial style of working and living together. They were independent-minded, which made them something of a scourge to Hollywood's stuffier commentators, but they were down-to-earth and inoffensively offbeat, which made them an enviable example to ordinary American couples with kids of their own and a yen for a little spice in their own lives.

Everyone said that *he* was the pretty one and *she* the real talent. And, in ways, they were famously mismatched: jumpy, go-go Paul who loved fast cars and boozy parties and bad bawdy jokes badly told, and low-burning Joanne, with her theater and ballet and books and dry wit and refined southern way with domestic and social matters. But everyone also recognized that it was a happy marriage, and if nothing else it was a growing concern: a second daughter, Melissa Stewart (Lissy), was born in September 1961, and a third, Claire Olivia (Clea), followed in April 1965. Throw in his children with Jackie, and you now had an even half-dozen, and their homes—various rented places around Los Angeles, a series of New York apartments, and a property they acquired in Westport, Connecticut, in 1963 and would remodel and expand over time—were big, merry ménages of casual comfort, home-cooked meals, rambunctious kids, and pet after pet after pet. For people who did their kind of work—and at their level of achievement—they were pretty mom-and-pop.

Perhaps because he found himself so invested in the future through the lives of this brood, he took an active interest in politics. He was, in general, a serious fellow who chummed around with writers rather than movie people—he counted among his friends Gore Vidal, A. E. Hotchner, Stewart Stern, and Mort Sahl. But his political concerns took him into places where none of them could follow: discussing nuclear disarmament with Hedda Hopper; agitating for civil rights in the company of Marlon Brando in Sacramento, California, and Gadsden, Alabama; funding a liberal think tank and attending its seminars and conferences whenever possible; appearing at Democratic National Conventions as a party host and a fund-raiser and, in 1968, as a voting delegate. He took his role as a public citizen seriously in ways that could raise eyebrows, if not hackles, in Hollywood. But he was precise and modest enough in his words and deeds that he never found himself alienated from the business. By the time he fully committed himself to having a voice in the affairs of his country, he was so big a star that he was given the platform of the cover of *Life* magazine from which to say so.

THAT WAS the public Paul Newman.

The private one was another fellow—related to the famous one, but quieter, cagier, more suspicious. He had a rascally streak to him and a need to explode—Peck's Bad Boy even as he neared forty. But he had a strong moral center and was quick to stand up when he believed in something and to learn from his mistakes. He did what he wanted to and didn't mind explaining himself, but he much preferred just being left alone to do it. If he wanted to grill steaks while living on location in Montmartre (Joanne held the umbrella above him against the Parisian rain), or wear shorts into a fancy hotel restaurant, or zip around Manhattan on a Lambretta scooter, or sneak homemade popcorn into movie theaters, or drive a Volkswagen Bug fitted out with a Porsche engine and a racing suspension, or drink so many beers in a day that he had to wear a bottle opener around his neck to keep up with himself, or go for a run every morning followed by an hour in the sauna with some fruit and the *New York Times*—why then, he would. He talked about his bosses and his pet peeves and his wishes that things were otherwise freely in the press, and he didn't seem to care how it came off. And he managed to do all of it in such a way that nobody could find serious fault with him or a weakness through which to bring him down to size.

If he had a taste for appearing idiosyncratic or flaky, he backed up his quirks with a lunch-pail work ethic. He went at the job of acting the way another man might physical labor; he was famous for poring over his scripts and making detailed notes about all aspects of them; for demanding extra rehearsal time, even unpaid; and for questioning the logic—particularly the emotional logic—of his scenes even as they were being shot. Joanne, who in comparison seemed born to act, would complain, not entirely facetiously, "I think he's crazy. When he's working, he breaks the whole script down . . . he's awful." In fact, she said, the more unhappy he was with the material, the more likely he was to become a bear about it: "If he doesn't like something he has agreed to do, he can be an absolute pain in the neck. He'll work much harder on a script he hates, and at the same time he'll drink too much beer."

He understood his own process and disposition at least as well as she. "For me," he explained, "acting is simply a matter of getting out there on stage—or in front of a camera—and getting the motor running and keeping it going. One trait I've always had is a kind of tenacity in whatever I set out to do." Indeed, his ability to dive wholly into his work, or indeed his play, was a point of pride. "I always go all out," he said. "When I drink, I drink, and no nonsense about it. When I study, I study."

He had a personal role model in his work, and it wasn't Art Newman Sr. "If I were a dog, I would be a terrier," he said. "I always see them as dogs that are trying to handle bones that are much too big for them, trying to dig up bones under fences when the fences are too deeply embedded. I am lucky to a fault, but I am also very determined. I will somehow get that bone." And he would guard his prize doggedly once he got his paws on it. "John Foreman, the producer, once gave a description of me that I love and cherish," he revealed. "He said, 'Paul Newman gets up every morning, walks to the window, and scans the horizon for enemies.' "

He recognized his limits—indeed, he had been surmounting them since the start—and he worked hard to smash through them to go further. But he knew too that his talent and application could take him only so far. "I know that I can function better in the American vernacular than I can in any other," he would say. "In fact, I cannot seem to function in any other." He feared being trapped in work that would bore him with repetition, and he was frankly jealous of artists with more malleable gifts. "I am beginning to get sick of acting," he told a friend, "not because it's a fraud, but because I am no longer able to find anything that I haven't done before. I have *had* me on screen in all my facets, and there's nothing unexposed of me. All I can do now is dig into the makeup kit and put on a false nose or add a regional dialect. Some actors of our generation, Guinness maybe or Olivier, never seem to exhaust themselves. Their inventions are always original." But when he strove to be original, the work suffered, and he knew it. "It isn't that I'm afraid to stretch," he'd admit. "It's simply that I've tried it and it's been a disaster." And he could hate what he did. "I'm glad you liked the show," he wrote to a friend who had written to praise a performance, "because I'm going to give up acting."

His determination led him to habits that affected the sort of father he was. When he was working on a script, he would disappear into an outbuilding on the Connecticut property; then he'd go off by himself to research his roles in other cities and countries; and then he would go off to shoot the film. So he didn't see the kids as much as he might have (which must have especially irked Joanne, seeing as she often had to look after a brood of six, half of whom weren't even hers); and then he could be overly bossy upon returning home—inevitably resuming his proper place, however, and contritely, when his woman told him to do so. Like a lot of dads who are frequently away from home, he could overindulge his kids and then suddenly take a stern tack with them. But he seemed genuinely to share their curiosities and enthusiasms, especially when they tended toward physical pursuits like swimming, riding, earth sciences, and motor sports. He wasn't as remote a father as his own had been; he had learned some kindness from Uncle Joe.

His sense of humor—well, that was a constant work in progress. His practical jokes got more elaborate, expensive, and thoroughgoing over the years. And he only hurt the ones he loved. His brother, Art, who became a working colleague on his films, was a favorite target for hustles and stunts. During one shoot Newman decided that he could no longer stand the sight of Art's ugly leather hat; he ripped it off his brother's head and tossed it into the air, where a stuntman he'd paid to do so blasted it with a shotgun. Art coolly picked up his mutilated headgear, put it back on his bald dome, and wore it every day until filming was through. Another time Newman was having trouble with his voice and walked around wearing a T-shirt that read "I have laryngitis. Joanne is fine. No autographs please." Yet another time he had 150 cartons of toilet paper made, each little square bearing the likeness of a famous actor and the motto "Greetings from Robert Redford." He loved bawdy jokes—just shy of dirty—and told them in mixed company, as it was known then, including his daughters, a tendency that was made even worse because the jokes he liked best were so often bad—and he told them poorly.

But somehow it was boyish, this enthusiasm for dopey humor and crude wit. And in truth in many ways he *was* boyish and always would be. He didn't like being looked at or talked about; he hated formal clothes; he bit his nails; he feasted on popcorn and burgers; he spit on the sidewalk; he couldn't remember people's names; he brought his own firecrackers to light off surreptitiously at Fourth of July barbecues; and he tried new sports all the time—tennis, scuba, go-karting. When he had to talk with an IRS man to work out a problem with his tax records, he pleaded immaturity: "In order to be an actor, you really have to be a child. And if that theory is correct, then it follows that the more childish you are, the better actor you are. If I'm a really good actor and I make a tremendous amount of money—from which I have to pay the federal government—then what you want me to be is an accountant. And if I'm an accountant, I'm a responsible human being. I'm mature. If I'm mature, I can't be a very good actor, which means I can't make any money!" The tax guy bought it; the matter died.

Despite the evidence of his film work, he played pool and poker passingly to badly; chess too. Bridge was his game, and he would often fight off boredom on movie sets or over dull dinners by working out bridge hands silently in his head. Probably he drank too much, although he never again made the papers for it; certainly he smoked too much, and he tried giving it up by substituting carrots and celery sticks when the urge struck. But he ate wisely and well, and he was a nut for physical exercise and being outdoors, so he balanced it out. And he knew that he was lucky—his original bit of luck, really: "In the business I'm in, I seem to have the right physical appearance. It's not just a question of attractiveness or unattractiveness. It means I have a metabolism that keeps me thin."

And there were those eyes, those uncanny lapis lazuli-cornflower-cobalt-summer-sky eyes that shot out and pierced and hooked people and were all you ever heard about him. They were a terrific asset but a terrific embarrassment too. He hadn't worked for them or chosen them, and the whole world seemed to have an opinion about them and to want to possess them, if only for a moment. Strangers would literally walk up to him and stare right into them, and when he took to wearing dark glasses, they would insist that he take them off. "There's nothing that makes you feel more like a piece of meat," he complained. "It's like saying to a woman, 'Open your blouse, I want to see your tits.'"

This was sticking his neck out, complaining about the studios and the publicity machine and the intrusiveness of fans. But he insisted that by choosing acting as a profession, he hadn't signed away his rights as a citizen. He felt that he owed the public a good performance but nothing of his personal life. He could get positively angry on the subject: "I've seen fan-magazine articles about Joanne and me that have made me want to puke. The most banal language—and the fucking nerve to put it in quotes attributed to me . . . I'm not your typical movie star. I can't even stand going to premieres." In time he turned down requests for autographs altogether. He saw himself strictly as a professional, a man who did a job with integrity and then went home. That his job happened to make him famous, that strangers felt a connection to him because of what he did for a living—well, that wasn't anything he had asked for or signed off on or thought up. He pissed off a lot of people in the business and the occasional pushy fan, but as he was fond of saying, "A man without enemies is a man without character."

So THIS was the man and the artist he became in the years between *Exodus* and *Cool Hand Luke*. And in many important ways it was who he would be for the rest of his life.

He had buried someplace behind him virtually all ethnic traces of the Newman family's religion while retaining its creative curiosity and intelligence and dogged work ethic and unimpeachable integrity. Of Theresa Fetzer's family, he held on to a kind of earthy realism and, perhaps, physical fearlessness. Cleveland and Kenyon and the navy still informed his sense of decency and hominess and fair play and humility and simple honor; Yale and the Actors Studio fed the side of him that aspired to art and to work for the elevation not only of himself but of his craft and his fellow man. He had married once in haste and accepted the responsibility for leaving that marriage, providing financially for his children and making sure that his home would always be open and welcoming to them. He had married a second time, for love, and again he had become a father, and he made sure that these children too were comfortable and happy. He was smart enough to respect his wife and her talent and to give her the freedom to do the things that pleased her, just as she allowed him the same license.

To this persona he would, in the coming decades, add dimensions, some quite vast and profound. And some of the more awful things of life would strike at him—not as often as they did others, perhaps, but inevitably, and at the cost of real pain.

It had taken him more than thirty years to become this Paul Newman, the one whom everyone would recognize for the remaining decades of his life. And this Paul Newman, in his fullness, contradictions, failings, talents, predilections, leanings, associations, habits, quirks, and humanity, was who he would be from then on.

Part Four

Twelve

*E*XODUS WAS SHAPING UP TO BE A MASSIVE PICTURE. LEON URIS'S novel about the struggles to found the Jewish state of Israel and to populate it in part with refugees from Europe had been a national best seller for more than a year. And even though Hollywood's moguls traditionally didn't like to draw attention to Jewish themes for fear of reminding the world that they themselves were Jews, any book that sold that well was always destined for the screen. Otto Preminger, just starting to fade from his standing as one of the most reliable of American directors, was planning to shoot in Israel and Cyprus for seventeen weeks, and the Newmans, complete with baby Nell (as infant Elinor was known), would be on location about half that time.

Newman was cast as Ari Ben Canaan, a composite of a number of paramilitary commandos who fought against both the British colonial rule of Palestine and the native Arab forces determined to hold on to it. Among the figures Uris based the character on was Yossi Harel, who led a series of ships filled with refugees from Cyprus to Israel, all strictly against British dictates. The most famous of these vessels, the *Exodus*, was physically repelled by the British, and global headlines about the incident resulted in a publicity coup for the Zionists. In Uris's doorstopping potboiler, Ari went on from this triumph to free Zionist prisoners from a British prison and then to protect a children's village from invasion by hostile Arab forces.

Lee J. Cobb would play Ari's politically moderate father, and David Opatoshu would play his radical uncle; John Derek was cast as his childhood best friend, an Arab prince; and Eva Marie Saint was his love interest, an American whose journalist husband had been killed in Palestine the year before. The British bad guys would include Ralph Richardson and Peter Lawford, and Sal Mineo played a Holocaust survivor intent on drawing enemy blood. Newman would be filling a big, heroic part in a big, epic film for the first time in his career, and Lew Wasserman had every reason to believe that it would make him a star of the first order.

The book wasn't exactly beloved by Arabs, and the filmmakers were under heavy security from the time they arrived in Israel. But the anonymous threats weren't nearly so hurtful, Newman found, as the way Preminger ran his film. "He's got the reputation of being such a fascist asshole," he told a reporter, "and he *is*, on the set. I mean, he can pick out the most vulnerable person and then walk all over him, you know. He could walk down a line of 200 people at a fast pace and pick somebody out and make lunch of him." (Preminger famously hectored a group of child actors on the *Exodus* set with the immortal imprecation, "Cry, you little monsters!") Their personal relationship, however, was cordial. "I found him articulate, informed, funny, absolutely lovable," Newman confessed.

Maybe he cut Preminger some slack because he knew the director was trying to film a genuine epic on a fraction of the budget he required; for all the time the production spent abroad, the footage had a rushed feeling. (Famously, Preminger left a shot in the finished film in which the shadow of the camera clearly passed over the trysting bodies of Newman and Saint.) Nevertheless, Newman felt he had a right to share his opinions on the material. He thought the script was "too cold and expository," and he couldn't find a way to turn the flatly heroic Ari into a living man. So he went to work on his own, rewriting the part, and then approached Preminger with the results. Newman "came to me one morning, after he'd been up most of the night writing his changes, with this stuff in his hand," Preminger recalled. "I told him I wouldn't even read what he had written. 'Why not?' he asked me. 'Because, I told him, what you have done may be good and I might be tempted to use some of it. And then tomorrow you would be back with more changes.' He studied me for a few seconds, and he twisted his mouth around a little, and then he said, 'Okay, I think you're right.' "

Tension governed their interactions from then on, and according to Preminger's widow, who worked on the film as a costume coordinator under her professional name, Hope Bryce, Newman did only what was required of him and no more. His final scene, a funeral speech over the bodies of principal characters who died defending the children's village, was meant to be an aria of mourning and hope. But despite Preminger's instructions, Newman played it more or less straight. And on the plane as the crew left Israel, Bryce claimed, he turned to Preminger and told him flat out, "I could have directed this picture better than you."

If the film was destined to be a thing of hits and misses, the Newmans' vacation in the Holy Land was also something of a mixed success. Joanne spent her days touring historic sights and taking Hebrew lessons. Or rather, she did those things until walking around became impossible. "The Israelis are movie mad," she explained. "We could not walk down the street because we would be followed by fifteen hundred people, and that used to terrify me. One morning, I was sitting having breakfast on the terrace enjoying the lovely spring day . . . I glanced over the side, and sure enough there must have been fifty people . . . standing . . . staring." Newman described the intrusions in a letter to Stewart Stern. "They stand in front of the hotel all day," he griped, "staring in at the lobby or hollering upstairs into unknown windows, eyeballs, hundreds of them, peering through the fence. Most people suffer from an excess of never being looked at, and here we suffer the opposite extreme."

He added that the accommodations were less than ideal:

"Booze is terribly expensive.
"Twin beds.
"Joanne's hair dye has yet to arrive and she's black at the roots, which is wonderful for her black disposition.
"Twin beds."

And it wasn't enough that the Israelis didn't respect his privacy or share his enthusiasm for cheap beer and large beds. No, they had other ways of bringing him down a peg, as Joanne remembered: "The day we left to come home, all of us in the *Exodus* company went to pay a call on Prime Minister David Ben Gurion. Mrs. Ben Gurion spent some time in Brooklyn and likes America. She said when we all walked in, pointing to Paul, 'Is he the handsome one they all talk about?' and then added, 'I don't think he's so handsome.' You should have seen Paul blush!"

BACK IN the States for the summer, Newman set up a production company with Martin Ritt who, among the directors associated with the Actors Studio, seemed most eager to work regularly in movies. It was, Ritt told the press, a unique alliance based on a simple principle: "I suppose the production association of an actor and a director is unprecedented. I can think of no other independent company formed by this combination. Paul and I simply found that we had something in common, a philosophy about making motion pictures. We agreed that every American motion picture should be a reflection of our American way of life, just as vital a motive in moviemaking as entertaining people and making money."

Before they could get to work for themselves, however, they were teamed for a project for Marlon Brando's Pennebaker Inc., *Paris Blues*, an adaptation of Harold Flender's novel about a black American expatriate jazzman who has a fling with a black schoolteacher who is on vacation in France. A succession of writers came in to expand the story by adding a second musician and a second teacher—white, naturally. The romance of the black couple had as a crucial subtext the question of whether the musician should avoid the civil rights struggle by living in dignified exile or form an alliance with this redoubtable woman and return home to make things better. The white guy's issues were more to do with pursuing an aesthetic dream and remaining committed to himself in a city that asked nothing of him; the woman he dated would thus be trying to domesticate him simply for the sake of marriage and family. Newman and Joanne would play that couple, while Sidney

Poitier and Diahann Carroll would play opposite. Louis Armstrong would appear in a featured part, and Duke Ellington would score the picture.

The Newmans arrived in Paris in autumn and moved into a two-story house in Montmartre. Newman took trombone lessons and liked practicing so much that he actually changed the musculature of his face. (His tone was never very good, he claimed, but he could find the notes well enough to convince real musicians that he was playing.) In his time off he slummed in local cafés, drinking beer with workers and practicing his French, dressed in rough clothes. Joanne did the museums and looked after Nell and the Chihuahuas and entertained her mother for three weeks. They both grew tired of the French food that the studio-provided maid, Desirée, prepared, so Newman found a barbecue and set it up in the back garden; in the dead of winter, he grilled steaks and burgers while the neighbors looked on aghast. And when that got to be a chore, they went to an American southern-style restaurant they'd found just below Place Pigalle. In the midst of this enviable escape from their regular lives, Joanne became pregnant with Lissy, who arrived the following September.

They sailed home from Paris, and Newman, under the influence of Montmartre, at the very least, wrote a postcard to Stewart Stern:

"We are drin
king
quite
a
b
i
t."

In December 1960, while they were making *Paris Blues*, *Exodus* was released. The problems that had bubbled just below the surface on the set were glaringly evident when spread across a gigantic screen and more than two hundred minutes of running time. Newman's Ari was a stiff and unlikable hero for a man who was supposed to be the center of a historical epic—and not necessarily because he was written that way; Newman played him as humorless, rigid, and dogmatic, as if he was more interested in presenting a stern aspect to his director than in weaving his character into the enormous, impassioned canvas Preminger was attempting. At the same time, Preminger had a kludgy story built around inert set pieces, awkward romances, and unengaging political posturing. For a film of its size and pedigree it was remarkably clumsy. But it had that wonderful Ernest Gold music and those authentic settings. And Newman looked great. So despite its flaws and its length, it drew people; it was one of the top five box office hits of 1961.

Newman had been threatening to pierce Hollywood's upper tier for a couple of years, and *Exodus,* for all its problems, made it clear that he had earned a place there: to make a hit of a long slog was the sign of a real star. It didn't matter that the film wasn't much respected in the business; his appeal as its marquee played was evident, and new opportunities were regularly falling before him. *Two for the Seesaw,* a hit Broadway play about the unlikely romance of a Nebraska businessman and a Greenwich Village dancer, was going to go before the cameras, and Newman was to star opposite Elizabeth Taylor. But somehow the thing fell apart. Indeed, he could have made an impressive career of the films he *didn't* make over the span of the next half-decade.

To wit, he was supposed to appear in *The Sixth Man,* a biopic about Ira Hayes, the Native American marine who helped raise the flag on Iwo Jima; *The Hook,* a Korean War melodrama with Sidney Poitier; *Sylvia,* a romantic detective thriller; *The Last Frontier,* based on the Howard Fast novel about the U.S. Army's war on the Cheyenne; the political melodrama *Seven Days in May;* an adaptation of *The Wall,* John Hersey's novel about the Warsaw Ghetto uprising; *The Enemy Within,* an adaptation of Robert F. Kennedy's book about his racketeering investigations; *The Great Race,* Blake Edwards's gigantic chase movie farce; *The Spy Who Came in from the Cold,* from the John Le Carré novel; *After the Fall,* from Arthur Miller's play about a man married to a ravishing second wife (they wanted Sophia Loren opposite him); an adaptation of *Tropic of Cancer* costarring Carroll Baker; *Night at Camp David,* in which he would play an aide to an American president who may be approaching a nervous breakdown; *The Sand Pebbles*, in the role that Steve McQueen ultimately won; and even *In Cold Blood*, when Columbia Pictures thought that Newman and McQueen combined would be boffo box office as the cold-blooded killers Dick and Perry. Twice Federico Fellini had to stand up to producers who wanted Newman: for the lead role in *La Dolce Vita* (imagine!) and for a never-realized film about a mad cellist. And François Truffaut made a pest of himself with his producers by repeatedly suggesting they try to build their adaptation of *Fahrenheit 451* around Newman, even going so far as to suggest setting it in New York. Only a handful of these films would get made—and without him—but their sheer numbers give an insight into the sort of stature he was achieving: a producer or a director just had to talk with him about a role or mention that he might want to use him in a picture, and it would make the papers.

So too would any word that he *wasn't* going to make a film. When *Two for the Seesaw* fell through, writer-director Robert Rossen (*All the King's Men, Body and Soul*) came to think that maybe Newman would be the right guy for the next picture he had in mind. "I think Robert Rossen had actually signed somebody else," Newman remembered, "and then he found out I was available and called me and said, 'Can I send you a script?' I read half of it and called my New York agent at six o'clock in the morning and said, 'Get me this film.' And he did."

Rossen's instinct was sharp, but he paid for it. Newman's stature on the heels of *Exodus* was such that Rossen, who was producing the film as an independent, had to give him 10 percent of the picture. But having Newman aboard meant the picture was a go, which was all that mattered to the director. Rossen, whose major Hollywood career had been interrupted by encounters with the House Un-American Activities Committee, was now hobbled by a combination of diabetes and alcoholism, but he was determined to make a film about a world that he knew well, the demimonde of smoky billiard halls and itinerant pool sharks. Writer Walter Tevis had published an acid little novel called *The Hustler*, about a dumb, gutty, foolish, gifted billiards player named Fast Eddie Felson who had to learn who he was and what mattered to him the hard way and to the occasional cost of innocent others. It was a bravura bit of pulp, tightly atmospheric, filled with pinpoint detail and spare, snappy dialogue. Rossen immediately recognized its cinematic quality, as well as the opportunity to expose an authentic subculture on the movie screen. And he saw in Newman an exciting Fast Eddie. The picture, known initially as *Sin of Angels*, would start shooting in the winter in New York.

Newman respected Rossen's knowledge of the subject matter and his commitment to the job. "He just pulled himself together to do the film," Newman remembered, "and he was incredible." Too, Newman loved the material and knew it was the best thing he'd ever had in front of him. Eddie Felson in his view was a guy trying to find himself, to express himself and his talents in an unorthodox way, to burst into the world and be a something instead of a nobody, and mostly, to realize his true self. Newman told an interviewer, "I spent the first thirty years of my life looking for a way to explode. For me, apparently, acting is that way." For Fast Eddie it was pool, and Newman knew it instinctively. He asked Rossen to infuse the script with more material supporting his interpretation of the character: "I told Rossen he ought to somehow liken what Eddie does to what anybody who's performing something sensational is doing—a ballplayer, say, or some guy who laid 477 bricks in one day." Or, he might have added, a squarejohn from Shaker Heights who was making himself into a successful actor.

"IT WAS one of those movies when you woke every day and could hardly wait to get to work," Newman said, "because you knew it was so good that nobody was going to be able to louse it up." Since no studio was hovering over him, Rossen was free to operate on the cheap and get an authentic feel; the picture was shot in midtown Manhattan during the winter and spring of 1961 over a span of ten weeks. They used the Greyhound Bus Terminal, some dive bars on Eighth Avenue, and, especially, Ames Billiard Academy on West Forty-fourth Street, where the gigantic figure of Jackie Gleason would appear to play his scenes as Minnesota Fats, the pool hall legend against whose figure Fast Eddie

measures himself.* In a stroke of genius Rossen cast the great comedian as a big, flamboyant, and shrewd gambler with courtly style and
deadly talent. And the director was equally lucky in the other parts.
George C. Scott, something of a shark among actors, moody and
powerful and diffident, was cast as a mysterious fixer and financier of
gambling scenarios. And Piper Laurie, a promising young actress with
a résumé rather like Joanne Woodward's of a couple years before,
would play the bittersweet role of the love interest, a fallen daughter of
privilege, drunken, overeducated, and partly lame.

To prepare for the film, Newman took lessons in straight pool
from Willie Mosconi, the famed champion; he moved a billiard table
into the Upper East Side apartment he and Joanne had bought, and
he got good enough, as with the trombone, to play a lot of his own
shots in the film. Naturally, being in a pool hall with Jackie Gleason
and being a good fella, Newman found himself tempted into a little
bit of a wager. He and Gleason, he recollected, played a little match of
four games; the first three were for a buck apiece, and Newman won
them; the fourth was for $100, and, said Newman, "He whipped my
ass." Gleason, of course, had been winning bets like this for years; he
was in life very like the man he was playing in the film. Newman, who
had learned merely to imitate the type for the role, respected and admired a man who lived it: "He was hustling me. He was looking down
my throat the whole time. And the thing that was marvelous, he had
such patience. Because everyone in the crew is standing around
watching these games going on. He had the patience to lose the first

_____

* The character Gleason played was not based on the living fellow who used to call
himself Minnesota Fats in the saloons, billiard halls, and casinos of America and who
became a minor TV celebrity in the 1960s and 1970s. Walter Tevis always swore that
Fats and Eddie were works of fiction, and he deeply resented the notion that he had
created two such memorable characters out of mere reportage. He complained to a
journalist that people asking him when he had met Minnesota Fats was like asking
Walt Disney, "When did you meet Donald Duck?" Tevis, who also wrote *The Man
Who Fell to Earth*, died in 1984 after writing a sequel to *The Hustler* called *The Color of
Money*. His widow would spend decades debunking the claims of those who pretended
to be the original Fast Eddie.

three to sucker me in for the last one." (As Gleason related, Newman paid the bet off in pennies.)

And Gleason could be very droll about Newman's actorly habits. Although Gleason had come up as an actor as much as a comedian, he was somewhat out of his element playing such dramatic material. One morning Mosconi was serving as a stuntman, in effect, by executing an exacting pool shot just off camera so as to make it look as if Gleason had taken it; after ten successive attempts, though, he couldn't get it just right, and Gleason bellowed, "Get Lee Strasberg in here immediately!"

After *The Hustler* wrapped, the Newmans spent the months leading up to Melissa's birth in a Beverly Hills house they rented from B-movie star Linda Christian (a nude torso of her, cracked by the weather, stood in the garden). Jackie had moved with her three kids to a home nearby in the San Fernando Valley, where she would live for more or less the rest of her life, eventually remarrying; Scott, Susan, and Stephanie would grow up there with her, but they invariably spent time with Newman when he was living and working in Hollywood and often lived with him for extended periods in New York and, eventually, Connecticut.

Newman shot the film version of *Sweet Bird of Youth* that summer, reuniting in the cast with Geraldine Page and Rip Torn and with Richard Brooks, who'd directed his previous film performance in a Tennessee Williams story. It was an unhappy experience. Brooks had rewritten Williams again, only this time in such a way that the actors for whom the piece had, in effect, originally been composed couldn't find their way back into it. And the studio forbade the stars from talking about the picture to the press, a fact to which Newman would allude as if with a raised eyebrow to indicate the damning truth of it. However, in consideration of his new pay rate—$350,000—he could respectfully comply with Brooks's wishes.

Newman then engaged in a project that had some of the savor of the live TV days of just a few years before—an epoch that, it was clear, would never be resurrected. Martin Ritt and Jerry Wald were filming an omnibus of Ernest Hemingway's Nick Adams stories that A. E. Hotchner had adapted into an episodic feature film. One of the stories was "The Battler," and Newman fancied getting into the persona and makeup of Ad Francis once again, "as an exercise in acting." His agents at MCA weren't too happy with his choice. He was highly marketable at the moment, and they could find lots of well-paid jobs for him if he'd let them. "They said I was a star," he remembered. "I couldn't cheapen myself by playing a bit part." But he was serious about seeing what he'd learned about his craft over the past six years. He sat dutifully for makeup each morning (photos of his transformation ran in *Life* magazine) and then played his scenes for Ritt opposite Richard Beymer (as Adams) and Juano Hernandez (as Francis's traveling buddy and minder). He looked forward, he told Hedda Hopper, to taking in both of his own performances as a form of quality control. "I want to run the old TV film and compare it with my present performance," he said. "I want to see if being a movie star has diluted my work as an actor."

IF HE was thinking overly about his status as a movie star, it was because his career had truly bloomed into something he had never imagined. In early 1962 the Newmans were given a free cruise from New York to the Mediterranean in exchange for being the featured on-ship celebrities on an ocean liner; they spent as much time as they could boozing and gossiping with Gore Vidal, who was also roped into the cruise, but they also had to present their films as part of the evening's entertainment; one middle-aged woman fell so under Newman's spell that she literally followed him around the boat like a puppy dog.

When they got back to the States, he found himself in the midst of Academy Award season, and *The Hustler* was in contention for an impressive nine prizes: best picture, actor, actress, director, screenplay, cinematography, and art direction, and two for best supporting actor.* All of these nominations were worthy, but Newman's was especially well deserved. He was the focus of virtually every scene in the film

---

* *West Side Story*, set, ironically, in a world not far away from Rossen's Midtown purgatory, had received eleven nominations and would be the big winner on Oscar night.

and carried it all—the swagger, the nervous tension, the sexual confidence, the not-quite-sharp calculation, the mercenary skill with the cue stick, the crushing humiliation, the hard-earned redemption—with appealing certainty. Sometimes he worked too hard, striking calculated poses as he had in Eve Arnold's famous photo of the Actors Studio. But there was fluency and daring in his work beyond what he'd demonstrated previously. Even Ben Quick of *The Long, Hot Summer* didn't have the cynicism of Eddie Felson, and Quick's rehabilitation was neither so arduous nor so convincing. *The Hustler* was hardly a blockbuster, but it was the first truly iconic thing Newman did, and it would be remembered fondly and deservedly for decades.

Still, it was a tricky moment in the business, and the Oscars had been particularly funny for him so far. He thought that he should have been recognized with a nomination for *Somebody Up There Likes Me*, but he had been ignored; he had stood by magnanimously when Joanne won for *Three Faces of Eve*; and he felt he had a real shot with *Cat on a Hot Tin Roof* (David Niven won for *Separate Tables*). This time he seemed the favorite against Charles Boyer in the little-seen *Fanny*, Stuart Whitman in the little-seen *The Mark*, and Maximilian Schell and Spencer Tracy, who seemed likely to cancel each other out for their performances in *Judgment at Nuremberg*. Schell, who had originated his part in a TV version of the Abby Mann script, had won the New York Film Critics Circle prize but was relatively unknown in the States. Newman had won the British Film Academy award and was emerging as a true Hollywood superstar; plus, he had been immense in the role of Fast Eddie. Surely it was his.

On an April night at the Santa Monica Civic Auditorium, Joan Crawford came out to award the best actor Oscar, and the TV cameras caught a glimpse of Newman so balled up in his seat that his pant cuffs had hiked up, exposing his calves. And then Crawford opened the envelope and called out the name Maximilian Schell. Schell gave a humble, tasteful speech, and Newman applauded him. But Joanne, who had presented the award for sound recording and was still backstage when Schell won, was another matter. "My husband behaved like a gentleman," she remembered. "He was, I'm sure, bitterly hurt and disappointed, but he didn't act as if he was. I'm ashamed to admit I was wild. I was furious and upset and in tears. Backstage, I made a terrible spectacle of myself. I wouldn't even speak to Max, and it certainly wasn't *his* fault!"

NEWMAN WOULD have another chance at the golden statuette sooner than later. With Ritt, he was developing a film based on *Horseman, Pass By*, a modern-day western that was the affecting first novel of a young Texan named Larry McMurtry. The narrator, Lonnie Bannon, orphaned by his parents, lives with his grandpa Homer on a family-run cattle ranch in the Texas Panhandle. Homer is old enough to be thinking about the day he'll have to leave the ranch to his sole surviving son—Lonnie's uncle. But the guy is a son of a bitch: mean and selfish and boozy and demanding. A handsome bastard with an ugly heart, carousing with other men's wives, forcing himself drunkenly on a black housemaid, accepting all comers in fights and dares and whatnot, capable and reckless, cocksure and narcissistic, he went by the name of Hud.

McMurtry's book was adapted by Irving Ravetch and Harriet Frank Jr., who had also written *The Long, Hot Summer* and who would join Newman and Ritt in producing the new film. From the start they had been looking for a more marquee-friendly title than the novel bore. For a time they tinkered with *Wild Desire*; McMurtry offered several suggestions, including *Coitus on Horseback* ("A title," he remembered, "I had long hoped to fit onto something"); then they tried *The Winners* and then *Hud Bannon Against the World* and then *Hud Bannon*. Finally they settled on the obvious and shortened it to one blunt syllable: *Hud*. Their choice—and the film's eventual marketing campaign, with Newman togged out as a lean and mean cowhand—was based purely on Newman's manly magnetism; the new title indicated how fully he had come to dominate any picture in which he appeared.

Next the filmmakers had to deal with complaints that the material was too dark. Even compared to the flawed fellows Newman had played in the past—Rocky Graziano, Ben Quick, Brick Pollitt, Chance Wayne,

Eddie Felson—Hud Bannon was detestable. And his comportment through the central crisis of the film, when the family's entire stock of cattle must be destroyed because of an incident of hoof-and-mouth disease, is inhuman. In the face of his father's sense of decency and the common good, he wants to sell the herd and let the next fellow worry about the contamination. And when his father stands up to him, he tries to maneuver the old man out of ownership of the ranch through legal chicanery.

The moneymen at Paramount, who'd put up $2,350,000, couldn't swallow it. "I remember when the studio executives were reading the script," Ravetch said. "They paled. One of them said, 'When does he get nice?' I said, 'Never.' " Indeed, Hud's unremitting cruelty was in part what recommended the material to Newman and Ritt: they wanted to make a movie that broke the mold of all the Hollywood films in which a leading man turned from heel to hero in the final reel. Newman had made a couple of such pictures himself, and he was eager to throw the formula away.

Ritt wanted to make sure the film's themes of corruption weren't overcome by a romantic image of fading cowboy life. So he and cinematographer James Wong Howe shot the film in black and white and did a deliriously beautiful, lyrical job of capturing the desolation of the Panhandle. They spent several weeks on location in Claude, Texas, an empty little town about thirty miles southeast of Amarillo. Newman got to bomb around the endless roads in a big Cadillac convertible and wrestle a pig in a dusty rodeo arena.

Along with his cast mates—including Brandon de Wilde, who had played the little boy in *Shane;* veteran Melvyn Douglas; and Patricia Neal, playing the maid, who'd been rewritten as white for the screen— he stayed at a large motel in Amarillo, and the place was swarmed by local women who seemed to have gone completely insane for him. "Women were literally trying to climb through the transoms at the hotel where I stayed," he remembered. Policemen had to be dispatched to the premises to keep intruders away. "If it was teenagers I could see it," one cop complained, "but it ain't. It's grown women, too . . . Somethin' like this comes to town, and you find out just how crazy the public is." To thwart the interlopers, Newman and de Wilde both changed hotel rooms several times. But calm would be restored only when the company returned to the Paramount lot in Hollywood to shoot the film's interior scenes.

NEWMAN HAD appeared in two films a year since 1956, adding two extra in 1958; he'd be in three in 1963. Gradually he was becoming a true marquee star, piercing the Quigley Poll, which measured actors' popularity with audiences, for the first time ever in 1963, when he finished ninth.* He was becoming a household name and, with his eyes and hard, lean body and angelic face and sardonic smile, a real sex symbol. "Some of the fan mail I'm suddenly receiving makes me blush," he confessed—in large part because he couldn't imagine that it was himself to whom these avowals of female passion were addressed. "I'm as sexy as a piece of Canadian bacon," he squirmed. He was a grown man, looking squarely at forty, but he had the vigor and appeal of youth—which, ironically, he hadn't quite had, or at least hadn't been aware that he had, back when he was young.

But if his coltish quality made him seem fresher than his years, he was also an adult with adult responsibilities: a wife, five children, an ex-wife, and so on. As his star rose, so too did his need to see to his private business on his own terms. As a respite from what had been a pretty steady diet of work and work-related travel, the Newmans had secured a redoubt not only from Hollywood but from New York and, indeed, the world.

Nook House they called it; Susan Newman came up with the name when the place was first described to her. A converted barn filled with bedrooms and a big open area to live and eat in, it stood on 2.5 acres ending on a bluff over the slender Aspetuck River in a wooded portion of Westport, Connecticut.

"It's the most beautiful house that was ever designed for a family

---

* He would rank in the poll every year from 1963 to 1975 (save 1965, when he didn't have a release) and would eventually appear in it fourteen times overall—seventh most frequently of all time—and rank as number one in 1969 and 1970.

with five children," Joanne declared. It was only the fourth or fifth house they saw on an impulsive real estate hunt, and Joanne's fancy was immediately taken by the tree house on the property. They took a quick look inside and bought it, paying $96,000 for house and property and spending a bit more than that again to renovate it and add improvements. Eventually there'd be a pool and cabana with sauna, a guest house that doubled as a den (complete with pool table and screening room), and a tombstone commemorating all the family pets who'd lived there and gone on to meet their reward.

In the main house the wooden beams and stone fireplace were complemented with antiques, including the famed brass bed, lots of framed photos of the Newmans and their family and friends, books and flowers and comfortable furniture, and a couple of bits of film and stage memorabilia, including Joanne's Oscar, tastefully off to the side on a bookcase. Joanne had some advice from decorators, including the stage designer Ralph Alswang, but she relied chiefly on her own eye and sense of gesture: the enormous dining table, for instance, which she explained was actually "a seventeenth-century Irish wake table. The coffin goes in the middle and everyone sits around and weeps and eats."

It was a country house but near enough to Manhattan to be, in effect, a suburban retreat par excellence. And Newman's life was circling about itself in grand, affirmative fashion. Art Newman had brought himself and his family from East Cleveland and Cleveland Heights to the curved, tree-lined streets of Shaker Heights, which was a real achievement. But his son was now a property owner in the sort of ideal Connecticut town on which the classic garden suburbs of the 1920s, like Shaker Heights, were based. Westport hadn't grown out of some scheme to re-create the pastoral past on the outskirts of a city; it was the real thing, first settled by white men in the seventeenth century, dotted with wealthy farms and farmhouses from the Revolutionary War era, with a quaint town center and plenty of exposure to the waters of Long Island Sound—and all within fifty miles of Times Square. For a small Connecticut town, it had a cultural sophistication: the Westport Country Playhouse, a respected regional theater, had been founded there 1931 and helped launch dozens of important acting, directing, and playwrighting careers; and the town had a long-standing reputation as an artists' colony, attracting famous writers, painters, musicians, and actors since the Civil War era.

Newman had been thinking of buying a home in Connecticut since he was married to Jackie. He was familiar with Westport, in particular, from the time he and Joanne shot some exterior scenes for *Rally 'Round the Flag, Boys!* there. And, too, Nook House was near the home of A. E. Hotchner, with whom Newman would become partners on a number of small boats, some bearing the name *Caca de Toro (Bullshit).* ("We were terrible fishermen," Hotchner remembered, and Newman concurred, stating of himself that he was "the worst fisherman on the East Coast.")

But it still struck many observers as unusual that a Hollywood star would make his home in such a place. To make it even odder, the Newmans were living not in the Gold Coast portion of Westport, with views of Long Island Sound, but in the wooded area of the town, on a busyish road, with a middle school right across the street: hardly the poshest spot, even in a town with a bohemian air.

From the first, Newman claimed that his residency in Connecticut wasn't a big or an unusual thing: "A dear friend of ours lived there, and we found a house that suited us," he'd say, or "I moved here from Ohio, went to school here. I moved to New York and did some plays and bought a house in Connecticut, and that's where I live." Of course, in the status-conscious movie business, it was crazy enough to live in New York. Living in Connecticut was like sticking a thumb in the boss's eye.

The Newmans would, in fact, keep apartments in New York for decades, and they rented homes in Los Angeles for long stretches, including much of the school years of their two youngest daughters. (Newman had a favorite spot: "Malibu in September and October is unsurpassed," he opined.) But they were easily put off by the parochial aspects of living in Hollywood—the continuous obsession with money, celebrity, and the next deal. They preferred to keep a quiet space to themselves, and if that made them seem aloof to people, that was their problem. No one was shocked when a banker or a lawyer moved his family to an appropriate home and turned into a commuter; why should it matter that an actor would do the same? "I love the seasons," Newman said. "I love the house that I live in. I like the people here. I don't know why there should be any excessive comment about that."

OF ALL the things that were special about Westport, the tree house that first caught Joanne's eye would become, perhaps, the most important in their lives. They created from it an adults-only space where they kindled their marriage in private. "That's where Joanne and I have cocktails," Newman said. "The kids are not allowed up there." They'd repair with newspapers and beer and sherry or, on special nights, champagne and caviar. At first it was a summertime idyll, but ultimately it was available to them year-round: Joanne had it winterized for him as a present.

Smart woman. If Newman had a tiger by the tail in his career, then Joanne had one in her marriage. If he was considered the most desirable man in America, she was the woman who had pried him away from his first marriage in an unlikely love match. He looked like a Greek god; he never took a bad picture, literally. Her own looks were mutable; she could be stunning or plain, ordinary or exotic, kittenish or tomboyish. And while it was clear that she still had finer acting chops than he did, surely he wasn't attracted to her for that; he could've married Helen Hayes or Ethel Barrymore if that was what turned him on.

She knew what the talk was like, about him and especially about their match. "I've long since adjusted to my husband's status as a superstar and a sex symbol," she would say. "The only place I'm a sex symbol is at home, and I'm very lucky that my husband thinks I'm sexy. I don't worry about women who come on strong with him, because I know what he thinks of them." Five years after they'd spent the shoot of *The Long, Hot Summer* in constant communion on the streets of Clinton, Louisiana, they were still that way. "They're the most hand-holding couple I ever saw," said a longtime friend, and the sense was that Newman reached for his wife's hand more often than the other way around.

For his part, Newman spoke of her in genuinely fond terms that were meant to emphasize her congeniality and allure but perhaps too often sounded laddish or indelicate. "She's the last of the great broads," he was fond of saying early in their marriage, and then a few years later, famously and to his regret, he asserted his monogamy by declaring, "I have steak at home; why should I go out for a hamburger?" (Chastened by Joanne for comparing her, in effect, to a piece of meat, he tried another metaphor. "She's like a classy '62 Bordeaux," he told a female interviewer. "No, make it a '59. That's a year that ages well in the bottle. Will I get in trouble for that?")

The mystery of their marriage fueled gossip and speculation for decades. While they were in France making *Paris Blues*, around the time of their third anniversary, the columnist Mike Connolly reported that they were close to breaking apart, and Newman, informed of the article, went ballistic. He fired off a cable to Connolly that read "You've always been irresponsible. Keep up the good work"; he denounced him to other writers as an "inaccurate dolt"; and he got Joe Hyams, a Hollywood correspondent who always enjoyed chummy relations with his subjects, to allow him an entire column in which to lambaste Connolly, mockingly declaring that he was going to take steps to ruin his marriage just to give the writer's words the scent of truth.

But it wasn't only ill-informed outsiders who wondered how the marriage of the world's most handsome man and his somewhat less glamorous wife held together. Otto Preminger, who had many chances to measure the Newmans' relationship during the months of shooting *Exodus*, put his finger on the secret of it, and it was the plainest one imaginable: "He's an oddity in this business. He really loves his wife." And Stewart Stern, best man at their wedding, vouched for Newman's love. "Paul has a sense of real adoration for what Joanne can do," he remarked. "He's constantly trying to provide a setting where the world can see what he sees in her."

She reciprocated his feelings by being at his side as colleague and partner as much as wife, lover, and mother. For one thing, she virtually gave up acting unless he was involved in a project. Between 1956 and 1963 he made eighteen films and she made ten, five of which starred both of them. "They're peculiar about their working," said a producer at the time. "They refuse to be separated. Many an actress has got her big chance in a role that Joanne turned down because it would keep her away from Paul." She herself acknowledged as much. "Acting is a career for Paul, but not for me," she declared, within mere years of winning her Oscar. "Being Paul's wife is my career. I don't forget that for an instant. And I never do anything which would let him think I won't be there when he turns to me."

Newman understood what a deal he was getting. For one thing, he was enormously impressed with Joanne's acting talent, which was much more instinctual than his burning-the-midnight-oil style. And because he was enjoying the life of a movie star, he understood what she had effectively given up for him. "We haven't had to be separated all that much," he acknowledged. "She's had many opportunities to go abroad or on location by herself, and she's turned these offers down in order to stay with me; she's done this to the detriment of her career, I'm afraid. But it's helped keep us together."

He tried to dote on her, but he was clumsy in the effort in an earnest and somewhat cloddish fashion. "For quite a while after we were married," she remembered, "he'd send me flowers on a certain day in September, which he thought was my birthday. Since I was born in February, I finally pointed out to him that his *first* wife was born in September."

(P.S.: She forgave him.)

Thirteen

IF JOANNE SEEMED CONTENT TO RIDE ALONG WITH HIM, MAKING the occasional film on her own but more often working with him, or indeed not at all, she still had some ambitions. So when Melville Shavelson, the writer-director of such innocuous comedies as *Houseboat* and *The Seven Little Foys*, approached her with a script called *Samantha*, about a tomboyish and opinionated fashion designer who poses as a courtesan to catch the eye of a sportswriter she meets in Paris, she took an interest. Rather than playing the sort of wallflower or dormouse she had portrayed in other films, a woman who would invariably blossom when shown the right attention by the right man, this script gave her character the upper hand; *she* would be the manipulator and the instigator of the relationship. "I love it," she told Shavelson. "It's the dirtiest script I ever read."

She imagined Newman playing opposite her and, as Shavelson was hoping to film a large portion of the picture on location, another working vacation for the family in Paris. She approached her husband with the script. "I read it," Newman remembered, "and I told her, 'Well, I don't think it's fun. I don't think it's *anything*.' She said, 'I was thinking we might do it together.' I said, 'No, *you* do it, and I'll watch and clap soundlessly from the wings.' "

But she was shrewd enough about the business and their respective places in it to know that his agreement to star opposite her would guarantee that the picture would be made, and she lit into him for his selfishness. " 'You son of a bitch!' " she hollered, in his recollection.

" 'Here I've made my career subservient to yours, I've raised your family, and not only my children but your children from another marriage . . . and now when I ask you to make a movie with me, you tell me there's nothing in it for you!' " To his credit, he performed an immediate about-face and agreed to make the picture, which in fact was shot in Paris and was eventually retitled *A New Kind of Love.* "That's how *that* project got off the ground," he told a reporter. "The family wash."

In fact, on the heels of *Hud,* he found himself gravitating to various uninspired projects for a number of similarly arbitrary reasons. He shot two more pictures in 1963, both with comic overtones. In *The Prize,* an adaptation of an Irving Wallace thriller about Cold War espionage in Stockholm during the week in which the Nobel Prizes are awarded, he played Andrew Craig, a wisecracking, boozing, womanizing novelist who has won the literature prize and stumbles upon a dastardly kidnap plot that no one else seems to realize is afoot. Director Mark Robson must have wanted the combination of effervescence and tension that Alfred Hitchcock could concoct, but he ended up with something far less, and Newman, delivering his lines in a droll snarl that sounded like a comedian's version of a sophisticated drunk, was awful. He followed it with a small but charming role in a white elephant called *What a Way to Go!,* in which Shirley MacLaine marries and buries a string of husbands who make fortunes and then die in absurd accidents. (Among the other victims of her love and poor luck are Dean Martin, Robert Mitchum, Gene Kelly, and Dick Van Dyke.) It was actually one of his most successful comic turns, lusty and earthy and foul-tempered, with a reasonable command of French and a saucy way with MacLaine. But it was a trifle, quickly forgotten.

Hud, on the other hand, succeeded brilliantly. The film opened in the spring of 1963 and met with rapturous reviews. Among the critics calling it not only the best American picture of the year but one of the best Hollywood productions in memory were Judith Crist in the *New York Herald-Tribune,* Brendan Gill in *The New Yorker,* Arthur Knight in *The Saturday Review,* and Penelope Gilliatt in London's *Observer.* In the *New York Times,* Bosley Crowther wrote about it twice, weeks apart, and compared it favorably with *La Dolce Vita* and *Room at the Top* as an indictment of contemporary mores. Newman, he wrote, "is tremendous, a potent, voracious man, restless with all his crude ambitions, arrogant with his contempt, and churned up inside with all the meanness and misgivings of himself." Even Dwight Macdonald of *Esquire*, who once wrote, "Paul Newman is simply not an actor and possibly not even alive," had to concede the power of his work, albeit left-handedly: "Newman's Hud is his best performance to date, a mild encomium." Pauline Kael, in one of the reviews that made her career, wrote a lengthy appreciation in *Film Quarterly*, comparing *Hud* favorably to such Hollywood classics as *Casablanca* and *On the Waterfront*.

Indeed, Newman was astounding—Ben Quick and Fast Eddie Felson combined, worked into fighting trim, filled with self-absorption and bravado and ambition and lust and unchecked by law or conscience or anyone in his vicinity who might take him down a peg. His Hud had been equipped with some psychological backstory that was meant to explain his awfulness—"My mama loved me but she died," he barks at his father during a heated exchange—but Newman was less comfortable with that sort of theatrical material than he was with the raw, manly, badass stuff of the role: the swagger, violence, competitiveness, cunning, and imperiousness. It's a well-acted film all around, and beautifully shot and scored and edited, but the unmistakable center of it is the evil, irresistible villain whom Newman builds and inhabits—a cross between Richard III and Elvis Presley.

The filmmakers always knew that they had good material on their hands and that the critics might go for it. What surprised them, though, was the response of the audience to such tart and morally ambiguous material. Hud was both the name and the face of the picture, and his callousness didn't repel audiences—rather, it seemed to lure them in. Ritt, Newman, and the Ravetches had intended an indictment of a certain strain in the American character, and they were genuinely taken aback when the film's strength at the box office was explained, in good measure, by the fact that a young audience saw Hud not as a heel but as a role model. Part of their miscalculation, as they saw it, was that Hud was simply too attractive. They had known that in order to get away with the things he did, the character would have to be handsome and appealing. "Most effective bastards are like that," Ritt said. "Otherwise they're not effective. They have to be very attractive and very charming." But in

Newman they had perhaps too much of a good thing. Moviegoers, particularly young ones, wanted to emulate his style, his defiant attitude, his uniquely American and modern brand of hip. "I got a lot of letters after that picture from kids saying Hud was right," Ritt recalled. "The old man's a jerk, and the kid's a schmuck, or a fag, or whatever they wanted to call him. And if I'd been near as smart as I thought I was, I would have seen that Haight-Ashbury was right around the corner. The kids were very cynical; they were committed to their own appetites, and that was it. That's why the film did the kind of business it did—kids loved Hud. That son of a bitch that I hated, they loved."

They weren't alone. When Oscar nominations were announced, *Hud* received seven in all: for best actor (Newman), actress (Patricia Neal), supporting actor (Melvyn Douglas), and director, adapted screenplay, black-and-white cinematography, and black-and-white art direction.* Newman felt sufficiently burned by his previous brushes with the Academy Awards that he decided to play down his interest in the prize, revealing in advance not only that he would skip the ceremony and stay at home in New York but also that he intended to cast his vote for one of his rivals, Sidney Poitier, who'd been nominated for *Lilies of the Field.* And in so doing he backed a winner: Poitier won, as did *Hud*'s Neal and Douglas and James Wong Howe for his gorgeous photography. *Hud* was a certified hit, but Newman was still standing just outside the screen door of Hollywood royalty.

NEWMAN HAD acted with Poitier in *Paris Blues,* but he'd come into more frequent contact with his former costar during the previous year as he became actively involved in political issues. Newman had long had an inclination to public affairs and what he took to be the responsibilities of citizenship. As a boy, he'd observed his father's softly spoken but ardent liberal leanings. While he was starting out in the acting profession, he looked on as various acquaintances fell victim to the

---

* Strangely missing was a best picture nomination, especially considering how inconsequential the nominated films would come to seem in retrospect: *America, America; Cleopatra; How the West Was Won; Lilies of the Field;* and the eventual winner, *Tom Jones.*

Hollywood blacklist. Striking closer to home was the ordeal of one of his cousins, Robert Newman. A son of Joe Newman's, he worked as a researcher with General Electric and was literally hounded out of the country because of his politics, his marriage to a woman of Russian origins, and his acquaintance with homosexuals through his work with the Cleveland Play House.*

Newman stuffed envelopes for Adlai Stevenson in 1952, spoke at rallies for Gore Vidal when he ran for Congress in upstate New York in 1960, testified to a New York State Assembly panel in 1962 about his belief that the government should not take a hand in censoring films, and took a public stand in favor of nuclear disarmament throughout the early 1960s, speaking of a desire to tour high schools and colleges to discuss the issue with young people and going so far as to tell Hedda Hopper that "people who can afford [bomb] shelters should put them in."

In the summer of 1963, though, his commitment took a more specific and potentially volatile form. Along with Marlon Brando and Burt Lancaster, he headlined and helped organize a rally at Los Angeles's old Wrigley Field in support of Martin Luther King Jr. and the Southern Christian Leadership Conference; after the big public event, at which King and California governor Edmund G. Brown were in attendance, a private fund-raiser was held at Lancaster's home, and Newman, Anthony Franciosa, Polly Bergen, and other Hollywood lights wrote checks to the SCLC. A few weeks later, on June 12, the very day Medgar Evers was gunned down in Mississippi, Brando and Newman joined the Congress for Racial Equality in a sit-in protest on the state capitol steps in Sacramento, drawing attention to the legislature's failure to pass a fair-housing bill.

---

* Robert and his family were relocated by General Electric to Mexico for a few years in the 1950s and then allowed back to work for the company in Stamford, Connecticut. When the Newmans moved to the same state, the two cousins became friendlier than they had been even as boys; Robert and his wife visited Westport regularly for screenings of classic films. Paul stopped by their house with a gift of eighty-eight bottles of beer on Robert's eighty-eighth birthday; Robert reciprocated a few years later on Paul's eightieth, presenting him with a Roman coin imprinted with a face of Caesar that he believed resembled that of his famous cousin.

Newman was hardly alone in supporting the cause of civil rights. As that crucial year in the movement progressed, such notables as Charlton Heston, Tony Curtis, James Garner, Rita Moreno, Sidney Poitier, Sammy Davis Jr., Sam Peckinpah, Blake Edwards, Robert Wise, and John Frankenheimer were among the cohort who joined him in making increasingly outspoken comments about the need for racial equality in American life. But he was willing not only to speak his mind politically but also to defend his right to do so in similarly unambiguous terms. "Because I am a motion picture personality, I am not prepared to ignore what happens around me," he told *Variety* that summer. "Is it necessary or desirable to abdicate your responsibility as a citizen just because it might be safer for business? . . . I cannot conveniently forget my responsibilities."

In August, just before the massive civil rights march on Washington, D.C., Newman joined Brando and Franciosa on a trip to Gadsden, Alabama, where hundreds of CORE activists had been arrested for picketing in favor of fair hiring practices at a local tire factory. The four flew into Birmingham, where Governor George Wallace watched their arrival without greeting them, then took a bus to Gadsden, meeting with local workers, many out-of-state activists, and, perhaps more to the point, the press. Brando took the lead as their spokesman, but Newman wasn't shy about his presence and was especially rankled when he and his companions on the trip were branded as "rabble-rousers" and "meddlers." He told reporters that he and the other actors had often gladly served the State Department as goodwill ambassadors abroad, adding, "We would like to hope perhaps that we can be considered the same kind of ambassadors in the South." What was more, he added, "It's all right when we come down South to raise money for a hospital. And it's perfectly all right when we are asked to donate our services for other humanitarian causes. They don't call us rabble-rousers then." That may have been true, but the actors failed to get a meeting with Mayor Leslie Gilliland or any other city officials; nor were they able to talk with representatives of the Goodyear Rubber Company, whose facility was the focus of the turmoil.

A few days later Newman and Brando attended a rally at the Apollo

Too small for football
at Shaker Heights
High School, 1942.
(Author's Collection)

Skinny arms Newman
(top, left of center) celebrating V-Day belowdecks
on the USS *Hollandia*.
(U.S. Naval Institute Press)

Hot date at Kenyon.
*(Greenslade Special Collections
and Archives, Kenyon College)*

As the Stage Manager in *Our Town* at the Wood-stock Opera House, 1949. *(Courtesy of Kurt Wanieck)*

Not as sexy as Ralph Meeker: in the original cast of *Picnic*. *(Photofest)*

One life to give for his country: as Nathan Hale in *You Are There*, 1953. *(Photofest)*

The man in the cocktail dress: *The Silver Chalice*. *(Special Collections, Cleveland State University Library)*

Rehearsing for the musical *Our Town* with Nelson Riddle and Eva Marie Saint. *(Courtesy of the Nelson Riddle Estate)*

Fasten your seat belts: Paul, Jackie, and Scott, then nearly five, in a publicity stunt for *The Desperate Hours*, August 1955. *(New York Daily News)*

Who's the boss: sparring with Tony Zale in preparation for *Somebody Up There Likes Me*. *(Greenslade Special Collections and Archives, Kenyon College)*

Joanne contemplates one of the faces of Eve, 1957. *(Photofest)*

Taking in the news with Joanne on the Louisiana set of *The Long Hot Summer*. *(Photofest)*

Theresa Newman *(front left)* and Art Newman Jr. *(to her left)* at the Cleveland premiere of *The Long Hot Summer,* 1958.
(Special Collections, Cleveland State University Library)

Honeymooners. *(Photofest)*

Otto Preminger directs lunch for, from left, Newman, Eva Marie Saint, Lee J. Cobb, Betty Walker, and Alexandra Stanley, in 1960's *Exodus. (Author's Collection)*

Learning the angles: Willie Mosconi preps the star of *The Hustler. (Photofest)*

A second bite of "The Battler": playing Ad Francis for the second time in *Hemingway's Adventures of a Young Man*, 1962. *(Author's Collection)*

Cool Hand Luke author Donn Pearce on the set with the Luke he didn't think cut the mustard (note the bottle opener around Newman's neck). *(Author's Collection)*

Campaigning in Indianapolis for Eugene McCarthy, 1968. *(Photofest)*

Preparing Nell for a shot in *Rachel, Rachel* in the summer of 1967.
(Author's Collection)

Accepting the New York Film Critics Circle awards for directing and acting in *Rachel, Rachel*.
(Author's Collection)

How I learned to drive: in 1969's *Winning* with Robert Wagner and beauty pageant queen Eileen Wesson.
(Author's Collection)

Theater in Harlem to raise funds for the march on Washington, and then they flew to D.C., where a modest Hollywood contingent was lost in a sea of more than a quarter of a million souls. He didn't think they'd accomplished very much in Gadsden—"We were wasting our time," he sighed (not to mention alienating southern theater owners, some of whom boycotted his films for a time). But of the march on Washington he rightly felt otherwise. "I'm proud I was there. There's never been anything like it."

JUST AS he was becoming more active politically, he had taken a proprietary interest in the Actors Studio, to which he would occasionally return for long, restorative spells of sitting, watching, and talking. By 1962, in the view of many of the people most intimately associated with it, the Studio had lost some of its impetus and centrality as a font of new theatrical talent. It was still a temple of acting, in a sense—where else could you see a star of Newman's stature workshop a scene from *The Taming of the Shrew* and then listen in as the likes of Lee Strasberg told him what was right (or more often wrong) about his performance? But it had lost the semireligious aura it had once had, and Newman wasn't alone in thinking that it had become more of a vocational institution than a spiritual one.

An idea for rejuvenating the Studio (and incidentally securing its always-shaky finances for the long term) was promoted by Strasberg and Cheryl Crawford. They thought that the Actors Studio could form its own theatrical company, presenting new plays and revisiting established works, bringing back a touch of the old Group Theater days and providing a basis for American stage acting akin to that provided English actors by such troupes as the Royal Shakespeare Company and the National Theatre. The plan that they and others devised was to create a Production Unit within the Studio that, separate from the workshop sessions, would develop plays and present them on or off Broadway. Various committees were formed (Newman served on several), and the sort of heated debate typical of the more radical past of many of the members ensued. There was fallout—among others, Elia Kazan decided to separate himself from the Studio altogether, declaring, "I wouldn't sit on a committee with Jesus Christ, never mind Stanislavsky, and you can quote me!"

In April 1962 the plan to present productions was announced in the press; the following March the Actors Studio Theater presented its premiere work, Eugene O'Neill's *Strange Interlude*, starring Geraldine Page and Ben Gazzara. And soon after that plans for a new play, the Studio's fourth production, were announced: Paul Newman and Joanne Woodward in *Baby Want a Kiss*, an original work by their old friend James Costigan.

"Lee was so happy that Paul, the big star, wanted to do it," remembered Geraldine Page. "Lee said, 'Paul has a play he wants to do; if we do it, he'll bring in some money.' " But others in the Studio had suspicions about the quality of the material. Costigan had written a one-act comedy about a pair of Hollywood stars (the Newmans) visiting with a reclusive writer friend (Costigan himself) in his remote country home, where his only companions were a parakeet and a sheepdog; over the course of a drunken evening, the three would reveal their darkest fantasies and desires. It was a quirky piece, with elements of absurdism and caustic commentary about the nature of celebrity and glamour. But it was short, so a curtain-raiser would be required; Costigan's *The Census Taker*, a two-hander, also to be played by the Newmans, was selected.

The Newmans agreed to premiere the show in the spring of 1964 and stay with it for four months, earning only Equity minimum— $117.50 a week each—for their work (big-name performers in other Actors Studio Theater productions commanded as much as $1,000 a week). And Newman did a tremendous job of publicizing the show, explaining the importance of the Actors Studio in his own professional development and of the liberating sensation of appearing on Broadway for a strictly limited engagement. "You get the luxury of developing a part for three months," he explained. "After four months it becomes a bore. You're working for real estate men and the play's backers. You're not satisfying the needs of an actor."

He was, according to Frank Corsaro, who directed the play, an exemplary collaborator. "Paul bent over backward," he said, "not to tread on toes, not to exert power, which he could easily have done." In the year between announcing the production and the first rehearsals, Costigan expanded *Baby Want a Kiss* into a full play, and the curtain-raiser was dropped. But there were still difficulties with the material, which was fantastical and strange and hard to describe. "It's an Irish fairy tale," Newman told a reporter while taking a break from rehearsals, "a theoretical comedy about the contradiction and ambivalence of friendship, of any relationship. It's a difficult script, full of non sequiturs." Joanne agreed: "We went home from the first readings exhausted. Right after dinner we'd disappear into the steam room and *memorize.*" She described the characters they would be playing as "an aging juvenile" and "a fading ingénue," adding with a chuckle, "Ourselves, no doubt."

After a few delays the play opened on the night of April 19, 1964—and it landed on the stage of the Little Theater like a soggy sponge. "What is it?" began Howard Taubman's review in the *New York Times*, praising the Newmans' performances before answering his own question with "a self-conscious, pretentious exercise in futility." Walter Kerr, writing in the *New York Herald-Tribune*, pronounced, "The play cannot find a firm, formal, satirical world in which it can make itself comfortable." *Time* declared that it was "better at cracking wise than being wise." And *The Saturday Review* sniffed that it was "closer to being a parody of *Who's Afraid of Virginia Woolf?* than it is to being its successor." (Even its most ardent partisans had to admit the truth: as Strasberg conceded, "A fantasy element in the play . . . didn't come across in the production," and Corsaro agreed, saying, "It exemplified a fallacious side of the Studio.")

Despite the poor notices, the play was a tremendous hit, selling out virtually every performance in an eighteen-week run and earning a $150,000 profit on the initial $25,000 investment. That was a real shot in the arm, considering how poorly other Actors Studio Theater productions fared: *Strange Interlude* had gotten wonderful reviews, for instance, but was believed to have lost some $60,000; likewise James Baldwin's original play *Blues for Mister Charlie*, which opened just after *Baby* and was well received by the critics, also closed at a financial loss. Later that year the Studio made a heroic effort to reverse its fortunes by sending its highly regarded production of Chekhov's *Three Sisters* to London (a trip in part subsidized by Newman); but there were many changes in the cast, and the show was savaged by the English critics and flopped commercially. And with that debacle the dream of the Actors Studio Theater finally died.

NEWMAN WAS luckier in politics. While still onstage with *Baby*, he took an active role in the 1964 Democratic National Convention in Atlantic City. Just prior to the main event, he cohosted a barbecue fund-raiser in honor of Lynda Bird Johnson, the president's daughter, at the Henry Ford estate in Water Mill, Long Island, and had a hair-raising adventure trying to get back to Manhattan for the evening's performance: the seaplane that was supposed to get him back to the city never showed up, and he wound up having to hire a small plane at the Easthampton air field to take him to the Marine Terminal near LaGuardia. During the convention he served as master of ceremonies at a fifty-sixth birthday party for the president. He created a small personal fund, the No Sutch Foundation, and used it to donate to various political causes, chiefly civil rights groups but also to the Center for the Study of Democratic Institutions, a liberal think tank based in Santa Barbara where he occasionally attended seminars, panel discussions, and lectures with a determination that he had rarely demonstrated back at Kenyon College. "I feel like an ass going up to these seminars," he admitted, "but I tell you, it is so refreshing to focus my mind on something."

Maybe so, but a lot of his free time was given over to less grave pursuits. When he was in New York, he enjoyed getting around town on a motor scooter—"The only way to get through midtown traffic," he swore. In Los Angeles and Connecticut he spent a couple of years and a not-inconsequential sum of money souping up Volkswagen Beetles with Porsche engines and racing suspensions. "This is such a discreet car," he explained, demonstrating one to a reporter. "You don't have people pulling alongside and waving at you." Some of his other souped-up sleds weren't so understated: "I also owned one Beetle that had a 351 Ford V8," he said. "It was really hairy. Great in a straight line, but, boy, it never did the same thing twice." He relished the reaction he got out of people when they did recognize him in what looked like a beater car and then he tore away from them at startling speed. He also acquired a small collection of motorcycles and would relax after a long day on the movie set by tearing out of his rented Hollywood homes. "Having that old brute bike on the front porch and driving it to the beach after dinner is marvelous," he said. "Within minutes you're looser."

AND HE wasn't fidgety only in his life; in his work he seemed restless too.

Before going onstage with *Baby*, he filmed an ill-conceived remake of *Rashomon* written by Michael Kanin and directed by Martin Ritt. It was set in the Old West, and Newman played the Toshiro Mifune role, which had been transformed into a bandit named Carrasco whose encounter with a prosperous Anglo couple in the desert begins as a robbery and then goes on to rape, perhaps, and murder, perhaps—depending, as in the original, on which version of the events you trust.

They couldn't find a name for it at first. The studio had quite naturally balked at *The Rape*, and when they shot it near Tucson and back in Hollywood, they were calling it *Judgment in the Sun*. Eventually it was called *The Outrage*, which was overselling its impact some. Despite the reteaming of the star, director, and even cinematographer of *Hud*, despite the casting of Laurence Harvey and Claire Bloom as the other players in the inscrutable triangle of theft, sex, and death, the film was tepid and altogether unconvincing.

Newman was as weak as he'd been in a drama in years, sneering and snorting and casting droopy-eyed gazes and leers from underneath a mop of straight brown hair and a dark line of goatee. The film was shot in black and white, which was good, because Newman wasn't able to do anything about the color of his eyes. "I tried brown contacts," he explained, "but my eyes are very sensitive. We were doing a screen test . . . I stood in front of the camera and all you had was this weeping Mexican." He was drawn to the role, he said, "because I had never played a primitive" (although, to be honest, Rocky Graziano was awfully close). And he traveled to find the skin of the part. "A friend and I went down to Mexico for two weeks. We got the accent from a soup salesman and the voice quality from a bellhop, over *mucho cerveza.*" But it all just seemed like a bad Anthony Quinn impression. And the reimagining of *Rashomon* convinced nobody.

He traveled again, both literally and within his craft, to make *Lady L*, which Peter Ustinov had written and was directing from Romain Gary's novel, about a woman who rises from a Paris brothel to become the dame of a fine English estate by riding a wave of sex and skullduggery propelled by anarchists, policemen, a pianist, and a titled eccentric. It shot in London, Paris, and Nice in the fall and winter of 1964–65, and Joanne and her daughters came along, joined, for a period, by Newman's older children.

As when they made *Paris Blues*, they rented a house in Montmartre. And as then, Joanne was pregnant. But this time she wasn't Newman's leading lady; Sophia Loren was, and, Gore Vidal recalled, "Joanne always suspected the worst." Vidal and she would try to get Newman to describe his unimaginably glamorous and sexy costar, and he would shrug and say things like "Well, she was late for work this morning." His evasiveness was almost like a tease.

One night the Newmans and Loren went out together to a fine restaurant, and the difference between the international sexpot and the serious actors with the houseful of kids in Connecticut was starkly evident. As Newman remembered, "She threw her sable across her shoulders and swept right through like the Queen of Romania, while Joanne and I were trying to enter the restaurant through the woodwork. Crabwise, you know? Skulking behind the headwaiter. I'll never forget that! I mean, [she] was not in the least uncomfortable about the attention she drew, while Joanne and I were." Ustinov, no doubt acutely aware of distinctions such as these, felt that Joanne had nothing to fear. In admiration of the Newmans' marriage, he declared, "They are one of the very few couples who are privileged to be in love, and because they love and quarrel occasionally, they can afford to be quite brash about each other. They have shut the window against the drafts of difference."

So much for *that* drama. On the set Newman was trying his hand at a new sort of role, an easily impassioned French bomb-thrower who treated his woman with macho entitlement and devoted his heart to his politics, someone pitched between Ari from *Exodus* and the modern painter from *What a Way to Go!* He fought the studio for the right to wear a mustache for the role—"I couldn't find one photograph of an anarchist without a mustache," he explained—and so he considered it a stretch of his acting chops. But the script provided him with hardly anything interesting to do, and he saw in the film's failure not the flaws in the script or the froufy treatment but his own inability to extend his range. "That film made me aware that I am stuck in an American skin," he said. "I doubt that I'll ever play a foreigner again." (Good to his word, he never would.)

His NEXT role would mine a distinctly American vein indeed: Lew Archer, the hero of Ross Macdonald's wonderful series of detective novels that had sustained the hard-boiled private eye tradition after the careers of Dashiell Hammett and Raymond Chandler. *The Moving Target*, written in 1949, was the debut Archer novel and would be the first one anyone filmed; screenwriter William Goldman had updated it—but only slightly—with the proper lacings of sauce and sizzle. Frank Sinatra had turned it down, which didn't mean much; the role was perfect for Newman. But for one thing: the picture would be made at Warner Bros., the studio he had left so angrily six years earlier. This time, though, he would be paid even more than the princely half-million dollars he once paid Jack Warner to release him from his contract; he could afford to let bygones be bygones. "A feud should live a full and colorful life," he told a reporter, "and then it should die a natural death and be forgotten."

Before going to California for the shoot, Newman stopped back east long enough to celebrate his fortieth birthday with friends at a party thrown by Gore Vidal. (Barbra Streisand was in attendance, and it was, Vidal remembered, the first time she'd ever tried caviar.) In April, Joanne delivered another girl, Claire Olivia, who would always be known as Clea. And then the family made their way to another rented Hollywood home.

At the studio, during rehearsals for the film, Newman was visited by his old nemesis, Jack Warner, and he couldn't resist giving him the needle. "I said, 'How are ya?' " he recalled.

Reaching into his coat pocket, he said, "You smoke cigars?" I said, "No, I only smoke people, Jack. You know that." He laughed, and the photographers came around and there were pictures of Jack and me smiling together. A few Christmases ago, I sent out greeting cards to the people who know about me and Warner. On the front they said, "Peace on Earth." You turn the page and find that smiling picture of me and Jack together again over the heart-warming line "Good Will Toward Men." . . . I sent one to Warner, too. He thought it was marvelous. What an extraordinary man. I've never known a greater vulgarian. Not even Khrushchev. He calls my wife "Joan."

The name of Lew Archer was changed in part at Newman's suggestion (he had done some rewriting of Goldman's work on a boozy flight from England to New York), and the film was eventually retitled after the new name, *Harper*; the H was meant to echo the titles of *The Hustler* and *Hud*. And whether the luck came from the new name or from his stumbling onto a good script, he was in luck; it was his best picture and most natural performance in years.

Compared to the struggles he had forced himself through for other roles, preparation for this one was a breeze: "I just got drunk." He stole a bit of physical business, he said, from Robert F. Kennedy, who had a habit of standing beside people and looking away from them with his head tilted when listening to them. It was a weird sort of engaged nonengagement, and it fit the character beautifully. The script was filled with California types, some depraved (particularly the characters played by Strother Martin, Lauren Bacall, and Shelley Winters) and some all-American (those portrayed by Robert Wagner, Arthur Hiller, and Pamela Tiffin). It was a completely breezy entertainment with a slick patina of modern sophistication, evoking comparisons with the films of Humphrey Bogart, the cinema's exemplary roguish private eye. A lot of director Jack Smight's work was perfunctory, but there was an undeniable cool to the film, and the plot was just lurid and twisty enough to create chatter.

The reviews were admiring—to a point. It was fun, most critics conceded, but it was sloppy. "Smight is a bungler from start to finish," carped Pauline Kael in *The New Yorker*, adding that the film featured Newman's worst performance since *The Silver Chalice*. In the *New York Times*, Bosley Crowther was kinder to both men, comparing Smight's work to Howard Hawks's and suggesting that Newman made too much of a smoothie of his private eye.* But it was a hit, Newman's first since *Hud*, and it marked his return, after a year's absence, to the top ten in the annual exhibitors' poll of top box office stars.

He jumped from one classic Hollywood genre to another, agreeing in the fall of 1965 to star in Alfred Hitchcock's latest film, *Torn Curtain*, opposite, of all people, Julie Andrews. In a script by Canadian novelist Brian Moore, Newman would play an American physicist who pretends to defect to East Germany so as to pry information from Communist scientists and help the United States build a missile system. Andrews was cast as his assistant and fiancée, who at first knew nothing of his plot but would become enmeshed in it, imperiling both of their lives.

Hitchcock was, at age sixty-six, nearing the end of his productive years. He had just made the commercial flop *Marnie*, which would go years before enjoying a revival in the estimation of critics, and he was becoming less patient with the process of making movies. Conceiving them, writing them, planning them: that was his game. As Andrews later recalled, "The first day of production, he announced that for him the fun was over—the creative part was finished with the script and storyboard preparation—and now, he said, the rest was a bore. You can imagine how that made us feel."

But Newman's trepidations about the film predated that first day. He had visited Hitchcock's offices to discuss the project before agreeing to make it, and he found that the director didn't have a finished script to share with him. "I know you should have script approval and

---

* No less an arbiter of taste than Yogi Berra offered a review of *Harper* to a reporter for the *New York Times* who undertook to divine the great malapropist's opinions on various current releases. "I saw it in Cincinnati," Berra declared, intending praise.

everything else," Newman remembered being told, "but I don't want to show you the script we've got now because it's not very good."

With filming imminent, Newman had to forgo his usual rehearsal period because he took a terrible spill on one of his motorcycles, skidding out on Sunset Boulevard and suffering burns on his legs and, more severely, on his left hand, where skin grafts were required on four fingers. "At first the doctors told me that I would never have the full use of my left hand again," he remembered. "They suggested that I should practice by gripping a tennis ball but instead I took a wet towel and wrung it all day. In the mornings my hand would have frozen and the towel would be as thick as a man's arm, but by the evening I would get it squeezed so dry that my fist was nearly locked tight."* He'd been wearing a helmet, for which he was grateful, and he got rid of all his motorcycles the next day.

But he hadn't given the script the attention he felt it needed. When he finally did show up for filming, he was unhappy. "I never felt comfortable with the script," he said. He drafted a memo for Hitchcock with questions about the character and the logic of the action, and he delivered it on a day when the director was receiving the magazine journalist and future filmmaker Peter Bogdanovich. Hitchcock, Bogdanovich recalled, was

> in a mood of quiet outrage. What was the matter, I asked. "Paul Newman sent me a memo," he said acidly, as if it might as well have been a letter bomb. A memo about what? "The script!" He was indignant. The four-page missive had evidently dealt with Newman's questions, misgivings, and complaints about various aspects of the screenplay and how these would affect his character. "His character!" Hitch muttered under his breath. "I thought to myself, 'What does it matter about your character? It's just going to be Paul Newman anyway.'"

---

* His injuries created a photographic problem on *Torn Curtain:* "If you look at the early scenes," he revealed, "I am always carrying a coat over my arm. That's because the stitches were still visible."

They went ahead with what they had, and Hitchcock managed a couple of thrilling scenes, particularly the one in which Newman and a woman have to kill an East German spy silently so as not to draw the attention of a taxi driver who's standing just outside the house. But Hitchcock was never happy with his stars, recalled Brian Moore. "He just lost his heart during the shooting," he said. "He discovered that they didn't fit the Hitchcock mold or the Hitchcock method. He just couldn't get a chemistry going with them, and he got very depressed and just went through the motions."

On the actual set, Newman recalled, Hitchcock was always a gentleman. "I think he treats actors with decency and respect," he said at the time, and he remembered later, "Hitchcock was very good to me." At the same time, Hitchcock was a master of publicity who knew that he could capture the imagination of the public by hinting that there had been friction on the set. "I always say," he told the *New York Times* upon the film's release, "that the most difficult things to photograph are dogs, babies, motorboats, Charles Laughton (God rest his soul) and Method actors."

His efforts to draw attention didn't change a thing. The picture was judged more or less a flop, both artistically and commercially—a real disappointment considering the great names involved. "There is a distracted air about much of the film," wrote Richard Schickel in *Life*, "as if the master were not really paying attention to what he was doing." And Bosley Crowther in the *New York Times* labeled it flatly "a pathetically undistinguished spy picture."

It wasn't long before Newman put the experience behind him by diving into yet another genre film, his third in a year. This one was a western that Martin Ritt and Irving Ravetch were producing out of a 1961 novel called *Hombre* by a writer named Elmore Leonard. Newman had an intriguing role that asked him at once to create an exotic persona and to inhabit it in a familiar American skin. John Russell is a white man who was raised in part by Apaches and in part by a rich Anglo who has died and left him a legacy. Cashing in his inheritance, Russell boards a stagecoach with a motley band of travelers who are set upon by thieves and left to fend for themselves in the desert. Russell, raised partly in the wild, is the only one among them with any chance to survive the ordeal, so even though the group can't abide him, they're forced to play by his rules.

Newman liked to say that he found the key to the character when he drove past a general store near an Indian reservation in Arizona and saw a man standing stock-still in the shade on its porch; a few hours later, when he drove back to his hotel, he saw the same man standing in the exact same spot in the exact same position. That stillness would, in his mind, become the patient, calculating, diffident, dangerous essence of John Russell.

Once again James Wong Howe was shooting the picture for Ritt, and a great cast was rounded up: Fredric March as a corrupt Indian agent, Barbara Rush as his wife, Richard Boone as the leader of the bad guys, Diane Cilento as the savvy woman of the West whose life has been upended by Russell's inheritance, and Martin Balsam as the Mexican stagecoach driver who maintains a friendship with Russell even when the latter is living among the Apaches.

But there were delays. Some could have been foreseen, such as the difficulty of working with the herd of horses that Russell, wearing the long dark bangs of an Apache, manages to corral from the wild in the opening sequence. Then Newman got the flu, missing work for virtually the only time in his life. And then unseasonable rainstorms struck the Tucson set for days.

Newman spent part of the time playing tennis. He drank. And he engaged in bawdy humor with Balsam. "We had to wait hours for the wind to let up one day," he remembered. "To kill the time, we decided to classify fucking. We got all the psychological classifications. There was sport fucking. There was mercy fucking, which would be reserved for spinsters and librarians. There was the hate fuck, the prestige fuck, and the medicinal fuck, which is 'Feel better now, sweetie?' It just goes to show you what happens when you're stuck on location on the top of a mountain. Your mind wanders slightly."

They were making a good picture, as it happened, a real grown-up story with beautiful photography, an engaging plot, and some fine performances. In ways it was a straightforward genre western, but Newman's eerie stoniness in the center gave it an air of modernity and menace. John Russell was a character who would have been on the periphery of other films—*Stagecoach*, say, which surely inspired some aspects of Leonard's novel. But placed at the center here, and embodied with thoroughly convincing coldness and steel by Newman, he quietly makes the case that the history of the Old West has been miscalculated—at least on-screen. In his political life, Newman could sometimes misstep by insisting too hard on his point of view; here, playing a man who in his very being was an argument for more equitable treatment of Native Americans, he was persuasively eloquent in his silence, sternness, and courage.

Hombre succeeded modestly at the box office, but it was well regarded. Not that Newman necessarily took such things to heart. In fact, he had come to feel a sense of diminishing returns from his film work. He was as successful as he'd ever been, but he was bored.

A combination of events within and beyond his grasp would, however, change that—and quickly.

Fourteen

"I SEEM TO PLAY THE CHILD OF OUR TIME," HE TOLD A REPORTER, and it was a canny insight.

Since the dawn of the 1960s, from *The Hustler* on, he had steadily built a screen persona that had a distinct American quality like, say, Fonda's or Gable's but that also included nuances that hadn't often been seen in movie heroes before Brando and Dean: vulnerability, weakness, a hedonistic streak, and a full dose of antiauthoritarian cockiness and cynicism—traits an older generation of stars and audiences would have ascribed to youth.

The twist was that Newman played not kids but grown-ups—more specifically, grown-ups who hadn't yet outgrown juvenile impulses, urges, and flaws and might never do so. As he portrayed them, Fast Eddie Felson, Chance Wayne, Hud Bannon, and Lew Harper (and in the coming years, Cool Hand Luke Jackson and Butch Cassidy) were grown-up rebels who felt kindred to a young audience getting ready to shake off traditional American paternalism forever. Despite each being a singular personality, they combined to form an echt 1960s type that Newman epitomized; indeed, part of what made those characters so emblematic of their era was the easy swagger and ridiculous charm with which he filled them. He was becoming the most popular actor in movies because he and his roles seemed so au courant and apt.

What was especially interesting in his assessment, though, was the use of the word *child* to describe his roles and, by extension, at least a little bit, himself. Somehow he had frozen time around him or, rather, in him. Movie stars didn't age like other people, but Newman didn't age like other movie stars. In his early forties he could seem half that old.

For one thing, he was in ridiculously good shape. He ran and rode a bike and saunaed and swam virtually every day, and he ate sparingly and smartly: steaks and soup and fruit and burgers and salads and buckets of popcorn. He had a flat stomach, a small waist, no hips, muscled arms—all on top of legs so thin that even he had to laugh at them. ("Old skinny legs," his kids would call him.) He wasn't a fanatic for fitness: he smoked, and he was constantly trying to quit by chewing gum or munching on celery stalks and carrots. And he drank: beer after beer after beer—a case or more a day, people said, often followed by the hard stuff, scotch mainly. Friends and colleagues and journalists and oglers would talk about him drinking beers on the set, in his office, at parties, during interviews, while watching TV, getting ready for dinner, relaxing after dinner; Mort Sahl recalled him filling a brandy snifter with ice and scotch and sipping it as he sat in a steam room; Newman himself joked about drinking even in bed. But he metabolized it or burned it up almost entirely. There wasn't a pint of fat on him, it seemed. He was famous for his lean, bright, spry, and confident face (dunked in ice water each morning, they said, just as he did at the beginning of *Harper*) and for those blue eyes, which maintained their uncanny color, it was whispered, with the help of imported French eye drops. And he still had a full head of curly hair. (He had a theory about this: he'd favored a brush cut as a boy, he said, but no one else in the family did. "My father, my uncle, and my brother became bald. I would have, too, except that I kept the short Germanic haircut and, from the time I was eleven to my mid-twenties, I brushed my hair every day with a stiff brush.") He had all the appearances of youthful perfection, but also the internal wisdom and self-awareness of mature age and, more, canniness and irony—in all, a devastating combination. Josh Logan was no doubt right when he declared that the soft-featured Botticelli angel of 1954 carried no sexual threat; the Paul Newman of 1967, on the other hand, not only carried it but *defined* it.

And perhaps because he stayed so attractive, he seemed youthful even as the years rolled by underneath him. "He got to be twenty-nine years old," said Joanne, "and then he stayed twenty-nine years

old year after year after year, while I got older and older and older."
That was something of a joke, but it was one of those jokes that revealed a truth and, perhaps, a painful one, if not for her then certainly
for Newman's son. Scott was nearing his seventeenth birthday, and
his relationship with his parents and stepmother was becoming
strained; he had no particular aptitude for school, and he was starting
to run with a dodgy crowd—when, in fact, he was in a crowd at all. At
the same time, his father was considered a hot number not only by
women of his own age but by girls of his son's age. Every boy grows
up in his father's shadow but can look to the passage of time as an inevitable leveler of the field, a promise of liberation; for Scott, Newman's seemingly perpetual youth must have seemed instead a
challenge and a taunt.

Joanne too could see her husband's boyishness as a threat. She herself would not turn forty until 1970, but she had already reached the
age when Hollywood actresses can't get the parts that producers give
to pretty girls. She had given birth to three daughters and was recovering her figure through the pursuit of ballet as a form of exercise. And
she—along with the rest of the family, true, but she most of all—had
to watch in silence as women walked up to her husband in public
places or at parties and literally threw themselves at him or went
knock-kneed (again, literally) at the very sight of him. She had a sense
of humor about the situation—"He's forty-four, has six children, and
snores; how can he be a teenage sex symbol?"—and the ability to make
him snap to attention when she demanded it. But it was an absurd burden to place on top of the burden of being married to a famous man.
Every wife of a celebrity must endure intrusions, of course, but being
married to a sex symbol was its own brand of punishment.

Professionally, Newman's agelessness made him a unique item in
Hollywood. He had all-American qualities, but he played against them
as if he hadn't yet grown into them, and that coltishness, combined
with an appearance that resembled the ideal of Greek and Roman
artists, meant that he could convincingly play characters who were significantly younger than his actual years. And it meant that audiences—
male and female, young and old—would accept him in those roles and

that he could become iconic in them in a fashion that no amount of studio publicity could manufacture. He had achieved a balance of Old Hollywood, with its polish and glamour and confidence and agreeable slickness, and New, with its roguishness, daring, and defiance. And if he had just the right project in front of him, he could make films that stood among the best of both epochs.

HE BEGAN making one in the fall of 1966, when he spent some time in West Virginia absorbing the atmosphere of small-town Appalachia and studying the ways in which the men in such places walked, spoke, and held their bodies. He had been cast in a new film being made by Jack Lemmon's Jalem Productions from a novel by Donn Pearce, a merchant seaman who became a counterfeiter and then a safecracker before writing about his experiences on a chain gang in a book called *Cool Hand Luke*. The film would mark the American theatrical debut of director Stuart Rosenberg, who'd been working in television for more than a decade and had, curiously, made a film in Berlin in 1961 about religious persecution. Rosenberg had actually discovered Pearce's book and brought it to Jalem, which hired Pearce to do the first pass at adapting it for the screen. But not only had Pearce never written a film, he had no idea what a script even looked like. And when his draft came in, another writer, Frank R. Pierson, was called in to recraft it.

There had been some thought of Lemmon himself playing the title character, Lucas Jackson, an incorrigible southern bad boy who gets arrested for a dumb crime (drunkenly wrenching off the heads of parking meters) and winds up in a prison work camp, where his increasing defiance of authority, logic, and even self-preservation makes him a target for sadistic jailers and a legend among his prison mates. For a while there was thought of offering it to Telly Savalas, who was stuck in England making *The Dirty Dozen*. But Newman heard about the project and asked in, even before the script was settled. "It's one of the few roles I committed myself to on the basis of the original book, without seeing a script," he recalled. "It would have worked no matter how many mistakes were made." It had elements that were irresistible

to him and would fit him perfectly: boozy prankishness, gutsy noncon-
formity, physical endurance and prowess, bawdy humor, and a human-
istic message that indicted the penal system (and by extension modern
society) for squashing anything that resembled free thought.

He went off to West Virginia to do his research, talking to various
locals, recording their accents, and quizzing them about their attitudes. He stayed in Huntington, causing ruckuses in nearby bakeries,
country clubs, and taverns when he stepped in for a bite or a drink; at
a Catholic high school he was introduced to a nun, who shook his
hand and said, "Nice to meet you, Mr. Newman. What do you do for
a living?"

While he developed his character, production ramped up in Stock-
ton, California, which would stand in for an unnamed southern state
in the film. The producers shipped tons of Spanish moss to the location and built a prison camp so realistic that a county building inspec-
tor passing by on his rounds mistook it for migrant worker housing
and ordered it condemned for code violations. The cast who would
inhabit that temporary prison with Newman was a motley crew of he-
men: George Kennedy, Harry Dean Stanton, Dennis Hopper, Wayne
Rogers, Ralph Waite, Anthony Zerbe, and Donn Pearce himself. Lord-
ing over them were Strother Martin, as the warden, and Morgan Woodward, who stood out from the pack of guards because of his reflecting
sunglasses and stony silence. There was a key female role—Luke's
mother, who comes to visit the prison one bittersweet day—and when
Bette Davis passed on it, it went to Jo Van Fleet.* Conrad Hall, who had
shot *Harper,* was the cinematographer. And there was a new face among
the lower-level production executives on the picture: Arthur S. Newman Jr.

Since his father's death more than a decade before, Art Jr. had
bounced around in a number of sales and management jobs in the automobile business, including stints with General Motors and various

---

* Van Fleet had played the negligent mother in Elia Kazan's *East of Eden;* Richard
Davalos, who beat Newman out for the role of one of her sons in that film, would also
appear as a prisoner in *Luke.*

auto parts manufacturers and dealers. He had married, and that wasn't going well, and he was sufficiently unsettled that he was able to move to California when his kid brother formed a film company and needed help in the number-crunching and quality-control sides of the business. Newman didn't have any stake in the production of *Cool Hand Luke*, but it would be an excellent opportunity for Art to learn the ins and outs of the movie biz at the very rarefied level on which Newman operated. Art would get credit as unit manager, one of those guys who stands around a film set making sure things got done on time and within the budget: a good job.

People would often be startled by the very sight of Art, who shared his brother's coloring—even the eyes—and a great many other details of his appearance. He was, said a writer in *The Saturday Evening Post*, "a larger and more heavily built version [of Newman] . . . a man whose features were roughly the same but had been assembled slightly differently." He distinguished himself—and hid the baldness that his brother had evaded—by wearing hats; at the time he was fond of old-fashioned newsboy caps, including a garish black-and-white-checked number. Newman used to kid Art mercilessly about those hats, but he was genuinely glad to have him around, if for no other reason than that Art was perhaps the only person whom Newman would fully trust when it came to matters of money. So just like that, another generation of Newman brothers was in business.

MONEY WAS much on Newman's mind. He once tallied up how many people he was supporting—wife, ex-wife, kids, mother, employees—and the number was in the dozens: staggering. He was nearing the absolute ceiling for Hollywood salaries, and yet he couldn't seem to parlay his success into real wealth. "I've never been able to make the kind of investments that people think I have," he told a reporter. "I have money, but it seems to go out quicker than it comes in." He lived well, yes, and he had money for charities—as much as $100,000 annually through his No Sutch Foundation and in 1967 $50,000 to Yale to help institute a permanent repertory theater there. But personal wealth, which he had long disdained as a goal in life, was increasingly important to him. In March 1966 he started to seek new ways to secure his finances, buying the 3,950-acre Indian Creek Ranch near San Luis Obispo as an investment. He began to restructure his film concerns. *Hombre* would be the last film he made with Martin Ritt either as a director or in some production capacity; he would instead spend 1967 forming a company with his own agent, John Foreman, who would leave the representation business to form the Newman-Foreman Company, to produce films both starring Newman and not.

He also became a partner in a West Hollywood nightclub called the Factory, which wasn't so odd a thing as it sounded. The mid-1960s were a transitional time in Hollywood nightlife. Old-style supper clubs like Ciro's and Slapsie Maxie's and Mocambo had closed or been converted to youth-oriented rock clubs or been replaced by a chic new style of night spot modeled on such French and English discothèques as Regine's or the Ad Lib. The only venue in Southern California that combined the new nightclub style with the classic veneer of high show-biz was the Daisy, a private club in Beverly Hills where you could see Frank Sinatra frugging with Mia Farrow or Cary Grant enjoying a night out with Dyan Cannon. Newman was a member at the Daisy, and he liked to shoot pool there, even though it carried risks: there was only one table, which meant that you always had a crowd watching. He loved to tell the story of the night he played a couple of games of eight ball on that table and was approached by a guy who'd been looking on and who declared, "Mr. Newman, I just want to tell you that I saw *The Hustler* three times and it was one helluva movie. I watched you play pool tonight, and it was one of the biggest disappointments of my life."

The Factory was pointedly meant to serve as an alternative to the Daisy. For one thing it had celebrity owners: in addition to the clothier Jerome K. Ohrbach and the restaurateur Ron Buck, its coterie of investor/directors included Newman, Sammy Davis Jr., Peter Lawford, Anthony Newley, Pierre Salinger, and the young director Richard Donner. Built in an abandoned bombsight factory off Santa Monica Boulevard, it had *four* pool tables in its third-floor bar (the one with red felt was reserved for the ladies), plus pinball machines. The second-floor discothèque featured live bands (including such immortal acts as Pacific

Ocean, which was fronted by a young singer from East L.A. named Edward James Olmos)—another leg up on the Daisy, which played only prerecorded music. And the Factory served food in a dining room and the bars; the Daisy didn't.*

In its opening months, even with membership capped at one thousand and costing $1,000 a year, it was a sensation. A galaxy of stars made their way past the bouncer, into a padded freight elevator, and then into dark, vast spaces decorated with Tiffany lamps, thrift-shop furniture, a leather-upholstered bar, windows made of stained glass and chicken wire, and other touches of hippie chic. On a given night, gushed *Time*, you might see "Roz Russell, Sonny and Cher, dress designer Jimmy Galanos, financier Bart Lytton, and fullback-turned-actor James Brown" among the crowd. Lawford purred with satisfaction at the place: "We needed a place to hang our hats. The Factory has turned out to be a big hat stand with lots of hats . . . melding the dinner jackets and the blue jeans. You dig? No one is embarrassed; no one cares."

The Factory was such a hit that it fostered imitators, including the Candy Store, partly owned by Tony Curtis. For a time there was talk of opening satellite Factories in San Francisco and Honolulu. A branch eventually opened in Chicago in 1970, with Newman on the board of directors, but it was robbed on opening night, and business never really took off. By then the novelty of seeing Roz Russell doing the Watusi had dimmed, and the original Factory had itself gone bust.

WHILE HE was in a buying mood, Newman once again went out of his way to help the Actors Studio. It had been a decade since he and Joanne and James Dean and other Method actors had come to Hollywood barely able to hide their contempt for the work it offered them, huddling at the Chateau Marmont like teenagers up to no good in a suburban basement. But by the mid-1960s a few score Actors Studio

---

* Not in the advertising: a rooftop deck that served as an unofficial spot for pot-smoking and quickie trysts.

members were living and working more or less full-time in Hollywood and doing estimable work, including Dennis Weaver, Bruce Dern, Lee Grant, and Mark Rydell. In 1966 the actor and teacher Jack Garfein thought that the Studio, which was still saggy after the Actors Studio Theater debacle, could be rejuvenated with a new branch in California. After some meetings, with Newman in attendance, it was agreed that they should establish the Actors Studio West.

Newman and Garfein were tasked with finding a spot, and they drove around L.A. and Hollywood in one of Newman's sports cars. They had a look at a dance studio near the intersection of Santa Monica Boulevard and Vine Street, and Newman was taken with it. "I like the smell of this place," he told Garfein. "It has the smell of Forty-fourth Street." He offered the landlady a check as a down payment, but she didn't like the look of his characteristically sloppy clothes. Garfein, though, was wearing a suit and tie; she accepted Newman's check once he'd cosigned it.

NEWMAN MAY very well have gotten a kick out of having his identity questioned, as he'd become increasingly frustrated with his inability to live privately. He felt he'd never asked for the intrusions that were part of being famous; he was notoriously reticent with reporters, and he tried almost too hard to play the ordinary guy: the frumpy wardrobe, the VW with the Porsche engine, the bottle opener worn on a dogtag chain around his neck.

And he talked about it. A lot. Just as he felt that he hadn't forfeited his right to hold political opinions when he became an actor, he felt that he hadn't signed away his right to have a private life, even if, like everyone else, he occasionally walked into public places such as shops, restaurants, hotels, or resorts.

"You can't really appreciate anonymity until you've lost it," he told a reporter. "People say that's sour grapes, but it really isn't. To be able to walk down the street without people paying attention to you is a real blessing. And you lose it when you become an actor."

He'd always had a self-contained nature; he had to learn how to step outside his skin to become an actor. And he was prone to brooding and stewing. "When Paul is angry," his brother told people, "he is very quiet." Longtime friends saw it clearly: "He is the most private man I've ever known," A. E. Hotchner once said of him. "He has a moat and a drawbridge, which he lets down only occasionally." He himself saw it a little differently. "I've been accused of being aloof," he said. "I'm not. I'm just wary." And, another way: "I'm a loner, and I'm always just a private person."

But it was clear that he didn't like the sort of attention he received. He took to wearing dark glasses—indoors, outdoors, day, night. This became a theme in itself, because so many of the oglers and intruders whom he resented specifically wanted to see those famous blue eyes.

The glasses, perversely, emboldened people, who would bluntly ask to see his eyes rather than just steal glances at them. It made him, he said, feel like a piece of meat. "If you have success, you'd really like to take credit for it," he explained. "It's really hard to take credit because some lady staggers across the sidewalk and says, 'Take off your dark sunglasses, I wanna see your baby blues.' " And he elaborated, "If you can get by on your baby blues, then what does it mean to be anything in the profession?"

He would make jokes to defuse the situation, replying to the most forward fans that if he took off his glasses his pants would fall down, or telling reporters that his tombstone would declare that he died a failure in life because his eyes turned brown. In a typical bit of Newmanish whimsy, he gave the matter some philosophical consideration: "The thing I've never figured out is, how do you present eyes? Do you present them coyly? Do you present them boldly?" But mostly he resented it.

And even worse, he resented requests for autographs. "It's just swell getting stopped seventy times going to the corner bar," he groused to a reporter while drinking a beer on a movie set. "If I never get asked for another autograph, I'll be a happy man." For a while he obliged, but then—after, he said, being asked to sign his name while he was using a urinal in Sardi's—he adopted a blanket policy of simply saying no to any and all autograph-seekers. He wasn't always diplomatic about it: one time he refused Henny Youngman to his face; another time he declined a request from the president of the Chicago Board of Trade—at the very moment when he had brought trade at the Commodity

Exchange to a dead stop merely by visiting the floor. He attended a charitable event for a school and refused autographs to the students. "With everything that's happening in the world," he asked them, "why do you collect autographs?" "It keeps us off the street," one of them said. "Isn't it better than smoking pot?" "Yes," he admitted, "and I'm sorry, but I still don't sign."

Once he thought he'd found a solution for being mobbed, but it didn't work. "I grew a beard so I wouldn't be recognized," he told a reporter. "So what happened: a couple of kids on the street saw me and said, 'Jesus! It's Paul Newman in a beard!' "

There was no end to it. He had been mobbed in Queens a couple years back when he took the kids to the World's Fair, and he wasn't able to take them to Disneyland without having a guide steer them to special entrances and exits around the park. When the family rented a home in Beverly Hills, rubbernecking tourists with maps to the stars' homes would snake slowly up the street searching for him; the Newmans slapped a sign on their front lawn that read "Please! They have moved! The Piersons." The most boorish of them would actually ring the bell—or wander up the drive of the farmhouse in Connecticut. Joanne joked that she'd need to get another sign: " 'Beware of Paul.' He doesn't take such things lightly."

RIGHT AFTER *Luke,* Newman shot an execrable World War II comedy that went through several name changes before being released— and bombing—as *The Secret War of Harry Frigg.* He tried to enjoy his role, a private with a penchant for going AWOL, by giving him a Graziano-esque simplicity and a goofy walk that he remembered from a guy he knew in the navy. He had a couple of sexy scenes with Italian starlet Sylva Koscina, but he never fooled himself about the quality of the thing: "I thought there was something there," he reflected. "The writer took it out."

But his next film was a different matter. In August 1967 *Variety* excitedly reported the scoop that Newman was making a new film—had been making it for weeks, in fact, without anyone's knowing. And what's more, he wasn't acting in it; he was directing. It was an adaptation of the novel *A Jest of God* by the Canadian author Margaret Laurence, and it was being filmed in and around Danbury, Connecticut, with Joanne cast in the lead as Rachel Cameron, a virginal small-town schoolteacher who decides, inch by inch one summer, to start taking chances with her life; Warner Bros.–Seven Arts, as the recently sold studio was newly called, would produce.

Newman's move behind the camera hadn't exactly come about without warning. He'd studied directing at Yale, of course, and he'd made *On the Harmfulness of Tobacco* previously, and he'd been talking for years about how he was more interested in the preparations for acting—the aspects most closely resembling the responsibilities of a director—than he was in actual performances. But it was still a newsworthy event, and the announcement of it indicated that Newman would direct a second film for Warner Bros. and star in two others, all in repayment for the studio's financial backing of *Jest*, which was believed to be in the neighborhood of $700,000.

The novel was actually discovered by John Foreman, who sent it in galleys to Joanne, figuring it was something she might appreciate. (He had a good eye; the book went on to win the Governor General's Award, Canada's most prestigious literary prize.) They took an option on the material and then surprised Newman with the news; he read it, and although he expressed some admiration for it and saw that she would be a good choice for the part, he deemed it "not movie material." So she took it to Stewart Stern, who had been mired in a dry spell since his script for *The Ugly American* had been shot as a Marlon Brando film in 1963. Despite having built up an enormous ambivalence about screenwriting—a couple of his scripts, commissioned as major projects, still sat unproduced on studio shelves—Stern set about adapting the book. When he had a draft, Foreman shopped it to prospective directors. As Joanne recalled, "[Stern] and I went around offering ourselves to everybody, but I'm afraid offering the package of the script and me was hardly like offering Elizabeth Taylor and Tennessee Williams."

As they kept at it, Newman took an interest in what they were doing, and he went from kibitzing over it to becoming engaged with it. The three went to Palm Springs to work on the screenplay. "I got involved in it about the same way the United States got involved in the Vietnam War," Newman joked. "I came in as an adviser and found the whole process was escalating until I was directing . . . There were a few conflicting discussions between myself and [Stern], until I gradually realized I just had to direct it. It was the only way to settle the conflict we'd been having."

For his part, Stern too recalled the process as arduous, "because of difficulty in communication. I tend to be very verbal. And Paul is minimalistic. Very often I won't get what he really means. Also, he is refined in a way that I'm not. He is selective in a way that I'm not. He refers to me as 'baroque,' and I refer to him as 'linear Cleveland mind.' To each other. I mean, that's how we talk to each other."

Despite the head butting, Newman the terrier had the scent of something. He would direct and produce—just the opportunity he'd been seeking to make a film but not act in it. He and Foreman offered the project to various studios, he remembered, "but all the companies turned me down flat." It was a wake-up call, he confessed: "I got total rejection of this picture, massive rejection. I finally had to go off in a corner and say, 'No, my taste is better; ultimately, I'm more perceptive than they are.' " Finally, they struck the deal with Warner Bros.: he and Joanne agreed to work without salary and to make additional films in exchange for the budget and for one-third of the profits. Newman formed a production company named Kayos (pronounced "chaos") to handle the deal, and he agreed to personally guarantee funding if he ran over budget.

He seemed enlivened by the sense of adventure and risk taking that directing entailed. "I'm curious about my taste, my dramatic selection, my technical ability with the camera," he told a visitor to the set. "There's no way to find out but to get up there and do it, and then let people hit you with baseball bats." Stern was impressed with his friend's determination. "He's the only man I ever met," he said, "who decides what makes him nervous—like directing a movie—and then, with his hands sweating and his feet sweating, goes right into it."

The film would shoot toward the end of summer in Bethel, Connecticut, near Danbury; they set up offices in a Danbury hotel and built soundstages in the gymnasium of the Danbury Veterans of Foreign

Wars hall. "There was some talk at one stage of shooting the film in California," Newman said, "but we finally did it in Connecticut because I very much wanted to contrast the schoolteacher's rather arid, dry existence with the lush, verdant spring background—it would have been far too obvious to have placed a barren life against a barren setting."

The cast included Estelle Parsons, James Olson, Kate Harrington, Donald Moffat, and Geraldine Fitzgerald in featured roles. Several of the key actors read for their parts with Paul at the house in Westport while Joanne and the kids and the pets all ran about. But others had more immediate paths into the film: Frank Corsaro, from the Actors Studio and *Baby Want a Kiss*, was also in it, as was Newman's auto mechanic, for that matter. And playing the role of young Rachel Cameron, who would be seen in the mature Rachel's memories and reveries of defining childhood events, was a debuting actress named Nell Potts—actually Nell Newman, the eight-year-old daughter of the star and the director. "It's cheaper to use your own children," Joanne cracked, and Newman explained, "She's not impressed with movies. The only reason she made this one was to earn money to feed her pigeons . . . I refused to subsidize them anymore, so she had to go out to work." But the truth was that Nell looked a great deal like her mother (with, lucky girl, her father's eyes), and the casting made perfect sense.

Art Newman was on the film as associate producer; the various department heads—cinematographer, editor, art director—were youngish for a studio project, among them editor Dede Allen, who had just worked on *Bonnie and Clyde*. Getting the thing together was a characteristic gung-ho spate of work for Newman: "In a little over a month," he said, "I had the perfect location, the perfect cast, and I was starting. That's the way to make pictures, when it's all in a rush and it's too late to back out." And as time is the most expensive item on any film's budget, he would have to be just as resourceful and expeditious in shooting it as he was in putting it together.

He was determined to get things done promptly and well, but it was also important to him that the crew felt it was a collegial set. "I called them all together on the first day," he recalled, "and confessed that I was a virgin and told them that I wasn't sensitive to criticism and that they would be able to make suggestions—once—on a given point. They did—sometimes more than once; but we got along fine." The crew recognized his limits ("He's sometimes stymied because he doesn't know how to express himself mechanically," one of them admitted to a reporter) but it was a genial shoot.

Indeed, in some aspects it felt like a summer camp: Newman reported to the set regularly in shorts and T-shirts and, often, barefoot. (One day, when some nuns from a nearby convent were visiting the set, the camera dolly rolled over his unprotected toes, and he sputtered out a stream of profanity just outside their hearing.) He drank beer and worried pack after pack of chewing gum; he'd nervously remove a wad of it from his mouth, shape it into a little ball, and then start chewing it again. Local hippies attached themselves to the peripheries of the production and decorated the crew's dining area with flowers and posters adorned with beautiful thoughts.

Newman and director of photography Gayne Rescher must have been tempted to get beautiful with the camera as well, and there would indeed be shots that could only have been composed in the Summer of Love. But they tried to maintain an aesthetic discipline. "My motto as a director is 'Fuck cool,' " he told a reporter. "I'd love to have it stenciled on the back of my chair and written on signs in letters a foot high. For my camera, I have a one-word motto: 'Eavesdrop.' "

He and Joanne seemed genuinely to enjoy working together. "We have the same acting vocabulary," he explained. "I would tell her, while [she was] reading a line, 'pinch it' or 'thicken it,' and she knew just what I meant . . . You could see her start off the day, and her toes would start to turn inward and her smile would become forced. She would just inhabit the part completely." She compared their collaboration to "the rapport Bergman has with his actors . . . About halfway through the film, we began to feel like the Moscow Art Theatre."

Parsons, whose performance in *Bonnie and Clyde* was just reaching theaters while she was working in Connecticut, was a little less rosy in her impression. "Paul Newman was very nervous and tense," she remembered, "but I liked his visual style . . . He knew exactly the way he wanted my hair to look, he told me how to wear my makeup . . . I learned how interesting it could be to get involved with a character from him."

And Stern, perhaps predictably, both *was* and *had* a nightmarish experience on the set. He came to Danbury to ensure that "the sense and intention of scenes that we had agreed about in calmer moments were not destroyed impulsively and under pressure." And he found himself fighting for his vision when Newman vacillated about including a scene in which young Rachel sees a dead classmate on the embalming table in her father's mortuary or one in which adult Rachel loses her virginity to a man she hasn't seen since high school. "Dede Allen and I had to practically break his arm with the argument that it's better to shoot it and have it than to make that kind of decision on the set," Stern recalled.

The battles between the writer and the director-producer were real. "To try and maintain the friendship throughout was very difficult," Stern admitted. "There were times when we simply didn't talk to one another. Still, every day I was on the set. My obsessive watchfulness became a very heavy burden for Paul and for Joanne. Finally, they had me sitting on a catwalk with a plank in front of me, looking through a knothole, so they couldn't see my expression. It bothered them that much."

Fortunately, they had a real foundation of trust beneath their differences. Near the end of shooting, when the budget had effectively been bled dry, Stern became one of the crew. "We were short of equipment," he remembered. "The dolly and everything had to go back because we were out of money. Instead of a dolly, for the last shot, the cameraman sat in a Safeway supermarket basket, and I pushed him. He had the camera between his knees."

Despite all the headaches and little quarrels, and despite the noises he'd made about being done with movies, Newman seemed to enjoy his first job as a director a great deal. "I didn't get anywhere near as tired directing as when I act. As an actor you stop and start the motor all day; it's like running a hundred yards two feet at a time. When you're involved with every facet of the production—script, attitudes, lighting, makeup, wardrobe—you're constantly pumped up and you don't have an opportunity to slow down."

Still, to unwind from the shoot, he and a Westport buddy, clothier Mike Hyman, took a boys-only trip to Florida, where they fished, bombed around in speedboats, and drank. He came home to battle with the studio over what to call the film. *A Jest of God* was out: too obscure, too religious. For a spell Newman thought about using a line from a nursery rhyme; later, the film briefly was known as *Now I Lay Me Down*. Finally, they agreed to call it *Rachel, Rachel*.

NEWMAN HAD had a blast making *Cool Hand Luke*, tooling around central California in a blue Mercury convertible—and sometimes even on a motorcycle—when he wasn't needed on set. He was open, too, to odd intrusions on the set, such as the day Dennis Hopper invited his San Francisco avant-garde filmmaker buddy Bruce Connor to shoot some footage of the actors clearing brush from a roadside under a blistering sun; Connor's seventeen-minute film, entitled *Luke* and featuring Newman, Hopper, and the rest swinging scythes in super-super-slow motion, would be studied in museum basement screening rooms for decades to come.

But it was a different matter for Donn Pearce, who hated movie people, thought Newman was too scrawny to play the hero of his novel, and capped his last day on the set by punching somebody out. Newman didn't seem to notice. He had thrived on the manly camaraderie and the outré pursuits in which his character indulged: fistfights and card games and physical labor in the hot sun and groveling two-faced to the road gang bosses—and, famously, taking on a bet that he could eat fifty eggs.

That scene would be a highlight of the picture, but Newman told an interviewer, "I never swallowed an egg."

"Isn't Method acting about doing the real thing?" came the follow-up question.

"Not if you have to swallow eggs."

He had, however, learned to play the banjo, if not particularly well, for the stirring scene in which Luke learns of his mother's death. As George Kennedy recalled, "Paul knew as much about the banjo as I do about baking cakes. But he wanted to play his own accompaniment, and Stuart Rosenberg and everybody else said, 'You don't learn to play banjo that easily.' And he said, 'I'm gonna try.' And in the scene you see, Paul makes an error. He wasn't doing it the way he wanted and became madder and madder, although you can only tell by the increase of the pace of his stroking the banjo. When it was over, it was magnificent. Rosenberg said, 'Print.' Paul said, 'I could do it better.' And Rosenberg said, 'Nobody could do it better.' "

It all boded very well. "There's a good smell about this," he told a visitor to the set. "We're gonna have a good picture." The film was released in November 1967 and succeeded on just about every conceivable level. In Lucas Jackson, Newman had found arguably the signature role of his career. He was lean and rascally and cagy and charming as all get out; he was tough and sharp and daring and loyal and manly. He could bleed and he could cut you, and he could be condescending and moody; but the flaws in him seemed only to magnify his better qualities. He was iconic—saintly and comely and true to himself. His story was like a modern-day gospel that resonated vividly in a time when so many young people were questioning the violent and arbitrary nature of social authority.

Rosenberg had made a brilliant job of it. It was a beautiful film— *too* pretty, indeed, in the eyes of some critics—with a fresh and vivid score by Argentine jazzman Lalo Schifrin; rich, lusty, plausible performances by George Kennedy and Strother Martin; and a script that furnished a drinking party's worth of memorable catchphrases: "Any man forgets his number spends a night in the box"; "Puttin' 'em on here, boss"; "Sometimes nothin' can be a real cool hand"; "Stay down: you're beat"; and most famously (and often misquoted with the addition of the article *a* where the ellipses are), "What we got here is . . . failure to communicate." From the bawdy humor to the attack on conformity to the martyrdom of the hero, it was a perfect picture for its moment. And it made money.

It was sure to be remembered at Oscar time—but 1967 was a watershed year in Hollywood movies. Among the films with which *Cool Hand Luke* would have to compete were such genuinely groundbreaking pictures as *Bonnie and Clyde*, *The Graduate*, and *In Cold Blood*, plus capable, sober Hollywood visions of the issues of the day such as *In the Heat of the Night* and *Guess Who's Coming to Dinner. Luke* was certainly a peer among that throng but not by any means unquestionably superior.

Still, even given the competition, it was disappointing that it would get only four nominations—acting for Newman, supporting acting for Kennedy (who had mounted an ad campaign for himself at his own expense), score for Schifrin, and adapted script for Pearce and Pierson. Rosenberg and Conrad Hall were overlooked; worse, one of the five best picture nominations had gone, embarrassingly, to *Doctor Dolittle*. In his own category Newman would be facing down stiff competition: Warren Beatty *(Bonnie and Clyde)*, Dustin Hoffman *(The Graduate)*, Rod Steiger *(Heat)*, and Spencer Tracy *(Dinner)*. Come the big night, Kennedy won for supporting actor (Newman beamed from his seat) and Steiger, whom Newman had truly admired ever since their days at the Actors Studio more than a decade earlier, won the best actor statuette for his role as a racist southern sheriff.

Newman was magnanimous; he had lost to a pro with unassailable chops. But, as anyone who kept score of such things would have noted, he was now 0 for 4.

Fifteen

C LASSIC HOLLYWOOD STORY, PERHAPS EVEN TRUE: NEWMAN IS walking through a studio commissary at lunchtime and comes upon a table at which John Wayne is dining. "Hey Paul," booms a voice every moviegoer in the world can imitate, "how's the revolution coming?" Newman smiles. "How can we possibly win, Duke, with you on the other side?"

They liked each other, Wayne and Newman, but they truly were competitors in several ways: at the box office in ticket sales, at the movie studios in their differing visions of what Hollywood films should be like, and increasingly in the arena of politics, where Newman became more intensely engaged in 1968 than he had been all his life. He certainly wasn't alone—millions of people felt that key aspects of the country were up for grabs that fevered year. But he was extremely visible and vocal, even for someone so uniquely able to command a platform as a movie star. He became a loud and prominent presence in the country's discussion of civil rights, the Vietnam War, the arms race, ecology, the farm and labor movements, and other issues. He campaigned for national and local politicians, and it was sincerely suggested to him more than once that he run for office himself.

As for many people, the war seemed to galvanize him—not only because of his ardent beliefs but, surely, because Scott would be turning eighteen in September. Scott hadn't been a good student; college wasn't a big attraction for him. He enjoyed daredevil pursuits like trampolining and skateboarding and, soon enough, skydiving. And he gave his parents trouble, Joanne included. Newman, who had so often played the flawed son in films and who held ambivalent feelings about his own father, didn't do very well in responding to Scott's troubles. Unable to corral the young man, he seemed to feel that changing a violent world might be a way to keep him from harm.

He had supported Lyndon Johnson in 1964, but like many others, he felt betrayed by Johnson's pursuit of a bloody and senseless war. "I had been severely had," he decided. But, again like many others, he didn't see an alternative to supporting Johnson for reelection until the advent of Eugene McCarthy, the bookish, hawkeyed senator from Minnesota who not only dared challenge a sitting president from his own party in the New Hampshire primary but beat him there on an antiwar platform. Newman was galvanized.

"I've admired the man for years," he said of McCarthy that summer, "but I admired the *hell* out of him when he came out against Johnson." He had himself become active in the peace movement before McCarthy's challenge. In January he appeared at a Lincoln Center fund-raiser in support of a number of sitting Democratic senators and congressmen who had come out against the war. When McCarthy determined to stand against Johnson, his staff called Newman and asked if he'd be interested in recording some commercials to air in New Hampshire. "I went back and checked McCarthy's voting record," Newman revealed. "I was so fed up with the present administration that I couldn't resist going to work for him."

He made some TV spots and appeared at rallies in New Hampshire, and then he took to the road in earnest as the campaign unrolled, visiting Indiana, Wisconsin, Nebraska, Oregon, Connecticut, New York. In the Midwest that spring he hopped around on a private plane and was met by station wagons driven by campaign volunteers and stocked with beer and sandwiches. He visited little town centers and factory parking lots where perhaps one hundred people came out, and college campuses and bigger towns where he could draw twenty times that. He went into the slums of Indianapolis with local Black Power leaders. He did as many as ten or twelve appearances a day, standing on the tailgates of trucks or on the trunks of cars and speaking simply and without pretense: "I am not a public speaker. I am not a politician. I'm not here because I'm an actor. I'm here because I've got six kids. I don't want it written on my gravestone, 'He was not part of his times.' The times are too critical to be dissenting in your own bathroom."

In New York he swelled the crowd of speakers at a political cabaret, Eugene's, where folks paid to be entertained by the likes of Peter, Paul and Mary; Elaine May; Phil Ochs; and Richie Havens and listened to speeches and poems read by such screen stars as Lauren Bacall, Myrna Loy, Lou Gossett, and Newman himself. He performed in a comic skit at a rally at Madison Square Garden where Albert Gore, the Tennessee Democrat, spoke about arms control prior to a Senate debate on the subject. He emceed an evening at the Manhattan discothèque Arthur, during which Joanne and Tammy Grimes hosted lessons in cooking crêpes, omelets, and fondues. Joanne spoke about her own wish for the election: complaining that she hadn't seen Newman since New Hampshire, she urged the attendees to vote for McCarthy "and help bring my husband home."

He brought madness on the road with him. In Kenosha, Wisconsin, he started his speech with the usual stuff about being a father of six. "Paul! Adopt me!" squealed a teenage fan amid a mob of teenage fans. Women rushed his car as it drove up to an American Motors plant. When an empty beer can fell out of his station wagon, a girl picked it up off the ground and kissed it. "All this for the star of *The Silver Chalice*," he muttered in chagrin.

Sometimes it got ugly: in South Bend, Indiana, he and the other McCarthy operatives with whom he was riding in the station wagon were met by a crowd that threw debris at them; Scott Newman, spending time on the road with his dad, was hit in the face with a rock.

Sometimes it was deeply humbling. In New Hampshire, Newman met a policeman whose son had died in Vietnam just the day before. Newman offered his sympathy and then, bucking his courage, looked the man in the eye and asked, "What did [the cop] think about some creep, some Hollywood peacenik, a functioning illiterate, coming in there and telling him about the war?" The cop replied that he didn't resent Newman: "Even if a war takes your boy . . . that doesn't make it right."

But Newman managed to find fun. In New Hampshire a local

Jaguar dealership loaned him a car for a couple of days. When he returned it, he learned that they were going to offer the same car to Richard Nixon the following day. He left a note on the dashboard: "You should have no trouble driving this car at all, because it has a very tricky clutch." Later in the campaign Nixon had occasion to speak with John Foreman by phone and told him, "Tell Paul I think he's a first-rate actor even if he thinks I'm a lousy politician."

ALONG WITH a number of Hollywood stars who had come out equally volubly in support of Hubert Humphrey and Robert Kennedy, Newman helped turn the Democratic presidential race into a newfangled media event. In May *Life* put him on the cover to illustrate a photo essay on various stars working for their various candidates: Shirley MacLaine, Bobby Darin, Sonny and Cher, and Lesley Gore (all for Kennedy); Robert Ryan, Rod Steiger, Hal Holbrook, Dustin Hoffman, and Tony Randall (for McCarthy). Frank Sinatra, the *New York Times* reported, was backing Humphrey, in a split with his Rat Pack buddies Sammy Davis Jr. and Peter Lawford, who had turned the Factory into a clubhouse for the pro-Kennedy crowd. ("Dean Martin is taking no part in the campaign," intoned the paper of record, "nor is Joey Bishop.")

In July he was named to the Connecticut delegation to the national convention; among the forty-three other members was Arthur Miller. In August, Newman joined Ralph Bellamy and Dore Schary in reading excerpts from the speeches of Adlai Stevenson from the podium. Later, as the streets outside the auditorium seethed, Newman was photographed snarling in anger on the convention floor, with Miller staring on intently behind him.

And he was on hand to witness one of the most famous battles of that mad week, when Gore Vidal and William F. Buckley, in their roles as analysts for ABC television, engaged in a series of inflamed debates. The Newmans had maintained their friendship with Vidal, sailing the Greek isles with him and Howard Austen a year or so earlier and keeping in steady touch. And Newman knew Buckley well enough to be allowed to help himself to booze and beer from the conservative columnist's dressing room at the convention hall. One night on the air, in the midst of a particularly rancorous exchange, Vidal had accused Buckley of espousing fascist tactics by supporting the actions of the Chicago police. A remarkable outburst ensued. "Now, listen, you queer," Buckley shouted. "Stop calling me a crypto-Nazi or I'll sock you in your goddamn face!" A few minutes later Newman confronted Buckley outside his trailer and told him, "That was the most disgusting display I've ever seen." "But Vidal called me a Nazi," Buckley replied. "That's political," Newman said. "What you called him is personal." Buckley stormed into his dressing room, unpersuaded.

In the fall Newman contributed money to and campaigned for Allard Lowenstein, the political activist and McCarthy organizer who was running for Congress from the South Shore of Long Island. In a single night, leapfrogging about in a helicopter, he appeared at a rally at the Green Acres shopping center, a fund-raiser at a country club in the Five Towns, and another fund-raiser in Merrick. Richard Weidman, a campaign operative who had some knowledge of piloting, was sent around as an advance man to ensure that there was an appropriate place for the helicopter to land.

When he got to Merrick for the evening's last event, Weidman realized that word about Newman's itinerary had leaked. "I come wheeling around the corner into this parking lot," he remembered, "and there's like five hundred people . . . I get there just ahead of the chopper. I can hear the whomp of the blade when I get there, and I'm trying to scream, 'Get out of the way!' I had set it up with the Nassau County police; they had one cop there. I go over to the cop and say, 'Do something!' and he said, 'What do you want me to do?' "

Weidman created a landing area, and when the helicopter was on the ground, he escorted Newman and the others to his car. "They're just like freaked by this scene," he remembered. "These screaming kids and middle-aged women acting like bobby-soxers, and Newman jumps into the front seat, and this woman, who is probably late thirties, early forties, in a white suit—very attractive . . . is like hysterical and jumps in Newman's lap! And Newman is actually pretty cool about the whole thing. He picks her up, pats her on the butt, and says, 'Thanks, dear.

Got to get out.' " The car was engulfed by women and kids, banging and rocking it; Weidman had to inch forward through the heaving mass until more cops arrived and cleared a path.

That campaign ended well—Lowenstein was elected. But McCarthy lost, and then of course Humphrey lost, and in the wake of those disappointments Newman tried to remember the good that he felt he'd helped accomplish. "We walked away from New Hampshire with the resignation of the president of the United States and with a whole new set of national priorities," he declared. "New Hampshire was the beginning of participatory politics." But at the same time, he recognized how entrenched and intractable the system was. "We blew the convention," he admitted. "We thought we'd go in there and the machine would have to respond. But the machine was a lot tougher than we hoped; the old bird's still got a lot of legs."

After Nixon's inauguration he continued to give voice to his beliefs. He and Joanne attended Senate hearings on the creation of a cabinet-level Department of Peace, and they carried protest signs in an antiwar rally outside the American embassy in London. He joined Alan Arkin, Peter Fonda, Arlo Guthrie, Dennis Hopper, and Jon Voight in asking moviegoers to boycott their own films for a day as a sign of solidarity with the antiwar movement. In the 1969 elections he undertook another barnstorming campaign in support of Reverend Joseph D. Duffey, who was running for the U.S. Senate seat from Connecticut; that was a losing effort too. "He really took it hard when Duffey was defeated," Joanne said.

He was so caught up in it that he blurted out to David Frost in an interview that he had "seriously considered" running for office: the Senate, even the presidency. "This might be facetious, but the issues are not," he pronounced. Frost pressed him, sensing a huge scoop, and Newman backpedaled: "I think I may have carried my credentials about as far as they can go."

He knew in his bones that he wasn't cut out to be a politician. "I've got sort of a short fuse," he admitted to an interviewer. "Besides, I don't have the arrogance to run for office. And I don't have the credentials." Another time he confessed, "I can barely, barely, just barely handle the aspects of my life that are public right now."

But he had said it, right? And so he was approached by political interests wondering if he would truly consider it. Gore Vidal joined them. "He had a chance to run for senator from Connecticut," he recalled, "and I urged him to do so. He declined, probably for financial reasons—he was supporting forty people at the time. I'm sorry he didn't run. He is one of the few people I know who has good character. That is rare in politics and just as rare in show business."

He knew his own limits, though, and demurred: "I chickened out. It would have been great for me but terrible for the public."

DURING THAT crazy political summer, *Rachel, Rachel* was released to respectful and even admiring reviews. Writing in the *New York Times,* Renata Adler called it "a little sappy at moments, but the best written, most seriously acted American movie in a long time." It was a strange and small and vivid film, rich in actorly moments, but unique too for its authentic air of lived-in, small-town realities—an American indie movie decades before there was such a genre. It was constructed with tasteful and sturdy craft that could sometimes strain when striving for poetic effect. But it was handsome and fluid and filled with fine and fresh moments: the intimate rewards of the careful writing and acting and observation of a tiny flame of life daring to burn brighter and higher, and the splashy, lurid bits that made it feel grown-up for its time: a lesbian kiss, a sex scene, a trippy visit to a newfangled Christian tabernacle.

Aside from a financial stake, Newman felt justifiable pride in the movie, and he went out and beat the drum hard for it. "I've never sold a film before, have I?" he asked columnist Sheila Graham over lunch. "I'm selling it because it's a special kind of film." He consented to photo shoots and dozens of interviews and small invitation-only screenings at which he would discuss the film with journalists and opinion-makers. There was a premiere in New York, and the Newmans did the rounds of the TV talk shows. And his publicist, Warren Cowan, launched a campaign for Oscar nominations for Newman, Joanne, Estelle Parsons, and Stewart Stern.

Newman rarely worked this hard to promote movies he was paid nearly seven figures to act in, but he told a reporter, "I had so much at stake. I was putting my taste up against eight major studios who refused to buy *Rachel*. I had something to prove, really. I was terribly afraid the film would get sloughed. I don't think the people who distributed it had any real faith in it."

"I hope it's successful," he told Rex Reed, "not because of any financial reward—hell, both Joanne and I did it for nothing—but to prove to Hollywood you can make a film about basic, simple people without violence."

The picture did succeed, grossing upward of $9 million at the box office: a real hit given the cost of making it. Eventually Newman was able to cash in on the success by selling Kayos, which owned a third of *Rachel* and 10 percent of *The Hustler*, to a realty holding company in exchange for about $738,000 of stock and the promise of another such payment if Kayos could produce as well again in the subsequent five years. Successful too were Warren Cowan's efforts to single out *Rachel* in a year in which there was such competition for Academy Awards as *The Lion in Winter*, *Rosemary's Baby*, *2001: A Space Odyssey*, *Funny Girl*, *Bullitt*, *The Odd Couple*, *Faces*, and *The Producers*. When the Oscar nominations were announced, *Rachel* was up for four, including best picture, best actress, best supporting actress, and best adapted screenplay.

But not best director. Which hurt. Newman had actually won the directing prize at that year's New York Film Critics Circle Awards. "Four critics walked out when the vote was counted," he crowed. "Being perverse, I take a good deal of the credit for that."* He was nominated for feature film direction by the Directors Guild. And he took the top prize at the Producers Guild Awards. But he was passed over by the Academy nominators in favor of Gillo Pontecorvo for *The Battle of Algiers*. Seemingly every year at the Oscars, one of the directors of a best picture nominee is shut out for his work; that year it was Newman.

As when her husband lost for *Hud*, Woodward was incensed: "I couldn't have been nominated for best actress or Estelle Parsons for

---

* Later he felt cowed by his own pleasure in the prize: "Christ," he admitted, "the high lasted two days, and then I hated myself for letting it get to me."

supporting actress without his being the director. This negates the whole purpose of the Academy. I'm not going to go. It's a total boycott!" Newman tried to talk sense to her: "You're being emotional." A few days later she demurred: "My husband decided I should go and do what he says." They showed up on Oscar night, and *Rachel* lost in all categories. The next day Newman griped about the whole ordeal. "There must be something wrong with a group that hands out awards and then has to send out telegrams saying, 'Please come,' " he said. "It should be fun to go to—not agony. There's something barbaric about it."

He had to admit there was a personal element to his complaint. "It was pretty hard to win the New York Film Critics Circle Award as best director for that film and then not even get nominated for the Oscar," he admitted. "But I'm not gonna whine about it."

AND HE had reasons not to whine: millions of them, in fact.

There was excellent reason to believe that he would profit immensely from the new production company he'd formed with John Foreman. Foreman had been wanting to produce for a while—agents were legally prevented from doing so—and he recognized that the best way to change careers would be to attach himself to Newman. He had plans to make a picture about a pair of western outlaws from a script by William Goldman. But for its first film the Newman-Foreman Company would make a film about auto racing called *Winning*. Universal Pictures was paying Newman $1.1 million to play a race-car driver in it—the highest sum ever offered to an actor in a deal for a single film, and nearly one and a half times the entire budget of *Rachel, Rachel.* Joanne was scheduled to play opposite him, and filming would take them to Indiana and the famed annual five-hundred-mile race at the Indianapolis Motor Speedway.

It was pure melodrama: a rootless race-car driver meets a small-town divorcée who leaves her world to marry him and join his; he bonds with her teenage son, but he becomes so obsessed with his work that she stumbles into an affair with one of his fellow drivers. It plays out against a backdrop of several races in several different classes of cars, but mostly it's set at the Indy 500, an event for which drivers and their teams often spend a month or more making preparations and living near the raceway. It would shoot in the spring and summer of 1968 for release the following year around Indy time. Written by veteran screenwriter Howard Rodman, *Winning* would be directed by James Goldstone, a TV hand with a couple of features to his credit. Robert Wagner and Richard Thomas would play the adulterous teammate and the confused teenager, respectively. The fourteen-week shoot would take them to Indianapolis; Elkhart Lake, Wisconsin; Riverside and Bakersfield, California; and studios in Hollywood.

Just as he had with boxing and billiards and the trombone, Newman seized the opportunity to research his character by learning about auto racing. He had long been enamored of speed, ever since he bought his scooter and, later, when he was commuting between New York and Westport or around Southern California in his Porsche-infused VWs. Lately he had owned a series of big, manly Corvettes and pacey Porsche coupes. He occasionally sponsored cars and drivers in races benefiting charities. And there had been the motorcycles, since abandoned. "I get 'stoned' on automobiles," he confessed. "For me it's a natural high, which is marvelous."

To prepare for *Winning*, he and Wagner were tutored by veteran racer Bob Bondurant, whose School of High Performance Driving was where James Garner and Yves Montand had learned the trade before making *Grand Prix* a few years earlier. Newman and Wagner would have only a couple of weeks to learn to drive a variety of cars—and their studies would be interrupted by the need to keep to the production schedule and to be in certain places when races were being held.

They started very slowly, with classroom lectures and then walks along the length of the test track. Then they sat while Bondurant drove and talked them through what he was doing and why. The emphasis was on technique: the heel-and-toe system by which drivers keep the right foot on the gas pedal and the brake at once; the calculation of approaching a turn and choosing and maintaining a course through and out of it; braking and steering; some emergency procedures. Bondurant started them out on small boxy Datsun sedans and then worked them up in size until they reached muscle-bound stock cars and, finally, racing Lolas that could hit speeds upward of 150 miles per hour.

Newman was an apt student. Within six days of his first drive he ran a 34-second lap on a track in Phoenix where the record was just under 29. Within two weeks he drove a lap at Indianapolis at 143 miles per hour. The filmmakers hadn't pushed him to such a pace: "I've told him time and again that anything over 120 doesn't show on camera anyway, but he wouldn't listen to me," Goldstone said. Rather, it simply felt good to him. "I never had any sensation of speed," Newman revealed. "The only time you're conscious of anything is if something breaks."

He got quite competent. For the Indy 500 portions of the film, Newman himself drove amid a field of professionals. In the final cut of the film, the wider shots showing the progress of Newman's character on the track were actually shots of Bobby Unser in the 1968 Indy 500. But when they cut in for close-ups, Newman was in the car himself, keeping pace with the camera car being driven by two-time Indy winner Roger Ward.

He had some laughs with his new pastime, taking his old navy pilot for a blistering couple of laps of the Road America track at Elkhart Lake and scaring the crap out of him. "They had to *pry* his hand loose from the roll bar," Newman cackled. And he even got Joanne into a car: "She actually did make one circle around the Indy track. Sure, she may be the only person who ever drove it at forty miles an hour, but she tried."

Actually, she wasn't at all happy. She came out to watch him only occasionally. The atmosphere of the racetrack was as uncomfortable for her as the ballets and dance recitals to which she would drag her husband were for him. She skipped his racing practices as often as possible, and when she did show up at trackside in Indy, she couldn't decide which was worse: the prospect of him killing himself in a crack-up or the clutches of screaming women holding up signs pleading "Paul, Please Slow Down" and clucking over him as he walked around the set. "I wish I wasn't married to him now," she grumbled to a reporter.

To his credit, Newman didn't see the film merely as an excuse to drive fast. He studied the world of racing and considered the sexual and emotional tensions of the story just as carefully as he did his clutching and shifting techniques. Roger Ward had been hired to teach him the finer points of open-wheeled Indy cars and of the Indy track. But he found that Newman was as curious about his teacher's private life as he was about driving. "He was interested in emotional attitudes," Ward recalled, "in my relationships with the mechanics and the car owners. He even spent a couple of nights in my home talking with my wife, reading her emotions."

The problem with *Winning* was that Goldstone was better at conveying the excitement of racing than the more intimate and dramatic aspects of the story. It got deservedly mixed reviews on its release in the summer of 1969, although it turned out to be a modest financial success. But in the long run Newman took more than money from the project. He had been introduced to a thrilling new fascination and challenge. He was thinking, he said, of continuing his auto racing education when his work schedule allowed. "I would hesitate to drive in competition now," he said, "not because I would be afraid to but because I'm too old. I started late, and my reflexes aren't really as hot as they should be. I'd hate to run seventeenth in a field of fourteen."

As soon as he'd put *Winning* behind him, he went to work on William Goldman's western, an account of the legendary outlaws Butch Cassidy and the Sundance Kid and the final days when a man could team up with some buddies to rob and rove and raise hell and flout the law and light out for the territory and feel the wild frontier in his heart just as vividly as he could behold it with his eyes. The script was written with a light touch, a sense of delight, jaunty dramatic pace and structure. It had a bit of modernish sex in it, inspired perhaps by *Jules and Jim*, and more than a bit of horseplay, inspired perhaps by Hope and Crosby. It felt youthful in its willingness to goose the formulas of the cowboy genre, but it felt old and wise and even sad, too, with its suggestion that the Wild West was no more and that such fellows as its protagonists could no longer run rampant in our world and our time: that perfect Newman blend of the traditional and the new.

Newman loved the script as soon as he read it and was excited to play the part of the Sundance Kid, the more headstrong and impetuous of the leads—the younger, sexier one. For Butch, a schemer, dreamer, and tactician who ruled the gang and eluded authorities with his wits and not his daring, Goldman had always imagined Jack Lemmon. But Lemmon was no longer right for this sort of film and was quickly erased from calculations.

In fact, the actor best suited to play Butch was Newman—but Newman didn't see it. In one of his first meetings with George Roy Hill, whom 20th Century–Fox had hired to direct the film, he kept talking about Sundance's motives and suggesting changes in his lines.

Hill was puzzled: "Why are we talking about Sundance? You're playing Butch."

"I'm Sundance," Newman told him.

"No, you're not."

"George, I was here first—I'm Sundance."

"I went back and read the script that night," Newman remembered, "and thought, hell, the parts are really about equal and they're both great parts. So I said, 'Okay, I'll be Butch.' "

Which left the question of who would play Sundance. As Freddie Fields recalled,* Warren Beatty had heard about the script and wanted in. That looked promising. But when Beatty learned that Newman was to play Butch, he insisted on the part for himself—and then he claimed he could get Marlon Brando to play Sundance. No one really wanted Brando, though, so when he finally got hold of the script and declared that *he* was prepared to play Butch, they had reason to pass on him, gratefully.

Then the inevitable idea of Steve McQueen's playing Sundance came up. McQueen was a star, but more to the point, he felt a kind of rivalry with Newman as a real man who didn't stand for Hollywood cant and gloss. They had some affection for each other; McQueen had recently introduced Newman and his brother, Art, to riding dirt bikes in the desert. But when it came to business, McQueen was plainly jealous of the more established star. He liked Goldman's script but got hung up on the fact that Newman—demonstrably a bigger earner and with a far more respected résumé—would receive billing over him.

---

* In his unpublished memoir written with David Rensin.

Fields tried a number of persuasive schemes to get him aboard, even creating mock-ups of advertisements that gave a sort of equal weight to both actors' names. But McQueen was never satisfied with what he saw.

Fields told Newman about his predicament: "We're going to lose McQueen on billing."

"What do you mean?" asked Newman, genuinely amazed. "I don't lose pictures on billing."

"He wants first star billing. What do you want to do?"

"I don't think that's nice," Newman answered. "No."

And McQueen walked.

It was Joanne, Newman remembered, who thought of an actor for Sundance: "She knew his work and thought he was the best." At thirty-two, Robert Redford, a handsome all-American sort, had been in the business for a decade and still had not broken through to stardom. He'd been in a half-dozen films, with featured roles in *The Chase* and *Inside Daisy Clover*; he'd appeared in TV series at the end of the Golden Age, and he'd had a hit on Broadway with *Barefoot in the Park*, in which he also appeared on-screen. But he hadn't established himself as a box office attraction, and he was, like McQueen, something of an ornery customer.

He'd been born in Santa Monica in 1936 and had excelled as an athlete at Van Nuys High School, winning a baseball scholarship to the University of Colorado. While he was there, he soured on sports and found his scholarship pulled—shades of Newman—after he got into some trouble with booze. By then he was interested in becoming a painter and wound up in New York, studying art at Pratt Institute and theatrical design at the American Academy of Dramatic Arts. That was where he drifted into acting, first landing a small role in the Broadway production of the campus comedy *Tall Story*. (He had an uncredited part in the film version of the play, which was directed by— shades of Newman—Josh Logan.) TV work—including episodes of *Alfred Hitchcock Presents*, *Dr. Kildare*, *Naked City*, *Route 66*, and *The Twilight Zone*—ensued, and film parts. And then in 1963 came *Barefoot in the Park*, wherein he played a New York newlywed opposite Elizabeth Ashley.

But as his star rose, something in Redford seemed to kick against it. He turned down the chance to appear in *Who's Afraid of Virginia Woolf?* and, more perversely, screen-tested for *The Graduate* just to prove to the producers that he *wasn't* who they wanted. He and his wife, Lola, who'd married in 1958 and had three children (one of whom died as an infant), lived neither in Los Angeles nor in New York nor even in Connecticut but in Utah, where they owned acreage, including a ski resort about an hour east of Salt Lake City. If Newman was offbeat as a movie star, Redford behaved as if the whole business was noxious to him.

Fields, who recalled first hearing about Redford from an agent in his New York office, visited the actor backstage on Broadway and gave him a script. But Redford was hesitant, suspecting at first that the studio was just trying to use his interest in the role as bait to lure a bigger costar for Newman. He wouldn't even read the script: "Suppose I liked it?" he remembered thinking. "Who needs the disappointment?" But Fields and Foreman and Goldman and his own agent kept after him, and he read it and agreed to meet Newman.

"We got together for dinner," Redford recalled. "We talked about car racing, where we liked to live, everything but the film. I don't think either of us enjoys talking about movies very much. And we didn't really need to, because right away there seemed to be this understanding that I would make the picture."

They had some things in common. They both despised the slickness of Hollywood and the way business was done in the town at the expense of art. Like Newman, Redford was an avid outdoorsman—skiing was a real passion—and he had convinced Paramount Pictures to front him a little money to make a film based on Oakley Hall's novel about Olympic skiing, *Downhill Racer*. And like Newman, he had matinee-idol looks and was suspicious of the advantages they accrued for him.

As they discovered in rehearsal and then again on the set, their acting styles were different. "Redford never intellectualizes," Hill recalled. "Newman will talk a scene to death . . . Redford would just stand there and squirm during all the intellectualizing." Redford took to watching his director and costar argue about scenes as a kind of spectator sport: "They were constantly into it, and they both have this habit of pointing with their index fingers when they argue, and during this one major, uh, discussion, they were both pointing and their fingers crossed, like locked swords. Hilarious. Everybody cracked up."

Cracking up was, more or less, the order of the day. They filmed for a while in the towns of Cuernavaca and Taxco in Mexico, where they caroused and drank and played Ping-Pong in shaded courtyards and had the sort of genuine fun that normally doesn't translate from the set onto the screen but makes for great stories in publicity interviews and at the premiere party. On the first day of shooting Newman was sitting by Redford, reached over, slapped him on the thigh, and said, "Well, kid, how does it feel to be in your first $40 million-grosser?" Redford thought his costar was some kind of egoist for such presumption, but he too came to realize that they were on to something. It was a "verifiable adult fairy tale," Newman was telling people. Like *Luke*, it felt good to him while he was making it.

After location work in Mexico, Utah, Colorado, and New Mexico, they returned to Los Angeles for several more weeks of shooting. Daredevil Newman impressed everyone with his trick bicycle riding, which was the focus of a breezily romantic scene between him and Katharine Ross that Hill had added at the last minute to create a bit of a romantic triangle among the characters. (Newman did his own riding. Hill had hired a stuntman, initially, and the fellow insisted that the old-fashioned bike they were using wouldn't stand up to trick riding; while they argued, Newman rode past them standing on the bicycle seat and holding on to the handlebars. Hill fired the stuntman on the spot.)

Throughout the shoot Newman and Redford drank and trash-talked and kept each other amused and rattled with practical jokes. Newman hated the way Redford was always late for work, dinner, whatever, and taunted him with the adage "Punctuality is the courtesy of kings." (He even had Joanne sew and frame a sampler with that caution and presented it to him.) Newman and Hill devised an elaborate plan to lure

Redford into a bet in which he'd have to prove his alleged fencing prowess, only to have it backfire when one of Newman's daughters warned Redford, "They're going to do something bad to you."

Hill had Conrad Hall as his director of photography and had the inspiration to get Burt Bacharach to write a score and original songs for musical interludes. The film was released in September 1969 and was an instant hit. They had revived a hoary genre—the buddy movie—by giving it a slightly camp sheen. It was a movie without sex or bloodshed, but it felt modern because it was played with winking comedy, antiauthoritarian cheek, and hints of a countercultural lifestyle.

Like any movie about men who are close friends, it had subtle hints of homoeroticism—and, lord knows, a pair of stars whom people might actually want to imagine in those ways. But this one excluded that possibility by introducing Ross's Etta Place character into the plot and giving the film the titillating suggestion of a ménage à trois. In many ways, it was an extremely simple film: two guys get chased. But the interplay between the leads was so breezy and infectious that it created a sense of depth: it wasn't a film about outlaws and a posse; it was a film about friendship. And it ended—like *Bonnie and Clyde, The Wild Bunch*, and *Easy Rider*—in the death of the protagonists (although, uniquely in that company, the deaths in *Butch* were implied, not shown). The idea that those two guys who were such good company were gone made the time spent with them seem that much sweeter. That there could always be another Hope and Crosby picture made the bunch of them seem indistinguishable from one another and forgettable individually; that Butch and Sundance were gone, hopelessly, made them beautiful, golden, immortal.

The critics weren't overly impressed. Vincent Canby in the *New York Times* called it "a very slick movie" and complained about "a gnawing emptiness"; Pauline Kael said the film left her "depressed . . . and rather offended"; Roger Ebert surmised that it "must have looked like a natural on paper" but found the completed film "slow and disappointing."

Didn't matter: the box office was astounding. Newman, who once complained that he'd never made a picture that grossed $20 million, had thought he named a big figure when he suggested to Redford that this one would double that mark. He was wrong, by a lot: *Butch Cassidy and the Sundance Kid* took in $102 million, ranking it among the twenty biggest ticket-sellers up to that time. It was eventually nominated for seven Oscars, including best picture and director, and it won four: best original screenplay, original song, original score, and cinematography. None of the actors were nominated—Dustin Hoffman and Jon Voight, who played the antihero buddies in *Midnight Cowboy*, took two of the five best actor slots, but both lost out to John Wayne for *True Grit*. But the thing worked out splendidly, and their agents and producers were already looking for something that would allow Newman and Redford to work together again.

IN A ballroom at Manhattan's Plaza Hotel, Newman sat one afternoon with two other stars, and they made a hell of a lineup: the number one box office star in America and Hollywood's reigning male sex symbol; the multimillion-selling recording artist who'd just won an Oscar in her first-ever film; and the number two box office star in America, also an Oscar winner, and an icon of the civil rights movement: Newman, Barbra Streisand, and Sidney Poitier.

It was June 11, 1969, and they had convened to sign contracts to form First Artists Production Company, a new business that would unite them as financiers, producers, stars, and distributors of films made outside the Hollywood studio system. There was nothing new about actors forming companies of their own to produce movies that they didn't feel the studios would want or know how to make. But this was a real murderer's row of talent and celebrity—with more stars to come, it was promised—and it made the business take notice. "As things now stand," *Variety* figured, "any one of the three can virtually write his own ticket. As a unit they pose an undeniable threat to the uneasy status quo in Hollywood filming."

Newman was vice president and secretary of the company, Poitier president, Streisand vice president and treasurer. As Newman explained, it represented a response to everything he felt was wrong and unfair about making movies:

It's a way to really exercise control of one's own films, a way to get rid of this great dinosaur of production and distribution we have now. The machinery takes a big bite for overhead and a bigger bite for distribution, and that isn't necessary. Why should the studios take all this money off the top? Who made up these rules, anyway? Sure, I have autonomy now. I can do pretty much as I please. But when it gets down to tricky stuff like the last cut of a film, that's where the control can get fuzzy. And that's where I want absolute control.

There was a precedent for all this: United Artists, a company founded by Charlie Chaplin, Douglas Fairbanks, D. W. Griffith, and Mary Pickford exactly fifty years earlier. That enterprise was also launched amid a splash of ballyhoo, and it was greeted with an immortal helping of skepticism when Richard Rowland, who ran Metro Pictures, declared, "So, the lunatics have taken charge of the asylum." It ended badly: the UA stars rarely worked for their own company, the films they did contribute to the communal effort tended to founder, and they finally lost the company altogether in 1951 when, ironically, it began a long run as a vital independent alternative to the older, established studios.

This new gang of lunatics was being chaperoned by Creative Management Associates president Freddie Fields, who had replaced John Foreman as Newman's agent and who had dreamed up the scheme more than two years prior. As Fields explained, each star had agreed to make three films for First Artists for no salary, working instead for a percentage of the gross, starting with the very first ticket sold. The films would be financed one-third by First Artists and two-thirds by an as-yet-to-be-determined distribution company, but the content of the films would be decided entirely by First Artists.* The company was also looking into television production and music recording and publishing. And it might consider a stock issuing down the line.

---

* The National General Company, a nationwide theater chain, wound up being First Artists' initial distribution partner, but it was soon replaced by Warner Bros.

Fields felt it was a "significant step in filmmaking." But when the company presented its bona fides to the Securities and Exchange Commission before making its stock offering public, it was ordered to tell prospective shareholders that its strategy of ceding creative control to artists—of handing the asylum keys to the lunatics—represented "a significant departure from traditional industry practice."

That was exactly true. But 1969 was the year of *Easy Rider, The Wild Bunch, Midnight Cowboy, Bob & Carol & Ted & Alice, Take the Money and Run, Medium Cool,* and *Z.* Traditional industry practice was falling apart, and First Artists looked less and less like a gamble. Within two years Steve McQueen joined the team. And then Dustin Hoffman. Newman and company might have been lunatics, but they had momentum.

Sixteen

IN MARCH 1971 BURT ROSEN AND DAVID WINTER, A PAIR OF TV producers who were at work on a project with Newman, attended an auction of movie memorabilia at Sotheby Parke Bernet's Los Angeles Hall, where two thousand items from the prop rooms of 20th Century–Fox were being sold. They had their eyes on a particular item and got into a heated bidding competition against composer Burt Bacharach and his wife, Angie Dickinson. Eventually Rosen and Winter won, paying $3,100 for the bicycle that Newman rode so charmingly and daringly in the "Raindrops Keep Fallin' on My Head" sequence of *Butch Cassidy*. The two producers made a gift of their prize to Joanne Woodward, who donated it the following month to a charity auction.

Maybe she didn't like bicycles. Maybe she didn't like clutter. Maybe she didn't like "Raindrops Keep Fallin' on My Head." Or maybe she didn't like—or didn't want to be reminded of—*Butch Cassidy and the Sundance Kid*. During the production of that film Newman began an affair with Nancy Bacon, a divorced Hollywood journalist whom 20th Century–Fox had sent to write a puff piece about the movie for magazine serialization. And rumors and publicity having to do with this liaison nearly scuttled the Newmans' marriage.

By Bacon's account, she and Newman spent several days together on the film's sets in Cuernavaca and Taxco—and nights in Newman's suite at a hotel then called the Vista Hermosa. When they were back in Los Angeles, they met in Bacon's apartment. There were periods when the affair cooled, but Newman kept coming back until midway through 1969, when he and Joanne briefly separated and he determined to repair the damage he'd done to his marriage. There were a few more secret liaisons, and then longer periods of absence. In time Bacon became disillusioned with the affair, and it died of its own inertia. "I finally said to myself, I can do better than this," she remembered. "I told him, 'You're always drunk, and you can't even make love.' I ended it."

The whole mess might have stayed between them had not Joyce Haber, a syndicated gossip columnist, announced in July that she'd heard "fascinating rumors, so far unchecked," that "the Paul Newmans are living apart, according to friends, and will soon get a divorce." In the next day's *Los Angeles Times*, the following half-page ad, which cost approximately $2,500 to publish, appeared:

(1) RECOGNIZING THE POWER OF THE PRESS —
(2) FEARING TO EMBARRASS AN AWESOME JOURNALIST —
(3) TERRIFIED TO DISAPPOINT MISS HABER AND HER
    READERS, WE WILL TRY TO ACCOMMODATE HER
    "FASCINATING RUMORS, SO FAR UNCHECKED" BY
    BUSTING UP OUR MARRIAGE EVEN THOUGH WE STILL
    LIKE EACH OTHER.

JOANNE & PAUL NEWMAN

This was a stunner, and it got folks talking. The Newmans' marriage, then eleven years along, was considered stable: all those kids, the famed Connecticut home, the films they'd worked on together, the collaborative success of *Rachel, Rachel*. It didn't seem right. Gossipy movie fan magazines had often tried to goose a few sales out of articles speculating that the Newmans were at odds with each other ("Shout by Shout: Paul Newman's Bitter Fights with His Wife"; "Strange Rumors About Hollywood's 'Happiest Marriage' ") or that forty-three-year-old Newman was feeling randy and seeking consolations outside the home ("Paul Newman's Just at That Age"; "Is Paul Newman's Joanne Too Possessive?"). Invariably, they all stopped short of actually announcing real trouble or accusing Newman of adultery. The Newmans were supposed to be examples. But this strange advertisement didn't so much squelch rumors as give people reason to wonder about them.

They didn't have to wait long for a fuller story. Later that year a gossip magazine published Bacon's tell-all about the affair, an article filled with details of Newman's life that had never before been printed and supported by a photo of Bacon and Newman looking quite chummy on the set of *Butch*. Saying that she felt the ad the Newmans had run was an unforgivable lie, Bacon shared an amazing portrait of Newman as a reckless, boozy, sneaky rat who was torn by impulses to act like a straight arrow and to career about like a rubber ball.

Bacon had been around Hollywood for a little while as a writer, an actress, and a scenester. A native of Washington state, she had been married to Don Wilson, one of the founding members of the surf guitar band the Ventures, and had a daughter by him. After their divorce she began running with a fast young Hollywood crowd. She'd been involved for a spell with Jay Sebring, the celebrity hairstylist (he had famously cut both Newman's and Steve McQueen's hair in modern styles) who was unlucky enough to be at Sharon Tate's house when it was attacked by Charles Manson's ghoulish minions. She had also been attached to Tommy Smothers and, when she started to hang around regularly at the Factory, had a flirtatious relationship with Robert F. Kennedy. Another beau, the producer Paul Monash, who was at work on *Butch Cassidy* and had a thing for her, was the guy who got her the writing assignment on his set.

And that was how she fell in with Newman. Everyone in Mexico knew about it. "Redford would kind of beard for us," Bacon remembered. "But we got out of the same hotel rooms and got into the same cars to go to the set." And the romance continued back home. "We were hot and heavy for about a year and a half," she said. "He was at my house almost every night for two or three weeks." He would return home, Bacon claimed, to see Joanne and the kids, to whom he explained his absence by saying that he was out making movies. But no such story would have worked to keep their affair hidden from their social circle. "It was the worst-kept secret in Hollywood," she said. "People used to joke about it: 'Paul may not go out for hamburger, but he sure goes out for Bacon.' "

Bacon wrote about the affair twice, each time revealing new details about the private Newman.* She knew what he drank (beers followed by scotch followed by more beers) and how much (a *lot*), what he drove (the VWs with the Porsche innards) and how (fast), how he dressed (jeans and moccasins, no socks), his favorite music (Bach), and details about the new film that he and Joanne had been shooting in New Orleans but that wouldn't premiere for more than a year (adapted from Robert Stone's novel *Hall of Mirrors*, it would be released as *WUSA*). She described his yearning and his lovemaking, his goofball jokes (he called himself "Mr. Sundance" when leaving messages for her), his dismissiveness toward his stardom ("I would say to him, 'Hey, Movie Star, make me a drink,' and he'd laugh"), and his obvious guilt about the affair. And she remembered his postcoital salutation: "It's heart attack time."

In her writing, Bacon measured herself against Joanne, bragging, "He left her at a party and came to my house . . . he missed a plane he was to catch with her because he was in my bed." But she recognized that she was on the outside looking in, a fact underscored for her once when she was dancing at the Factory and Newman walked in "with Joanne and about four or five of his six kids." And she knew too that she was destined to be dumped: "He was really a square. He was really sinning. And he was always drunk." So she moved house and went on with her life, even as he kept calling and visiting. And when she finally decided to end things by telling him, falsely, that she was getting married, he said, according to her account, "Great. Good luck. Hey—could we get together a couple of times more before you do it?"

This was stupefying stuff, and there wasn't apparently much that could be done about it. The Newmans didn't take out any ads to counter Bacon's assertions. They didn't sue her or the magazine that

---

* Newman earned an entire chapter in her gossipy 1975 autobiography *Stars in My Eyes . . . Stars in My Bed*. At the time, according to Bacon, the publisher's lawyers vetted all her claims about Newman by interviewing her friends. The stories stood up.

printed her accusations or the others who reported them. Rather, they went on vacation—without the kids—to London, their honeymoon site, as soon as production on their film wrapped.* Newman was still harboring guilty feelings about the failure of his first marriage. He wasn't going to give up a second one, even if it was he who had placed it in jeopardy.

Much of the work that went into mending things between them was undertaken, obviously, in private. But with their publicist, Warren Cowan, the Newmans hit on a strategy of guarded openness about their marriage with select press—especially women's magazines and female reporters from major news outlets. (In this way they directly countered Bacon's original story, which was written in the first person and explicitly addressed to an imagined woman reading it in a beauty salon.) Within a year of the Joyce Haber column and its unchecked rumors, the Newmans were regularly giving interviews to *Good Housekeeping*, *Redbook*, *McCall's*, *Ladies Home Journal*, *Cosmopolitan*, and once, *Playgirl*. They would share and be frank, but they would do so on their own terms and in venues of their own choosing.

For instance: "Joanne and I have had difficult, body-bending confrontations," Newman told Maureen Dowd some years later in *The New York Times Magazine*. "But we haven't surrendered. I've packed up and left a few times, and then I realize I have no place to go, and I'm back in ten minutes."

And: "Being Mrs. Paul Newman has its good and bad days," Joanne told *Good Housekeeping*. "Obviously, since we're still together, most of them have been good. But it hasn't been easy, and I don't think any valid relationship is."

As with *Rachel*, Newman demonstrated his loyalty by committing himself to Joanne's work. Almost everything he would produce or direct going forward would include her. And he learned to accommodate her interests and moods just as she had always tolerated his specific ways and tastes; he encouraged her love of ballet by attending dance

---

* That's how they happened to be in Grosvenor Square for the antiwar march at the U.S. embassy that fall.

recitals, by giving her gifts of ballet-inspired artworks, and by helping her to fund a dance company of her own.

It would often be praised as a fairy-tale marriage. And perhaps because it contained and overcame a dark and perilous episode, it was worthy of the name.

THAT FALL Newman took Joanne on a trip to San Francisco so that he could be fêted at the San Francisco Film Festival. One thousand folks at the Palace of Fine Arts theater watched a couple of hours of clips from his career—all of it, including *The Silver Chalice* and *WUSA*. Newman took questions afterward. There were parties—a private do in John Foreman's suite at the Mark Hopkins (Newman drank beer), then a hop up a hill somewhere to the mansion of some festival board members (Newman stopped the limo at a grocery store so he could grab a sixer), then another party someplace else, complete with a Black Watch Piper. Later in the weekend there was the premiere of a Newman-Foreman production, *Puzzle of a Downfall Child*, in which photographer Jerry Schatzberg directed his girlfriend, Faye Dunaway, as a fashion model who makes it big and then has an emotional breakdown.

As usual, the sheer presence of Newman wowed the locals. At the fancy party a society matron who'd been heard sniffing about "movie people" went absolutely speechless when introduced to him. In the hotel the staff were so dazzled that they sought relics of him. "They even took the dental floss out of the trash can," a friend recalled. "I don't think many people could handle that as well as Paul." He demonstrated a bit of heroism, or at least Eagle Scout–ishness, when he was visiting Ghirardelli Square with Joanne and reunited a lost girl with her mother; the woman, who was in a panic, was so stunned by the appearance of Newman with her daughter on his shoulders that she stammered a thank-you and walked away without the child. "Haven't you forgotten something?" Newman asked her.

NEWMAN WAS inordinately proud of *WUSA*, which he several times described as the "most important" picture he'd ever done. A story about race, social unrest, changing morals, and political demagoguery in New Orleans, it had cost $4.8 million to make, partly because so much of it was shot on location. It had meant to shake up America's sense of itself as a nation being overrun by tyranny, but it was a clumsy, shrill, confused, and unappealing picture that barely got a release. Newman had fought Paramount Pictures to get the thing made, accusing executives at the studio of cowardice. "There aren't many smart people who have power," he declared to the studio's vice president for production, Peter Bart, "and you have to use your power to advance truth. What's money and power worth if you don't do that?" But Newman was one of very few people convinced of the film's incomprehensible sexual and racial politics. And nobody found the film entertaining. Even the genteel Vincent Canby went out of his way to slap at it, writing an essay about its half-baked politics and excoriating its "self-conscious pretensions" and "narrative incoherence."

Still, Newman was fond of Robert Stone's vision and language, and he was drawn into another film with a similar pedigree, a true American epic with as much to say about the national character and the changing times as it did about nature, family, physical daring, literary narrative, and indeed English prose itself. *Sometimes a Great Notion* was the second novel of the wrestler, vagabond, poet, and prankster Ken Kesey, a brawny, earthy, foxy American original cut, in some ways, like Newman himself: handsome, unpretentious, educated, and as connected as someone of his talent, position, and fame could be to the common ground from which he had sprung. Various filmmakers had been struggling for a couple years to bring his classic first novel, *One Flew Over the Cuckoo's Nest,* to the screen (there had been a successful Broadway adaptation starring Kirk Douglas in 1963), but that task seemed a lark compared to attempting to make a film of *Notion,* a sprawling novel of dense stylistic experimentation and shaggy, parochial narrative.

In prose as thick and dreamy as Faulkner's, Kesey told the story of the Stampers, an iconoclastic Oregon logging family who insist on fulfilling their timber contracts even when all their neighbors, who belong to a union, have put down their chain saws in a strike. In the midst of this labor crisis, the Stamper family is tearing apart. Flinty old paterfamilias Henry is laid up with a broken arm; his gung-ho son, Hank, and nephew, Joe Ben, keep up the business; their obliging, subservient wives feed and bed them like maids, without complaint; the delicate household balance is shattered by the arrival of Leland, Hank's estranged half brother, who is there to demand his place in the family in the wake of his mother's death.

It's a notoriously complex text and hard to imagine pared down for the screen: Newman had initially put Stewart Stern to the task of adapting it, but the version that was eventually filmed was credited to another veteran screenwriter, John Gay. An impressive cast was assembled: Newman as Hank Stamper, Henry Fonda as his dad, Lee Remick as his wife, Richard Jaeckel as his cousin, and Michael Sarrazin as his long-lost brother. They would shoot in the summer of 1970 in the southern Oregon towns of Newport and Lincoln City, where the Siletz and Yaquina rivers supported the local fishing and logging economies: just the sort of places the Stampers—and indeed Kesey—called home. Newman and Foreman entrusted the project to director Richard Colla, a relative novice who had a single feature film and a fair bit of episodic TV to his credit. (He had worked with George Kennedy, which was perhaps how he came to Newman's attention.)

Newman planned to spend the summer commuting from Oregon to Los Angeles, where he was having fun running a Formula One race car around Ontario Speedway, taking driving lessons, and competing, in a low-stress way, in pro-am fund-raisers for charity. In Oregon he rented a house on a spit of land stuck into the Pacific and had an Irish wolfhound for company, as well as a train of Hollywood visitors, including Marlon Brando and John Derek. Scott Newman would be there as well, working with the second filming unit between semesters at Washington College in Chestertown, Maryland, a small liberal arts school actually founded by George Washington. And Joanne and the girls visited a fair bit.

Newman had gone up early to Oregon to get in with the loggers and absorb their work ways and personalities. As usual, he committed himself physically to the job, even learning to climb eighty-foot-tall trees with a full load of chain saws, axes, and safety equipment—despite a phobia of heights. "It takes a lot of acting to cover up that fear," he said. (Perhaps to help, he was hitting the sauce: whiskey, and lots of it, on top of his daily diet of beers. And he had a new trick: crushing beer cans with his feet so that they formed clanky shells that stuck to his shoes.) His role included a scene in a motorcycle race at a loggers' picnic, so he was learning the ins and outs at the feet of champion desert racer J. N. Roberts. He killed time roaring around on a motorcycle right on the beach outside his rented home.

The shoot began in late June 1970, and right away there were problems. Colla had decided to employ a fluid camera style to impart some of the savor of Kesey's prose in the visuals. But his approach was working against the actors, who felt that he was emphasizing their position relative to the camera more than their interaction with one another. After two weeks Newman and Foreman weren't happy with what they were getting from the young director, and they put him on notice that he had to change his technique.

The big test would come when Colla filmed one of the dining room scenes in the Stamper house—big, noisy, manly affairs with old Henry scarfing food and cracking wise and mean, Hank and Joe Ben joining in, the kids all carrying on, and the women doing the serving. On the set that day was Ted Mahar, a reporter from the *Oregonian*, the state's biggest daily paper. As he recalled it, Colla had contrived a long, elaborate tracking shot with the camera gliding above the actors' heads and coming to rest on specific faces as they spoke. "It required intricate planning and rehearsal," Mahar recalled, and the crew had to "pull back a wall so the camera could orbit the table in one smooth take."

They did it again and again and never got it right. And the next morning, according to Mahar, "Colla wasn't even in Oregon anymore." During the evening Newman and Foreman had fired the director, and now they had to replace him. Although he had not chosen the material for himself to direct, and had not prepared at all to fill that role, Newman agreed to do it himself. As he put it, "Rather than close down and find another one [director], and then have him learn about the whole logging thing, it just seemed better for me to take over."

Newman, who the previous day had been happy enough to have a reporter around that he'd offered Mahar a beer from the fridge in the

Stamper kitchen, was now stuck somewhere by a phone, working out the situation with Foreman and the money people back at Universal. Mahar passed the time talking with Fonda and cinematographer Richard Moore and learned the whole story. Mahar wrote up his hot scoop at his hotel before dictating it over the phone to his editors. And then he went back to Portland, where Foreman called him the next day after seeing it in print, "furious to the point of tears."

Newman meanwhile enlisted the help of George Roy Hill, who flew up to Oregon to look over all of Colla's footage and give Newman a sense of how he could incorporate it into the stuff he was preparing to shoot. As Newman recalled, "He said, 'You need twenty setups, you need a point of view on the kid, you need his walking-away shot, and so forth.' And then he got in his airplane and left."

Stuck in this stressful situation, Newman plowed ahead and went a little crazy. "To act and direct at the same time is like sticking a gun in your mouth," he said. "I don't think I'd ever do it again." He coated his exhaustion and stress with drink. "I drank whiskey a lot," he admitted years later. "For a while it really screwed me up. There are periods of my life in which I don't take any particular pride . . . I gave up hard liquor because I simply couldn't handle it. That was my sledge-hammer. We were finishing shooting *Notion*. I don't know if it was the pressure of the picture, but I was *really* out of line." He imperiled the film further by cracking up on a motorcycle, busting his left ankle, and bringing the production briefly to a halt. He flew to Los Angeles for X rays, and as it turned out to be merely a bad sprain, he actually resumed riding. Sue Bronson, a novelist who visited the set to do research for a book about a Hollywood film crew shooting a movie on location, saw Newman skid and nearly dump a bike on the beach one day while his foot was still in a cast; he came up unhurt, laughing at his clumsiness and urging her with a shushing gesture to keep what she'd seen to herself.

Bronson was on the set a few days later when the most memorable scene in the film was shot. In the aftermath of a landslide, Joe Ben finds himself trapped in the mud of the estuary underneath the weight of a fallen tree; Hank tries a number of ways to free his cousin, but the tide is coming in and he's working against it. After several exhausting efforts, the two realize that they must wait for help; but the tide is liable to drown Joe Ben before help comes; the stillness and strangeness of the setting become almost intoxicating, and they break into laughter. When the water finally swallows Joe Ben, Hank keeps him alive by breathing gulps of air into his mouth. But that too becomes impossible after a while, and Joe Ben drowns.

The incredible drama and pathos of the scene, and its implicit theme of the power of nature over man, was what recommended the project to Newman in the first place. "Our company really bought the book because of that one scene," he said. "To me the film was worth doing because of the impact there." The close-up work was done in a large water tank, Bronson recalled; Newman and Jaeckel, forced in effect to kiss each other over the course of several hours of work, "could not stop laughing." But the finished scene played magnificently, and Jaekel would eventually get an Oscar nomination for his work in it.*

Newman had hopes for the picture: "It wasn't great, but it certainly wasn't a *lousy* movie," he said. The finished film wasn't released until the spring of 1972, a full eighteen months later. Reviews were mixed: admiring the effort, the naturalistic acting, the scenery, and the scene of Jo Ben's death, they generally cited it as muddled and bland. Vincent Canby, who championed the film in the *New York Times* more than once, called it "happily impure" and compared it favorably to classic films about workingmen by Howard Hawks and John Ford. But the studio had no clue what to do with it even after all that time. "Those schmucks at Universal released it in sporadic spurts across the country, mostly at drive-ins," Newman complained. "They killed it before it got a chance to attract any serious attention." He conceded that the title didn't help: "*Sometimes a Great Notion* didn't give any idea of what it was about." And he did achieve a milestone of sorts with it: on November 8, 1972, it was the very first attraction presented on the world's first pay-cable station, Home Box Office, or HBO.

---

* Even more impressively, an Oroville, California, man who had seen the film would actually save the life of his eight-year-old daughter in 1985 by using the same technique until he could free her from beneath the family's houseboat.

By the time *Notion* was finally released, Newman already had another picture out, *Pocket Money*, a lackluster attempt to make Newman–Redford hay out of the more dubious seed of a Newman–Lee Marvin pairing. A comedy about the half-baked get-not-too-rich-not-too-quick schemes of a pair of chums who are kind of grifters and kind of cowboys, it was adapted from J. P. S. Brown's novel *Jim Kane* by Terrence Malick. Stuart Rosenberg was directing, and John Foreman was producing under the aegis of First Artists, marking that company's first screen credit—more than two years after the starry announcement of its formation.

Much of the picture was shot on location in Santa Fe; when Joanne and the girls rode through on a train to New York, the production company arranged for it to slow down sufficiently for them to wave at Newman as they passed through. Newman and Marvin hadn't worked together since *The Rack*, a full seventeen years earlier, and they didn't bond. English photographer Terry O'Neill visited the set to shoot some publicity snaps, and he found Marvin on edge. "He'd decided everyone was against him," O'Neill recalled. "He was always being cast as the ugly one. It was difficult standing up next to Paul Newman, who was so fantastically good-looking."

Vogue magazine sent a young reporter to the set for a few days, and she turned in an insightful and beautifully written piece. Her name was Candice Bergen, and she captured Newman with great vividness: "His face is so handsome you almost start laughing. It's like a joke . . . He is a physical phenomenon. We should bequeath him to the Museum of Natural History." She was a careful observer, noting his nail-biting and his complaints of insomnia, reporting that he had been calling himself "the Old Fox" around the set, "A nickname," she recalled, that "he originated and no one else ever took up. Consequently, his calling, 'Hey, get the Old Fox a beer,' is met with people shifting positions to see who the Old Fox is." She came to a wise understanding of his acting too: "His working technique is rigidly logistical and linear. He is an intellectual actor, dealing in motivation, and uncomfortable in an extemporaneous or improvised situation. His style is subtle and cerebral. And he is constantly refining it. 'The Master of Underplay' they call him."

Marvin was less impressed with his costar, though, and when the picture was released, he complained to a reporter that Newman had "finessed" him into a subordinate role in the film. Newman was stunned to hear such a claim: "*I* finessed him? I never even looked at the picture." Nor did most anybody else: the film had a lazy charm—Newman's obliquely comic performance was like a pared-down version of his Harry Frigg of a couple of years earlier—but it had no real bite or energy. The reviews were tepid and so was the box office, and the two uncomfortably matched stars never worked together again.

NEWMAN FOLLOWED Joanne and the girls back home to Connecticut and a chance to reunite the director of *Rachel, Rachel* with the film's star and costar on a new movie. *The Effect of Gamma Rays on the Man-in-the-Moon Marigolds* was the unlikely title of Paul Zindel's play about Beatrice Hunsdorfer, a dumpy, bitter mother of two teenage girls, one a misfit epileptic, the other a brilliant science scholar. Beatrice is mean and awful and lives, like an especially acrid Tennessee Williams character, on a diet of sour and selectively sweetened memories and impossible schemes for bettering her situation. Newman and John Foreman had acquired the Pulitzer Prize–winning material specifically for Joanne to star in and Newman to direct. But even given the success of the play and of *Rachel, Rachel,* they were unable to get funding from a studio unless Newman signed away his right to the final cut of the film. ("Perhaps if I played Beatrice and Joanne directed there would have been more interest," he joked.)

The film was shot through the late winter and the spring of 1972 in the abandoned parsonage of a deconsecrated Hungarian church in Bridgeport, Connecticut, about fifteen minutes' drive from the Newmans' home. To add to the familial atmosphere, fourteen-year-old Nell, once again working under her childhood nickname Nell Potts, was given the featured role of Matilda, Beatrice's younger, more gifted girl. (Early on there had been thought of having Nell play the older sister and Lissy, then eleven, the younger, but the role of Ruth went instead to a debuting young actress, Roberta Wallach, the daughter of Eli Wallach and Anne Jackson.)

Despite the family atmosphere, the shoot wasn't entirely happy. It rained a lot, continually causing scheduling backups and changes. More important, Joanne didn't seem to much like the project—the wardrobe, the awful hair, the makeup that made her look worse than if she'd simply worn none, the dreary set of the Hunsdorfer house, the hopelessness and boorishness and negativity of the character. As Newman later recalled, in all their years working together as costars or as director-actor, it was the only time she let herself get overwhelmed by a role: "Joanne *never* brings a character home with her. Never. Except once. She brought home Beatrice Hunsdorfer . . . She brought home that—that miscreant—that vulgar—that punishing—that *impossible* woman. She just hated that woman so much, hated what it brought out in her, and she brought home that—that hostility *every single night.* And I would just *flee.*"

Again, as with *Rachel*, he tried to keep the atmosphere on the set lively and collegial. Perhaps taking a cue from Martin Ritt, he wore a jumpsuit a lot of days—comfortable, equipped with plenty of pockets, and definitely not stylish or showy. He allowed visitors: a writer from the *Christian Science Monitor*; a couple of Yale students making a documentary about the production; and English journalist Charles Hamblett, whose interviews with Newman in Bridgeport and at the house in Westport would form the basis of a biography that appeared in 1975—the very first book about him.

But all that effort to build goodwill for the picture couldn't overcome the forces working against it: the indifferent studio, some brittle material, the opaque title, and, especially, the lukewarm critical reception, which Newman resented to the point of telling a reporter from *Rolling Stone* that Vincent Canby's mixed review in the *New York Times* was "bullshit." The film had its champions: Roger Ebert called it "hard-edged enough to be less depressing than it sounds," and *Variety* declared, "Newman has gotten it all together here as a director, letting the story and the players unfold with simplicity, restraint and discernment." Joanne won an acting prize at the Cannes Film Festival for the film, but somehow it was like it never happened; decades later, it would be, with *The Rack* and *WUSA*, one of the hardest-to-find things he ever did.

HE HIMSELF wasn't hard to find. By the time *Gamma Rays* rushed through theaters, Newman had already played another part—a bigger and more public one than he had in years. Throughout the early part of the year and into the summer and the fall, he was active in the presidential campaign, trying to stop the reelection of Richard Nixon, first by supporting Nixon's upstart Republican opponent Pete McCloskey and then by backing the Democratic challenger, George McGovern.

Even though the two men were in different parties, they were rivals in New Hampshire. McGovern was running against a group of Democrats including Edmund Muskie of Maine and Sam Yorty, the mayor of Los Angeles. But he was courting the McCarthy voters of four years prior—the independent, antiwar, even libertarian-leaning New Hampshirites, the same sector to whom McCloskey, a congressman from California's Bay Area, was appealing in the name of casting direct votes against Nixon and the war. Using New Hampshire as a kind of referendum on the war was how activists toppled Johnson in 1968, and McGovern's camp feared that the enticement to do the same to Nixon would lure its natural constituency into voting as Republicans and ceding the Democratic primary to a more moderate candidate.

So oddly, the two candidates of different parties fought it out that winter for the hearts and minds of the old McCarthy gang. Newman, one of its most famous faces, was more convinced by McCloskey. (As a principled contrarian, it suited him to tilt at windmills in politics.) He had lobbied Nixon to install a Department of Peace in the cabinet; he had joined the likes of Ramsey Clark, John Lindsay, and Tom Seaver (!) in forming a Citizens Committee for the Amendment to End the War; and just the previous year he'd become a director of the Center for the Study of Democratic Institutions in Santa Barbara. He didn't mind speaking out for a hopeless cause. "It was important Nixon got his wrist slapped," he said later of McCloskey's effort. From his Connecticut base, he hopped up for three or four days in New Hampshire, making scores of appearances. But when McCloskey, inevitably, got his head handed to him, Newman, inevitably, returned to the Democratic fold.

He skipped the convention in Miami that year but showed up at Madison Square Garden in June as a celebrity usher at the Warren Beatty–produced "Together with McGovern" rally. He was in fairly amazing company: Julie Christie, Raquel Welch, Gene Hackman, Dustin Hoffman, Shirley MacLaine, Bette Davis, Jack Nicholson, and Goldie Hawn were among the other very famous escorts who led the more generous guests—and some lucky stiffs from among the mob—to their seats. Simon and Garfunkel; Peter, Paul and Mary; and Dionne Warwick would all perform. Big night.

Somebody had the idea to lead all the celebrity "seat escorts" out in a kind of introductory parade rather than have them just be present when folks showed up. And somebody else, maybe Newman himself, had the idea to stick Newman in the upper deck among the real people. So when he started to climb to the cheap seats, beer in hand, he became the focus of a small melee, with men and women mobbing him, despite the pair of policemen keeping watch. "My God, they're going to kill him," someone said aloud, and the cops ran him into an elevator and got him backstage where he belonged. Before long they took the precaution of wrangling all the celebrities to safety.

During the general campaign Newman appeared in fund-raising TV ads for the Democratic Party, becoming so visible and persuasive that Nixon's backroom operatives watched him. In June special White House counsel Charles Colson wrote a memo to John Dean, the president's counsel, naming twenty people in public and behind-the-scenes life who should be considered enemies of the president and explaining why. The list included such politicians as Allard Lowenstein, John Conyers, and Ron Dellums, the journalists Daniel Schorr and Mary McGrory, and bizarrely, nineteenth of the twenty, "Paul Newman, California; radic-lib causes. Heavy McCarthy involvement '68. Used effectively in nationwide TV commercials. '72 involvement certain."

There was a longer list, but in the view of the most nefarious guys on Nixon's team, these were the real biggies: the twenty fund-raisers, agitators, and conspirators most liable to bring the president down. In

1973, when the list came to the attention of the public during the Watergate investigation, it was a shock to learn the extent of the Nixon team's paranoia. People who found their names on the roster had good reason to feel rattled: who'd been watching them, and when, and why? But, too, there was a bit of status in being singled out, a recognition that one was big enough for one's voice to be heard. The longer list cited more than two hundred enemies, a mere ten of whom were "celebrities," a group in which Newman was joined by Carol Channing, Bill Cosby, Jane Fonda, Dick Gregory, Steve McQueen, Gregory Peck, Tony Randall, Barbra Streisand, and, bizarrely, Joe Namath—none of whom appeared on Colson's annotated list.

It obviously wasn't a thorough account of liberally active entertainers and athletes. (Shirley MacLaine was excluded, and Joanne revealed, "She's furious!") But it was, Newman would say ever after, his proudest achievement. He cited it in official biographies and public-relations announcements over the years. It touched, in fact, his very sense of family. Speaking of his father's politics, he declared, "My one great regret is that he didn't live to see his son named number 19 on the White House Enemies List of Richard Nixon. My dad would have been puffed up over that!" On the anniversary of the list's appearance, he told Daniel Schorr, "I have been fortunate in my lifetime to be tapped for a reasonable abundance of honors, but none delighted me or elevated me in the eyes of my children more."

IT WAS odd that he would associate a quirky bit of fame like this with his children's impression of him. If anything, the kids were overly aware of how famous he was. "When they go anywhere with Paul," Joanne said, "they may be pushed aside literally by fans who want to get near him. As if they don't count at all; as if they're nothing in themselves. And then think how disturbing it must be for a girl to know that her friends are madly in love with her father!" (This was no joke: Susan remembered that at age twelve a friend asked her if she wanted to "rape" her father. "Do *you* want to rape *your* father?" she replied.)

Joanne understood that it was exceedingly hard for the two sets of kids to grow up on two coasts, in multiple homes, at multiple schools, in a bohemian household with celebrity parents. "Children like a normal life," she said. "They don't like oddity. Our children have all gone through that stage of really hanging out with their close normal friends and wanting to be at their houses, where Mommy and Daddy are home and people don't come up to them and ask them for an autograph."

But there was more to it. As Newman himself admitted, "I didn't have any talent to be a father." He had never really felt a connection with Art Newman, and when required to forge bonds with six young people, he was at a loss. "The process of really connecting is very long and painful for me," he confessed, even with his own kids. "I sometimes have a hard time talking because I have a hard time talking to anybody." Add to that the fact that he tended to brood about his work when it was approaching, and then disappear for months on end to do it, and then overcompensate for his absence with effusions of generosity, and there was a real potential for disastrous parenting.

"When they were growing up, I wasn't there much," he acknowledged later. "I was very inconsistent with them. I was all over the place, too loving one minute, too distant the next. One day they were flying on the Concorde, and the next day they were expected to do their own laundry. It was very hard for them to get a balance." Despite the privileges they were granted, the kids went through rough patches.

For Joanne's girls, it was a little bit better, if only because they were younger and lived more of the time with their father than did Jackie's children. Nell changed schools quite often and wasn't terribly interested in academics, but she was brilliant with animals, especially birds. She'd become absorbed by in falconry at age eight and appeared in a TV special about eagles and hawks four years later; by the time she was fourteen, she had been specially trained in handling birds of prey and had been granted a rare license to keep a hawk as a pet. A few years after that, she was working as an ornithological researcher out in the field in Idaho. (Her acting career was limited to working with her parents, who had forbidden her from even auditioning for the role of Reagan in *The Exorcist* when the opportunity arose.) Lissy, eleven in 1972, was into horses, and Clea was still just a little girl of eight; neither would ever stray too far outside the lines.

But Jackie's kids were another story. Scott wasn't doing anything especially permanent or promising by his early twenties; he drifted in and out of private high schools and attended college sporadically. Far more interesting to him was the sort of neck-risking stuff that his dad enjoyed. He was tall and strapping—bigger than his dad—and handsome, though not as shockingly as his father. Susan, also not much for school, had thoughts of acting and was involved, to the dismay of her parents and stepparents, with a much older guy. Stephanie was artistic too, with craft skills and a love of building and making things; like her brother and sister, she didn't stick with her schooling, though she did attend some college.

In part the woes of the older kids had to do with being the children of divorce and simply being young people at a time when a lot of young people were feeling troubled or confused by the changing world. And, of course, they weren't the three little blond girls with the Oscar-winning mommy. So they had to feel somewhat like outsiders even when they were in rooms of their own in their father's various homes. Joanne admitted that she had a difficult relationship with Jackie's children. "I think that I experimented on them to their detriment," she said, "and maybe to the betterment of *my* children. We are all six friends, but we've had some rough times. I mean, Scott and I didn't speak for several years. He was going through difficult times, and I resented the fact that he wasn't standing on his own feet and was using Paul. That made me angry, for Paul. And Susan and I had a to-do, and now Susan and I are very close."

Like Newman, she wasn't afraid to take at least some blame for some of the kids' problems. "I had a baby because that's what you did, right?" she revealed. "You had a baby. I didn't know anything about it; I was scared to death. I still don't like children. I don't like children. *I . . . don't . . . like . . . children!* I like my own children; I occasionally like other people's children. But I don't like babies per se." And yet there she was with six of them to see to and a public career that required that she be more vain and egoistical than an ordinary working mother would have to be. It was a poor mix. "My career has suffered because of the children," she said, "and my children have suffered because of my career . . . The only child I have raised out of the six children, three of whom are mine, is Clea. She is the only child I didn't immediately turn over to a nanny—while I went off to make a movie. I suffered great guilts."

But she made sure that Newman took on his share of the burdens, feelings of inadequacy included. "Sometimes I come home," he said, "and there's this woman wandering around the house muttering 'What am I doing cooking for seven people? What the hell am I doing?' " And worse, when he would insist on a little time off after a movie job, to go drinking and fishing and racing cars, he often did so without recognizing that he was offering his wife the merest short end of a stick. "For chrissakes," she complained to a reporter once, "he has been gone all fall on location with his new movie and then he comes home for two weeks, you know, like King Faisal, and then off he goes again on vacation. I said, 'When do I get my vacation?' "

He learned to make space for her needs—gladly, even. Having severely tested his wife at least once, having become wealthy and given up hard liquor and begun to talk about himself as an Old Fox, he settled into his marriage as a staple of his life and became, at nearly fifty, the sort of old married man who listened to his wife and usually answered "yes dear" when she spoke. And as long as she let him raise a little hell with the boys now and then, they were both content.

Part Five

Seventeen

ACK IN 1969, ON THE HEELS OF MAKING *Winning,* NEWMAN treated himself to a brand-new Corvette Sting Ray, and he drove it from Westport to Lime Rock, a quarry town in the Berkshire foothills of northwest Connecticut. His destination was Lime Rock Park, a 325-acre racetrack that had been built on the site of a gravel pit about a decade prior. The track was available once a week for anybody who wanted to pay a fee and test out their wheels or their driving skills. Newman had a yen to do both, but he didn't want to look like a fool. So he approached Jim Daley, who ran the track, and asked him for some pointers. Daley in turn introduced him to Bob Sharp, a racer, auto dealer, and racing-team owner who often gave driving lessons to wealthy guys with a jones to go fast.

One thing Sharp wasn't was a film buff; introduced to Newman, he reacted to him as if he was just another guy, which naturally Newman loved. "The name didn't register, ring a bell, whatever," Sharp explained. He gave Newman some tips, and he treated him with no special deference—"This is not a publicity stunt," he warned his new pupil, once he realized who he was. Newman, always an apt and determined student, learned and thrived. "He was higher than a cloud," Sharp remembered. "All of a sudden a vehicle becomes the medium that lets you show that athlete you want to be."

If he'd merely been exposed to the racing bug during the making of *Winning,* now Newman had caught it for good. Back in California working on film projects, he ran some laps at the Ontario Motor

Speedway and wound up taking a spot on the board of directors of the track, along with other celebrities who liked driving such as Kirk Douglas and Dick Smothers. In the spring and summer of 1970, when he was working on *Sometimes a Great Notion* in Oregon, he returned to Ontario as often as possible and drove in a race to raise money for charity along with James Garner, Steve McQueen, Robert Redford, Robert Wagner, Pancho Gonzalez, and a complement of race-world superstars.

For most of those other actors, racing was a rush and a goof: they did it only occasionally and for fun. Newman, though, was getting more serious. In late 1970 he traveled throughout the United States and even to Germany, visiting a variety of tracks and driving a variety of cars on them; he had a small film crew in tow, with an eye toward turning the footage into a TV special.* In the summer of 1971 he again found time to get out to Lime Rock and Ontario and other tracks, and his driving was showing steady signs of improvement.

He was well and truly caught up in it: it was a real hobby, to rival beer drinking as his favorite pursuit. And it was an escape from Hollywood and a houseful of kids, carrying the savor of danger and thrills, steeped in macho liveliness and male camaraderie. "Some people play golf," he said. "I like cars. It's just kicky, very natural. It may not offer as much exercise as some sports, but I love it."

Joanne, predictably, was made anxious by his choosing to risk his neck like this—and at an age where most drivers would concede that they were losing sharpness of vision and reflexes. "She thinks it's the silliest thing in the world," Newman said. "It's also very scary to her, and she doesn't much care for it." But that didn't deter him. Nor did the very real specter of life-threatening injuries. The columnist Earl Wilson visited Newman and his producing partner, John Foreman, that year, and the talk turned to motor sports. "It is dangerous, isn't it?" Wilson asked.

---

* The final product, *Once Upon a Wheel*, was produced and directed by Burt Rosen and David Winter—the fellows who bought Joanne the *Butch Cassidy* bicycle—and aired on national TV in April 1971.

"Oh, something could break, I suppose," Newman replied. "But as for driving, I'm not off the road a lot."

"Two drivers we used in *Winning* got killed," Foreman interjected.

"Not in the picture," Newman shot back. "They went on to another race and got killed."

"They *did* get killed," Foreman replied.

But Newman wasn't afraid of the potential harm that could come to him; like the terrier to which he was so fond of comparing himself, he had the scent of auto racing and was determined to go after it.

IN LATE 1971 Newman approached Bob Sharp with a proposition: he would lease a Datsun 510 race car from Sharp and pay to have it prepared and maintained by his mechanics. Thus equipped, Newman planned to devote himself in the summer of 1972 to driving on the Sports Car Club of America circuit, in which amateur competitors raced in a half-dozen regions of the country in order to accumulate points that would qualify them for a series of national championship races held annually outside Atlanta. He went to the SCCA training schools in Connecticut and New Hampshire and was admitted to the rolls as a driver.

That summer he entered a number of races at Lime Rock and took the same sort of attitude toward them as he had toward sessions at the Actors Studio twenty years before: watching, absorbing, going step-by-step through his paces. Sam Posey, a professional driver, didn't think much of Newman's skill at the time: "He drove it smoothly—and slowly—seemingly oblivious of the other cars around him. He rarely fought for a position."

But Newman, knowing his own learning curve, stuck to his plan. "Like everything else," he'd say of his driving,

> it took a long time. I really don't have any natural talent for any of that stuff, and I suspect the guys on the circuit were calling me a real balloon foot. I'm a very slow learner. The same with acting. But one thing is interesting to learn in acting: you cannot let it affect you when people laugh at you. If you don't take chances in

rehearsals, you might just as well get out of the business. You've got to have enough courage to fall on your ass and not pay any attention to what the people are saying.

He took that philosophy to the track with him that summer. "I particularly wanted to avoid the trap of getting in over my head just to satisfy what other people might have thought I should be doing," he explained.

> There are a lot of guys who would have jumped in at the deep end, and I was determined not to do that. I'm a slow study. I knew that before I started . . . But I'm not dumb, and when I got the car I was determined to learn my craft at whatever speed seemed sensible. I knew I had my way of doing things, so it never really bothered me. What *did* bother me was that it took me so long to get going. The first few times I had the car on the track I was having a lot of fun with it—before it dawned on me that I really wasn't very good.

By 1973 he was confident enough to enter more races around New England and at the Nelson Ledges raceway, about an hour southeast of Cleveland. (When he ran there, he often made a stop in Shaker Heights to visit his mom.) He managed to qualify for that fall's SCCA championships—the Runoffs, as they were called—at the Road Atlanta raceway. But he didn't fare well, skidding out into a dirt back in a practice run, in full view of a film crew, and finishing ninth in his class.

The following year movie obligations limited his ability to get back to Lime Rock and accumulate enough points to make it to the Runoffs. But he found other racing outlets—and got in a little too deep. In February he drove in a Porsche against the pros in the International Race of Champions at Daytona Speedway in Florida; he was a catastrophe, spinning out on the first turn, causing another driver to spin out later, and finally blowing his engine on just the sixth lap. (To make matters worse, the racer A. J. Foyt called him "Steve"—an obvious dig suggesting that Newman didn't drive as well as Steve McQueen.)

He could squeeze in only the occasional race that summer, but in September he took on a truly foolish challenge. As part of a team of four drivers that included Graham Hill, who had twice won the championship of Formula 1, the most prestigious auto circuit in the world, Newman went out to the Bonneville Salt Flats in Utah in order to attempt to break seventeen speed records that had been set ages before and were rarely challenged because they were in such obscure categories.

The North American Racing Team, which drove Ferraris, sponsored the strange effort, and they had managed to bring Ragú spaghetti sauce on as a sponsor and CBS television along to film it for a special. Newman balked at the latter: "I'm not a professional driver and I don't pretend to be as good as Graham . . . Just racing around out here with them is fun. But doing it in front of a national television audience where I'm the slow guy—or maybe I'm the guy who breaks the car— that's showing my butt in a way that I'm not prepared to do." Eventually his publicist, Warren Cowan, came out to Utah and negotiated a deal with CBS, allowing for Newman to be filmed in certain conditions.

In retrospect, he may have wished they hadn't reached an agreement. He wasn't driving badly, but the open course was pebbly and featureless and marked only by stakes with flags on them. Compared to the paved and maintained courses he'd been driving on, it was "like driving on the moon," he told a reporter. "Like nothing I expected." He wasn't able to get up to the same speeds as Hill and the other pros, and his pride was hurting, until Hill pointed out, "Frankly, I'm bloody glad you're not as fast as I am!" Still, he knew he'd stretched too far. "It really was a foul ball," he confessed later. "I didn't exactly drench myself with glory."

The team suffered mechanical problems and had to settle for breaking only five of the low-hanging records they were shooting for. The only consolation Newman took away from the experience was the sheer pleasure of being among other members of the racing fraternity in a faraway location: hanging out at the Hideaway Lounge in Wendover, Utah, drinking beer and shooting pool and telling crude jokes and laughing and whatnot. Inevitably he drew a crowd of local gawkers—one woman was seen retrieving his discarded apple core from a wastebasket. But the folks at the bar didn't seem to think he was a big deal, and that pleased him immensely.

Indeed, as much as the driving, he seemed truly to love the atmosphere of racing—the vagabonding travel from one track to another in regular annual rhythms, the joking around in the pits and the garages, the long days of hanging out inside or outside or even on top of motor homes drinking beer and talking about cars and races and nothing in particular. At first he was considered a dilettante and a freak by a lot of the drivers and spectators, who harbored some resentment against a fellow with his money and creaky skills barging into their small world. "Sure he won," griped a spectator at Lime Rock to a reporter. "So what. He's got the best car money can buy. That's a class for little guys, and he's driving a car set up by Bob Sharp. Most of those other guys set up their own car in their backyard."

But nobody who was around him much in the racing world ever felt he pulled rank or expected special treatment. Skip Barber, a veteran SCCA racer and champ who operated a driving school at Lime Rock, said, "There's an awful strong sense of entitlement around Lime Rock. Everybody acts like it's theirs. He didn't do that. He was good for Lime Rock, and in turn people didn't bother him. The road-racing community was good that way when it came to him."

He did what he could to blend in, hiding his celebrity by racing under the name P. L. Newman. And as his driving improved, and as he demonstrated to members of the racing world that he was serious about learning the craft and not interested in publicity, his stature among them rose, and he became one of the boys. He swapped an ongoing series of practical jokes with SCCA racing rival Bob Tullius. Once he had a garbage truck painted with Tullius's colors and number and arranged for it to take a ceremonial lap on the track before a race. Another time he hired an airplane to drag a banner through the sky over a raceway bearing the legend "Tullius Gobbles"; when Tullius pointed out how upset his mother would be to see such a lewd message, the plane returned the next day with a banner that read "Tullius: Call Momma."

He barbecued steaks and his famous hamburgers for his race buddies; he had cases of Coors shipped in from Colorado for race weeks. He would sit around the Winnebago bullshitting and then stand up and stretch and say, "Well, the time has come for the old man to do a little driving," and then go out and race hard and fast and sometimes quite well. He was in heaven—if only, perhaps, because he was away from the movies. "I enjoy the people in racing a lot more than the people in Hollywood," he said. "It's like being around circus people."*

ALL OF this running around—this literal running around—wouldn't seem to leave him time for making films, but Newman was terrifically busy as an actor during the years in which he honed his racing skills. And even when the results weren't of especially high quality, he reliably chose to make films that had a sense of purpose or potential to them. In most every case, you could see why he'd made a film and what he'd hoped it'd become.

In 1972 he made a pair of pictures back-to-back with John Huston, the larger-than-life character who'd debuted as a director with *The Maltese Falcon* and gone on to make *The Treasure of the Sierra Madre*, *The African Queen*, *Moulin Rouge*, *The Asphalt Jungle*, *The Night of the Iguana*, and, most recently, *Fat City*. Huston was a man's man in a vein that Newman admired: a boozer, gambler, brawler, and womanizer with culture and huge appetites and no fear of pissing off Hollywood bigwigs and a knack for landing on his feet in the most improbable ways. They were meant to work together.

Huston approached Newman with a script by a young writer named John Milius, a western about the infamous Roy Bean, a self-appointed judge whose liberal use of the noose and confusion of his own prejudices with actual statute made him an icon of frontier justice, eccentricity, and severity. Milius had serious ambitions for his script,

---

* Newman's love of motor racing would be celebrated in a cameo in Mel Brooks's 1976 comedy *Silent Movie*. He played himself as a movie star waylaid with a leg injury who tears around the grounds of a hospital (actually the University of California at Irvine campus) in an electric wheelchair.

which he imagined could reveal the rancid truths behind the myths of the Old West—something like *The Wild Bunch* or a Sergio Leone film with a villainous central figure who resembled Richard Nixon in his unambiguous contempt for the law. But Huston and Newman saw the chance for a mock-heroic comedy in the vein of *Butch Cassidy and the Sundance Kid*—a tall tale, a whopper. And they were big enough, and had paid Milius sufficiently, to get their way.

So a lark it would be: Newman would get to spend some agreeable weeks in Tucson dressing sloppily, drinking, playing cards, cavorting with an actual bear and lion, making eyes at Victoria Principal, and generally behaving like a rascal. Huston went even further: in delicate health as he approached seventy years of age, he drank vodka all day and brought along the woman who would become his fifth wife, a hell-cat by the name of CiCi who was less than half his age and whom he himself compared, in a sentence of his fine autobiography that didn't even deign to mention her name, to a sea snake.

It was a shambles. Ava Gardner, on set only briefly, was always drunk and impossibly ornery the whole while. And she hated Newman. "I can't stand that man," she told a biographer. "He's one of my un-favorite actors. He's an egomaniac, and so false. He's 'on' all the time." (For what it's worth, she thought Kirk Douglas and John Wayne were just as bad.) Tony Perkins complained to Newman that Huston picked on him—he feared it was to do with his sexuality—and Newman or-chestrated the bisexual actor into a fling with Principal. Huston and his CiCi were often off by themselves (Newman dubbed the woman "a functional voluptuary"), and Newman gave Principal a lot of direction for her scenes. She in turn babysat for him and Joanne so they could go off on *their* own. Gardner too went on walkabout, wandering drunk-enly into the brush one evening; Milius was sent after her. Marlon Brando came by the set. Clint Eastwood visited. The script called for Bean to take in a bear as a pet, and the trainer of the animal that played the part brought a lion to Tucson with him; Huston liked to release the big cat in his trailer when he had guests over to play cards and drink.

And the picture they made was stilted by forced goofiness, chocka-block plotting, and an indistinct tone, alternately satirical, elegaic, comic, and laconic. At times you could see the bawdier, bloodier, colder film that Milius had wanted to make, and at times the ghost of *Butch Cassidy and the Sundance Kid* overwhelmed it. (The utterly insipid tune "Marmalade, Molasses and Honey" made "Raindrops Keep Fallin' on My Head" seem as profound as a Schubert lied.) Newman had great sport with the gruffness of the role—some of the sloppy, seedy characters of his late career can be traced to Roy Bean—and clearly with a scene in which he swears at, yells at, and finally punches the bear. But Huston never made anything more than a pastiche of it. And reviews and the box office were, given the potential of the thing, pretty dismissive.

STILL, THE star and the director had enjoyed working together. They may have been a pair of superannuated juveniles with tastes for the ribald and the macho, but they truly collaborated. Huston was willing to entertain Newman's questioning and analytic sides and to chew scenes over with him and to bounce around new ideas, engaging in the workshop and preparation aspects of the craft that Newman so loved. "We kept nattering at each other all the time," Newman remembered fondly. He did little to disguise his admiration for Huston: "I always felt very bourgeois around him. One always feels a certain sense of uneasiness around a man of genius. I was intimidated." (Filial, even. "Paul would never do anything to cross John," remembered someone on the crew. "Paul was a bit of a boy scout.")

Naturally Huston thought the world of Newman, calling him "the Golden Lad" and declaring that "among the gods he would surely find a place as Hermes of the Winged Heels, forever in motion—graceful, stylish, with an inborn rhythm." So when Newman hit upon a thriller named *The MacKintosh Man* that a young screenwriter named Walter Hill had adapted from *The Freedom Trap* by Desmond Bagley, he thought of Huston to direct it. It was a sweet package: they'd film in London, Ireland, and Malta; it would get Newman-Foreman out of its commitments to Warner Bros.; and there was money on the table. Why wouldn't Huston go along?

The problem was, they really didn't have a fully baked film. "I was vaguely ashamed of the whole thing," Hill later said. "The story didn't make any sense." Newman would play Joseph Rearden, an American in London posing as an Australian and engaged in a jewel heist. He's caught and sent to prison, where the agent of a racket specializing in arranging escapes offers to break him out—for a price. He agrees and escapes along with another prisoner, an upper-class traitor who sold Britain's state secrets to the Soviets. Then we learn that Rearden's actually a British security agent trying to bring down the escape ring. And *then* we learn that Rearden's boss is using the operation against the escape ring in a still bigger plot to catch a high-ranking member of Parliament who is himself a Communist spy. Or something.

It was shot sharply and smartly, with a couple of thrilling chase scenes and atmospheric settings and intelligent terseness. But too much of it was off: Newman with his awful Aussie twang, French starlet Dominique Sanda almost impossible to understand as his lover and collaborator, a cardboard villain (who is given life simply because James Mason played him), and an abruptness that felt less like a stylistic choice than a lack of confidence. As Huston confessed, the filmmakers didn't quite know where they were going as they made it: "The story lacked an ending. All the time we were filming we were casting about frantically for an effective way to bring the picture to a close." It closed on its own, as it happened, without making a ripple.

Box office failures rolled off of Newman's shoulders, though, in part because he had been such a reliable earner and had hit such a peak with *Butch Cassidy and the Sundance Kid.* Indeed, the success of that picture was so massive that it inevitably spurred talk of the dream team of Newman and Redford pairing up again. In 1971 word circulated that the two would appear in a torn-from-the-headlines story as a couple of real-life New York City policemen who testified before the Knapp Commission corruption investigations into crooked goings-on in their department; Newman would play Sergeant David Durk and Redford would take on the role of Detective Frank Serpico.*

---

* Obviously, it never happened, or at least not in that way. Newman's old *You Are There* director Sidney Lumet wound up directing the story as *Serpico* with Al Pacino in 1974.

Instead, chance brought them a script by yet another young writer, David Ward, who had been researching the world of conmen and had an idea for a story set in the 1930s. It had twists and atmosphere and drama, and it was built around a pair of guys jauntily paired as a team, kind of like *Butch Cassidy:* a buddy movie, or "dick love story," as one of its producers, Julia Phillips, called it. She was a fiery kid who had been working as an acquisitions and management factotum at First Artists, a protégee of David Begelman, who'd left the agenting biz to run the company. She had working relationships with Barbra Streisand and Robert Redford, whom she had convinced to make *The Way We Were*. Now she and her husband, Michael, and a third producer, Tony Bill, had bought the rights to Ward's smart, engaging script and gotten Redford interested in playing the lead—a conman out to take revenge on a gangster.

They needed a director. Ward wanted to do it himself, but Redford said he'd drop the project if that happened. Someone got the script to George Roy Hill, who said he'd do it. Then Newman asked Hill if he could have a look at the script, and he surprised everyone by leaping into what was, in reality, a supporting role: Henry Gondorff, the older of the two conmen, the one who's in on the caper less for honor than for kicks. "I don't give a damn about the size of the part," he told Hill. "It's terrific. I want to play it." While he was in England making *The MacKintosh Man*, Newman hand-delivered a copy of the script to Robert Shaw, who signed on to play the villain. The thing was falling into place almost too easily.

As with *Roy Bean*, the writer envisioned something darker, colder, and harder than the director did. The film was set in the midst of the Depression, but Hill, a one-time Yale music major who played Bach on the piano every day in order to unwind, found himself gravitating toward the ragtime music of decades earlier as he conceived of the treatment. "It's not the right period," he said, "it's the right *spirit.*" (This same gap between what the script called for and how the film was made appeared in the performances of Newman and Redford; as the latter explained, in comparison to Butch and Sundance, they took the attitude that they were "different characters but played them the same way.")

The film was set mainly in Chicago, but the crew filmed for about five weeks in studios in L.A., where the Newmans rented a house in Malibu, and then for a mere couple of days in Chicago, where a springtime snap of winter weather messed up the shooting schedule. Despite Redford's rising popularity—he had parlayed *Butch Cassidy* into a career that was rising to the stature of Newman's—it was Newman who grabbed all the attention wherever they went. When the pair, with costar Shaw, showed up at Union Station for a day's work, Newman got a standing ovation from the extras.

Shaw, a bona fide intellectual who wrote novels and plays, was dumbfounded by the adulation Newman received. He compared Newman to Laurence Olivier in terms of sheer magnetism, but he saw a crucial difference in the way their personal charisma was integrated into their acting techniques. "I certainly don't feel in any way as an actor that [Newman's] overawing at all," he remarked to a reporter. "I tell you candidly that what he does always seems to me to be better in the dailies than I think it is at the time. . . . There's something photogenic—a chemistry. What the hell is it? I don't know, but he certainly has it. If Newman were a completely unknown actor and had two lines in a potboiler he would absolutely stand out."

Newman, as always, only wanted to stand out for doing his work well and honorably—and maybe for busting George Roy Hill's chops when he had the chance. Making *Butch*, Newman had come to learn that his director was tight with a buck, and the insight took on a life of its own during their second film together. One day Hill invited Newman to his trailer for drinks but offered him only hard liquor, which Newman had sworn off; Newman repaired to his own trailer to fetch beers from his own fridge—and then sent Hill a bill for them. Hill responded with a memo about abusing their friendship, to which Newman replied by cutting the director's desk in half with a chain saw—a trick his character pulled in *Sometimes a Great Notion*. Hill sicced Universal on Newman; the studio dunned him for the money to replace the desk; Newman never paid.

Despite the tomfoolery and the weather problems, the film was finished by the summer, and Universal realized it had something special. Not only had the stars of one of the biggest studio films in the past decade been successfully reunited, but Hill had put it together with pep and charm and that undeniably delicious music. They had a prestigious picture on their hands, but it was a crowd-pleaser too. Normally, a film with hopes of Oscars and positive reviews would have opened on a small number of screens in New York and Los Angeles and then spread out gradually into the national marketplace; wide national releases were reserved for lowbrow action fare and comedies. But Universal took the gamble of opening *The Sting* on Christmas in the top thirty-five markets in the country, and it paid off splendidly— even against so formidable a competitor as *The Exorcist*, which opened the very next day.

Screenwriter David Ward suggested that the film worked because he and Hill managed to keep viewers unsteady. "The trick was not just in working the con game," he said, "but in conning the audience as well . . . You didn't want people leaving the theater saying, 'Well, that was nice, but I'd never fall for anything like that.' " It wasn't a total love fest. "This isn't a movie," carped *Time*, "it's a recipe." But audiences lapped it up, particularly the camaraderie of Newman and Redford, which was drawing comparisons with such immortal screen pairs as Clark Gable and Spencer Tracy and James Cagney and Pat O'Brien. The film rolled up an amazing $156 million at the box office— representing nearly 100 million tickets sold, one of the top ten gates in movie history at the time—and capped that success with a staggering ten Oscar nominations: best picture, actor (Redford), director, original screenplay, cinematography, art direction, sound, adapted score, editing, and costumes. Newman was skipped over, a slight that was magnified, perhaps, when Joanne was nominated as best actress for *Summer Wishes, Winter Dreams.** At the end of the evening, which would long be remembered for the spectacle of a streaker darting nakedly past host David Niven, *The Sting* had won seven prizes, including best picture

---

* Stewart Stern wrote the script, as he would for the TV movie *Sybil*, which was made just three years later and afforded Joanne the first of her seven career Emmy nominations. (She would eventually win two.)

(only Redford, the soundmen, and cinematographer Robert Surtees lost), making it by a wide margin the most successful movie Newman had ever been part of in a career dotted with some fairly prominent successes.*

HAVING MADE two titanic hits together, Newman and Redford were surely destined for a third pairing, but it never came, despite years of rumors indicating that they were considering something: *The Man Who Would Be King* (John Huston himself sent the script to Newman, who set him straight: "For chrissake, John, get Connery and Caine!"— which, it happened, he did), a stage production of *What Price Glory?*, a screen adaptation of Bill Bryson's *A Walk in the Woods*, one directing the other in something, and so on.**

And since both actors' personal value had been increased enormously by the two films, each was associated with any number of potential projects in the coming years. In Newman's case, some of the films wound up being made, and quite successfully, with other stars instead: *The Eiger Sanction* (Clint Eastwood), *Dirty Harry* (also Eastwood), *Robin and Marian* (Sean Connery), *Cry Freedom* (Kevin Kline), *Bobby Deerfield* (Al Pacino), *Superman* (Marlon Brando), *Romancing the Stone* (Michael Douglas), *I Will, I Will . . . for Now* (Elliott Gould!), *Ragtime* (James Cagney!), and with his daughter Nell, *Paper Moon* (Ryan O'Neal, of course, appeared opposite his own daughter, Tatum). Other films to which he was attached were never realized: a Mandrake the Magician film, to be directed, perhaps, by Alain Resnais; an Andrzej Wajda film about the Polish-Jewish social activist Janusz Kor-

---

* He was paid $1 million for his part and earned more than half that again in his percentage of the enormous gross. And he had to fight the state of California over the amount of taxes he owed on those earnings, which, the state contended, should be treated like income earned in the state even when dispersed years later to someone not residing in the state. The state Supreme Court finally sided with him, sparing him a $41,000 tax bill.

** A sequel to *The Sting* finally appeared in 1983, starring Jackie Gleason, Mac Davis, and Oliver Reed in the Newman, Redford, and Robert Shaw roles, respectively; mercifully, it tanked.

czak; an adaptation of Irving Wallace's paranoid political thriller *The R Factor*; *Hillman*, about a man who built a home out of trash; *Madonna Red*, in which he would have played a Vietnam vet who has turned to the priesthood; and *Where the Dark Streets Go*, a melodrama in which he would have played a priest who finds himself drawn into a murder mystery.

Now that he was a producer and a director, there were also unrealized projects in which he was to serve behind the camera: *The Trip Back Down*, about a stock-car racer with a broken marriage; *A Fairly Honorable Defeat*, in which Peter Ustinov was to have directed James Coco; *Precious Bane*, the cinematic directorial debut of Actors Studio cofounder Cheryl Crawford; a secret project in which he was going to direct his First Artists partner Barbra Streisand; and *The Tin Lizzie Troop*, a comic action picture about a group of National Guardsmen chasing after Mexican border bandits just before the start of World War I.

He had in mind to direct Dustin Hoffman and George Roy Hill in that latter one, and he commissioned a script from the writing team of Robert Benton and David Newman, who'd written, among other pictures, *Bonnie and Clyde* and *What's Up, Doc?* "The phone rang one morning," Benton recalled, "and somebody asked, 'Is this Newman and Benton?' And I said, 'Yes.' And he said, 'This is Paul Newman.' And I asked, 'Is this a joke?' And he assured me it was him and that he was serious, and he told me about this book. And we did several drafts for him and had a wonderful time. He was great to work with—he really understood a lot about characters. But the thing never quite pulled itself together."

Newman tended to brush off these missed—or indeed, avoided—chances but for two. He passed up the role of Joe Gideon in Bob Fosse's *All That Jazz*, and asked by a reporter how he felt about the decision after seeing the finished film, he made a gesture of raising a hand to his temple in the shape of a pistol and pulling the trigger. "It was just dumb of me," he confessed. "I was just so stupid, I didn't take into consideration what the contribution of the director was going to be. That was a terrible oversight."

The other was a controversial project that would bounce around

Hollywood for decades: Patricia Nell Warren's novel *The Front Runner*, which dealt with a track coach in love with his star runner—his *male* star runner. Newman would play the coach, and there was talk that Redford would be cast as the athlete.

By the time he acquired rights to the book, Newman was no longer in business with John Foreman, who had gone out as an independent producer; his new partner was George Englund, whom he had known socially as Cloris Leachman's husband and who had produced such films as *The Ugly American* with Marlon Brando and *The Shoes of the Fisherman* with Anthony Quinn. The company that Newman and Englund formed, Projections Unlimited, contracted with United Artists to produce eight films, four starring Newman, and had no less than Sargent Shriver, the brother-in-law of John and Robert Kennedy, as its representative for international deals. Its formation effectively signaled the end of Newman's connection to First Artists, which had frankly done nearly no business at all on the meager output of its founders: Newman had provided the company with *Pocket Money* and *The Life and Times of Judge Roy Bean*, neither of which generated much revenue, and he was planning a sequel to *Harper*; Streisand had made the disappointing *Up the Sandbox*; Steve McQueen had given the company a moderate success with *The Getaway*; and Sidney Poitier had a comedy in the works, *Uptown Saturday Night*, which would become a tremendous hit for the company and spawn a sequel, *Let's Do It Again*. But it was clear that the enterprise was dead.*

Newman and Englund went through several writers attempting to adapt *The Front Runner*, including the playwright John Bishop. And Newman insisted that he wasn't afraid of risking his image to play a gay man on-screen. "I'm not ready for a cop-out," he declared. "I won't tolerate this project being turned into a watered-down love

---

* First Artists struggled on until 1980, with one substantial hit—Streisand's *A Star Is Born*—and a couple of minor critical successes (including Dustin Hoffman's *Straight Time*) to its credit. By then it had issued public stock, diversified into such holdings as a casino and sports shirt manufacture, lost about two-thirds of its stock value, and been served with a lawsuit by Hoffman. It had produced barely twenty films in its decade of existence—fewer than a single large movie studio might release in a year.

story, or substituting a female for the role of [the runner] . . . I'm a supporter of gay rights. And not a closet supporter, either. From the time I was a kid I have never been able to understand the attacks on the gay community."

But personal beliefs aside, he was fighting an uphill struggle. At one point Newman's *Winning* costar Richard Thomas was being considered for the younger role; at another, it was said that Newman was shooting second-unit footage at the Montreal Olympics. Articles about the film started appearing in gay publications such as *Blueboy;* movie magazines ran stories with appalling headlines like "Will Success as a 'Homo' Spoil Paul Newman?"

All the negatives were too much for Newman and Englund to overcome. "We could never get the script right," Newman said later on, disappointed. *The Front Runner* seems to have influenced *Personal Best,* Robert Towne's 1982 movie about a track athlete's lesbian affair with a teammate, and in 2007 the novel was rumored to be back in development as a project for Brad Pitt. But no adaptation of it ever appeared.

Eighteen

WHEN JOANNE WAS OUT PROMOTING *THE EFFECT OF GAMMA Rays on the Man-in-the-Moon Marigolds*, she went on Dick Cavett's TV show and brought along a clip of herself playing a scene with Nell. After it had run, Cavett remarked that he didn't mean to be rude, but he thought that the daughter might be even more beautiful than the mother. "Well, it's no surprise," Joanne told him. "*My* father wasn't Paul Newman!"*

That was part of Newman's legacy to his girls—both Jackie's daughters and Joanne's. The five of them, from twenty-one-year-old Susan to nine-year-old Clea, were pretty not only because they had lovely mothers but also, of course, because of their father. But when they traveled with him, they stood in amazement—and no little discomfort—at the attention he received from women, who would sometimes literally bowl the girls over to gain proximity to their father. It was a puzzlement, a curiosity, and a joke. And it bled into their self-images.

Susan, the oldest girl, had genuine troubles in her late teens. In high school she had a crush on her French teacher but decided she was too chunky to woo him, so she went on a fasting diet for more than a

---

* Both Newmans liked Cavett and appeared on his show gladly. When Newman appeared once, Cavett remembered, there was an audible gasp from a woman in the audience: "Oh my *God*! There he *is*!" "I almost asked her, 'Did you think I was kidding?' " Cavett said.

month, losing forty pounds and becoming unhealthily weak in the process. She was moody and would often retreat into her bedroom, talking to nobody in the household for days on end. "I was intolerable," she admitted. "I was known to lock myself in my room for a year of my life and only come out when I had to. I'd come home from school and read or crochet in my room."

When she hit her early twenties, she got involved romantically with a guy about a decade older, going so far as to move in with him, to the distinct disapproval of both her sets of parents. (Jackie, who worked as a high school English teacher in the San Fernando Valley, had remarried and had a daughter with her new husband in the late 1960s.) She had no interest in college. She was tart and cynical and quarreled with Joanne. She was a handful.

But her troubles were nothing compared to Scott's. The only son, having to carry the legacy of his famous father, he was less apt to shrug off the strange accoutrements of Newman's celebrity than to see them as tokens of achievement—standards, in effect, that he would have to live up to in order to reckon himself a real man. The girls had their mothers to emulate; Jackie was an ordinary working mom, and Joanne had her feet sufficiently on the ground—for a movie star—that her daughters didn't seem to be cowed by her example. But Scott alone felt compelled to follow in the footsteps of a titan, and predictably, the prospect overwhelmed him.

From the time he was a teen he dabbled in drugs and alcohol, and as his indulgences and inherent wildness took their toll on his schoolwork and his ability to fit in with classmates, he was forced to leave one school after another. He'd spent two years at Washington College but never went back after working in Oregon on *Sometimes a Great Notion*. Rather, he was drawn to a lifestyle even more exciting than the one his father was falling in love with on the race circuit. At college Scott discovered skydiving, and he became sufficiently enamored of it that he left school to learn the craft, taking more than five hundred parachute jumps in pursuit of certification to be an instructor.

Newman was impressed. "I went down to Maryland to see him the other day," he told a reporter. "You ought to try watching your son jump out of an airplane sometime . . . It was all I could manage to watch from the ground . . . It must be quite something. Really thrilling, I guess."

Scott managed to get work teaching parachuting to midshipmen at the U.S. Naval Academy, but he wasn't offered a full-time position, and he drifted on. He got it into his head that he wouldn't accept any money from his father but would live on his own, and he next turned up at a California ski resort, where he drove a bus shuttling skiers around and, for less than three dollars an hour, cut down trees to build new ski runs. He worked construction for similar wages, borrowing money from friends rather than asking for help from his father.

The help came anyway. In late 1973 George Roy Hill, who had fallen in love with flying as a boy in Minnesota and served as a marine pilot in the Korean War, sent Newman a script about old-time barnstorming stunt pilots. Newman passed on the picture—Robert Redford wound up playing the title role, *The Great Waldo Pepper*—but he thought there might be work on the movie for Scott, maybe as a stuntman. He forwarded the script to Scott, and Scott contacted Hill, and after Redford and Hill refused to let him do any wing-walking or similarly risky business, he was cast in a small role as a rival pilot to the hero.

Before he made his way to Texas for the shoot, however, Scott found himself in a mess. One February night in the eastern Sierra Mountain town of Bridgeport, California, he got stinking drunk and vandalized a bus, slashing its tires. Three Mono County sheriff's deputies responded to calls about his behavior, and it took all three to subdue the six-foot, 180-pound twenty-three-year-old when they got there. When they finally got him into the rear seat of a patrol car, he squirmed loose and kicked the driver in the back of the head, causing him to veer off the road. And at the county lockup he tore apart the jail cell into which they stuck him. At the station he identified himself by his birth name— Alan Newman—and was charged with public drunkenness, destruction of public property, and, most seriously, felony battery with a dangerous weapon—namely the boot with which he kicked the deputy who was driving him to jail.

It was an ugly but unexceptional incident; but the bad guy in it was the son of a movie star, so it made headlines across the country. Newman learned about it in a middle-of-the-night phone call; asked a couple years later how he'd reacted, he confessed, "You go into the kitchen and you get about three ice cubes, and you chill a beer mug, and you sit there and think awhile. Listen, there's not much you can do except offer what support you feel is required."

Right there was the problem, or at least part of it. Scott was clearly having substance abuse issues, but Newman himself, a functioning alcoholic, was in no position to lecture him on the evils of drink. Newman would tell friends that he had no means at hand with which to reach his son, but the truth of the matter was that to be an effective voice and example of reform for his son, he would have had to make a significant self-accounting and changes in his own lifestyle.

That spring, when Scott appeared in court, he was found innocent of felony battery but guilty of misdemeanor battery; the judge fined him $1,000 and sentenced him to two years' probation. Again Newman took an odd tack in response, seemingly blaming the press for making a big deal out of nothing: "The incident with him was blown all out of proportion. And I think that's deliberate. The accusation is always on the first page and the retraction on page nineteen." But if he didn't ascribe blame for Scott's brush with the law appropriately, it nevertheless seemed to encourage him to take a more active role in his son's life. He steered him toward acting classes with Peggy Feury, an L.A. teacher with an Actors Studio background, and he helped him get a role in his own latest film, a big-budget movie about a fire in a skyscraper entitled *The Towering Inferno.*

LOOKING BACK, it would be hard to accuse Newman of choosing his movie roles simply for the money. But in the case of *The Towering Inferno,* not much else can explain why he agreed to appear in a film in which, as he put it, "the real star . . . is that damned fire." The movie was the creation of producer Irwin Allen, who'd made his name in television and then invented a new formula for blockbuster movies with 1972's *The Poseidon Adventure:* take a big cast of well-known names, stick them in some sort of disaster, and let a bunch of extras die at the hands of special effects while the stars—minus a sacrificial lamb or two—fight their way to safety. Already he had a second iteration in the can—a seismic disaster film called *Earthquake*—and now he had acquired the rights to not one but two novels about high-rise fires and had no less a writer than Stirling Silliphant, who'd won an Oscar for *In the Heat of the Night*, working to combine them into a script.

Newman was cast in the entirely unchallenging role of the architect who designed the dizzying tower and doesn't know that the financiers have cut corners on fire safety in building it. On the skyscraper's gala opening night fire strikes, and everything that can go wrong does. To play the key role of the fire chief, who must risk his own life and those of his men to save the very people whose penny-pinching had created the catastrophe, Allen had scored the coup of casting Steve McQueen, meaning that the film would pair two of the biggest stars in the world; surely it would be a moneymaking machine. The cast was filled with impressive names—William Holden, Faye Dunaway, Fred Astaire, Jennifer Jones, Robert Wagner, Richard Chamberlain, even O. J. Simpson. And Scott Newman would play in a small role opposite McQueen as a rookie fireman with a bad case of the jitters.

He'd gotten onto the film not only because of his father but because he was legitimately capable of stunt work. In preparation, he learned how to rappel down a sheer wall on a rope line. And he even made a sweetheart of a young stuntwoman, Glynn Rubin, whom he met on the shoot. But McQueen was chary of him. McQueen had a genuinely neurotic relationship with Newman, whose career and stature he frankly envied. The two had worked together, in a small way, on *Somebody Up There Likes Me*, and McQueen was still smarting from having passed on *Butch Cassidy* over essentially an ego issue. He had seen to it that he would get slightly more desirable billing on *Towering Inferno* than Newman, and that the two would have equal amounts of dialogue and screen time, but he was cross to learn that he would have to carry his rival's kid through a big scene. As it happened, though, he took a liking to Scott, praising his work and allowing Allen's writers to add a couple of lines for him. Later, when the film was released, Scott was employed heavily in the publicity campaign, touring the East Coast and doing interviews with print and TV journalists. It was a big moment for him.

Newman didn't do much either in *The Towering Inferno* or in support of it—"I knew that the quicker I got off the screen and the stuntman got on, the quicker the picture would start rolling," he told a writer for *The Atlantic*, whose readers could hardly be considered the film's target market. It was an agreeably slick film, with little in the way of credible human drama but reasonably tense action. Newman thought of it as "distinguished junk" and was remunerated impressively for holding his nose, taking home a guaranteed $1 million, as per usual, and a percentage of the gross that was estimated to be more than eight times that: nearly a $10 million payday all told.

And that sum turned out to be gravy: "*Towering Inferno* was the first and only picture I've ever decided to do for money—up until then," he explained. "After I'd accepted the role, though, the money from *The Sting* started coming in, so I put *that* aside and pissed away the *Inferno* money."

Putting money aside surely had something to do with another impressive number that was facing him: fifty, which was how old he turned that January, a fact that magazine covers would wonder about in genuine disbelief: how could a fellow so fit and spry and sexy be fifty years old? He celebrated his birthday—January 26—by assembling Joanne and the girls (but not Scott) in Westport to observe his morning swim in the gelid waters of the Aspetuck River. A family luncheon followed, during which he was given, among other gifts, a wicker wheelchair.

That night a coterie of friends—Stewart Stern, George Roy Hill, Robert Redford, A. E. Hotchner, Edward Villella, Cheryl Crawford, Anne Jackson, and Gene Shalit—were among the fifty guests who joined the seven Newmans at La Cave Henri IV in Manhattan for an evening of dining, laughs, and music. (Neil Sedaka performed a few standards for which Sammy Cahn had rewritten the lyrics.) Among the gifts for the Old Fox, as the printed menus called him, was a cache of fifty cans of Coors, then still a cult beer available only in the West. (Redford presented him with a smashed-up old Porsche, which Newman later had compacted and delivered in a shipping crate to Redford's home on *his* birthday.) The birthday boy and his wife sent the kids home and spent the night at a Park Avenue hotel.

Approximately three months later he was being celebrated in

Manhattan once again, this time alongside Joanne, as an honoree of the Film Society of Lincoln Center at a gala benefit retrospective of their careers. Newman was embarrassed at being given an honor that had previously been accorded only to Charles Chaplin, Fred Astaire, and Alfred Hitchcock. "I depreciate my own work," he told a reporter over a lunch of omelets and beers. "When they're good, they're okay; when they're bad, they're really horrid." Joanne didn't exactly crow about herself either: "We're a kind of an artificial couple. Paul is a great star. I'm a character actress."

On the night of the gala, an array of stars turned out—Myrna Loy, Martin Balsam, Maureen Stapleton, John Houseman, Anthony Perkins, Geraldine Fitzgerald, Richard Thomas, Shelley Winters—plus directors Otto Preminger, George Roy Hill, Arthur Penn, Gil Cates, and Stuart Rosenberg. The Newmans were seated with New York mayor Abe Beame and his wife, and they had to endure, along with everyone else, an endless program of twenty-seven film clips: eleven of "his," ten of "hers," and six of "theirs." Tennessee Williams introduced the Newman portion of the program and got an unintentional laugh by calling the star "Paul Goodman." ("Why are you all laughing?" Williams asked. "I'm really not that funny.")

When he finally got to speak, Newman poked fun at how he looked in that infamous "cocktail dress" from *The Silver Chalice* (a clip from which he insisted be included); when Joanne spoke, she apologized to the audience for a show that ran "longer than *Gone with the Wind.*" The evening went on for several hours, with the honorees standing patiently at a reception to which the most generous donors were invited. Newman passed the time by draining can after can of Coors.* The next morning he met some reporters for a casual press

---

* Tales of his beer drinking had become legendary. An old joke was resurrected and ascribed to him—"Twenty-four hours in a day; twenty-four beers in a case: Coincidence? I think not." And students at Bates College in Maine—and then, more famously, at Princeton University—began to celebrate Newman's Day, dedicating themselves to putting two dozen beers away in the span of a single day. Along with university officials, Newman tried to get the students to stop, but he never succeeded. And he eventually gave up Coors in the late 1970s when he was told—falsely, as it happened—that the Coors family had donated large sums to Anita Bryant's antigay political campaigns in Florida and California.

conference and once again drank beer after beer throughout, even though it started at ten A.M.

LINCOLN CENTER was actually an increasingly familiar place for the Newmans. Having turned to ballet in the late 1960s to tone up after her pregnancies, Joanne had become an avid attendee, donor to, and even patroness of the ballet, and her husband frequently accompanied her to recitals, galas, and benefits in support of dancers, dance education, and new dance companies. The Newmans were spotted at performances around the country, most especially in New York. And they were generous with grant money, giving, for instance, $50,000 to the Los Angeles Ballet in 1975 to help it open a school for dancers, as well as donations to the Royal Winnipeg Ballet, the Paul Taylor company, and many small troupes around the country.

Newman wasn't exactly keen on dance—"I enjoy all aspects of the theater," he told a reporter, "though after I'd seen *Giselle* for the nineteenth time, I became resistant." But he understood that his attendance at and appreciation of dance served as a way to pay Joanne back for all the weekends she'd been forced to spend doing needlepoint beside Winnebagos on dusty racetracks. "I trade her a couple of ballets for a couple of races," he explained. He regularly gave her gifts from the world of ballet—posters and sculptures of her favorite dancers; she actually hung a large framed photo of Rudolph Nureyev in their bedroom. And he funded her passion. In 1975 she made a gift of $120,000 in seed money and became a founding board member of a new company, the Dancers; Dennis Wayne, a devilishly handsome and fiery-tempered thirtyish New York native and alumnus of the Joffrey Ballet and the American Ballet Theater, was its artistic director.

She was up and at the barre bright and early every morning—just as Newman was engaged in his daily routine of jogging or biking or swimming followed by a long sauna and a shower. In a marriage that could sometimes seem incongruous, their shared passion for fitness was one of their most reliable bonds. Joanne couldn't quite drag him into all of her enthusiasms, though. When she and the girls turned to vegetarianism in the mid-1970s, he did so only grudgingly, and then lived on steaks and burgers whenever he was away from home. In 1975 Joanne attended est sessions—self-awareness training—and got so much out of them that she encouraged Scott, Susan, and Nell to do so too. But she never got her husband involved, even though, she said, "he complains of feeling left out of what's became an exclusive little clique within the family."

Nor did he follow her in her next bid for self-enhancement, when she enrolled at Sarah Lawrence College in Westchester County, New York—convenient to both their Connecticut and Manhattan homes—to take the classes she'd been promising herself since she dropped out of Louisiana State more than twenty years earlier. She studied philosophy, art history, astronomy, and other miscellaneous subjects without intending to fulfill a degree or, indeed, without any aim in mind other than enrichment. It was as if she had decided that the subjugation of her career to her husband's wasn't going to be the end of her growth. If she was going to be seen as an appendage to an internationally famous movie star, she was going to be a cultivated one.

As a sort of working vacation away from their strange multilimb juggling act of careers, homes on two coasts, and passions for auto racing and ballet, the Newmans went to New Orleans to make a film in 1974, the first in which they'd acted together since *WUSA*, which was also shot there. This one would be a sequel to *Harper*, initially entitled *Ryan's the Name* but renamed *The Drowning Pool*, like the Ross Macdonald novel on which it was loosely based.

The plot had Lew Harper called to the Crescent City by a former lover, Iris (Joanne), who is married to a local big shot and is being blackmailed. In trying to ferret out the source of the threat, Harper encounters any number of depraved, dangerous, and dastardly southern types, from Iris's sexpot daughter (an impossibly young Melanie Griffith) to a vaguely corrupt police lieutenant (Tony Franciosa) to a Cajun mogul (Murray Hamilton) determined to get his hands on the land owned by Iris's mother-in-law.

Like all of Macdonald's books, this one was originally set in Southern California, but Joanne, according to Newman, suggested they shoot in New Orleans. That allowed the filmmakers to imbue it with some exotic textures—French Quarter bars and antique shops, bayou speedboats, a warehouse full of Mardi Gras floats, and so on. The location had echoes of *The Long, Hot Summer,* with Newman as the outsider visiting an incestuous Louisiana town and sharing an attachment with Woodward while the presumed prince of the place, Franciosa, watches helplessly. And Stuart Rosenberg, who had made *WUSA,* was directing Newman for the fourth and final time.

In one exciting scene Harper and the bad guy's wife (newcomer Gail Strickland) find themselves locked in the hydrotherapy room of an abandoned sanitarium, then fill it to the ceiling with water in an effort to burst out through the skylight; Newman wears boxer shorts and is incredibly fit on the cusp of his fiftieth birthday. But little of the old *Harper* magic—let alone that of *Long, Hot Summer*—was evident. The film didn't carry the same saucy charm as the first; the slick irony of the Harper persona felt less fresh and timely than it had a decade earlier. Newman was obviously having a grand time. "I simply adore that character," he said, "because it will accommodate any kind of actor's invention . . . It's just lovely to get up in the morning, it's great to go to work, because you know you're going to have a lot of fun that day." But this was one of those grand times that didn't translate from the set to the movie house, and the picture was released to indifferent reviews and business.

His commitment to auto racing had begun to dominate his film choices; he deliberately avoided working during the race season, meaning he either had to develop projects around that schedule or, worse, take the work that was available when he would be finished racing. "If I've been available in October," he explained, "I've taken the first picture that's available in October." That strategy would lead him down some artistic and commercial dead ends. But his next project—which, yes, was filmed in the fall—was one that he'd been nurturing for years. In 1969 Newman and John Foreman, along with agent David Susskind, had spent $500,000 to acquire the rights to *Indians,* a scabrous play by Arthur Kopit concerning the abhorrent treatment of Native Americans by the white man. The intent was to have Kopit write a script and George Roy Hill direct it.

After five years of back-and-forth, however, the film had come to bear a different aspect. The Buffalo Bill project was in the hands of Dino De Laurentiis, the Italian producer famous for his alternating output of awful schlock and genuine quality. And rather than Kopit and Hill, the chief creative force behind the project was the celebrated independent writer-director Robert Altman, who was riding a string of hits including *M*A*S*H*, *McCabe and Mrs. Miller*, and *Nashville* and who had written a new version of the script with his protégé, Alan Rudolph. What they had created was less an indictment of the Anglo-American conquest of the Indians than a gimlet-eyed send-up of the notions of fame, myth, and history, a pastiche of the life of a celebrated American hero and charlatan. It was meant to be released during the national observance of the Bicentennial—a pie in the face, as it were, at the big patriotic party.

For his role as the great self-aggrandizer, Newman grew a jaunty goatee (which made him look rather like Altman, who wore similar facial hair most of his adult life) and sported a long, blond wavy wig and the sort of ornate leather outfits favored by the actual Buffalo Bill Cody. He was surrounded by a cast of Altman regulars (including Shelley Duvall, Bert Remsen, and Geraldine Chaplin), Native American actors (including Will Sampson, the giant who had played Chief in *One Flew Over the Cuckoo's Nest*), oddball cameo actors (opera star Evelyn Lear), and various curiously chosen screen icons: Joel Grey (the former Cleveland Play House Curtain Puller and an Oscar winner for *Cabaret*) as Cody's producer, and Burt Lancaster as Ned Buntline, the pulp novelist who helped sell Cody's myth to a public eager to be gulled.

Once again Newman was as keen on making merry on the set as he was focused on his performance. The company were staying in Calgary and took a bus each day out to the set on the prairie, but Newman had a Porsche with him and drove himself. "I went out with him to the set in the mornings," recalled John Considine, an actor on the film, "and he was always trying to break his speed record. It was a little hairy." As with *The Drowning Pool*, Newman spoke fondly of the freedom he felt in the character he was playing—a description that often meant he was reaching a little too hard for the quirky affect at the expense of real feeling. "I'm using this stance for my Buffalo Bill character," he said to a reporter on the set. "Know where it comes from? Baryshnikov! His curtain call! Actors are sponges. Terrible, terrible sponges. You steal from friends."

He had long had the habit of treating film shoots as a kind of version of summer camp: practical jokes, cookouts, beer blasts, getting up to no good among the locals. On the relatively isolated and dull *Buffalo Bill* set near Calgary, Alberta, Newman reached virtuosic heights of sophomoric invention, and he was goaded into them by, of all people, his own director. Altman was himself a famous enfant terrible, a pothead given to outrageous acts of defiance and tomfoolery. He made sport of Newman's constant diet of popcorn and contrived one day to have the actor's trailer packed with the stuff so that it spilled out all over him when he opened the door. Newman laughed it off, but then he issued a dire warning to his director: "You shouldn't have done that, Bob. I'm richer than you are, and I've got more time."

In the coming weeks he made Altman's life hell. They were filming in Canada in autumn, and Altman wore calfskin gloves to protect his hands from the nippy weather. Newman had them stolen, breaded, deep-fried, and served to the director as a garnish on his lunch plate. The two had debated whether Newman's daily river of beers or Altman's similarly voluminous stream of chablis was more manly; Newman called Altman's tipple "goat's piss" and presented him with an actual goat kid with a sign around its neck reading "Now you can have your own vineyard." He had Altman's trailer filled with a couple hundred live chickens, imparting a scent that could never be entirely eradicated. He hired a helicopter to fly over Calgary and drop invitations to a party at the rented home where Altman was living. In his most elaborate gag, he arranged for a local radio disk jockey to record a false news report, saying the film company needed 2,500 extras for the next day's shoot and would pay each $155 for their work instead of the going rate of $17.50; interested parties, the announcement continued, should call . . . and then came the sound of Altman's private phone number. Newman arranged to have the tape broadcast on radios on the set as if it were really going out over the airwaves, then sat beside the director to watch him as it aired. "Bob just turned white, pure white," he beamed.

To mark the end of the shoot, Newman flew in hundreds of live lobsters and ears of fresh corn for a prairie clambake. He tried to get Robert Redford to show up in Buffalo Bill garb to startle the party-goers, but he couldn't make that last bit work. Instead, he had a plan to auction off a pretty girl to a high bidder as a date—a bit of hijinks. As John Considine recalled,

> I was given the job of finding the young lady, and I thought that it was the perfect opportunity to get one back on Paul. So I got together with Tony Powell, the wardrobe guy, and told him that I would like to be the young lady. And he had to go into town and find a dress for a six-foot-four woman, which he said was the most embarrassing thing he'd ever done, and then he and Monte Westmore, the makeup guy, got me ready, with the hair and heels and everything. And they brought me out for the auction, and I sashayed onto this little stage, and there was Paul with this look on his face like "What is this?" And right beside him was Joanne, who had just flown in and whom I'd never met. So they auctioned me off, and I walked over to Paul and leaned in and said, "It's me, John," and I tried to kiss him. Well, boy did he fight back! I couldn't believe how strong he was!

Newman had obviously enjoyed himself, as had the rest of the cast, but Altman didn't manage to convey that pleasure on-screen as, say, George Roy Hill had done in his two Newman-Redford pictures. Joel Grey was of the opinion that the studio had ruined the film. "They were trying to make a straightforward film," he said. "What we'd made was really about the subtle relationships between all these characters, but they took all that out. It wasn't allowed to be what we had intended it to be."

Buffalo Bill and the Indians, or Sitting Bull's History Lesson, as it had finally come to be called, confused and even angered critics who'd made a darling of Altman. (Typical was a head-scratching *New York Times* review by Vincent Canby that began, "What are we going to do about Robert Altman?") The box office was, again, disappointing. And this was becoming a worrying trend: since *Butch Cassidy,* Newman had made two gigantic hits—*The Sting* and *The Towering Inferno*. But he had also made seven other films, including *Buffalo Bill*, whose grosses, all combined, didn't earn as much as *either* of those films. And it could be argued that the stars of those hits were actually the dream buddy team and the flaming skyscraper, not Newman himself. In 1976, for the first time since 1965, he failed to be named one of the top ten attractions in the country by the Quigley Poll.

He'd consistently chosen interesting material and collaborators, and his performances had often been pleasurable and authoritative, if not exactly sincere or heartfelt. But he had begun to falter, somehow, or misfire, and audiences felt it. In part, he confessed, he had simply, after more than twenty years of pursuing it as a profession, become bored with acting. He was tired of being offered scripts that reminded him of *Hud* or *The Hustler* or *Cool Hand Luke* or *Butch Cassidy*. He was tired of the grind of finding a decent project and then using up to his capacity to make it feel that the work was worth his while. And he was even tired of Paul Newman the actor. "The thing that I'm concerned about right now," he confessed to a reporter, "is that I'm running out of original things, and I'm falling back on successful things that I can get away with. I duplicate things now. I don't work as compactly as I used to work, simply because the demands aren't asked of me anymore."

His artistic and spiritual exhaustion became a trope of his interviews. "My teeth hurt," he told Gene Shalit as he drove him speedily along Connecticut highways. "I've been so busy holding up the tenuous career with my teeth, holding my family together, holding up the political structure of the country, that my teeth hurt, and I just want to stop having them hurt." He had thought of alternative ways of life, he said, but then he realized that he wasn't up to the challenge of adapting to them. "I'm too tired," he said, "to go through what I would have to go through to become a marine biologist. I don't think I can handle the hassle as well as I could have thirty years ago."

And while he was taking the long view, he expressed a confusion about himself and his achievements that sounded like the existential musings of a young man. "Sometimes I wonder what have I accomplished," he admitted. "I've become famous, something I never wanted, and I've made a lot of money, something I was not opposed to having.

But what have I accomplished? [Becoming] an American celluloid sex symbol? Whoopee! I'm not miserable. I'm just not happy. I don't have inner serenity, and I don't have the guts to do anything else."

WELL ACTUALLY, that wasn't entirely true. Guts, in fact, were an essential component to something else he was as deeply engaged in as moviemaking: auto racing. "I think it takes a certain amount of sensible bravery," he mused about his pastime. As his film career slowed down, he took every opportunity that presented itself to get away and gun a car around a track in pursuit of his racing education.

His progress was evident, but he could still find it bumpy going. During the filming of *The Drowning Pool,* he'd run a Porsche at a course near New Orleans and had a terrific crash. "Neither of us had a seat belt," he explained about himself and a passenger,

> and for a time we rode on two wheels. Then the car went on its side but we weren't thrown out. The windshield shattered. Fortunately it was European glass that breaks into powder on impact. We climbed out of the windshield. Neither of us was hurt. We hardly had our hair mussed. As I stood by the car, somebody slammed the door on my hand. Fortunately the door was sprung or I would have lost the tips of my fingers. "Open the door," I said quietly. When they did, I ran to the beer cooler and stuck my fingers in the icy water. I didn't even lose my fingernails.

Most of his racing exploits were tamer, if sensational in their own right. Back in Connecticut he had gotten into the habit of traveling back and forth between Westport and Lime Rock by helicopter. In Westport he landed on the playing fields of the middle school right across the road from his home, and it was a kick for neighborhood kids to see him pop out of his helicopter with his suitcase. But the folks who lived near Lime Rock weren't so pleased; a group of them who felt that the track had outgrown its original intentions got an ordinance passed in 1975 to ban helicopter flights to the place. By then Newman's race appearances had become such a big deal that he was besieged by media and women fans wherever he appeared: Connecticut; Ohio; Bridge-hampton, New York; Pocono Raceway in eastern Pennsylvania; and in the fall, Road Atlanta, where he once again competed for a national title and once again came away empty-handed.

But his driving was improving—markedly, according to observers. Bob Sharp had originally agreed to outfit him but hadn't put him on his SCCA team; gradually Newman improved so dramatically that Sharp asked him to join the team—even when it meant, as it often did, that the two would race against each other. In the 1976 season Newman raced cars in two classes—the Datsun 510 he'd been driving for a few years and a Triumph TR-6. When he got to Road Atlanta that fall, everything fell into place for him. He ran third in the championship race in the Datsun, but he won the national championship in the Triumph, and his combined performance was rewarded by SCCA officials with the President's Cup for overall excellence, the highest honor accorded at the Runoffs.

At the party following the awards ceremony, he was ebullient. "In a spectrum of ten, this ranks in the high nines," he told the assembled drivers, crew members, and spectators. "Screw the Oscars. This is terrific." And then he got a little reflective. Speaking generally to the racing fraternity that had initially received him as an oddity, he confessed, "It's good to finally be on the inside."

The championship gave him the confidence to commit himself more fully to racing. He allowed Sharp to use him for certain types of publicity and sponsorships (including Budweiser, which paid him in unlimited cases of beer). He tried driving different types of cars, some much faster than he'd been racing previously. His natural instinct for the sport started to kick in. "Newman has something that drivers can only be born with," said Sam Posey, "a soft touch. He can get the most out of a car without hurting it." Increasingly, his driving style came to resemble those of top professionals. "Newman liked the car best when it was sliding the most," Posey said. "He liked to hang it out. This was the sure sign of the true racer." His dogged learning technique had yielded real results. "Look at that man," Bob Sharp said admiringly of Newman as he ran a race. "Same line through the turn every time. Consistent as a clock. So smooth you can't hear him shift."

He had an appropriate respect for the sport, and in truth he was aptly built for it, with a compact body that made him more comfortable in the tight, airless confines of a race car than a bigger man would have been. For the first time since he was a boy, he felt like a jock. "I always wanted to be an athlete," Newman said, "a football player or a baseball player. I tried skiing for ten years. The only thing I ever felt graceful at was racing a car, and that took me ten years to learn."

And, too, he was lucky. As he drove faster cars in more competitive races, he started to experience the spectacular accidents—and lucky escapes—that all veteran drivers had to their names. At Nelson Ledges another guy's car got airborne and flipped on top of Newman's in the middle of a race. At Lime Rock he lost his brakes at upward of 140 miles an hour and aimed his car toward an escape path designed for such emergencies. Track manager Jim Haynes witnessed the near-calamity:

> The car never slowed. Before he reached the end of the chute, he veered to the left and plowed into some trees. It wiped out the left side of the car, and I thought, "Oh, lordy, he's liable to be killed." I was really scared. By the time we got to the car, he stepped out, not even scratched. It was a right-hand-drive Ford Escort. He'd hit the trees deliberately to slow down instead of ramming into the woods head-on. It was quick thinking, but it scared the hell out of me. How did I know it was an English car?

Walking away from such accidents seemed only to embolden him. And as his personal wealth grew—the money he'd earned from *Butch Cassidy*, *The Sting*, and *The Towering Inferno* was bolstered with investments, including an ownership interest in a shopping center in Merced, California—he made a major decision: he would take 1977 off from moviemaking and concentrate on driving. Connecticut, Florida, Ohio, New York, Pennsylvania: he raced everywhere. He didn't have a very successful campaign—his team fought mechanical troubles all season—but he was dedicated.

That February he returned to Daytona for the twenty-four-hour race, and this time he shone. He and the other drivers with whom he shared the driving duties finished fifth overall, and he fell in love with endurance racing. "I'd never driven at night before," he said. "I'd never driven a car with this much horsepower, and I'd never been involved in a race more than three or four hours long. Would I like to do it again? You bet your life."

In June 1979 he fulfilled that wish in spectacular fashion. With team owner Dick Barbour and the German pro Rolf Stommelen, Newman drove a Porsche 935 in the only other twenty-four-hour race in the world: the Le Mans road race in southern France. After taking in the Monaco Grand Prix with Joanne from a balcony in the palace alongside Princess Caroline, Newman went to Le Mans and drove all day and night at speeds upward of two hundred miles per hour in rainy conditions and on a course he'd never seen before. "Boy, it sure gets your attention," he said during a pit stop. The awful weather knocked a number of teams out of the race, and in the end it came down to two cars, both fighting engine trouble: the Whittington brothers of Florida, who had bad fuel injectors, and the Barbour team, which grabbed the lead in the final laps only to have their engine die, leaving them to limp over the finish line in second place.

It was an enormous achievement: a close second place in one of the world's most storied auto races at age fifty-four. But in a sense it was a disappointment—victory had been so close, and it would have been monumental. Worse, the press and the paparazzi dogged him in a way that they never did at lower-profile races back home. "They were insufferable," he groused. "I never, ever had an experience as bad as that. When I went out jogging in the morning they were there, like locusts. So I just ran along holding my middle finger up." Even during the race he felt assaulted: "You're strapping yourself in the car in the middle of the night and they knock off about 150 flashbulbs. I just wish I had a grenade." Finally, he swore never to return. "My racing here places an unfortunate emphasis on the team," he said. "It takes it away from the people who really do the work."

Back home he followed up this success with a string of eight straight wins on the SCCA circuit and another national championship victory at Road Atlanta. "It took seven years," Newman said, "but all at once things have started to pull together. I can feel it." He was especially proud of having earned the esteem of fellow racers, who, he feared, had initially dismissed him as a dilettante. "Perhaps now," he said, "people will stop taking me for a stupid actor who's playing at racing and accept me as a serious racer."

They did. Said one SCCA rival, "The man's a freak. There's no way he should be out on the track driving as well as he does at his age. He's just got talent coming out of his ears."

Nineteen

I N THE 1960S THE NEWMANS BEGAN TO SHARE THE WEALTH and good fortune they'd enjoyed with people they didn't know, sponsoring a girl from a mountain village in Colombia with monthly donations to the organization Save the Children, which was based in Westport. Over time they added six other children to their makeshift family and became spokespeople for the organization, appearing in magazine ads and TV commercials. But there was a sad irony that they should become involved in any organization by that name. In the mid-1970s some of the Newmans' biological children were as in need of saving as any of the kids they "adopted."

Scott, as ever, was in the worst shape. Despite the patronage of such Hollywood stalwarts as his father, George Roy Hill, Robert Redford, Irwin Allen, and even Steve McQueen, he hadn't exactly taken the town by storm after *The Great Waldo Pepper* and *The Towering Inferno*. He got a small role in a Charles Bronson action picture, *Breakheart Pass*, and appeared a few times on television—in episodes of *Marcus Welby, M.D.*; *S.W.A.T.*; and *Harry-O*, as well as a visit to Merv Griffin's talk show. But the bigger prizes kept eluding him.

The media were interested in him, and the attention made him nervous. "I sometimes feel compelled to dispel a public myth that I get work because of my father," he said. "The only thing my dad helps me get is my foot in the door."

But even that wasn't happening much, and he was hardly his own best friend in the matter. He was still drinking heavily, still using drugs. He had enrolled in acting classes, yes, but he was something of a catastrophe in them. He would miss sessions, sabotage rehearsals, and disappear from school and even his apartment for days on end, not answering his phone, not responding to his classmates' pleas for cooperation. He could go through bursts of self-improvement and self-rescue, hitting the gym, running, laying off the booze and the pills, slurping down health-food drinks. And then he'd relapse into a diet of liquor and drugs and junk food. In one thing he remained steadfast: he adamantly refused to turn to his father for financial or professional assistance. "I'm flat broke," he told a reporter. "I don't even have a bank account. Everyone assumes I have tremendous funds, but I haven't got a cent."

By this time he wasn't the only one of the kids in trouble. Nell, who had tasted acting twice by the time she was thirteen, seemed to have a stable foundation in her love of birds. ("I was really frustrated because I couldn't fly," she said, "seriously.") She and her sisters had appeared on TV with their parents in *The Wild Places*, a consciousness-raising 1974 documentary program about hiking and camping in the White Mountains of New Hampshire. She was their earth child, the keeper of the Newman menagerie. But she was confronted by the burden of two famous parents and a childhood spent inconsistently in multiple homes on two coasts, and when she hit her teens, she dropped out of high school and flitted dangerously close to the same lifestyle that had trapped her brother. When she learned to drive, she had several accidents, alarming Newman sufficiently that he had her take driving lessons from racing professionals. According to Joanne, "Nell . . . also got into drugs. Not like Scott, thank God, but she did miss a whole period of her life." She didn't fall terribly hard, but as her mother explained, "What she did was to screw up school and everything else in her life . . . She finds herself way behind her peers."

Stephanie too was drifting, leaving Bennington College to apprentice in a number of building trades—bricklaying, carpentry, electricity—and then working on a photojournalism project in Mayan communities in Guatemala. The youngest girls, Lissy and Clea, seemed to be doing well, pursuing interests in equestrian sports; Lissy actually dabbled in acting, once, appearing opposite her mother in

the made-for-TV film *See How She Runs*, about a housewife who becomes a top-class marathoner. But the family pattern was certainly
disconcerting.

There was hope amid the roiling: Susan had blossomed into a pretty
and unusually forthright young woman and had begun to pursue a performing career of her own. She attended acting classes in New York at
the Circle in the Square Theater School, making her home in the
Newmans' luxurious coop apartment on East Fiftieth Street, and she
got roles in a few small off-Broadway shows and workshop productions
and in at least one Broadway bomb. Like her brother, she found that
there were natural advantages in being Paul Newman's kid. "The terrific part is that I can get in to read for most roles," she said. But she
also recognized that the people whom she would be auditioning for
would have a set of preconceptions about her: "Everyone in that room
already knows ten or twelve things about me, right off the bat. And I
don't know a thing about them." She also found that some people felt
that there were disadvantages to casting a famous actor's daughter: it
could be seen purely as a publicity stunt and had the potential to dwarf
other aspects of the production. For a while she went professionally by
her first and middle names only—Susan Kendall. But that didn't fool
anybody, and she struggled along like any other young actress, albeit
with the most sensational of lineages.

In 1976 her father offered her a leg up. He was off to Johnstown,
Pennsylvania, to film *Slap Shot*, a movie about minor-league ice
hockey that struck him as something he would enjoy doing. He offered Susan a chance to work for him as his secretary on location as
well as a cameo role in the film. Johnstown was nobody's idea of a vacation, but the film looked like a hoot. She went.

George Roy Hill was directing from a script by Nancy Dowd, who
had written a ribald and shaggy story centered on Reggie Dunlop
(Newman), an over-the-hill player-coach who responds to the threat
that his team might fold for economic reasons by turning them from
also-rans who play by the rules into goons who win games by taunting,
goading, and fighting with their opponents. The script, based on the
experiences of Dowd's younger brother, Ned, who played for the Johnstown Jets of the North American Hockey League, was by several

measures the most vulgar thing Newman had ever done, and it was filled with violence, albeit of what Newman called the "Tom and Jerry" stripe.

Much of the film had to do with Dunlop's relationship with his star player, an Ivy League grad who refuses to play on the base level that his coach demands of him. Several rising young actors were auditioned for the role, including Nick Nolte and Peter Strauss, but none could skate well enough. (Strauss actually broke his leg trying to learn.) So the part went to Michael Ontkean, the Canadian-born star of the TV series *The Rookies* and a former hockey player at the University of New Hampshire. The roles of virtually every other member of the team—rechristened the Charlestown Chiefs—were taken by actual hockey players, including a trio of brothers, Steve, Jeff, and Jack Carlson, who were cast as the Hanson brothers, the gooniest of goons, whose arrival signifies the transformation of the Chiefs from a team that played hockey into a gang engaged in something more like professional wrestling.*

Newman, who'd spent his boyhood skating on frozen lakes in the wild spaces around Shaker Heights and had kept up his skating occasionally when the Aspetuck River beside his Westport home froze over, spent seven weeks training to do most of his own stunt work. "It was hard to go back to using the muscles again," he admitted, adding, "I'd forgotten how much fun it is." He was fifty-one, though, and he had his limits. "On the eleventh day of shooting the hockey scenes, I really ruined myself," he said. "It was a big fight sequence on the ice. You have to brace yourself very differently when you get into a brawl without good solid footing. So I strained all the muscles on the inside of my thighs and in my abdomen." He actually loved it, though—"Isn't the movie business great? I've learned how to drive a race car, to ride a horse, to play the trombone, to shoot billiards, and to play ice hockey." But he confessed there was a cost: "This has been the toughest physical film I've ever done. And believe me, I've done some rough ones."

---

* Before filming started, Jack Carlson got a contract to play actual professional hockey and was replaced by another player named, bizarrely, Dave Hanson.

For the duration of their stay in Johnstown, the production had rented a house for Newman in one of the nicer sections of town. But he preferred to be closer in, where he could hang out with the other player-actors and get in on the fun. So he spent his nights at the Johnstown Sheraton unless Joanne was in town, when he would use the big rented house. He hit bars with the guys, took them to nearby racetracks to watch him run practice laps, and even brought a couple of them along on the movie studio's private jet when he flew to Watkins Glen to do some racing. One afternoon he stopped by Dave Hanson's apartment to watch a car race on TV and have a few cold ones. They all loved him. "He's a great guy, not at all like a big shot," Jeff Carlson told a reporter. "We'll go out for a beer, and he'll buy a round, then we'll buy a round. It's not like he's always laying out a hundred-dollar bill."

Jeff's brother Steve recalled Newman behaving as if he had as much to learn from the young hockey players as he had to teach them as a veteran actor. "We had no clue what to do and how to do it. He would pull us off to the side and say, 'Try to do it this way. Try it that way.' Vice versa, we were the hockey players. He didn't know how to do something, and he'd ask our advice. He wasn't shy about that. He was a perfectionist." Newman made an impression, as well, on a young actress named Swoosie Kurtz, who was playing one of the players' wives. "It's interesting to watch his decisions in acting," she remarked. "When there's a choice of being sexy or funny or macho, he'll choose the last two every time, even though he *comes off* sexy."

His daughter certainly saw the evidence of that. On-screen she was limited to the tiniest of roles as a drugstore clerk with whom the players flirt during their idle afternoons. But as the gatekeeper who opened her father's mail, she was privy to a truly exclusive and provocative glimpse of the world. "I'll tell you one thing I've learned," she told a reporter. "Women in America are absolutely not getting laid! Maybe they're unhappy in a lot of different ways, but they're *also* not being satisfied by their husbands. Whatever crushes I've had on rock stars or actors have been fantasy-like things, but these women are *actively* pursuing my father."

It was as Kurtz said—even if Newman tried not to attract them, he attracted them. In *Slap Shot* he wore a garish wardrobe of polyester slacks and gaudy shirts and a cheap leather bomber jacket. But he looked great. The set of his character's apartment was the actual apartment of one of the Johnstown Jets—the one least capable of keeping a neat house—and Newman walked around it guzzling from beer cans in a T-shirt and boxer shorts, and he still looked good. (But at the film's first preview, one female member of the audience got a load of his infamously skinny legs and blurted aloud, "You mean he skates on *those*?") And although he swore like a sailor—the film was rated R almost entirely for its language, which Dowd had adapted from actual tape recordings that her brother had made for her in hockey locker rooms—he still exuded charm. Indeed, the film was released at approximately the same time as a new celebrity magazine, *US*, and it slapped Newman on the cover, salty mouth and all.

Slap Shot did startle audiences with its profanity: one woman from Indiana wrote Newman to say that the high point of her life had come a couple years earlier when he had raced his car at a track she owned; having seen *Slap Shot*, she said, she would turn her dogs on him if he ever came around again. But it was an entirely successful sports movie in which the clichés of triumphant underdogs were skirted for something that felt more like a slice of the real, asymmetrical, organic life of an obscure but vital subculture. Dowd's plotting was pleasantly shaggy, and Hill had captured the mood of it without any of the forced frivolity of *Butch Cassidy and the Sundance Kid* or *The Sting*. The reviews were admiring. Pauline Kael raved that *Slap Shot* was Newman's best work: "the performance of his life . . . His range isn't enormous; he can't do classics . . . But when a role is right for him, he's peerless . . . He's one of the few stars we've got in a normal emotional range . . . His technique seems to have become instinct. You can feel his love of acting."

The ticket sales, however, never materialized. The movie grossed $28 million in the same year that *Star Wars* and *Smokey and the Bandit* were released: in one regard, a respectable take, but really peanuts. Perhaps it was the very subject matter—hockey is at best a kid brother in the American sports pantheon. Perhaps it was the language and violence. Perhaps it was because Newman's star was itself in decline. But he was splendid in it: raunchy and cockeyed and filled with piss and vinegar. And the film caught on with the frat-boyish male audience, who made it—and much of the dialogue, and almost everything to do with the Hanson brothers—the object of a cult.

Newman was truly fond of the film. "I'm not usually happy with my work," he said, "but I loved that movie. It rates *very* high as something in which I took great personal satisfaction." The secret, he thought, was that "the picture was the star of the picture." He did harbor one regret from the shoot, though: he'd begun to swear too much, even at home. "You get a hangover from a character like that," he said, "and you simply don't get rid of it. I knew I had a problem when I turned to my daughter one day and said, 'Please pass the fucking salt.' "

THE PACE of his life was incredible. At the same time that he was skating and drinking with the boys of *Slap Shot*, he became a founding member of the Energy Action Caucus, a group that was trying to counteract the impact of big oil lobbying on the political process, with special focus on the environmental consequences of some oil industry practices. Along with a group of five others, described in the press as "liberal businessmen," Newman donated some money and helped raise some more to give the group $500,000 in funding for its lobbying activities in Washington. That summer he popped up at several events during the Democratic National Convention, which nominated Jimmy Carter at Madison Square Garden. He had done a little campaigning for Ramsey Clark, the former U.S. attorney general (and fellow director on the board of the Center for the Study of Democratic Institutions) who ran unsuccessfully for a Senate seat from New York. In January 1977, when Carter was inaugurated as president, both Newman and Joanne spoke at the star-choked gala held that night. (His old political sparring buddy John Wayne gave a speech at the event, declaring his allegiance to the new president as a member of the "loyal opposition." "That was simply the class act of the evening," Newman said admiringly. "I never forgot that.")

The following year, knowing of his long interest in halting nuclear proliferation, Carter's White House asked Newman to serve as a so-called "public delegate" at an upcoming United Nations General Assembly Special Session on Disarmament. He would be seated alongside Andrew Young, then the U.S. ambassador to the UN, W. Averell Harriman, George McGovern, and Charles W. Whalen, a Republican congressman from Ohio. For the five-week appointment he would be paid approximately $5,000 in salary and living expenses (which would not be a problem, since he owned an apartment mere blocks from the UN). In preparation he attended a briefing at the White House and happened to bump into the president as he was walking through a corridor. "What are you doing here?" Carter asked him. "Nothing." "Why don't you come on up?" He went into the Oval Office for what he felt was a rare opportunity to discuss the arms race with the leader of the free world, only to find out that the president was just like virtually everyone else he met outside of Hollywood: "I wanted to talk to him about SALT II,* and he wanted to talk about how you made movies."

During his tenure at the UN, Newman was respectful, private, and alert. As ever, he was afraid of being over his head in something. "I'm just learning the job," he told a reporter. "I'm trying to feel my way in." He realized he was out of his element and that his participation could be seen as frivolous. "I'm not a great negotiator," he admitted, "and I'm not a great drafter of initiatives. But I can get on the idiot box, and my goal is to spotlight what is going on at the UN."

Of course, he could cause a commotion simply by walking through the halls of the place. But when he finally was charged with making a major presentation, he spoke to a relatively small crowd about the United States' offer of its ground-based and satellite-surveillance technologies to help monitor the compliance of signatory countries to arms treaties. The speech was reportedly read in a monotone, but it was well received—and he did get a bigger crowd than Soviet foreign minister Andrei Gromyko had, which was something of a coup. But in general the permanent staffs of bureaucrats and diplomats seemed not

---

* The second round of the Strategic Arms Limitation Talks.

to miss him when his tenure was over. "He's a wonderful person, I'm sure, and I love his movies," said a Latin American ambassador. "Need I say more?"*

As AUTUMN approached and the racing season ended, Newman went off with Robert Altman again to make *Quintet*, as bizarre and wrongheaded a career choice as he'd ever made. Set in a frozen, desolate, postapocalyptic future, it starred Newman as a seal hunter who arrives in a city with a populace facing certain extinction. Life has been reduced to crude basics, enlivened only by a cryptic game called "quintet," which is played for life-and-death stakes. Filmed in Quebec, it boasted a cast of international stars—including Fernando Rey, Bibi Andersson, and Vittorio Gassman—but it flopped everywhere. The stolid sense of gloom and existential angst that pervaded the film; the nearly collegiate arbitrariness of its story line and plot; the wooden dialogue that was meant to be gnomic—it made for neither great art nor the sort of food for thought that brings adventurous moviegoers out of their homes. And Vincent Canby of the *New York Times* went out of his way to rip the film twice in two weeks, comparing it to "all the terrible little-theater plays I'd seen in my youth."

Funny he should mention the theater. Not long after completing work on *Quintet*, Newman found himself directing a play for the first time since he'd been a graduate student at Yale. And he was doing so at, of all places, the Bolton Theater, the brand-new facility on the campus of Kenyon College.

Newman had never let go of memories of Kenyon, and he kept in touch with the school. Starting in 1958, Kenyon began granting the Paul Newman Award to the best student actor of the year. The following year President F. Edward Lund of the college offered to present Newman with an honorary Doctor of Humane Letters degree at the

---

* That December Newman donated $25,000 to stage a one-day "Nuclear War Conference" in Washington, D.C. He attended and sat on the dais but never spoke.

spring 1960 commencement. He wrote back that he'd be in Israel on the proposed date. The following winter Lund wrote him again, and he replied that he was uncertain about his availability:

> I would like very much to accept the Degree but I cannot at this time commit myself to be in Gambier on June 4th simply because I do not know what my schedule will be. It makes me feel badly because I might give you the impression that I am indifferent, which I am not. This business gets crazier and crazier every year. I could be in New York on June 4th, or New Orleans, or Italian Somali land . . . I am not sure quite which.

But in fact he was available, and along with Joanne and his brother, Art, and Art's then-wife, Margie, he was at Kenyon on that date, accepting an honorary doctorate predicated by these encomia:

> We are proud of the eminence you have achieved, but for our own pleasure we like to think also of the lively and irreverent young man who was a student on this green hill not very many years ago. Such recollections have the effect of assuring us that something of you remains in this place, and that something of Kenyon goes wherever you go . . . It is a particular pleasure to confer a degree not as the culmination of a well-spent life but as an expression of our confidence in the good things you will do in the many years that lie ahead.

The Kenyon brass weren't entirely sentimental in their motives; internal correspondence of college officials discussed their plans for asking Newman for money. He complied to the generous tune of $10,000. And a decade later he sent more money to fund a Joanne Woodward Award for the best female student performance at the Coordinate College, a women's school affiliated with Kenyon.*

---

* Joanne herself would be awarded an honorary doctorate of fine arts by Kenyon in 1981.

In 1975 he was back on campus for a single day, flying in from Connecticut to nearby Mount Vernon, Ohio (site of the epochal Sunset Club brawl), to confer with school officials, including his old drama instructor and director James Michael, about the possibility of a new theater to replace the antiquated Hill Theater inside the Speech Building, where Newman had performed so memorably as an undergraduate. The reception was low-key and homey: Newman, dressed in denim, had a lunch of beer and sandwiches, sat on a lawn "rapping" with the college drama club, then met to discuss nuts and bolts, dollars and cents, with college president William G. Caples.

They were trying to coax him into donating enough to build the theater—about $2 million would be required—or, barring that, to allow them to name the building after him. He balked at both suggestions. Would he appear in the premiere production? No, he said, but he'd be willing to *direct* the premiere production for free. "It's less than we wanted," Newman recalled being told. "But more than I can afford," he responded.

His visit generated headlines, though, and those headlines gave the theater project traction. Eventually the necessary sum was raised, in large part through a grant from Cleveland industrialist Kenyon (Kenny) C. Bolton, a third-generation member of the college's board of trustees. An additional $20,000 for the premiere production was awarded by the Ford Foundation.

With the Ford money the college hired Ted Walch, a 1963 graduate who had been running the summer theatrical programs at Kenyon for several seasons. For material Walch managed to secure the services of writer Michael Cristofer, whose current play, *The Shadow Box*, was enjoying its initial run in New York en route to winning the Pulitzer Prize for drama. Cristofer had appeared in several summertime productions at Kenyon as a young actor (although he was never a student at the school) and happened to be in Gambier to witness the groundbreaking for the new theater when he learned of *The Shadow Box*'s success with the Pulitzer jury. He agreed to provide a completely new script based on an idea about a forgotten character of the American past, a 1920s entrepreneur and showman who had barnstormed with Red Grange and Bill Tilden and promoted a cross-country walking race in 1928 that became known as the Bunion Derby: *C. C. Pyle and the Bunion Derby*, it would be called.* And Newman, reminded of his promise of a couple years earlier, committed to coming back to Gambier to direct the finished play.

TALK ABOUT second boyhoods: Newman made several visits to Gambier in the summer and fall, then arrived on the first of November, planning to stay for upward of a month. He brought along a portable sauna and installed it in the antique-filled house of Kate Allen right in the middle of Gambier. (He never made his bed, she reported, but he always apologized for the failure.) He tried as much as possible to blend in, going for beers and pizzas, and beers and burgers, and beers and popcorn at the hamlet's watering holes, the Village Inn and Pirates Cove. (His own old haunt, Dorothy's, had long since closed down.) He was part of college life—or, at least, as much of it as he could enjoy without disrupting it with his mere presence; he attended a glee club concert and one of the monthly Sunday brunches at which students and faculty mixed. He invited folks over for grilled steaks and burgers and popcorn and beer and vintage wine. "We adults in the project would get together almost every night," Walch remembered, "and Paul was like a little kid, organizing it: 'I'll make the burgers and salad, and you guys do the rest.' " He screened *Rachel, Rachel* in the big campus assembly hall one night and took questions from students, even producing Joanne from the audience to join in the Q&A.

Thrill of thrills, he was named honorary coach of the football team on November 11. Coach Tom McHugh allowed him to give the boys in purple a pep talk before the game, and he told them about his own ignominious career (including a game against Otterbein College, when the opponents scored against Kenyon so often that they ran out of the fireworks they lit to celebrate touchdowns), promised to fill the locker room with Jacqueline Bissets if they won, and admonished the

---

* The actual Bunion Derby walked through Cleveland—not three miles from Shaker Heights—when Newman was a three-year-old.

players to "go out there and beat the shit out of them." Kenyon beat Bethany of West Virginia 34–33—huzzah!—but alas, no Jackie Bissets appeared.

With the theater people he was even more generous with his time and resources. He forked out for the construction of a turntable in the stage, as well as $12,000 toward video equipment to record the making of the play. He worked with the various craft departments, sewed costumes, painted scenery, and donated his weekly allotment of ten cases of Budweiser to the cast and crew.

Naturally he worked closest with Cristofer and the actors. Two professionals were in the cast—John Considine as C. C. Pyle and New York stage actress Susan Sharkey as Euphemia, his wife. James Michael, who had just retired from teaching, would play Pyle's father. And the remainder of the roles were filled by students, all of whom Newman knew by name instantly and would greet matter-of-factly on campus as they went about their days. (Among the cast was a lanky young actress from Dayton, Ohio, who passed her audition by explaining to speed-crazy Newman that she'd made the three-and-a-half-hour trip in two hours and forty-five minutes; her name was Allison Janney.)

The young actors were shocked and flattered by the treatment they got from the superstar. He would provide them with handwritten notes after rehearsals, or take them aside individually after they'd run through a scene to give advice or propose ideas. "He's an actor's coach," opined Michael. "The thing he does best is the intense one-on-one. In rehearsals there are a lot of people around, almost like a movie set. He'll go up onstage and tell an actor something in a quiet voice. It's something like movie directing." Indeed, Newman had a tendency, noted by several cast and crew members, to use movie lingo in his direction, saying "roll 'em," "put a wrap on that," "you've moved out of your frame," and so forth. But Considine remembered that Newman offered him an especially helpful bit of direction right at the start: "He said to me, 'I think C. C. Pyle has itchy palms,' and that was a nice little physical thing for me to work with."

But for all the control he exercised, he was ceaselessly collegial. Ted Walch said, "One of the fabulous things about Paul is that if Michael [Cristofer] or I thought something was wrong with a scene, we'd feel no compunction about telling him. He loves to listen. He can say he was wrong." He could get a laugh out of them. When they were working on a scene in which Red Grange made a sudden appearance among the contestants in the coast-to-coast race, he told them, "Think that you're meeting a big superstar . . . like Robert Redford." And he could shock them, too, with his sense of being just another guy working on the show. When Chris Smith, who had a small role, invited Newman to hear his singing group, Newman failed to show up; the next day a car driving past Smith near campus came to a sudden stop, and Newman jumped out with an apology: "Hey, Chris! Sorry I didn't make it. But I have a good excuse." (Smith gave him the needle: "What kind of excuse can you, Paul Newman, have for not coming to see us?") As Thomas Turgeon, a drama professor at the school put it, "He's practically one of them."

That was the remarkable thing. He was fifty-three years old, and yet he had the zest and energy and appetite of someone one-third that age. He had been a young man on those campus paths and hills and playing fields three decades before, and walking them once again in the chill light of a midwestern autumn, he could feel that he was one again. He was still, in middle age, the Golden Boy, "lively and irreverent," as his honorary degree had put it, eternally young, restless, inquisitive, iconoclastic, intrepid. He may have seemed like one of the kids, but he was the biggest kid, in many ways, of all.

OF COURSE, he had kids of his own, and for them his youthfulness and accomplishments could be crushing. He recognized it, at least in the abstract: of being the child of a superstar, he surmised, "There are liabilities and assets. Some of my children have focused more on the liabilities and others have been able to enjoy the assets."

In the eyes of Susan Newman, who spent some time at Kenyon while her father worked on the play, the most burdensome aspects of Newman's fame and image fell truly on one child: Scott. "Some children of public figures hold up well," she said, "and some get mad as hell and walk away or become the ugly duckling in the family. Because he was a man, it was much harder for my brother. Much as people might want to compare me with my father as a performer, some of the heat was off me because we were different sexes. A lot of outsiders regard this as a very privileged life, but in many ways it can be draining and very painful."

According to A. E. Hotchner, who'd known him since he was a boy, "Scott was a big, handsome, outgoing man. He felt the burden of being Paul Newman's son." Scott may not have been as handsome as his father, but he was, as Hotchner said, a good-looking young man (Joanne compared him to a French movie star), and he was taller and, when he was feeling well, friendlier than his dad. He was at least as willing as his father to risk his neck with cars or bikes or skydiving, and he had his father's taste for hijinks. But he continued bootlessly to butt his head against a performing career and to batter himself with liquor and drugs and danger as if in punishment for his failures. "People expect more of me," he said when asked about being Paul Newman's son. But nobody, seemingly, expected more than he himself.

In 1977 he got a featured role in a film made by some University of Southern California grad students. Set in the 1950s and called *Fraternity Row*, the film cast Scott as Chunk Cherry, the frat-house sadist who bullies the protagonist and his buddies. It was a dreary, sober portrait of fraternity life gone sour that wanted for humor, drama, and charm. It did almost no business, which was probably a good thing for all involved. Then he tried singing, appearing in cabarets and night spots around L.A. under the stage name William Scott and angling for a record deal with Don ("American Pie") McLean. It came to naught.

He was increasingly erratic in his behavior. Kathy Cronkite, the daughter of famed newscaster Walter, knew Scott socially and recalled him being in his cups at a party and angrily dismissing someone as being interested in him only because of his father; as it happened, the other fellow had no idea that Scott was the son of a movie star. Later at the same party, Scott puffed up at someone else and sneered, "Don't you know who my father is?"

The Newmans knew Scott was in trouble, and they got him into the care of a highly regarded addiction counselor, who saw the problem plainly, explaining that he found Scott "terrorized by the idea of trying to be a professional actor. The risk of failure scared the hell out of him, so he relied on drugs and alcohol." It was a teeter-totter of emotions, and it always seemed to end with him on the down side. And it left Newman, a self-confessed flaky father, desperate for a solution. "We were like rubber bands," he said later. "One minute close, the next separated by an enormous and unaccountable distance." It had even crossed his mind to force his twenty-eight-year-old son physically to hew to the straight and narrow, but as he confessed to a friend, "The kid's bigger than me, and I can't tell him what to do anymore."

Soon it would be too late for even that.

On Sunday, November 19, 1978, Scott spent the day in L.A. watching football on TV with a friend. He'd been doing some stunt work—he'd just filmed a car jump for a "Circus of the Stars" TV special—and he'd recently crashed his motorcycle, which made him more eager than usual to chase away his pains. The day began with rum drinks, but they had no effect on his discomfort. "It hurts right here under my ribs and behind my shoulder," he said. His friend had some Valium on hand, and Scott swallowed five of them. An hour later he took three more.

Then he went off to see a psychologist whom the Newmans had hired—along with a nutritionist—to help Scott find an even keel. Scott and the doctor spoke for a while, and when they were finished, Scott was given a sample bottle of Darvon and sent off in the keep of an associate of the practice. He went back to his friend's place for some more rum drinks, then sometime after nine P.M. decided to call it a night. He had recently moved out of an apartment in Brentwood and had been renting a set of rooms at a Ramada Inn in West Los Angeles; he repaired there.

At the hotel Scott chatted with his keeper, ate a little supper, retired to the bathroom, popped a couple of quaaludes, chased them with some cocaine, and emerged to declare himself ready for bed. By ten he was asleep, snoring loudly. After about an hour and a half the attendant noticed that he could no longer hear the noises from Scott's room. He went in to check on him and found that he'd stopped breathing.

Paramedics were summoned, and they brought him to the emergency room of Los Angeles New Hospital. But it was too late. At 1:07 A.M. on the morning of November 20, Scott had succumbed to

what the coroner called "acute proxpoxyphene and ethanol intoxica-
tion": an accidental overdose of drugs and booze. To make the
tragedy complete, the hotel in which he had died—with a minder in
the very next room—was right across the street from the hospital
where his death was pronounced.

THIS WAS a thunderbolt from hell, compounded by the fact that Newman would get the dreadful call about Scott while encamped at Kenyon, site of his early triumphs and of the blissful second youth he was
living all that month. It was like a smackdown from the gods: in exchange for his vitality, his energy, and his boyishness, he would pay the
price of the only son who would carry his name, his genes, his aura. All
the talk of Newman's Luck seemed suddenly a bitter joke.

"In a way, I had been waiting for that call for ten years," he said not
long afterward, about that day. "Somehow my body mechanism built
me an anesthetic for when it really happened. I was . . . *a lot of things*
when I got that call. I was probably more pissed off than anything."

He claimed that he and Scott had both contributed to their es-
trangement and, by extension, to Scott's fate. "Scott and I had simply
lost the ability to help each other," he explained. "I had lost the ability
to help him, and he had lost the ability to help himself." But he took
responsibility for his own failure to find a solution: "I just realized that
whatever I was doing in trying to be helpful was not being helpful at
all. In fact, it could have been harmful."

Still, he recognized that he was the father and that he should never
have stopped being involved, making the effort, looking for signs of
real danger in his son's behavior: "You know, for someone who is supposed to be in the business of observing people, to have a whole series
of signals being sent out and having them go right by without any
recognition at all, it troubles me."

When the call came, Newman was, despite the detachment evinced
in these retrospective observations, devastated. John Considine happened to be visiting him at his lodgings in Gambier, and as he recalled,
"It was a horrendous moment. He could barely talk. We got out into
the air and walked around the campus for hours, and he was deciding

what to do and whether or not he could go on with the play. I went back to my room, and he came around later to say that he had decided that the best thing was to keep busy and carry through. He came back and said, 'I'm gonna do it.' "

Later that day he gathered himself to attend rehearsal. He walked into Bolton Theater and stunned the assembled cast and crew with the awful news. But he insisted that they continue as they had been, that their efforts and energy would be invaluable to him: "What I need right now—I need the show, I need all of you, I need the rowdiness." After work had finished for the night, Claire Bass and Breezy Salmon, a couple of girls from the chorus line, dressed up like clowns and, along with another cast member, Kevin Cobb, showed up at Newman's front door with a case of Coors and a bottle of Jack Daniel's. Newman took a slug of whiskey—"That's the first time I've touched the hard stuff in eight years," he told them. And then he shooed them away gently.

In L.A. someone in the office of Newman's publicist, Warren Cowan, was reached by a reporter who asked if Newman had anything to say. "No," he responded. "What is there to say?" Cowan's office issued obituaries that, appropriately in the circumstances, painted a picture of a warm relationship between father and son. But a lot of people knew better, and Scott was offered up by the press as another of those children of fame who lived in pain and had recently died young: Jonathan Peck, Dan Daily III, Diane Linkletter, Diana Barrymore, Edward Robinson Jr., Jenny Arness—an awful tally.

The next day Newman and Joanne drove to Cleveland, where they had a makeshift Thanksgiving dinner with Theresa Newman, who was still in the house on Brighton Road. Then they flew to Los Angeles for Scott's funeral, a small private affair to which none of his friends were invited. On November 27 Scott's body was cremated and his ashes interred at the Westwood Village Mortuary.

The family issued no official statement in Scott's memory, but not long afterward Susan, speaking independently but truthfully, revealed how they may have felt, saying, "I think Scott was a troubled individual from the time he was born. I believe in Karma. I believe certain things in life may be preordained. I believed from the time I was twelve years old Scott was not going to live to be an old man."

Scott's friends, organized by actor Allen Goorwitz (aka Allen Garfield), director Mimi Leder, and psychologist Burton Kittay, met on that Friday for a memorial at, with painful irony, the Actors Studio West. Kathy Cronkite was there, taking notes for a book she was writing about the children of superstar celebrities, and she recorded some of what was said:

> I remember when Scott first came to acting class. He seemed so self-assured—and that smile! But what I always remember is the nervous laugh *behind* the smile.
>
> He was always competing with his father's image—lover, actor, race-car driver.
>
> In Scott, the panic was always *right* there, and he was always trying to find a solution. It was so powerful he didn't know how to help himself.
>
> I don't think I ever saw him jump into a pool; he always did triple flips.
>
> Scott didn't die because he was a celebrity's kid; he died because he had a terrible disease called alcoholism. And alcoholism doesn't care who your father is.
>
> Scott was the talented one. He just was.

And then, because he had made the commitment, Newman returned to Kenyon, to finish rehearsals. As Ted Walch recalled, "The kids in the play were the healers for him—at least at that moment. When they realized that he was coming back to work with them, they just leaped back into it with love and appreciation. Their youthful resilience really buoyed him. And Paul just went on with his work. He wouldn't talk about Scott." John Considine, who would lose a child of his own later on, was aware that Newman was still in pain: "You could tell at times that he was distracted, but he carried through."

The play finally premiered on December 9 to a sold-out gala crowd who'd paid $100 a pop to see the show and rub elbows with the Newmans. (The press were banned from the production, but the *Plain Dealer* of Cleveland sneaked in a reviewer, who found the show "a delight.") Newman stayed on through the couple of weeks of performances, giving further encouragement and instruction to the actors, leaving everyone deeply impressed with his ability to work on through unimaginable pain.

But, he said, it was the cast and the crew and the play and the college that had given him so much, that had restored him in a time when he might've self-destructed.

"When the college finally called in its chit—my longtime promise to direct the first play in a new theater—it was the last thing I really wanted to do," he confessed. "But I felt I owed it to Jim Michael and to Kenyon. Now, as I'm getting ready to leave, I feel like I owe Kenyon all over again."

Before many years had passed, he would find a way to repay that debt, and others, both directly and indirectly, and many times over.

Twenty

PERHAPS THE MOST TERRIBLE, THE MOST GNAWING THING ABOUT Scott's death was that Newman had been aware for years of the dangers that drugs posed to kids. As early as 1968 he was narrating public-service documentaries about opiate addiction, and over the years he would occasionally speak to student and youth groups about alternatives to drug use.

It could have been taken as a sign of hypocrisy. After all, he was famous for how much he drank, and he admitted to being curious about stronger vices. "I've smoked grass," he confessed to an interviewer, "but I've never done anything else. I'm a square." (In fact, he was: when he first saw someone wearing that great icon of 1970s cocaine use—a gold-plated razor blade hanging on a chain—he thought it was a joke about slashing your wrists when the going got tough.) But his awareness of drug abuse could also be seen as part of his long-held belief that a man must be engaged in the issues of his time, and as the father of six, he was palpably aware of its specter.

In 1979, mere months after Scott's death, the Newmans served as narrators for a TV documentary about the dangers of angel dust; the film was made by David Begelman, the former agent and studio boss who was caught forging checks against Columbia Pictures' accounts, as part of the community-service portion of his sentence. Two years later Newman helped out yet another mogul in trouble, Robert Evans, who was making a series of public-service announcements about the perils of drug use as part of *his* community-service obligation after conviction on a misdemeanor charge for cocaine possession.

He wouldn't speak about Scott—interviewers were specifically warned away from the subject. But Joanne occasionally did, and the wounds she revealed were fresh and deep. "Maybe it would have been a good idea if we had been able to stand up somewhere along the line and announce to the public, 'Wait a minute. Here is what is happening in our household,' " she said, singling out for praise comedienne Carol Burnett, who spoke openly about her daughter's drug problems.*

But Newman wasn't the confessional sort. And he had to find something more tangible to do, so as to feel there had been a reason for this terrible loss. Soon after Scott's death, several friends of the Newmans— John Foreman, Stewart Stern, and Warren Cowan principal among them—combined their resources and connections to form the Scott Newman Foundation, which would dedicate itself to the cause of promoting antidrug education through films, TV shows, and lecture tours. The Newmans were involved, although not as founders. And Jacqueline McDonald, as Scott's mother was known after her second marriage, joined the staff full-time and stayed on for the rest of her working days.

Again, Joanne spoke publicly about the effort. "This may sound corny," she said, "but we didn't want Scott to have lived in vain. His life didn't seem to have much point, and we wanted—even after the fact—to make it have a point." At first the foundation was a very small operation, dedicated to lobbying for drug-prevention programs, to educational film production, and to an annual awards ceremony honoring people who made films or TV shows with antidrug messages. But because the Newmans were involved, the foundation drew Hollywood stars to its fund-raisers and to the casts of its informative programs. Within a few years the Newmans had upped their stake in the fight against drugs considerably, donating $1.2 million to the University of Southern California to create the Scott Newman Chair in Pharmacy and the Scott Newman Center for Drug Abuse Prevention and Health

---

* More than a decade later Joanne would star in a made-for-TV movie about a U.S. congresswoman whose daughter (played by Laura Linney) is a cocaine addict.

Communications. Newman himself was present at the press conference announcing the gift, and it was one of the rare times he spoke
publicly about the toll that drugs had taken on his family.

"The biggest problem is when the subject is swept under the carpet,"
he told reporters. "Communication has to be brought out in the open. It
can be tough. You have to keep the lines of communication open."

Had he done that with Scott? he was asked.

"I don't know," he answered, on the verge of tears. "I really can't
answer that."

BESIDE HIM on the dais that day was Susan, now the oldest of his children and the director of special projects for the Scott Newman Foundation. When her brother was playing out the last chapter of his life,
Susan was still a struggling actress, drawing publicity because of her
famous lineage but compiling a rather ordinary résumé of roles and
performances. After *Slap Shot* she had a small part in Robert Altman's
A Wedding and then a featured role in *I Wanna Hold Your Hand*, an
early film of Robert Zemeckis's that concerned the hysterical reaction
of American girls to the 1964 arrival of The Beatles.* She was saucy
and outspoken: when *People* did an article about her, she revealed,
"Losing my virginity was hard. I was always asking myself, 'Do they
want to lay me for myself or because I am Paul Newman's daughter?' "
A few years later, reflecting on her brother's death, she told a newspaper, "That predisposition to compulsive behavior is present in every
Newman. My addiction is food. I am a compulsive overeater."

Statements like that, along with her willingness to participate in
Kathy Cronkite's book about the children of superstars, might have
driven a wedge between her and Newman. But Susan gave up acting
as she reached her thirties and sought other outlets for herself; most

---

* She had an anecdote that revealed how out-of-touch her dad was with the realities of
a young actor's life. When she phoned to tell him that she'd been cast in Zemeckis's
film, he asked, "How many points did you get?"—referring to the percentage of box
office gross a star of his caliber commanded. "Dad, I hate to tell you this," she replied,
"but I was glad to get the *salary.*"

important, she found a way to bond with her father, partly out of their shared grief at losing Scott. "In the last year," she admitted to a reporter, "he has been reaching out in a more direct way. Less guarded. More open. We've become closer. Daddy has really made an effort recently. Perhaps his priorities have changed. Scott's death had something to do with it. Maybe he's going through some sort of midlife crisis. He's changing physically; he's changing mentally."

Before she dedicated herself to the foundation that bore her brother's name, Susan had a chance to collaborate with her father professionally. With a documentary filmmaker named Jill Marti, she had acquired the rights to *The Shadow Box*, the Tony- and Pulitzer Prize–winning play by *C. C. Pyle and the Bunion Derby* author Michael Cristofer that dealt with the lives of patients in a cancer hospice. Susan and Marti had the idea of producing it as a television movie, and they brought it to Joanne—there's a juicy role as the flamboyant ex-wife of one of the patients—who in turn suggested that they ask Newman to direct it. Having directed a play of the author's previously, and seeing an opportunity to present the "voluptuous, kinky" Joanne he knew to the world, he agreed. And he went to work with Cristofer on adapting the stage play for television.

The two neophyte producers, meanwhile, shopped the idea around to the TV networks, which initially all balked at the idea of entertaining their audiences with such grim material. Susan and Marti were prepared for this reaction. "We got together all the reviews of the play," Susan recalled. "If they said, 'But it deals with death,' we said, 'But look at this review, which talks about how funny it is.' So when we walked in with this package, which included Joanne and Paul, it was pretty impressive. It was hard to say no."

Having the Newmans in the mix attracted a stellar cast: Christopher Plummer as Joanne's ex, James Broderick and Valerie Harper as a blue-collar couple, and Sylvia Sidney and Melinda Dillon as a crabby old woman and her dutiful, selfless daughter.* ABC agreed to fund the

---

* Sidney's part had been a woman's role onstage, but Newman had the idea to rewrite it for Laurence Olivier, who ultimately passed on the offer to play it.

film to the tune of $1.9 million—a hefty sum for a TV film—and granted the production a couple of real liberties: the right to a two-week rehearsal period (Newman, as ever, was particularly insistent on this) and a twenty-two-day shooting schedule.

The Newmans rented a house in Malibu for the month, and the production set itself up not far away, at a former Salvation Army camp in a canyon of the Santa Monica Mountains. The weather that winter, though, was brutal; Southern California had some of the worst rains in memory, and the old camp cabins that were being used as sets and offices were actually in danger of being swept away in landslides or flooding.* And yet somehow—perhaps because they had prepared so well during rehearsal—the film was finished more or less on time.

Everyone was aware that Newman was doing the film in large part to bolster Joanne. "I was fed up seeing her play frumps," he declared proudly of her glamorous, brazen character. "She finally got into the part the day she glued on her fingernails." Plummer, whose character has divorced Joanne's after acknowledging his own homosexuality, was especially pleased that the Newmans' collaborative instincts extended to the whole company. "It's always slightly uncomfortable for the other performers when a husband directs a wife," he said. "But Paul and Joanne have none of the secrets you find in that situation. I have the distinct impression that when Paul and Joanne go home they don't talk about this at all."

But the working rapport between the director-father and the producer-daughter was a trickier matter. "I'm an actress," Susan reminded a reporter. "I always wanted to be directed by my father. Now I have to argue over the phone with him about renting some piece of equipment." She spoke of "complex role playing" and "testy waters" and joked, "It's hard to tell your father 'No helicopter shots,' but we did." And Newman ultimately realized, after a little head-butting, that she was serving the project—and its director—very well. "I know

---

* In fact, after the film wrapped, the facility was partly destroyed by the rain, and a nearby creek, which can be seen in the finished movie, drowned two people.

Susan's not going to make any deals that are not in my interest," he admitted. "She watches everything like a hawk."

She was especially vigilant over the press. For a made-for-TV film, *The Shadow Box* had an impressive pedigree, and so it drew a lot of interest from reporters. But in all the coverage of the film in national magazines and in the most prestigious newspapers, not a word appeared about one of the most obvious aspects of the project: Newman and his daughter were making a film about saying good-bye to a loved one just a year after Scott's death. Newman only hinted at a personal stake in the project when he described the film's themes: "The statement is that we should have reverence for what happens today, tomorrow, and the day after tomorrow, not throw time away." It was not a statement of grief, certainly, but evidence nonetheless that a certain costly knowledge of life's pains had informed the film.

After shooting wrapped and Newman began the editing, he found that the film was too long for the traditional two-hours-minus-commercials slot for which he made it. ABC magnanimously agreed to let the film run seven minutes overtime, bumping the evening news. And while they failed to find a major underwriting sponsor for the film—too much honesty about death and homosexuality, perhaps, for the prime time of the era—the network agreed to let the final thirty-five minutes air without interruption.

Unfortunately, they aired it on December 28, when even a funny, tasteful, and exquisitely performed movie about such grim themes was a tough sell. The reviews were respectful but not exactly enthusiastic. The acting was quite fine, but the production had a flatness that kept it from becoming truly evocative emotionally. Joanne was dazzling as a wise, boozy floozy, and Plummer, Broderick, Dillon, and Sidney were good, as was Harper. But the film didn't really make a splash, either in the ratings or among TV insiders; it was nominated for three Emmys (including one for Newman) but won none.

If the makers of *The Shadow Box* had to content themselves with a *succès d'estime*, that was more than was available to the folks behind *When Time Ran Out . . .*, Newman's second bit of work-for-hire for Irwin Allen. The disaster movie craze had come to an end once Steven Spielberg and George Lucas showed up with their special-effects pictures, but Allen was still chugging along, and he paid Newman $2 million to come to Hawaii, along with the likes of Jacqueline Bisset, Red Buttons, Ernest Borgnine, William Holden, and Burgess Meredith, and confront a volcanic eruption. James Goldstone, who had made *Winning*, was on board as director, and—and nothing. It was dreadful makework, stodgy and laughable and thrust into the marketplace well past its sell-by date. Nobody wanted to see it in theaters, and it had such an unpromising air about it that it was retitled for video release *(The Day the World Ended)* and then again when it aired on television *(Earth's Final Fury)*. Newman had rarely worked solely for money, and he hadn't, since he left Warner Bros. more than two decades earlier, appeared in something that bore absolutely no potential for artistic innovation or experiment. This time he had done both.

At least he was putting the money to good use. In 1981 the Newmans expanded their Connecticut property significantly. Their original parcel had been gradually improved over the decades with outbuildings and so on, but they were hemmed in a bit. Their property ended at a small bluff above a finger of the Aspetuck River; across that waterway, in which Newman swam virtually every day he was in Westport, sat another, much larger parcel, owned by a widow whom the Newmans feared would someday sell out to a new owner who would build a modern monstrosity and ruin their view. They had approached the woman and asked to buy the portion of her acreage that faced theirs, but she didn't want to break up the property. At the time Newman put a proposition to her: When she was ready to sell, he said, "You get two appraisals made, and I'll get two made, and we'll add 'em up and divide by four, and I'll write you a check."

Now she was ready, and the Newmans acquired her land, bringing their holdings up to nearly fifteen acres, plus the two main houses and the outbuildings on both properties. They built a footbridge across the river—after hassling with the town over where the hundred-year high-water mark should be set—and gradually turned the newly acquired house into their main residence, giving their original house to their girls as a home for holidays and vacations. In time they converted several of the buildings on the new property; Joanne had a dance studio, Newman installed thousands of dollars' worth of fitness equipment, and there was a barn that they turned into a screening room/rec room/guesthouse. It was a world unto itself.

They had another property too, also expensive: Far West Farms in West Salem, just over the border from Connecticut in Westchester County, New York. A fifty-four-acre riding school and horse farm, it boasted a riding arena, stables, a Grand Prix jumping course, and business facilities. The farm operated as a business, but it was also a family playground. Joanne rode, as did Lissy and especially Clea, who was becoming one of the most accomplished show-jumping riders of her age, competing regularly for national titles in the sport.

What with the horses to feed and transport, and the expense of new property and new construction in Westport, and the ongoing cost of auto racing—which was threatening to balloon as Newman considered adding the responsibilities of owning and operating a race team to his driving career—there came a sense of fiscal reality: Newman hadn't been managing his career well for some time. It had been more than six years since he'd had an agent in Hollywood; in that time his movie deals had been made through his production companies and overseen by lawyers and business managers.

In 1980, though, he reversed himself and signed with the most powerful and cutthroat agent since Lew Wasserman, Newman's original hired killer, had left the business: Michael Ovitz of Creative Artists Agency, the Death Star of the Hollywood agenting business. Ovitz was nothing like Freddie Fields, the likable, kibitzy fellow who'd previously looked after Newman's movie deals. Rather, like an old-time studio boss, he was a warrior willing to crush anyone to get his way. He studied martial arts and philosophies of war. He operated like a ninja: quiet, decisive, deadly. Newman once described Ovitz, admiringly, as "a combination of barracuda and Mother Teresa." And he learned right from the start just how valuable it was to have such a fellow working for you.

For the first deal that he cut for Newman, Ovitz delivered a whopper: $3 million or 15 percent of the gross, for him to appear as a veteran policeman navigating a perilous course of romance, mentorship, loyalty, justice, and appalling crime in the treacherous terrain of New

York's worst ghetto, in a film called *Fort Apache the Bronx*. Considering that Newman hadn't starred in a genuine hit since *The Towering Inferno* and that he was fresh on the heels of the deadly one-two of *Quintet* and *When Time Ran Out . . .* , this was a staggering deal. But it also marked a transformative moment in Newman's work, in which his characteristic attraction to top-flight collaborators and socially compelling themes melded with an enriched acting style born of the experience of three decades in front of movie cameras and the real sense of loss and mortality with which he'd been struck when Scott died. The massive fees Ovitz would wrest from movie studios were almost secondary. As each of his next films would reveal, Newman had begun to evolve into not only a new style of acting but a new version of himself.

FORT APACHE was made of the raw stuff that could help Newman scour his résumé of his recent cinematic missteps. The South Bronx of the late 1970s and early 1980s was a blighted-out urban hellhole, so decayed and desolate that people compared it to Dresden or Tokyo after World War II. Jimmy Carter had visited the place as president in 1977 as if it had been the site of an earthquake or a hurricane and pledged aid and restoration. But there wasn't much hope for change. A script about life in the local police station—the 41st Precinct, nicknamed Fort Apache by the cops assigned there*—had been floating around for a few years; at one time Steve McQueen had been attached to star. David Susskind, the former agent and talk show host turned producer, set the film up at 20th Century–Fox with a budget in the range of $15 million—a big chunk of which, of course, would go to Newman.

The story was loosely based on the experiences of two detectives, Tom Mulhearn and Peter Tessitore, who had each put in several years at the 41st; a series of rewrites of former journalist Heywood Gould's original script led to the version that director Daniel Petrie would

---

* A few years later, after spates of fires and foreclosures had isolated the precinct house even further, it became known as the Little House on the Prairie.

shoot. Opposite Newman, the filmmakers sought a dynamic younger actor to play his protégé and, as events unfold, conscience. John Travolta was considered, but the part eventually went to the actor Ken Wahl. Ed Asner was cast as the precinct commander; Danny Aiello, a Bronx native, as a cop with a sadistic bent; and newcomer Rachel Ticotin as the Puerto Rican nurse with whom Newman's character has a brief and painful fling.

The film began shooting in March 1980 on location in the Bronx, a choice that might have been intended in part as an economic boon for the community but that turned out to have distracting consequences for the film. A couple of weeks into production, copies of the script leaked out to various community groups, and they were incensed at what they saw as a racist attack on the people of the South Bronx. They complained to the filmmakers that all of the black and Hispanic characters in the film were criminals or junkies or bad guys, while the largely white police force was depicted as besieged and helpless. The filmmakers met with the protesters, who had formed a group called the Committee Against Fort Apache, and found themselves at loggerheads; the committee wanted changes to the script, but Susskind and Petrie wouldn't accommodate them. CAFA escalated by sending picketers to the set to disrupt filming: when Petrie called for action, they would start chanting, "Get out of the Bronx." Next CAFA filed a libel suit against the production in the New York State Supreme Court; William Kunstler argued their case.

The attacks on the film made great fodder for journalists. The *New York Post* was especially keen on the story, as it showed Newman and Asner, famed advocates of liberal political causes, to be hypocritical about helping the urban poor when their own paydays hung in the balance. Newman tried to countervail the protests and actually invited one of the most fiery—and desperate-looking—picketers into his trailer to discuss the issues; he managed to turn the fellow around. But it wasn't enough. On April 7 Newman took part in a press conference on the set intended to defend the film from CAFA's attacks. "It is not a racist picture," he contended. "It is tough on Puerto Ricans, blacks, and the neighborhood, but the two villains are Irish cops who throw a Puerto Rican off a roof." He explained that a movie about police work would necessarily focus on criminals, prostitutes, and drug users, and that he was hopeful that making the film would open the eyes of audiences to the very real problems the South Bronx was facing. "About 90 percent of the people in this country don't know what urban blight is," he said, pointing out that the area policed by the 41st Precinct had neither a hospital nor a high school in its boundaries.

But this sort of pleading only made the protests seem based in something true. And when Newman admitted later on that he truly knew nothing about the South Bronx ("To realize that you live on its doorstep and never realize what's going on inside your own city came as something of a shock to me"), he wasn't strengthening his position. CAFA's lawsuit was dismissed by the court—the judge commented that it contained "only speculative connotations and ideological innuendo"—but the production had work to do to make things right with the community. Newman met with a representative of the Ford Foundation, which was investing in South Bronx community groups and even funding home-ownership programs in the area, and he was sufficiently impressed to insist on two changes in the film: adding a disclaimer at the start of the film that declared that the South Bronx had many individuals and groups who were working to improve the community and giving lines to Asner citing the honest citizens of the neighborhood as the reason that the officers of the 41st needed to be exemplary.

But when the film came out the following February, protesters picketed the Manhattan theater where it was supposed to have its premiere. ("Supposed to" because the management of the theater—which stood in one of the poshest parts of the Upper East Side—had passed on booking the film and instead sent it uptown to a theater in a more racially and economically diverse neighborhood.) They were joined in their condemnation of the film by no less a cinema maven than Mayor Ed Koch, who agreed that it was a racist movie but wasn't worried that audiences would be fooled by it: "People can smell something that is not kosher. This film is not kosher."

The box office vindicated Koch, unfortunately, totaling less than $30 million. *Fort Apache* had some quite good scenes—real tension having to do with the killing by the cops, a climactic standoff with gunmen in a hospital, and a last-minute tragedy that brought out an especially poignant reaction in Newman's character. But it felt like a message picture too, at a time when that genre was distinctly out of favor with the public.

FEELING THAT he had been badly burned by the press, and particularly by the *Post*, Newman must have been especially pleased when, at the end of the 1981 auto-racing season, Ovitz presented him with the offer to replace Al Pacino in a film about journalistic malfeasance that was to shoot in Miami during the winter. *Absence of Malice* was based on a script by Kurt Luedtke, a former executive editor of the *Detroit Free Press*, and dealt with an investigative reporter who is manipulated by a federal investigator into putting pressure on a private citizen in order to jump-start a stalled Justice Department probe. As a result of the newspaper's decision to run a front-page story claiming that the man was the suspect in an infamous unsolved crime, the fellow, who has done nothing wrong, loses his business and sees a good friend commit suicide. He finds that he must fight back by framing the prosecutors and the newspaper in the same way that they attempted to frame him.

Newman had taken potshots at the press before; after Scott's death, he objected to a *Newsweek* article about his time directing at Kenyon by writing a letter to the magazine, which it published, in which he declared, "I've canceled my subscription to *Newsweek* and replaced it with *Screw* magazine. At least that publication doesn't have any pretensions about what it is." He was pretty keen, then, to play Michael Gallagher, the gangster's son—and legitimate businessman—wronged by the press and the government. A substantial cast was assembled: Sally Field as the reporter, whose violations of professional ethics would include actually sleeping with the fellow she was writing about; Bob Balaban as the nervous and unscrupulous prosecutor who used Gallagher as a Judas goat; and Wilford Brimley as the Justice Department official who must sort the whole mess out.

Sydney Pollack directed, meaning that the performances would be of guaranteed quality but that a certain slickness and patness would pervade. He and the producers actually rewrote and reshot the ending after test-screening audiences balked at the notion that Gallagher and the reporter had no chance to reconcile; a tacky little hopeful coda was included in the final cut. That said, they left tough stuff in: in one grueling scene Gallagher physically attacks the reporter, coming close to rape. As Field recalled, Newman "had to push me around and he really didn't want to do it. He was so afraid he would hurt me, he could have cared less what the scene was. I had to act like such a booger, and he finally did it. I was completely black-and-blue, but I couldn't let him know so he wouldn't feel bad."

If the shoot went smoothly, the release was another matter. When the film came out at the end of 1981, in time for the Oscar season, Columbia Pictures decided to launch it with a luncheon for the press at Tavern on the Green in Central Park. Newman refused to shake the hand of the woman representing the *New York Post*, telling her, "I hate your paper," and ignoring her questions. He assailed a reporter from the *Village Voice* who he claimed, wrongly, had misquoted him in a story about the *Fort Apache* controversy (the writer *had* written an unfavorable story, but Newman was not quoted in it); the fellow was so rattled that he stood up and left rather than submit to more of Newman's scorn. Newman didn't care who knew why he'd made the picture. "The movie was a direct attack on the *New York Post*," he acknowledged. "I was emotionally receptive to doing a piece about sloppy journalism. I wish I could sue the *Post*, but it's awfully hard to sue a garbage can."

The attack on journalism in *Absence of Malice* occasioned a lot of soul-searching in the newspaper trade, which was, as ever, eager to critique itself in public. But press critics who searched the film for cautionary lessons generally came away satisfied that the script distorted their work. Newman knew they'd close ranks against him. "They protect themselves just like doctors, dentists, and gangsters," he said, "and not necessarily in that order." He had one more plan for revenge on the *Post* and its owner, Rupert Murdoch: "What someone might do is invent something, something really insulting. Like Murdoch can't spell and has to carry a pocket dictionary. That he got picked up at a very early age for having sex with chickens." It would not be the last skirmish of the war.

The sensational offscreen aspects of *Fort Apache* and *Absence of Malice* nearly obscured the fact that Newman had delivered two remarkable performances in 1981: tough and feeling and cunning and desperate in turns, with moments of profound emotion and thoroughly realistic spontaneity throughout. It had been at least a decade since he'd been so good in two pictures, and he was good in a way that he'd never really been before: contained and disciplined and sinking into the sides and backgrounds of movies rather than dominating their centers. There was no doubt about his stardom, about the power of his lean, handsome appearance, about the steel and gravel in his voice. But there was something truly poignant in the spectacle of a middle-aged Newman with frailties and problems and vulnerabilities. Perhaps because of the pain in his private life, he had developed a spare style in his maturity, as if the death of Scott had killed off the eternal adolescent inside him. *Malice* earned him an Academy Award nomination— his fifth overall and first since *Cool Hand Luke*—and although he didn't win (Henry Fonda won his only competitive Oscar for his final role, in *On Golden Pond*, that year), he had demonstrated clearly that he was back in fighting trim—and in a new guise. "I was always a character actor," he told a reporter. "I just looked like Little Red Riding Hood." Now, having been battered inside and out by life and aging, he could, ironically, feel more comfortable in his skin and his craft.

His newfound mettle would soon be tested in a surprising arena. In 1980 Newman had jumped from the Democratic ship and supported John Anderson for the presidency, and he was appalled when Ronald Reagan swept his way into the White House. On election night, with Reagan's victory assured, the Newmans held a party at which they screened Reagan's infamous comedy *Bedtime for Bonzo;* they and their well-lubricated friends banged spoons on pots and pans to drown out Reagan's dialogue until the reality of the situation dampened their giddy mood and they turned the film off.

In response to Reagan's Cold War fervor, Newman became a founder of the Center for Defense Information, a lobbying group that sought to counter the public statements of the Pentagon and the Reagan administration with what the CDI regarded as a full and true picture of the Cold War arms race that Reagan was ratcheting up. In 1982 advocates of a freeze on the development of nuclear weapons and stockpiles managed to get a proposition on the California state ballot that urged both American and Soviet authorities to cease nuclear escalation and development. Newman was especially visible in the campaign, and he became an easy target for Reagan's allies.

The trouble began when Newman declared, "The Russians have honored their obligations [to limit nuclear development] as well as we have." That statement drew fire from a group named Californians for a Strong America, which had been formed to oppose the ballot initiative, and more unusually from Charlton Heston, who held a press conference on the tennis court of his Beverly Hills home to declare, "Paul is a good man and a good actor, but if he is going to speak out, he has a responsibility to check the facts first."

Over the next few weeks a pattern emerged: Newman would appear on some TV or radio show to discuss his support of the nuclear freeze, and Heston would pop up the following day and dismiss whatever Newman had said. "Heston is riding piggyback on me, really sabotaging us," Newman complained to Los Angeles radio host Michael Jackson. "He's refuting my points, but I'm not getting any rebuttal." He finally got something like a chance to actually talk to Heston when the latter was a guest on the late-night ABC news show *The Last Word*; via phone, Newman put questions to Heston in the studio. The exchange was brief but intriguing, and when Newman suggested that the two appear together on *The Last Word* and have a proper debate on the issue, it was agreed and scheduled for the week before Election Day.

On the day of the debate Newman spent hours boning up on the issues, taking time to meet with experts from the Jet Propulsion Laboratory in Pasadena and composing notes and introductory comments for himself. (Habitually, he read from notes when he discussed political matters.) But throughout the broadcast Heston ran circles around him. Newman alternated between stolid repetition of data and unscripted reactions and even outbursts; at one point he rudely dismissed a caller who had been selected to interject a question. Heston came off as a cool customer, referring to his opponent by his first name, calmly provoking Newman with selective points of information, and finally comparing the advocates of a nuclear freeze to the Europeans who appeased Hitler in the 1930s. By most accounts, he walked away with the evening. Newman tried to brush it off. "I've done better and I've done worse," he said. But the following year he insisted that the Scott Newman Foundation rescind its invitation to Heston to appear on the dais to introduce him at a benefit.

Throughout the decade, though, he continued to speak out against nuclear proliferation and the Reagan administration's arms policies in general. He had letters and op-ed pieces published in the *New York Times*. He appeared at benefits for Physicians for Social Responsibility and the Nuclear Weapons Freeze Campaign. He narrated a TV documentary about the presumed consequences of a limited nuclear war. And he continued to work on a long-gestating film project about the dangers of nuclear weapons. "I've been trying for ten years to write a film on this subject," he told a reporter. "The only thing is, if you write a bad melodrama, who cares; if you write a bad comedy, who cares; but if you write a film about an important subject, it has to be absolutely impeccable. If it isn't, it's simply food for the enemy. He uses it against you." And he certainly wasn't going to let that happen again.

In the summer of 1982 he experienced a sad milestone: Theresa Newman died of metastatic lung cancer after an illness of approximately eighteen months.

She had stayed on at Brighton Road in Shaker Heights for decades, keeping the big house by herself and putting in time as a volunteer at a nearby nursing home, still hale. In 1980 she parted with her household belongings in an estate sale and moved to the desert region of Southern California, near Art Jr.'s home in Lake Arrowhead. After her death her sons brought her remains back to Cleveland, where she was buried in the mausoleum at the Mayfield Jewish Cemetery beside her husband.

Some of the mysteries about her early life were buried with her. Her death certificate said she was eighty-eight, and an obituary in the *Cleveland Plain Dealer* gave her age as eighty-three—but neither, according to her own sister's suspicions, may have been the case. The newspaper also claimed that her maiden name was Fetzer—while at the same time identifying her surviving siblings as Andrew and Jewel Fetsko, perpetuating that family's shadowy history.

Newman spoke about her very little, in comparison to what he shared with interviewers about his father. But soon after her death he described her as "an absolutely gorgeous woman with a volcanic emotional makeup." It was the kindest and most vivid phrase he ever used about her—he could have been talking about the traits he admired most in his own wife—and the nearest thing he would provide her as a eulogy or an epitaph.

Twenty-one

I n July 1956 showbiz columnist Sidney Skolsky was profil-
ing the star of *Somebody Up There Likes Me* and shared an amusing
bit of information about Newman with his readers: "He is an enthusiastic chef. He is proud of his 'Newman Celery Salad' [chopped
celery, oil, vinegar, seasonings]. Dining out, he is likely to prepare
the salad himself."

Decades later Joanne Woodward averred that her husband had always insisted on having his salad just as he liked it. She remembered a
long-ago dinner they shared at Chasen's, one of Hollywood's most
clubbish and exclusive restaurants, back when it was an open secret
that they were an item: "It was one of our first stylish meals out. He
took an already oiled salad to the men's room, washed it clean, dried it
with towels, and returned to the table to do things right, with oil cut
by a dash of water."

In fact, Newman always held an amateur craftsman's pride in his
way with a small but select number of foods: hamburgers, steaks, popcorn, and salad—and particularly salad dressing. In restaurants from
Westport to Eleuthera to Beverly Hills to Manhattan to Paris to
Hawaii he would stand beside his table mixing a salad dressing from
scratch while chefs and waiters and goggle-eyed customers looked on.
And he truly did take the trouble to wash improperly dressed salads
clean and start from scratch when he had to.

At home, inevitably, his dressing was the house brand. And when his
grown-up kids would come home to visit, he would often whip them up

a batch and send them off with a wine bottle full of the stuff. Like his endless showers, his daily saunas, the ice baths to which he submitted his face, his cases of beer, and his notoriously sloppy clothes, it was one of the homey touches about him that became the stuff of legend.

In December 1980 he had a nifty idea. The Newmans had a Yuletide tradition of going from house to house in their little section of Westport and singing Christmas carols, joined by A. E. Hotchner and his wife and anyone else who was moved to join the throng as they made their way. That Christmas Newman decided to regale his neighbors with bottles of his fabled salad dressing. He and Hotchner repaired to an unused barn on Newman's property and—armed with gallons of olive oil and red wine vinegar, large containers of seasonings, and bowls of chopped garlic and onions—mixed up a huge batch of the stuff, more than enough to fill all the empty wine bottles Newman had on hand.

Indeed, there was enough left over that Newman suggested that they bottle the rest of it and sell it at gourmet shops around Westport to raise beer money. Hotchner knew just enough about the world to talk him out of the idea; glancing around the barn, he later recalled, he told Newman, "Look at this place! The bugs can't even stay alive here! If somebody croaks from ingesting this stuff, you'll be in court, with no liability insurance."

Newman heeded the advice. But the idea of bottling and selling his salad dressing had taken hold. He convinced Hotchner to put up $20,000, which he would match, to see if they could get a little business off the ground. Throughout the next two years he kept after Hotchner to find out more about the bottling and selling of salad dressing. "He was off making films, and I was trying to write a book," Hotchner remembered. "But when he makes a film, he's in his trailer most of the time, waiting for lights to be set up and all that. So we were constantly on the phone. At first I didn't think he was serious about trying to bottle his dressing, but the more he persisted, the more I realized that if I wanted to get him off my back, I'd better get the dressing in the bottle."

They consulted with various grocers and manufacturers and discovered that what they wanted to sell—a fresh-made salad dressing without preservatives or dehydrated ingredients at a reasonable price—wasn't possible, at least not in the way the business was then run. You needed chemicals to ensure the shelf life of the product, they were told; ingredients like fresh onion and garlic would spoil over time; olive oil prices would drive the cost up too high; you needed at least $1 million to compete for shelf space against Kraft and Wishbone and other giants of the business; and so forth.

Even as they dickered with their advisers, they tinkered with a recipe for the dressing that could be produced in mass quantities; they arranged a tasting at Newman's home organized by a Westport chef named Martha Stewart, who had catered several parties there. Newman's dressing won the blind taste test and then won another at Stew Leonard's Dairy, a locally owned grocery store. And they got some good news from a laboratory that they'd hired to run some tests: the combination of red wine vinegar, fresh-ground mustard seed, and olive oil in their recipe formed a kind of natural preservative. They would still have to use flaked and dehydrated onion and garlic, but they could sell the stuff without fear.

Now they needed a name, packaging, and a marketing plan. Newman and Hotchner had been dreaming of opening a restaurant in Westport to serve plain American food and calling the place Newman's Own. Wisely, they backed out of the restaurant business (although Newman did fund a place in Hollywood called Hampton's, conceived on a similar theme and owned principally by Ronald Buck, one of the investors in the Factory). But they liked the name, so they decided to use it. Their original plan to sell the dressing in wine bottles was nixed; the bottling facilities they looked at all required the more familiar salad dressing–size containers.

And as for the label, one of their associates put it simply: "If your dressing is really good, you've got a good shot at it, since you'll sell the first bottle because your face is on the label." Newman, who had never endorsed anything, not even the Rolex watch that he wore in *Winning* and that became known to collectors by his name, was appalled: "I couldn't think of anything tackier than putting my name and reputation on a bottle of salad dressing." But somewhere in him, buried under decades of denial, was the genius of Art and Joe Newman, and he came to see the logic of it. So he let them draw a picture of him for the labels, and he wrote copy for them that made fun of himself and generally treated the whole thing as a gag. Probably they'd lose their money anyhow, right?

They rented a small suite of offices in Westport and furnished it with chairs and tables from Newman's swimming pool—plus an old Ping-Pong table that served as a conference table. They called themselves Salad King (after a brief stint as Newhotch Company) and set the business up as a class S corporation, which tied their fiscal year to the calendar year. That didn't matter much to them, as they had no plan to make any personal or corporate profits: before they sold the very first bottle of dressing, they had agreed to give every penny they ever made—if indeed there were any pennies—to charity.

In August 1982 they started selling the concoction at Stew Leonard's for $1.19 a bottle—about a quarter more than the national brands went for; the big promotion was "Buy two bottles, get a head of lettuce free." In the first three weeks, without a nickel's worth of promotion, they sold ten thousand bottles. And suddenly calls were coming in to the bottler from national supermarket chains wanting to stock the dressing.

So they upped production and did a promotional launch for a national media audience. Newman and Joanne sang special lyrics to Gilbert and Sullivan songs at Hanratty's, a bar and grill on the Upper East Side of Manhattan, before a befuddled but amused press. And they repaired to Westport to see what would happen.

What happened was that nationwide sales were as brisk as those at Stew Leonard's. Supermarkets that would normally order a case of a specific bottled salad dressing per month were ordering three times as much of Newman's Own. In the first six months they sold $502,000 worth of dressing, with a profit of $65,000, and they gave it all away, mostly to the Scott Newman Foundation.

But there was a hiccup in their early success. The stuff was popular, but it wasn't exactly what Newman wanted to sell; in the opinion of Mimi Sheraton, a food critic for the *New York Times*, Newman's Own suffered from an "unpleasantly oily feel" and "overpowering dehydrated onion and garlic flavors." That observation hit Newman right where he felt it: his palate. He ordered that the recipe be rejigged, and the bottlers were able to find a formula that allowed for real bits of garlic and onion to be put in the dressing. By all accounts, the new formula was better.

Inspired, Newman had another idea: a bottled spaghetti sauce, with chunks of tomato and mushroom instead of the pureed ingredients then found in most jarred brands. Again, he and Hotchner were told all the reasons it wouldn't work; again, the simplicity, naturalness, and savor of the product put it over. Newman's Own Industrial Strength All-Natural Venetian-Style Spaghetti Sauce hit the market in 1983. In 1984 a lifetime's worth of popcorn scarfing culminated in the release of Newman's Own Old Style Picture Show Popcorn, a blend based on Newman's finicky rejection of dozens of kernel samples. "He wanted a better popcorn than Orville Redenbacher," remembered the Ohio farmer whose kernels finally passed muster with him.

Each year the profits—and the charitable donations—rose: $397,000 in 1983; $2 million plus in 1984. In 1987 Newman's Own broke the $5 million barrier for a single year—and the $15 million barrier in total contributions. By then a microwave popcorn and Newman's Own Old Fashioned Roadside Virgin Lemonade—based on a family recipe of Joanne's—were in the product mix. Then came more varieties of salad dressing and pasta sauce. It was an empire.

With each new product line, Newman, Hotchner, and Joanne would engage in another corny snake oil–type launch at an unlikely location—Central Park, a Manhattan chophouse, Ronald Buck's Los Angeles burger joint. And with each passing Christmas season another remarkable collection of donations would be made. Newman gave money to Kenyon College, to Yale's School of Drama, and to the Actors Studio; Hotchner supported his own alma mater, Washington University, and the Scholarship Foundation of St. Louis. They funded major charities such as hospitals, clinics, and organizations that supported research and care for those suffering from various diseases and conditions. But they did a kind of homemade grassroots charity as well, such as buying a school bus for a rural school catering to the children of farmworkers in Indiantown, Florida, or buying a fridge for a school in New Mexico, prompting a letter that said, in part, "Now our chocolate milk won't spoil."

Newman was dazzled by what was happening: "We have no plan," he told a reporter. "We never have had a plan. Hotch and I comprise two of the great witless people in business—none of this is supposed to work, you understand. We are a testament to the theory of Random—whatever that means!" Major corporations approached them with offers to buy them out for millions, tens of millions. "We won't meet with them," Hotchner said. "It's more fun to have a couple of bumbling idiots running the company."

In the most amazing of ways, a wild hare of an idea had brought Newman full circle in his life. The young man who had become an actor to flee the sporting goods business suddenly saw the point of what his father had spent his too-brief lifetime doing. "I begin to understand the romance of business," he said, "the allure of being the biggest fish in the pond and the juice you get from beating out your competitors."

And along with being named to Richard Nixon's list of enemies, he had a new feather in his cap to brag about. The success of Newman's pasta sauce led Frank Sinatra, of all people, to come up with a signature sauce of his own, Artanis (*Sinatra* backward). It came and went from the marketplace in barely eighteen months. Henceforth Newman's publicity bio would include the boast "He ran Frank Sinatra out of the spaghetti sauce business."

He was having the time of his life.

AND HE was a titan of more than just dressings and sauces and snacks.

In 1981 Newman reconnected with the Actors Studio, sitting in on a few workshops at West Forty-fourth Street, just for a shot of artistic refreshment, as it were. That little visit would turn into something more the following February, when Lee Strasberg died suddenly of a heart attack at age eighty. The tenacious old lion of acting teachers had enjoyed a remarkable final decade or so: he revived his acting career with his role as gangster Hyman Roth in *The Godfather: Part II*; he had two sons by a pretty young third wife; he was acting and teaching and fêted and honored and out and about almost until the day he died.

But the Actors Studio he left behind wasn't the place that had turned Newman from an Ohio boy with a yen for the stage into a cultivated Method actor with the ability to talk about his craft. Once the Actors Studio West had formed, actors who took their art seriously enough to keep studying it even as they enjoyed some success had one less reason to live in New York, where stage opportunities were increasingly rare. A lot of the original crew—Newman's class and those just before and after—had evolved into supportive but usually absent alumni. Too, Strasberg was never especially fortunate as a businessman and hadn't managed the finances of the operation well. The Actors Studio still had enormous cachet and respect and quality, but it had become a skeleton of itself.

Strasberg's death shook the community of mature and seasoned Actors Studio veterans. People who had moved on in their lives and careers started to come back. Newman had watched Strasberg's memorial service from the back of the Shubert Theater, where he stood alongside Anthony Quinn, and he soon found himself so drawn into rescuing the Studio that he allowed himself to be elected president of its corporate board in October. Among the people joining him in the new administration were Arthur Penn, a face from his first days at the Studio; the artistic director's position that Strasberg had held for decades was to be shared by Ellen Burstyn and Al Pacino. The Actors Studio West would have new leadership too, including the likes of Sydney Pollack, Martin Landau, and Martin Ritt. They were planning a renaissance.

But from the start there was trouble. In 1983 the Studio was drawn into a messy legal battle with Strasberg's widow, Anna, over the tape recordings of more than one thousand workshop sessions in which Strasberg and other participants—but mostly Strasberg—critiqued a piece of work they'd just seen. Anna believed these recordings were the equivalent of a professor's lecture notes and belonged to Strasberg's estate; the studio saw them more as collaborative artifacts produced as part of the organization's ongoing activity. The matter came to the surrogate's court in Manhattan, and Newman spent two and a half hours one November afternoon testifying on behalf of the Studio, explaining that in his view the material on the tapes was "criticism by your working peers." Eventually Anna got the original tapes, and the Studio was given copies for educational purposes.

In 1984 Pacino resigned his co–artistic directorship, leaving Burstyn, who was also involved with Actors Equity and had a career as an actress and a director, on her own. In the coming years there was grousing from within the ranks of the Studio about its lack of coherent leadership. In 1987 the twice-a-week workshops were actually suspended—not for the first time, but still a significant step. In January 1988 a group of administrators, including Newman and Burstyn, who were believed to be at odds with one another, sat down to discuss what needed to be done to save the place. It was apparently a dramatic meeting. "We thrashed out all our problems and hopes," Burstyn said. "It was a healthy period of reexamination." The upshot: she let go of the reins. She and Newman were joined by the playwright Peter Masterson on a search committee for her replacement, and in a few months they settled on Frank Corsaro, a member of the Actors Studio for almost as long as it had existed (and the Newmans' director in *Baby Want a Kiss*), as the institution's first-ever full-time, salaried artistic director. Speaking at the news conference announcing the hiring, Newman acknowledged Burstyn's efforts and admitted that she had saved the Studio from potential closure.

From that point on his involvement with the Studio would be more promotional and financial than administrative, even as he kept his name at the top of the board of directors until 1994. ("His contributions after that were more in the way of donations," Arthur Penn recalled.) Whenever a significant documentary or book about the Studio appeared, Newman would be interviewed; he hosted the New York premiere of his film of *The Glass Menagerie* as a benefit for the Studio; he appeared as the guest on the first episode of the popular TV talk show *Inside the Actors Studio*. And he gave a lot of money to the Studio, personally and through Newman's Own. But he had lost his appetite for actually running the thing.

OR MAYBE he was just too busy running a race-car team.

He still raced himself—and pretty well. Better than pretty well, even, considering that it was his second or third profession and that he was sidling up to sixty years of age. In 1981 he set a lap record at the Bridgehampton raceway on Long Island. In 1982, racing on the professional Trans-Am circuit, he won a victory at Brainerd, Minnesota, in a race that he considered the best he'd ever run, beating a field of top-class drivers in a hundred-mile sprint race on a rain-soaked track. The very fact that he was in the race was a testament to his uncanny improvement as a driver. Several times, in fact, he'd been invited by Bob Sharp to race more powerful cars against stiffer competition. It was no publicity stunt. (Indeed, Newman was very strict about what Sharp could do with his name.) Rather, Sharp saw that Newman was actually improving—and getting faster—with age. He said, "He's racing against truly professional drivers . . . comes in on weekends and does a darn good job."

He made the Runoffs at Road Atlanta as a finalist in 1982 and again in 1983, but he had engine trouble the first time and lost the second when he crashed late in the race; Joanne was on hand for that crack-up, and she had some hot words for him when he managed to get his crippled car back to the pits and emerged unhurt. But he had matured into the sort of driver who could handle wrecks without undue alarm. In 1980 at Sonoma he'd rolled his Datsun 280Z three times before it skidded to a stop on its roof; not only did he refuse to be taken to a hospital, but he was put out that anyone thought enough of the accident to ask him about it. "Why are you making such a big deal of this?" he replied testily to a curious reporter. "I lost control, and you either do something smart or you don't. I tried to muscle my way through. It didn't work. So what can you do?"

He became known as a methodical and mechanical driver—fast, yes, but also precise and deliberate. "He's amazing to watch on the racetrack," said a fellow driver. "He's so consistent. His concentration has to be outstanding to run lap after lap like that." His sometime teammate Sam Posey agreed: "He has this incredible ability to focus, and he memorizes and knows a track inside out before he starts driving, and this makes him a fine driver." Newman had a theory about his own style on the track: "I think as a racer you can either be violent and aggressive or you can be smooth. I've always found it compelling to see if you can go fast and do it very gracefully."

But like many successful drivers before him, he knew that he would one day be too slow in his bones to be fast—or even safe, let alone graceful. And so his thoughts turned from driving to managing a racing team—owning and maintaining cars for others to drive at levels higher than he could himself compete in. He began small, with a company called Broken Wheel Racing in the Can-Am series, a racing circuit that, as the name indicates, split its seasons between Canada and the United States. In the five years he had the team, he employed such drivers as Bobby Rahal, Danny Sullivan, and Al Unser. But the series shut down for financial reasons in 1982.

That winter Newman got a call from Carl Haas, an owner on the Can-Am circuit with whom Newman felt a competitive rivalry that wasn't always friendly. Haas was thinking of starting a team on the Championship Auto Racing Team, or CART, circuit—a competition among the fastest open-wheeled race cars in the world, with the most famous drivers in the world inside them. As Newman later recalled, "We had not been exactly friendly during the Can-Am days, because he provided my cars for the Can-Am series late and overweight. But that was another discussion. And he said, 'How'd you like to start a championship car?' And I said, 'Well . . .' And he said, 'What if Mario Andretti was the driver?' And I said, 'When and where would you like to meet?' "

Newman and Haas put aside their differences—or rather they managed to subjugate them sufficiently to work together, speaking only when necessary and almost never socializing, at least not in those early days. In 1983 they formed Newman-Haas Racing, with Andretti as their lead driver in a Class 7 Lola, one of the fastest classes of cars in the world. Despite the fame that the team would later earn, it wasn't a success out of the gate; the first season, in fact, ended so poorly that Andretti threatened to leave when it ended. Newman visited the champion driver that winter at his home in Nazareth, Pennsylvania, to urge him not to quit. "He had been so loyal, such a good friend," Andretti remembered. "How could I tell him no?"

Andretti and Newman truly did become friends, and Andretti didn't know which was more amazing: Newman's genuine racing ability or his ferocious competitiveness, which would come through in practical jokes, contests of various sorts, and absurd bets. One night the Newmans were dining in New York with Andretti and his wife when the two men fought over who would pay the check; they settled it by betting on how long it would take a bottle to hit the floor after being knocked off the table. Another time Newman and Andretti argued in the middle of another Manhattan meal about how many people were out on the street at that very moment. "He says, 'At least seventy-five,' " Andretti said. "I said, 'No way: at the most fifty.' Our wives roll their eyes and head for the ladies' room. Paul and I get up and head out to the street to check out our bet. The poor maître d' thinks we're running out on the check."

Newman's friendship with the great driver paid off for his racing team immediately: Newman-Haas claimed the CART championship in 1984 by winning six races outright. And each spring Newman would relish the nearly monthlong visit to Indianapolis and the Indy 500, the most prestigious race in American open-wheel racing. Just as when he made *Winning* more than fifteen years earlier, he spent hours in the pits and garages talking about technical aspects of cars, drinking beer, and schmoozing with the boys. And the boys liked having him around. Jim Fitzgerald, a veteran racer a couple of years older than Newman who raced both with him and against him, recalled, "He never played the big-time movie star routine with us. I mean, he was never, 'Okay, I'm Paul Newman, give me room.' He's someone who genuinely cares about cars and racing, like the rest of us, and really doesn't like to have special attention paid to him."

He had enormous fun too. CART had an annual race in Portland, Oregon, and Newman became famous there for his antics during race week. At the press conference for the very first race, Newman was asked to say a few words in honor of Mildred Schwab, the Portland city councilor who supervised parks and gave raceway officials much-needed help in obtaining noise-restriction abatements and other considerations for the event. Schwab was, in the words of one of the race organizers, "the homeliest woman you ever saw—never dressed well, didn't wear makeup, really a sight." In front of the assembled press Newman was called up to the podium to thank her for her efforts. He grabbed her up in both arms, leaned her backward, and gave her a big kiss. "She turned red as a beet," a witness remembered. "And she was speechless: both firsts."

Another time Newman learned that the CART drivers would be competing in a go-kart race for charity the following day, and he found the suburban Portland venue where the event would be held. He asked the staff which was the fastest kart and then spent a couple of hours gunning it around the track. The next day he organized a betting pool to see who could run the fastest first lap; with the quickest rig and some freshly acquired local knowledge of the course, he won easily.

He couldn't necessarily get other folks to share his passion. One race week he flew John Huston and his lady of the moment up to Portland and arranged for them to get VIP treatment at the track, including a police escort from the nearby airport. Huston watched about an hour of the race and then stormed out, barking, "This is the stupidest thing I've ever seen."

Maybe. But for Newman, it was heaven on earth.

AND SOMEHOW all this new energy—the food business, the charities, the engagement with the Actors Studio, the driving, the management of a racing team—fed the career upsurge that had begun with *Fort Apache* and *Absence of Malice*. The coolness in his screen persona that used to come off as flippancy had coalesced and hardened into something crystalline, pure, and solid. Not only was he enjoying working more than he had a decade or so earlier, but he was working better. According to Newman, Joanne had told him that it was all due to the car racing: "She says I was getting bored as an actor, maybe because I couldn't get out of my own skin any longer. And that I was starting to duplicate myself. She says that she thinks that part of my passion for racing has now bled back into my acting. I don't know. It's as valid a theory as any other I've heard."

In 1982 the proof of her surmise would emerge as Newman embarked on a new film, one with as distinguished a pedigree as any he'd ever made. Sidney Lumet, with whom Newman had worked nearly thirty years earlier in those episodes of *You Are There* on television, was trying to make a film of Barry Reed's novel *The Verdict*, about an alcoholic Boston personal-injury lawyer who finds in a desperate and probably unwinnable case a path to personal salvation. David Mamet had adapted the book, and his script was tart and piquant and filled with scenes of the protagonist doing what Lumet liked to call "kicking the dog": behaving so contrary to ordinary morality that the audience would have to struggle to like him.

Frank Sinatra, a curious first choice, had turned down the role, but Lumet landed an even bigger star, arguably, when Robert Redford got interested. The trouble, as Lumet recalled, was that Redford wanted to replace all the kicking-the-dog material with petting-the-dog scenes. A string of writers rewrote Mamet's script, eliminating the raw and coarse stuff and turning the story bland and dull. After the third or fourth neutered version of the original came to his desk, Lumet reread Mamet's work and told Redford that he was going to make *that* film. Redford walked. And Newman signed on to play Frank Galvin: rummy, ambulance-chaser, and quixotic champion of a lost cause.

Newman had played flawed, broken, and troubled heroes since the 1950s; some of his greatest roles—in *The Left Handed Gun; The Long, Hot Summer; The Hustler; Hud*; his Tennessee Williams adaptations *Cat on a Hot Tin Roof* and *Sweet Bird of Youth*; and *The Life and Times of Judge Roy Bean*—were predicated on his willingness as an actor to play kick-the-dog scenes. Even the good guys he played in films like *Somebody Up There Likes Me, Harper, Cool Hand Luke, Butch Cassidy and the Sundance Kid*, and *The Sting* had antisocial and even criminal streaks to them. Perhaps because of his looks, perhaps because he could be such a Boy Scout in real life, he came most alive when playing a scoundrel or a rogue.

But Galvin was another strain of mutt altogether. "He's panicked. He's frightened. He's out of control. He's on the edge of things all the time," said Newman. "It's a relief to have an unprotected character to play. The guy's an open wound. As the curtain rises, he is face down in a urinal. Sensational." Simply by embracing the role, Newman felt, he had made a breakthrough as an actor.

Nevertheless Lumet, who had directed such remarkable perfor-

Butch, Etta, and Sundance.
(Author's Collection)

At a Vietnam War
protest in Grosvenor
Square, London, 1969.
(Special Collections, Cleveland
State University Library)

The lunatics who
tried to run the
asylum: First
Artist principals
Steve McQueen,
Newman, Barbra
Streisand, and
Sidney Poitier.
(Special Collections,
Cleveland State
University Library)

Camping in New Hampshire with Joanne, Nell, and Lissy in the 1974 TV special *The Wild Places*. *(Author's Collection)*

After the billing battle: with Steve McQueen on the set of *The Towering Inferno*. *(Photofest)*

Thrilled to be in a tux on Oscar night. *(Special Collections, Cleveland State University Library)*

Hitmakers: with George Roy Hill and Robert Redford on the set of *The Sting*, 1972. *(Photofest)*

Kenyon professor James Michael *(in glasses)* helps his prize pupil identify faces in a photo (note the Coors ad on the sleeve). *(Greenslade Special Collections and Archives, Kenyon College)*

Scott Newman in *The Great Waldo Pepper*, 1975. *(Author's Collection)*

The Doug and Mary of the Jet Age feted by the Film Society of Lincoln Center; note can of Coors, then unavailable in New York. *(Special Collections, Cleveland State University Library)*

Directing *C. C. Pyle and the Bunion Derby* at Kenyon, 1978. *(Greenslade Special Collections and Archives, Kenyon College)*

The face of genuine loss: as Frank Galvin in *The Verdict*. *(Photofest)*

The gift of concentration: at a Trans-Am race in Seattle, 1983.
(Jim Culp Photo/ProRallyPix.com)

"Like sticking a gun in your mouth": directing himself in *Harry and Son*,
1984. *(Author's Collection)*

Gramps and Cruise: *The Color of Money*. *(Author's Collection)*

"Shall I order a wake-up call?": Directing John Malkovich and Joanne in
The Glass Menagerie, 1987. *(Photofest)*

An old married couple consider their assets: as *Mr. & Mrs. Bridge*. *(Photofest)*

The Iron Horse: *Nobody's Fool*, 1995. *(Author's Collection)*

Acknowledging luck: Performing at a benefit with some Hole in the Wall campers, 2005. *(Kevin Mazur/Wire Image)*

"Those two guys could have gone on in films forever": shooting a TV special with Robert Redford, 2005. *(Photofest)*

A triumph of understatement: as the Stage Manager in *Our Town* on Broadway. *(Photofest)*

mances as Rod Steiger's in *The Pawnbroker*, Al Pacino's in *Serpico* and *Dog Day Afternoon*, and Peter Finch's in *Network*, felt his star wasn't wholly revealing himself. After the two weeks of rehearsal were over, Lumet asked Newman to sit for a chat. "I told him," Lumet recalled, "that while things looked promising we really hadn't hit the emotional level we both knew was there in David Mamet's screenplay. I said that his characterization was fine but hadn't yet evolved into a living, breathing thing." Newman explained that he hadn't yet memorized his lines and would soon have a better sense of the flow of the script. But Lumet held firm: "I told him I didn't think it was the lines. I said that there was a certain aspect of Frank Galvin's character that was missing so far. I told him that I wouldn't invade his privacy, but only he could choose whether or not to reveal that part of the character and therefore that aspect of himself. I couldn't help him with the decision." When they met again to begin shooting, Lumet recalled, "sparks flew. He was superb. His character and the picture took on life."

Newman, echoing his wife, credited his activities away from acting with helping him reach the breakthrough. "Racing has destroyed every iota of conservatism that was in me," he said. "Only at this point in my life could I have played such a splattered character as Frank Galvin. Any time before, I'm afraid, I would have held back and played him much too cautiously."

The film shot in New York and Boston in the early months of 1982, with a cast that included James Mason as Galvin's rival counsel, Milo O'Shea as a hostile judge, Jack Warden as Galvin's loyal old friend, and Charlotte Rampling as a barroom beauty with whom Galvin has an unlikely affair. Newman had a real feel for the character, prodding himself with reminders to do less, to let the emotions bubble up from an internal place and not play them out broadly. He let his hair grow out a little, to give Galvin the look of someone who was too distracted to have a sense of his own appearance. (His dresser on the film nevertheless found him almost impossible to clothe so that he looked seedy: the wardrobe just fit him too well.) He even enjoyed a bit of Newman's Luck on the set in Boston when he got up off a couch minutes before a huge chandelier fell right on it. "God was with us," producer David Brown swore.

When it was over, Newman was delighted with the work he'd done and the film they'd made. "I welcomed the opportunity to let the blemishes, the indecision—the wreckage—show through," he told an interviewer. "There's a tendency for an actor after a period of time to protect himself. You couldn't get away with that in this part. You just had to let everything hang out. And that was refreshing."

Milo O'Shea described Newman's transformation this way: "He personally has been through a great deal. Losing his son was a terrible blow both to him and Joanne. You can't push that off, not when you have a great wound like that. It has had a great effect on his work and his life. He really is feeling his way into a deeper part of himself, to a layer that has never been exposed before."

And the response to the finished film was unanimously favorable. "Newman always has been an interesting actor," wrote Roger Ebert, "but sometimes his resiliency, his youthful vitality, have obscured his performances; he has a tendency to always look great, and that is not always what the role calls for. This time, he gives us old, bone-tired, hung-over, trembling (and heroic) Frank Galvin, and we buy it lock, stock and shot glass." "This is as good a role as Mr. Newman has ever had," Janet Maslin added in the *New York Times*, "and as shrewd and substantial a performance as he has ever given." And people came out to see it: at $54 million, it reaped the highest gross of any of Newman's films since *The Towering Inferno*.

Surely he would now win an Oscar, after having gotten to the altar five times only to be jilted. Around the corridors of the publicity department at 20th Century–Fox, *The Verdict* had been referred to as "Paul Newman's Oscar picture." The studio sponsored a TV special, aired nationally on ABC, to promote the film and its star: *Paul Newman: The Man and His Movies.* But when the Academy Award nominations were announced, Newman found himself amid a formidable pack of competitors: Dustin Hoffman *(Tootsie)*, Jack Lemmon *(Missing)*, Peter O'Toole *(My Favorite Year)*, and the relatively unknown Shakespearean actor Ben Kingsley, who had played the title role in *Gandhi*.

Newman was in Florida at work on a new film when word of his sixth nomination reached him. "I told him that *The Verdict* got five nominations and that he was one of them," recalled a friend who was on the set with him that day. "He just smiled and said that would be good for the movie. He's not making a big fuss."*

But a big fuss was being made. The film was released at more or less the time his food business began, and at around the same time that Newman was doing public-service TV ads to remind drivers to buckle their seat belts: he seemed to be everywhere. When the film premiered, he was on the cover of *Time*. Naturally, *Newsweek* saw all the publicity as an orchestrated plot and ran an item suggesting that Newman was campaigning for an Oscar. "He's a willing participant," said an unnamed studio executive, "no matter what he says about hating awards." Warren Cowan shot back a tart riposte: "As Mr. Newman's public-relations representative, we would know if there were a campaign on his behalf. There isn't. He would not permit it."

And it didn't matter anyway. On Oscar night Kingsley took home the Academy Award as part of *Gandhi*'s haul of eight trophies. Newman, who had to be prodded into attending, joked afterward, "I flew to the Coast only to prove I'm a good loser." When he got back to Florida, his colleagues presented him with a T-shirt bearing an image of himself with his hands wrapped around Gandhi/Kingsley's throat. He had the good grace to laugh the whole thing off, but his failure to win Hollywood's most glamorous acting prize was beginning to make everybody concerned look a bit ridiculous.

AFTER *The Verdict* had finished shooting, the Newmans took a family vacation to Europe—Paris, Nice, Florence—and then split up again on their separate but parallel tracks: he spent the summer racing, she went to Kenyon to appear in a production of Noël Coward's *Hay Fever*. (Newman caught her performance and was dazzled: "I thought, 'I don't know that woman. She must be a real scorcher.' ") They were reunited for the holidays in Westport, as per the traditional custom, and again in January 1983, when they marked their twenty-fifth an-

---

* *The Verdict*'s others nominations were for best picture, best director, best adapted screenplay, and, for James Mason, best supporting actor.

niversary in front of a small group of family and friends by renewing their vows, with their five daughters standing as bridesmaids. That same month they moved into a new apartment in Manhattan, a place with Central Park views, a large terrace, and a custom-installed sauna.

And then they set off to Florida to work on a film together. Ronald Buck, the Los Angeles lawyer with whom Newman had owned the Factory and the burger joint Hampton's, had written a screenplay called *Harry's Boy*, about the relationship of a widowed blue-collar squarejohn and his bookish, sensitive son. Buck had been peddling the thing around Hollywood to various stars; Henry Fonda, Telly Savalas, Jason Robards, and Anthony Quinn had all considered it. But he'd had no luck, and then he showed it to Joanne, who he thought would be a good choice to play the gal who lives next door to Harry and carries an unrequited torch for him. Joanne, in turn, showed it to Newman, who called Buck and asked to be allowed a chance to direct it.

After two years and several rewrites (he once claimed there were as many as twenty) Newman felt they had a picture worth making. He showed the script to various studios and producers—and was rebuffed everywhere. "I thought it was stageworthy," he said, "but a lot of people didn't. That pissed me off, and I find I work very well when I'm pissed off."

So he decided to commit himself to the project even further. "It reminded me of *Rachel, Rachel*," he explained, "which was turned down by every major studio. And this was turned down by about five, I guess, which just served to get me angry. So I finally agreed to act in it." Buck was astounded at his good fortune. "It never dawned on me that Paul was right for the role," he admitted. But with Newman on board as star and director and Woodward on board in the role Buck had thought of her for, they got a $9 million green light from Orion Pictures.

For the role of Howard, the son, Newman and Buck looked at dozens of young actors, finally settling on twenty-eight-year-old Robby Benson, who was trying to transform himself from teen idol to serious actor. A strong supporting cast, including Ellen Barkin, Wilford Brimley, Judith Ivey, and Morgan Freeman, was added. The film was shot in the early months of 1983 in southern Florida—Fort Lauderdale, mostly, to emphasize the ordinary working-folks aspect of it. Newman had directed himself once before, on *Sometimes a Great Notion*, and he'd sworn he'd never do it again, but he thought he had a way to make it work. He asked Joanne, who had recently directed a television film called *Come Along with Me*, to keep an eye on him, serving as a director surrogate when he was acting. But it didn't quite work out. "She felt uneasy about asserting herself," Newman said, "and I felt uneasy about delegating responsibility." As a result, he thought that he had given a less-than-committed performance. "There are places where I caught myself on film watching the other actors instead of playing the character," he admitted. "I think we got it all out in the editing. But I don't think I'll ever do that again."

To be sure, he hadn't given his all to the production. He was in the habit of getting away on the weekends, going to Tampa to see Clea in an equestrian competition, to Arizona to race his car, to Los Angeles for the Oscars. The crew respected and liked him; they waived union rules to create some time to allow him to attend the Academy Awards, for instance, and they came to rely on the snack of popcorn he provided them in the afternoons. ("It's incredible how cranky those guys would get if they didn't get their popcorn exactly at four," Newman said.)

Most of all they avoided the obvious: making comparisons between the material they were shooting and the real-life tragedy of Scott Newman's death. According to Buck, "The name Scott Newman never came up" during the screenwriting process. But, he continued, "How could Paul not think of him? He had to be drawing on that experience. He never said so, but he had to have those feelings." When the picture, retitled *Harry & Son*, finally appeared the following year, Newman refused point-blank to make the comparison or indeed talk about Scott at all. "That's not in the public domain," he told a reporter for *People*.

Unfortunately, *Harry & Son* wasn't either—or not for long, at any rate. It was a stilted if sincere film with little of the credible intimacy of Newman's other works as a director. Benson seemed grown-up at some times and half-witted at others. From a directorial standpoint, Newman flubbed the script's light comedy and made a hash of a pair of risqué scenes focused on a man-eater played by Judith Ivey. His own performance was grounded and true, but the film seemed unreal, despite all the efforts to give it blue-collar cred. It fizzled, deservedly.

HE HAD taken 1977 off from making movies so that he could concentrate on auto racing. And he had so much going on in 1984 and 1985 that he could have done more or less the same—dedicated himself to his own driving and to the activities of the Newman-Haas team, tended to the unexpected growth of Newman's Own—without excuses.

He wasn't tired of work, that was for sure: in January 1985 he joined with a group of his fellow Connecticuters in forming a limited partnership to acquire and run the Westport Country Playhouse, a treasure of a small-town theater housed in a converted barn that had hosted legions of the greatest names of Broadway's and Hollywood's golden ages since 1931, when its opening season had starred Dorothy Gish. He and Joanne would remain intimately involved in the operations of the theater for decades.

Like so many other things they did, this decision to roll up their sleeves and help the local theater in its hour of need endeared them to their fellow Westporters. The town had many celebrity residents, but the Newmans were granted special status, left to be their unassuming selves, to shop, to play badminton at the Y, to carol or trick-or-treat, to eat at ordinary restaurants, to pick through ears of corn at roadside produce stands, to play softball in the summer league in the park, to participate in the reading-aloud-to-kids program at the local library.

Those simple pleasures gratified Newman and sustained him into his later years. But at the same time, he grew increasingly dissatisfied with the script opportunities that were coming his way: films that weren't written to the standard he would hope for or that asked him to repeat something he felt he'd done—perhaps overdone—before. So whether by plan or whimsy or mere circumstance, he stayed out of it for a while, aloof, remote.

That same January he turned sixty, and the milestone caught him a bit unprepared emotionally—and even in something of a downspin. "Joanne was working," he remembered, "and I was at the beach, letting her support me, which is terrific. I kept going down, down, down. I thought, 'Well, that's interesting. You say it doesn't make any difference, eh? Then why are you stretched out on a sofa with a wet cloth on your forehead?' And of course the next day I had a temperature of 103. I had the flu! And I thought, 'Thank God! At least it's legitimate!' "

As an actor, he felt he'd finally come of age. "Until eight or nine years ago it wasn't organic," he said of his own work. But more recently, he explained, he had come to a wiser understanding of his craft: "In the last, I don't know, four or five years, I've just tried to make the character come to me, to find the elements of the character that are part of my personality and incorporate them. If you go back and see the early films, you can always see the machinery and the disconnection between me and the character. You see the actor working. But after a while, instead of working your way up every canyon and every crevice, you know how to get rid of all this peripheral stuff that you're not going to use anyway. You don't waste as much time."

In fact, the idea of Newman's being sixty made people realize that his time was a precious commodity. In October the Screen Actors Guild presented Newman and Joanne with its most prestigious honor, a life achievement award, and there was talk around Hollywood of finally enshrining him in the even more exclusive pantheon he'd been denied access to for nearly thirty years. Late in the year the Academy of Motion Picture Arts and Sciences approached him, through Warren Cowan, to ask if he would be willing to accept an honorary award for his life's work at the Oscar ceremony the following March. It was one of those backhanded honors: having ignored or forgotten or overlooked or skipped him six or more times, they were trying to make amends while he was still hale enough to walk up to the podium and make a speech.

He had joked about not winning an Oscar until his extreme dotage: "They'll carry me out on a stretcher and I'll reach my wizened hand out from the coverlet and grab it." Now, he felt, they were trying to put him on that stretcher before he needed it.

Besides, how could they honor him for his career when his career wasn't even over?

Hell, he had found another script worth shooting.

Twenty-two

THINKING BACK ON *BUTCH CASSIDY AND THE SUNDANCE KID,* Newman sighed. "It's too bad they got killed in the end, 'cause those two guys could have gone on in films forever." Of course, as the ongoing failure to follow up *The Sting* with a third Newman-Redford picture showed, he might have had an aversion to repeating a role. Indeed, he often declared his frustration with scripts that reminded him too much of things he'd done before: "Wherever I look, I find parts that are reminiscent of Luke or Hud or Fast Eddie. Christ, I played those parts once and parts of them more than once. It's not only dangerous to repeat yourself, it's goddamned tiresome."

That said, he had returned to the role of Lew Harper in *The Drowning Pool.* And he was convinced in 1984 or so that there was a good reason to go back even further to an early, crucial moment in his career: Walter Tevis had written *The Color of Money,* a sequel to *The Hustler,* concerning the later life of Fast Eddie Felson. It was a tale of maturity, the gaining of wisdom and empathy, and small-scale redemption. It fit the mold of films Newman had most recently been making. He decided to see if there wasn't a script waiting to be teased out of it.

He had a director in mind. A couple of years earlier he'd been so blown away by *Raging Bull,* the extraordinary boxing film starring Actors Studio member Robert De Niro and directed by Martin Scorsese, that he took the remarkable step of writing Scorsese a fan letter. (He addressed it, alas, to "Michael.") He took in Scorsese's newest film, the dark, offbeat comedy *After Hours*, and got in touch with the director again, asking if he'd be interested in working on a film about the middle-aged Fast Eddie. Scorsese, a feverish movie buff who'd grown up watching Newman, agreed to have a look at the script.

It was, Scorsese felt, too like the novel—which, in his view, meant staid and static and dull. Tevis (who had died after writing the book) had turned Felson into a pool-hall operator who has a romance with a college English professor. Scorsese, who had a much more vivid sense of darkness and redemption even than Tevis, felt that it was likelier that Fast Eddie would turn into a version of Bert, the evil, manipulative fixer played by George C. Scott in the original film. He passed the project along to a writer who he thought would help them realize a really pithy version of the story.

Richard Price was a novelist *(The Wanderers, Bloodbrothers)* who had been tapping on the windowpane of the movie business for a while and had been working on updating the film noir *Night and the City* for *Raging Bull* producer Irwin Winkler. Scorsese had no interest in that project, but he admired Price's work and thought he would provide an angle on the Fast Eddie story that would make a better film than would a faithful adaptation of Tevis's novel. Price was delighted with the opportunity—"Finally I would get to work with someone my mother had heard of," he said—and he and Scorsese flew to California to meet with Newman, who was living in Malibu.

"We're sitting there on the porch," Scorsese remembered. "Too bright. I've got on a blue blazer, jeans, sunglasses. Richard's all hunched over. Y'know, we're these two New York scuzzballs. And Newman's out in the sun in a bathing suit and he says, 'Come on out.' And he's saying things like, 'You know, this morning I got in the shower and ate an Israeli melon.' And Richard is looking at me as if to say, 'What is he talking about?' I don't know what he's talking about. Does he realize he's talking to two New York Lower East Side–type guys? Israeli melons? He's talking about a sensuality we have no idea about. We were lucky if the showers were working."

Cultural identities aside, Newman agreed to give Scorsese and Price's version of the story a hearing and then proceed to a treatment. Price produced an eight-page outline of a new script and submitted it to Newman, who admired it but threw up his hands. "Fellas," Price recalled him saying, "this is not me. I can't do this. This is too grim and dark and down." He agreed, though, to see if they couldn't all steer it toward some happy medium. The three would meet and discuss some scenes and ideas, and then Price and Scorsese would go off to work the changes that the meeting had suggested. "As I kept telling Richard," Scorsese said, " 'We're making a three-piece suit for the man. He's the main character and the reason we're involved in this thing. He's got to look a certain way, and the words have to come through his vocal cords.' "

They spent about a year, on and off, working out a script they could all live with—a story in which Fast Eddie would discover a young version of himself to mold and manipulate. Newman, Price recalled, would read his work with care and then often, and always respectfully, find another way to do it. "Sometimes Newman would say, 'Guys, I think we're missing an opportunity here,' " he recalled. "And the minute I heard that, I would groan, 'Oh, no, here we go again.' Unfortunately, he was rarely wrong. But there were points when I thought, 'If I hear, "We're missing an opportunity" one more time, you're gonna be missing a writer.' "

They were keen on experimenting—Newman called the writing process "as good a communal experience as I've ever had"—and even tried to work Minnesota Fats into the script so that Jackie Gleason could make an appearance. (Approached, Gleason demurred, said Scorsese, because he felt his role was "an afterthought.") Finally, script in hand, they went to 20th Century–Fox, which had made *The Hustler*, with the project. The studio passed. But a newer studio, Touchstone, which was run by Michael Eisner and Jeffrey Katzenberg, early champions of Scorsese, was interested. The problem was, Touchstone was a division of Walt Disney Studios, and Newman had no interest in being in business with them, not even with the portion of the studio that made grown-up fare. Eisner managed to convince him that the studio wouldn't interfere with Scorsese, and the film was green-lit with a budget of more than $14 million. (Newman and Scorsese each pledged one-third of their fees as guarantees against running over budget.)

Part of the reason that Touchstone—which based its business model on making films for less than $10 million—was willing to spend more than usual was that Newman, Scorsese, and Michael Ovitz (who would soon start to represent the director) had managed to secure a hot young star to play Vincent Lauria, the untutored hotshot whom Eddie finds and polishes. Tom Cruise had actually auditioned for the role that Robby Benson played in *Harry & Son* and been passed over ("I saved your career, kid," Newman told him later); now he was a rising star and had a tremendous hit on its way into theaters, a picture about navy pilots called *Top Gun*. With the premier sex symbols of two generations and one of the most respected directors in the world on board, Eisner and Katzenberg weren't exactly betting a long shot.

That said, though, they were still very anxious about the film. "That was one of the few pictures they went out on a limb for," recalled Peter McAlevey, who worked at Disney as a development executive at the time. "Jeff Katzenberg was scared of the picture, and they didn't want to do it at first. But Martin Scorsese wrote an impassioned personal letter to him from his heart of hearts, and Katzenberg didn't want to walk away from him." So the picture went ahead, with a few provisos: one was that everyone was working for less than their usual price; another was that Newman would have to make special arrangements to get to the Chicago sets each weekend. "Normally the star would come in on the morning of the shoot, on Monday," McAlevey explained. "But Katzenberg made Newman agree to fly in from Connecticut each weekend on Sunday morning because they were shooting in the winter in Chicago, and O'Hare Airport was liable to be shut down a certain number of days during the shoot."

At Newman's insistence, as per usual, the actors and the director and, for a time, Price met for two weeks of rehearsal before shooting began. Once production proper began, Newman was immensely impressed with Scorsese's command of the technical aspects of directing. "Everything was comprehensively prepared," Newman remembered. "I thought, 'My God, how long do you have? Ten weeks?' We had 392 set-ups. We were able to do it because the planning was so complete."

But Newman was also taken with the way Scorsese would coax depths out of his actors. "Scorsese's got an incredible eye," he said.

"You just don't get away with anything—he's on you *like a hawk*. You can't fall back on inaccessible mannerisms. He would hesitate, kind of creep over like a crab, and I would say, 'Spit it out!' I couldn't quarrel. He'd be right on." With even so fine a performance as the one he gave in *The Verdict* fresh in his mind, Newman felt he was finding a new level of quality and commitment in collaboration with Scorsese. "I keep thinking of him as a siren on the rocks," he told a reporter, "constantly beckoning. Every once in a while you'd crash, a couple of times you'd sink, and he grabs you by the hair and asks, 'You okay?' "

By all accounts, it was an immensely pleasurable production. Newman and Cruise both did most of the billiard shooting in the film themselves after taking a course with Mike Sigel, then the world's top straight pool player; they developed a friendly rivalry in games played for small stakes. They constantly teased each other on the set, Cruise calling Newman "Gramps" and Newman calling him "Kid" or "Cruiser" and telling him to go get his diaper changed. On Newman's sixty-first birthday he was fêted by the producers; Cruise presented him with a garter belt and a bra from a local sex shop. The two sneaked off for a weekend so that Newman could teach the kid a little about race-car driving.

Newman genuinely enjoyed working in Chicago, which had a big-city feel but none of the distracting fripperies of New York or Los Angeles. At one point Stewart Stern came to visit him, and the two went for a postprandial constitutional. "We were walking through a blizzard," Stern recalled. "He said, 'Oh, God, I love this town. Think how far we've come and nobody has stopped me.' 'But Paul,' I said, 'we haven't passed anyone for fourteen blocks!' "

Indeed, he was so happy there that he stayed in town on the night of March 24, when Sally Field stood at the podium of the Dorothy Chandler Pavilion in Los Angeles and presented him with an honorary Oscar "in recognition of his many memorable and compelling screen performances and for his personal integrity and dedication to his craft." It was, Academy president Robert Wise noted, "an honor long overdue for one of the screen's most versatile and dynamic performers." Newman spoke to the assembled crowd and the massive television audience via satellite. "I'm especially grateful that this does not come wrapped in a gift certificate to Forest Lawn," he said. "Tonight has provided a lot of nourishment and a kind of permission to risk and maybe surprise myself a little bit in the hope that my best work is down the pike in front of me and not in back of me."

WHEN IT appeared in theaters in October 1986, *The Color of Money* was received warmly by both critics and audiences. Grossing more than $50 million, it was Scorsese's biggest hit to that time, and it was a media sensation. *Life* magazine put out two different covers with a photo of Newman and Cruise lying on a pool table head to head, their bodies pointed in opposite directions; each half of the run of issues had a different actor faceup and the other upside down.

And then there were the reviews: Paul Attanasio, writing in the *Washington Post*, declared, "Newman's confidence in his own instincts gives Fast Eddie a remarkable gravity, so that Newman can accomplish with the slightest of intonations, or the choice of a simple prop (like the tinted glasses he wears), or an almost indetectable shift in his eyes, what would take another actor the course of a movie to attain." Roger Ebert, slightly drunk on expectations, was underwhelmed by the film as a whole but nevertheless acknowledged, "In many of Newman's close-ups in this movie, he shows an enormous power, a concentration and focus of his essence as an actor." The *New York Times* ran a glowing review by Vincent Canby ("Mr. Newman appears to be having a ball . . . a wonderfully funny, canny performance") and followed it with an equally appreciative essay by Janet Maslin ("[Newman] brings the weight of a moral victory in a man's struggle to regain his faith and proficiency").

Newman should have been luxuriating in all of this, but instead he found himself embroiled in a public pissing contest with his old arch-nemesis, the *New York Post*. It began with a harmless little joke in a *New York Times* profile intended to draw attention to *Money*. The writer, Maureen Dowd, related an anecdote from Gore Vidal, who said that he had heard echoes of his old friend Newman's fame in the unlikeliest of places, namely the Gobi Desert of Mongolia. "This KGB agent from the Foreign Ministry who was following me around asked if he could see me privately because he had something very special to talk about," Vidal said. "When we were alone, he whispered, 'How tall is Paul Newman really?' " Cute. Later on in the story Dowd provided the answer, describing Newman as "a lean 5 foot 11": more or less what every article and official bio of him ever stated.

The *Post*, which had taken up the policy of reporting on Newman only in a negative light since the *Fort Apache* imbroglio and his subsequent outbursts during the *Absence of Malice* publicity tour, flat out called Dowd a liar. "Anyone who has met Paul face-to-face," wrote "Page Six" columnist Richard Johnson, "says he has never hit 5′-11 except in heels." As proof of its certainty, the *Post* offered to pay $1,000 to charity for every inch that Newman was above five foot eight in bare feet.

Newman, who was truly closer to five-ten at that age, hit the ceiling. He made arrangements to appear on television with *New York Daily News* columnist Liz Smith to debunk the *Post*'s claims and challenge them to an even more impressive wager. If he was five-eight, he said, he'd write a check to the paper for $500,000. After all, he said, a couple thousand was pocket money. "For a newspaper that loses $10 million a year," he explained, "it strikes me that losing 1,000 bucks on a bet is irrelevant." Instead, he said, if he was correct about his height, the *Post* should put up $100,000 for every inch he measured above five-eight. "These guys threw down the gauntlet," he explained, "but it has the moral force of a powder puff. Real men don't eat quiche, and real men don't bet only $1,000."

The back-and-forth went on for a couple of days. The *Post* made a show of looking for corroboration of Johnson's claims and consulting gambling experts on whether they were being set up for a hustle. Newman, in private, made calls to an orthopedist to find out how to make himself as tall as he possibly could if he actually had to have himself measured. (It was recommended that he have it done early in the morning and that he hang from gravity boots the night before being measured and again immediately prior.) The *Post* shilly-shallied and finally dropped the matter, and Newman got the last word, firing off an angry letter (shared with the *Daily News*) that said, among other things, "Finding truth in the *New York Post* has been as difficult as finding a good hamburger in Albania . . . Sorry you guys turned chicken when it got to the Big Time . . . I'm sorry I got sucked into operating on the same level that you guys do but give you points on winning that one. Never again."

The episode absolutely cemented Newman as persona non grata in the pages of the *Post*. According to Susan Mulcahy, who worked on "Page Six," he was on the paper's "shit list" for years; she was forbidden even from mentioning Newman's Own products and charitable donations. "For a time," she remembered, "his name was stricken from the *Post's* TV guide. If a Paul Newman movie had been scheduled for television broadcast, the *Post* would describe it without mentioning Newman: *Hud* starring Patricia Neal and Melvyn Douglas, or *The Hustler* starring Jackie Gleason."

Newman held on to his portion of the grudge for years as well. Speaking of *Post* owner Rupert Murdoch nearly a decade later, he railed, "I may be dead wrong. He may be the most charitable person in Australia. He might have a whole hospital complex somewhere. He may have built sixty-three Presbyterian churches. But I think he's a real bloodsucker. He'll take and squeeze and take anything he can get and never give anything back." He added, in fact, that he refused to work for 20th Century–Fox, which Murdoch owned: "Not," he confessed, "that anyone gives a shit." (And he never did.)*

Just a few months after this distasteful dustup, Newman found himself getting his hands dirty once again—but for a far more uplifting reason. Charity had become more and more natural for him. "I don't think there's anything odd about philanthropy," he told people. "It's

---

* One last press ruckus—in the summer of 1987 the Newmans were on their way home to their Manhattan apartment from seeing a Broadway show when they were set upon by paparazzi. "The shits are out tonight," Newman sneered at them. Photographers actually followed them into their building. Joanne swung her purse at one photographer; Newman shoved another, a woman. When the photographer complained about Newman's actions, he responded, "I couldn't have manhandled that broad with a Mack truck."

the other stance that confounds me." That fall he had awakened with a vision for a new charitable venture, one that would be a way, he later said, of sharing his lifetime of personal good fortune.

Specifically, as he revealed to Joanne and to his Newman's Own partner, A. E. Hotchner, he had it in mind to build a camp for children suffering from cancer: a place that felt like the Wild West of childhood fantasy, with fishing and swimming and animals and rowdy play and no visible reminders of the daily grinds of hospitals and doctors' offices to which those unfortunate kids were subject the rest of the year. Campers would be afforded the very best health care, he conceived, and their families wouldn't be charged a cent for the privilege of having a child attend.

Hotchner was immediately on board with the idea, and the two men set about a series of tasks: finding a campsite, finding funding (tax regulations required every dollar donated from Newman's Own to be matched from other sources), finding physicians to staff the camp, and finding somebody to build the place to Newman's quirky specifications. After one costly false start, the first item on their to-do list was satisfied when they discovered a nearly three-hundred-acre lot in the northeast corner of Connecticut, straddling the towns of Ashford and Eastford. It was relatively flat—a boon, considering that many potential campers would be in wheelchairs—and included a forty-seven-acre lake. They bought it, and in December 1986 they broke ground on the site.

Seeking designers to build the camp and doctors to staff and equip it, they turned to Yale and came away with both. Dr. Howard A. Pearson, chairman of pediatric service at Yale–New Haven Hospital, assembled an advisory board of pediatric hematologists and oncologists. And Thomas H. Beeby, dean of the Yale School of Architecture, agreed to oversee the plans for the camp personally, even when his invaluable input was scotched by Newman in favor of some specific and idiosyncratic idea that he had for the place.

While plans for construction and the medical program were developing, Newman and Hotchner sought funding from various entities with which Newman and/or Newman's Own had relationships, and they were received with open arms and checkbooks. Anheuser Busch donated $1 million for construction of the central building in the camp. The U.S. Army Corps of Engineers volunteered its services in dredging and shoring up the lake; the U.S. Navy Seabees built bridges and piers. An organization of Connecticut swimming-pool manufacturers dropped professional rivalries to donate the time, labor, and materials to build an Olympic-size pool. It was impressive and gratifying, but it was still short of equaling the $7 million that Newman's Own was donating to build the camp and endow its operation.

That hurdle was overcome in October 1987, when Newman was introduced to Khaled Alhegelan, the twenty-five-year-old son of a Saudi Arabian diplomat. Alhegelan had grown up with thalassemia, a form of anemia that had severely limited his activities as a boy, and after meeting with Newman and learning about the camp's intentions and needs, he took advantage of a law that permitted ordinary Saudis to petition their king for assistance in personal matters. A few days later he phoned Westport and told Newman and Hotchner that if they would come to the Saudi embassy in Washington, he would present them with a gift from King Fahd. The little makeshift delegation from Connecticut made the trip and were stunned when the Saudi ambassador handed them a check for $5 million. It allowed them to begin construction right away.

In June 1988 the Hole in the Wall Camp, named for the group of bandits led by Butch Cassidy and the Sundance Kid, welcomed its first class of campers. The facility that they encountered resembled, in Newman's words, "a turn-of-the-century lumber camp in Oregon." There was a town center, complete with buildings that looked like Old West saloons and general stores. There were small, unmatched cabins scattered in adjacent fields. There were delicately inclined paths and doorways wide enough to accommodate wheelchairs, electric scooters, and gurneys. At Newman's insistence, nothing about the place resembled a medical facility. "These kids spend too much time in hospitals already," he said. Even the infirmary, staffed by highly skilled volunteers and filled with the most up-to-date equipment, was hidden behind rough wooden walls and marked by signs as the O.K. Corral.

That first summer provided something of a dry run, with only half of the available spaces for campers actually being used. But before long word got out about the level of care the camp provided—and of the miraculous elation it afforded the campers. The original plan of two sessions per summer was expanded, as was the range of illnesses that made a child eligible to attend. Raising money to maintain the camp's operating funds became a simple matter of asking—or of hosting an annual celebrity-filled gala revue in which the likes of Newman, Joanne, Julia Roberts, Robin Williams, Mikhail Baryshnikov, Glenn Close, Jason Robards, Nathan Lane, Gregory Hines, Rosemary Clooney, Jerry Seinfeld, Bobby Short, Tony Randall, and dozens of other high-wattage names cavorted in fractured fairy tales and over-the-top pantomimes on stages in New York, Los Angeles, and Connecticut. In one of the most memorable benefits, Newman and Hotchner revived their first project together—the Hemingway adaptations for TV and the big screen—as *The World of Nick Adams,* a star-studded evening of celebrity readings (Newman, Joanne, Julia Roberts, Morgan Freeman, Meryl Streep, Matt Damon, and more) accompanied by the performance of a score that Aaron Copland had written for the script decades earlier; Carnegie Hall was sold out at $2,500 a seat and up.

In 1993 a sister camp, the Double H Hole in the Woods Ranch, opened in Lake Luzerne, New York. The following year another facility, the Boggy Creek Gang Camp, sprouted up in Lake County, Florida. Other camps followed in Ireland, France, Israel, California, and North Carolina, and at a rotating series of sites in Africa. In the first two decades of their existence, the various associated Hole in the Wall Camps, eleven in all, served nearly 120,000 children from thirty-one U.S. states and twenty-eight countries, including the Soviet Union, from which eight children stricken ill by the Chernobyl nuclear accident made the trip to Ashford.

For Newman, the camps were the summation of his life's work: the sweetest fruit from the tree of charity that had grown from the seed of his acting career—the reason, he might even have allowed, that he had been born with those eyes, that metabolism, that terrier determination, and that deep reservoir of luck. And his luck included the good fortune not only to live to see the camps thrive but to be able to visit them and interact with the children: fishing, teaching them practical jokes, singing campfire songs, playing badminton, telling tale tales. He could be counted on to make at least one visit to Ashford during each camp session, usually unannounced. He ate with the campers, delighted in their ribbing, marveled at their resilience. He could overwhelm himself by relating stories such as that of the girl who told him, "Coming up here is what I live for—what I stay alive for during those miserable eleven months and two weeks is to come up here for the summer."

As Colneth Smiley Jr., a Hole in the Wall camper, later recalled, "That camp was friggin' awesome. It was even better than some family vacations, because I got to get away from worried relatives who constantly reminded me that I shouldn't do this or shouldn't do that. At Paul Newman's camp, a kid—as sick as he or she was—was allowed to be a kid." There were hundreds, thousands, of similar testimonials.

"If I'm going to leave a legacy," Newman would say, "it's not going to be my films or anything I do politically. It's going to be these camps." And like so many philanthropists, he felt that it was he who benefited from his work and generosity and not the people he was helping. He cherished his encounters. John Considine recalled that after one of the first camp sessions Newman wore continuously a bracelet made for him by a little girl who didn't have very long to live after her visit to Ashford. "Even if he was in a tuxedo he had it on," he said. But Newman reveled too in how unimpressed the campers were to meet him: "Two of the kids came over, pulled at my pant leg, and said, 'You a movie star?' And I said, 'Yeah, I've done some films.' They said, 'Did you do *Cool Hand Luke*?' I said, 'Yeah, I did *Cool Hand Luke*.' They said, 'Boy, them movies sure make you look young!' "

IN THE winter of 1986, as *The Color of Money* was making its way into theaters, Newman was on a soundstage in Astoria, Queens, involved in yet another directorial project based on yet another play. This time it was *The Glass Menagerie*, Tennessee Williams's heartbreaking semiautobiographical tale of an itchy young man, his physically and emotionally hobbled sister, their overbearing, self-absorbed mother, and a gentleman caller who visits them for dinner one fateful evening. For this small and emotionally charged story, Newman had most of the cast of a production that had recently been staged in Williamstown, Massachusetts, and later in New Haven, Connecticut: Joanne as the suffocating mother, Amanda Wingfield; Karen Allen as her daughter, Laura; and James Naughton as the man whom Amanda hoped would rescue Laura from a sentence of spinsterhood. The actors who had played Tom Wingfield onstage—John Sayles in Williamstown and Treat Williams in New Haven—were unavailable. But while he was working in Chicago on *The Color of Money*, Newman heard tell of the well-regarded Steppenwolf Theater production of the play from a few years earlier, in which John Malkovich played the role. He called the actor, who was working in Florida, to discuss it.

As Malkovich recalled, "I said, 'Here's the thing: I have some really specific ideas about this which are based on a fairly intense study of it. So I kind of more or less know how I want to do it. So maybe we should meet, and if you talk me out of that, great, or if you think that the way I see it is not your way, then you shouldn't use me.' And he said, 'That sounds fair.' So he came down to Miami, and we had lunch at a club where Hedy Lamarr lived, and we had a good chat. Although I do remember him dropping the sunglasses at one point when I said the only 'seamen' Tom was interested in was not the kind you find in a club for sailors." Newman overlooked the blue remark and hired Malkovich for the role.

As was his practice, Newman had the actors come to the studio for two weeks of rehearsal, along with the cinematographer, Michael Ballhaus, whom Newman had met on *The Color of Money*, and Stewart Stern, Newman's old screenwriter chum who was on hand as a kind of fly on the wall.* The principal intention of the film, as Newman saw it, would be to bring the theatrical experience of *Menagerie* to the screen

---

* Newman had, in fact, asked Stern to begin research on materials for a prospective autobiography, in order, he said, "to avoid the hostile takeover of my body." Stern did hundreds of interviews and solicited documents from schools, the navy, movie studios, and so on, but the project never achieved fruition. "We have 10,000 pages of interviews about my life going all the way back to grammar school," Newman said. "There's stuff in there about the war and my early days in Hollywood. But it's so boring. I have no handle to grab it all by. It's just a chronicle of what I did."

as fully as possible. "I was curious what would happen if you didn't rewrite Williams but still shot the play as a film," he explained. A highly detailed but more or less stagelike set was being built at the Kaufman Astoria Studios (which, as it happened, Stern's uncle by marriage, Paramount Pictures founder Adolph Zukor, had built). Newman didn't intend to shoot it through a proscenium arch—it wouldn't *look* like a stage play—but he wanted to maintain the domestic intensity that Williams had concocted and that had been embodied in the stage production he was filming.

Newman was working very hard, but to a notable degree, this show was Joanne's. The play had always spoken deeply to her. Having grown up in a world of manners not unlike those it depicted, she had once shared with Williams himself remembrances of her mother that startled the playwright. "My mother was a little Southern belle," she recalled. "She had no education. She *was* Amanda Wingfield. Tennessee once said to me, 'I thought in writing Amanda I was writing about *my* mother, but it seems like I was writing about *yours!*' "

Malkovich, an experienced theater director himself, understood quickly that Newman was as interested in preserving Joanne's stage performance as he was in creating a memorable version of Williams. "Once," Malkovich remembered, "he told me that he found me a little too rough with her, or cruel. But I saw that as part of how Tom communicated. He had a tendency to protect Joanne or to feel like he was protecting Joanne, and God knows that was perfectly understandable."

The two butted heads occasionally in rehearsal, but never with animus, and they seemed to agree, if only tacitly, that they would let the evidence of what they captured on film settle some of their differences about matters of interpretation or authorial intent. Stern, watching them work together as if he were Newman's cornerman in a boxing match, never felt entirely comfortable with Malkovich. "He has made it clear already that as a student of this play, and as a director, he may consider himself more experienced about its possibilities than Paul," he wrote in his book-length diary about the production. (Malkovich would recollect no such power struggles.)

There was, though, the matter of the alarm clocks. After the final day of rehearsals on *Menagerie*, Malkovich made a quick trip to London.

Arriving back at his New York flat the night before shooting began, his biological clock failed him; he awoke well before dawn and started to set off to work, only to realize his mistake and get back into bed. When he awoke, after midday, it was to the sound of the manager of his building letting himself into the apartment to see if he was okay; he was seven hours late for his appearance on the set, and the production company had become concerned. He raced to the studio, made his apologies, was assured by Joanne that his tardiness was nothing to worry about, and helped get as much as possible done in the time that remained to them.

When they broke for the day, Newman beckoned for him to walk out of the studio with him. "And as I left the set," Malkovich said, "about sixty or seventy alarm clocks went off. There were cars, there were ducks, there were golf balls, there were fancy alarm clocks and not-fancy ones and electric ones and battery-powered ones and song-playing ones. And he pushed his sunglasses down and said, 'They're all for you.' And I said, 'Thank you, that's very kind. But tomorrow, if my car breaks down on the way to work, does this mean you'll buy me a Ferrari?' And he said, 'Try me.' And I thought, 'Probably I won't.' They packed up all the clocks and gave them to me, and I gave them away for years. It was such an incredible thing that you could give someone an alarm clock that Paul Newman had given to you because you were such a dick as to sleep through your call on his film."

NEWMAN WAS editing *Menagerie* when he heard that he was nominated for the seventh time as best actor in the Oscar derby for his role in *The Color of Money*. He had joked for years about how elusive the honor was, and now that he finally had one, albeit honorary, on his shelf, it was almost comical to find himself in the running yet again. He was up against a comparatively weak field: Dexter Gordon (*'Round Midnight*), Bob Hoskins (*Mona Lisa*), William Hurt (*Children of a Lesser God*), and James Woods (*Salvador*). But he'd lost in such races before. So he decided, somewhere in the process, not to go to Los Angeles for the ceremony and to stay in New York and watch what happened on TV.

On Oscar night Woods, fidgety in his seat, repaired to the bar at the Dorothy Chandler Pavilion for a nerve-soothing drink, and he found Hoskins and Gordon there chatting. "We talked a bit," Woods remembered, "and then the three of us drank to Paul Newman." It was a propitious toast. When Bette Davis opened the envelope to announce the winner, it was Newman's name that she read. Robert Wise, who had directed Newman in a career-making role as Rocky Graziano more than thirty years earlier, accepted the award for his old colleague. Newman, who wouldn't even touch the statue until it was presented to him at a dinner party at Warren Cowan's house a few weeks later, released a statement through Cowan's office: "I'm on a roll. Maybe now I can get a job."

IN RETROSPECT, it amused him that *The Color of Money* should have been the film he won an Oscar for. "I don't think they gave it to me for the film," he said, "but for a body of work, which is funny because I got it for a body of work before I got it for a body of work." But in fact he *was* on a roll. Buoyed by the success of *The Color of Money*, he had signed a three-year nonexclusive development and production deal with Disney that winter. Peter McAlevey was the production executive on what was called "the Newman account," and he found a couple of projects that he thought might interest the actor, including *Seven Summits*, an account of Disney president Frank Wells's effort to climb the highest mountain peaks on each continent, and something called *Monte Carlo Cop*, a *policier* in which Newman and Richard Dreyfus would play a father and son trying to find Billy Baldwin, their grandson and son, respectively, after he has gone missing while investigating an arms-smuggling ring on the Riviera. The problem, McAlevey said, was that Newman made it clear that "he would rather be driving race cars than acting in a formulaic programmer to fill out an opening on the release date. He was either going to work with the finest people on the best stuff, or he was just going to race."

And why not? He had won national racing titles at the Runoffs at Road Atlanta in 1985 and 1986—giving him four overall. He'd won a second race at a higher level of competition, the Trans-Am circuit, in 1986 at Lime Rock. And he'd followed Henry Fonda as only the second actor to win a competitive Oscar the year after being awarded an honorary one.

The Glass Menagerie premiered at the Cannes Film Festival in the spring of 1987 to respectful if not adulatory reviews. Gene Siskel called it "a surprisingly emotional version of the play," while his partner in the balcony, Roger Ebert, averred, "Paul Newman is a very good director, very quiet, and he respects the material." In the *Washington Post* Hal Hinson disagreed almost violently: "The simple fact is that Newman is a bad director. And, even worse, sitting in the director's chair, he seems to forget everything he ever knew about acting . . . Newman has failed to do the one basic thing a director must do: He has settled on a style for his adaptation without arriving at an interpretation." In the *New York Times* Janet Maslin fell somewhere in between, concluding with a passage that Newman cited as especially annoying in his conversations with other reporters: "Quiet reverence is its prevailing tone, and in the end that seems thoroughly at odds with anything Williams ever intended." That fall the New York Film Festival passed on showing it (in large part because Newman and his distributor insisted it be made the opening- or closing-night showcase), but it was the centerpiece of a lucrative fund-raising gala for the Actors Studio.

Once again he was complaining that there wasn't anything worth doing as an actor, but now he seemed genuinely content to take time away from the movies. As ever, projects passed through his hands, some of which were made without him (*Witness, Rollover, Who Framed Roger Rabbit*, and two adaptations of A. E. Hotchner books, *Papa Hemingway* and *King of the Hill*) and some of which were never made at all, including an English-language remake of *Das Boot*, a sequel to *Rachel, Rachel*, adaptations of the police thriller *The Man with a Gun*, and the western *The Homesman*, as well as biographical films about journalist Walter Lippman, Nazi hunter Simon Wiesenthal, and controversial World War II–era general "Vinegar Joe" Stillwell. For the first time since he broke into movies, he went two years without premiering a new one in theaters—and by the time he finally got around to choosing a film, it would be three.

He was still racing—he introduced Tom Cruise to full-scale competitive driving that summer, and he watched on in horror that autumn when Jim Fitzgerald, one of his best friends in the automobile world, was killed in a Trans-Am race in Florida; Newman was ahead of Fitzgerald in the race, and he found himself unable to continue driving after the pause caused by the fatal wreck.

He maintained his loud and public interest in politics. He outright refused to appear in an antidrug ad with Nancy Reagan, claiming, per a spokesman, that he "just couldn't find the time." And he augmented his activism by becoming vocal about the preservation of various landmarks in New York City: theaters in the Times Square area, the traditional architecture of the Yorkville district of the Upper East Side, and the neighborhoods around the New York Coliseum and the Guggenheim Museum.

After decades of resisting the temptation to hawk products for money, he allowed himself to get a little bit pregnant, as it were, appearing in commercials for coffee and automobiles in Japan, then showing up on American TV screens in an ad for American Express, donating his fee to the Newman's Own charitable funds.

In May 1988 he appeared in New Haven to accept an honorary degree from Yale University in recognition of his artistry and philanthropy. And in June he appeared in a courtroom in nearby Bridgeport, defending himself and Newman's Own in a lawsuit filed by a Westport delicatessen owner who claimed that he had been a consultant in the formation of the successful salad dressing business and was due a percentage of its profits. Newman took the stand and angrily sparred with the lawyer for the plaintiff, defending the operating model of his company and its method of dispersing funds, which, it was revealed, included a small salary to A. E. Hotchner and some donations to fledgling race-car drivers. Newman's frustration with the trial spilled out into the street; leaving the courtroom after a particularly contentious session, he bumped into a Westport newspaperman who had sided with the *New York Post* in declaring him five foot eight; he loudly berated the fellow, calling him, among other things, an "asshole"; the reporter, fearing for his safety, later said, "My first thought was, 'Would he hit an old man?' Then I realized we're the same age."

After eighteen days of sometimes explosive and sometimes comical courtroom wrangling, a mistrial was declared when the judge learned that someone had accidentally left copies of several pretrial depositions in the jury room. Two years later another judge, with a much firmer hand, presided over a more sedate and expeditious trial, which was decided in Newman's favor after little more than a week. Newman's Own, the jury decided, was indeed Newman's own.

Part Six

Twenty-three

FIFTY MOVIES, OR THEREABOUTS, IN THIRTY-ODD YEARS.
It sounds like a lot, but it wasn't really. Clark Gable, Cary Grant, James Stewart, Henry Fonda—guys like that averaged two pictures a year for decades, easy, even with hiatuses for war service, even when they were old and frail.

But those actors were employees of movie studios, with their workloads lined up for them and their images—on-screen and off—carefully managed by their bosses. Newman was a step further along in the evolution of Hollywood. He had put in only a few years before the studio model fell apart and was, for most of his career, an independent operator. He chose his projects one by one and built his career and résumé and persona on his own. In charge of himself, he made decisions about what movies to make and how to present himself to the world in the same way he made decisions about his performances and race cars and salad dressing recipes: studying, mulling, checking his instincts, and, finally, paying careful attention to his gut. There was serendipity to his career—luck, coincidence, happy fortune—but there was also hard application and righteous effort. Being an actor was his job, and he was raised to work at work.

From the vantage of movie theater seats, though, audiences don't see the machinery or understand the intention of it or really want to know anything about it. Audiences want the magic, the illusion, something to disappear into and lose themselves in. And movie stars, carrying the weight of our collective aspirations, self-projections, jealousies, dreams, and sexual urges, are a means through which audiences achieve that escape. They reassure, inspire, beguile. We *want* them; we want to *befriend* them; we want to *be* them: a chain of desire. And the greatest stars are the ones who can sustain that chain for the largest number of people over the longest span of time and in the widest variety of vehicles.

Whether he knew it or intended it or was comfortable with it or not, Newman managed that. From *Somebody Up There Likes Me* to *The Color of Money* and on into the dozen or so films that remained to him, he was able to pique an audience's interest or lust or envy or sense of camaraderie sufficiently to forge a golden career. He made shifts over time—whether because of commerce, art, age, inclination, whimsy, opportunity, or calculation. But he sustained a screen self for, eventually, a half-century, and in sum it would be one of the most estimable movie careers ever built.

NEWMAN GREW and shed a series of actorly skins through the decades, but his transformations from one to the next were always subtle; watching his career unfold, taking his films as he made them, you wouldn't necessarily think he was moving in any direction; look up, though, after twenty or thirty years, and you could see real development—improved craft, deepened humanity, palpable wisdom.

In the first films in which he had an impact, he was an unformed, psychologically delicate brooder of the classic early Method stripe: the oedipally tortured young men of *Somebody Up There*, *The Rack*, *The Left Handed Gun*, *Cat on a Hot Tin Roof*, and several of his best TV dramas could have come right out of Actors Studio workshop pieces. He's trying things out in these roles: accents, physical postures, attitudes, angles of attack. His undeniably Brandoish Rocky Graziano booms through *Somebody* as if crashing a party, demanding center stage, and always on the edge of violence. But the savor of the performance wasn't as indicative of what he would go on to do as was the energy of it; the only roles like it in the rest of his career were one-offs without resonant impact: *The Desperate Hours*, *Hemingway's Adventures of a Young Man*, *The Secret War of Harry Frigg*.

Far more central to defining Newman as a star are the cowed, cracked psyches of his troubled POW in *The Rack* and his Billy the Kid and his boozy, self-lacerating Brick Pollitt: roles that recall James Dean and Montgomery Clift. Not only does he look more like his iconic self in these roles, but he starts to evince some of the qualities that became intrinsic to his lifelong persona. Although Newman is in his thirties in these pictures, he gives these characters a plausibly adolescent feel; they're young men trying to find a way to fit into a world that demands more of them than they can perhaps bear. There's hesitancy in them and self-doubt and real struggle to define themselves. They're wounded; you want to hug them.

There's a tremendous difference, of course, between the psychological math problem set up for him in the Rod Serling–Stewart Stern script of *The Rack* and the declawed but still splashy soap opera that Richard Brooks made of Tennessee Williams's *Cat*. But the characters Newman plays in them are kindred: timorous sons who've gone errant and squandered their patrimony in their neurotic failings. There's calculation in these performances: Newman deliberately tamps himself down so as to set up an explosion or a fracture late in the drama. But there's also something very personal in his playing the disappointing heir: Art Sr. had been gone about eight years when his son played Brick Pollitt; confronting a character named Big Daddy in a basement filled with family heirlooms must have been more than a little bit creepy for Newman.

BUT BY then he'd already begun to develop a second skin: the knave. There were hints of the character in the no-good schemer of *The Helen Morgan Story* and again in some of his TV dramas. But he truly cracked it with *The Long, Hot Summer*, in which he blends sexual swagger, animal energy, and frank on-the-make-ism in a way that would surely have impressed Josh Logan sufficiently to give Newman a shot at filling Ralph Meeker's shoes in the road cast of *Picnic* had Newman been capable of it sooner. Newman based his Ben Quick on the stillness of Brother Fochee, his friend and protector in Louisiana, and that afforded him the firm foundation he required at that stage of his craft. Secure on the ground, he freed himself. The physical confidence he gained in the boxing ring; his fully avowed happiness at being on the set with Joanne; a certain breezy elation at feeling comfortable, athletic, in his work: all of it oozes out of him deliciously. He's the cat who not only ate the canary, the cream, and whatever was left on the table after supper but is also rubbing up against you electrically asking for more and confident of getting it.

This guy, or versions of him, made Newman a movie star, the guy men wanted to be like and women wanted to eat on a cracker. You see him starched and cold in *The Young Philadelphians*, gifted and reckless in *The Hustler*, hot and icy in *Paris Blues*, rancid and sweaty in *Sweet Bird of Youth*, and, climactically, wild and mean in *Hud*. It's not a self-projection; not really. There's about as much of Newman the man in this character as there is in, oh, the humorless Ari Ben Canaan or the moony schmuck in *From the Terrace*—and surely no more. But it was something he found that he could do, at least in the discreet doses in which he needed to do it to build a performance for a movie: sell himself, anticipate luck, say exactly what he's thinking, kill with a smile.

Eddie Felson is that way, and so is Hud Bannon. They're not the same guy, of course: Fast Eddie is a martyr who almost gladly wills his own crucifixion, Hud the jaundiced centurion who'd prick him with a spear for kicks. But they're equals in self-possession, and they're equally guilty of overselling their gifts and their charm and their status and power: Fast Eddie is neither the hot item that he thinks he is nor the legend that Minnesota Fats most surely is, and Hud's domain stretches only so far as his Caddy can go on a tank of gas and shrinks to the size of an empty house by the end of the film.

They're devastating characters, with their crooked grins and their wantonness and their physical abilities—whether those are expressed in boozing or screwing or fighting or shooting or enduring hours of mortal combat in a pool hall. And they've gotten beyond the whole daddy business—or at least learned to sublimate it and transform it into something they can use. Ben Quick is happy to latch on to the coattails of the big man in town and supplant the neurotic prince who should, by rights, inherit things; Hud does just about everything he can think of to offend, alienate, disenfranchise, and damn near kill his old man. Fast Eddie is the nearest of the three to the older Newman persona, with his agent and his awe of Fats and his apprenticeship to a gambling fixer; but he's sufficiently evolved to realize, after great pains, that if he's to be his own man, he needs to overcome not a father figure but himself.

Newman's confidence in these roles is ravishing. It's hard to believe that little more than a decade earlier he couldn't bring himself to be heard weeping offstage in *Saint Joan* at Yale and now he was capable of pulling off such a raw and bold and magnetic and hurtful character as Hud. He spoke of Fast Eddie Felson as a technician who was performing at a high level of his craft, and for the first time he himself was that guy—masterful, deep, inventive—and making it look easy. It's clear to see how he cemented his status as a movie star at this moment: he's beautiful and he's charming and he's got depth—a keeper.

BUT AFTER *Hud* Newman grew restless. He had found a groove but was chary of it, hitting the limits of his patience with repetition just as, in an unfortunate coincidence of timing, he was reaching the limits of his technical versatility. He tried to stretch, in *The Prize*, *The Outrage*, and *Lady L*. But these films simply didn't fit him, and he knew it. What he didn't know was where to go or how to present himself next. And then he found not a new path or a new mask but a new attitude. He became an ironist, a rascal, a scamp. Again, there was some hangover from prior roles—Ben Quick especially, who it seems would be perfectly content to walk out of the movie he appears in and come face-to-face with whatever might be next for him.

That cocky mien was shared by Fast Eddie and Hud, but it didn't define them. It was an essential component, though, of the persona Newman wore in the most popular films of his career and during the longest single chunk of work he did: from *Harper* to *Slap Shot*, a string of ne'er-do-wells who can laugh off both adversity and good fortune with a cynical, breezy chuckle. Harper, who seems more interested in getting drunk with a buddy than in solving a case, operates, in this light, just across the dotted line of legality from Cool Hand Luke Jackson or Butch Cassidy or Henry Gondorff or Roy Bean or—insofar as the rules of hockey are laws—Reggie Dunlop. They're all rambunctious and smart-alecky, these characters, unable to hold on to marriages or well-paid jobs or to settle in homes or, really, to grow up.

Newman made these pictures in his forties and beyond, and he carries himself like a man—like a boy, really—half his age or less. Between *Hud* and *When Time Ran Out* . . . he made two dozen films, and he played married men in only two of them: *Winning*, which was about a failed late-life marriage, and *Sometimes a Great Notion*, in which the Stamper women are treated as chattel by their macho husbands. At a time when Newman was continually celebrated (rightly or not) for the stability of his real-life marriage, the characters he played continually failed to mature into the responsibilities that his generation commonly associated with manhood. And an unwillingness to be tied down was, quite often, the least of the boyish aspects of these fellows. They boozed and brawled and skirted the law and cussed and drove too fast and were disagreeable when they felt like it and generally carried on like superannuated kids.

It might seem a risk for a man old enough to have served in World War II to try to sustain a top-flight Hollywood movie career in the 1960s and '70s by playing rakes, roués, renegades, and other countercultural types. And yet such was Newman's appeal and such was his nose for a project that fit him that he was embraced by audiences his own age as well as by the younger crowd that was otherwise turning on to actors like Dustin Hoffman, Jon Voight, Robert De Niro, and Al Pacino. He could at once color inside the lines and impart the air of somebody who didn't care a whit where the lines were. And even as his instinct for choosing projects became spottier in the 1970s and he turned his most engaged attention to auto racing, he could still, if only in flashes, rekindle his most charismatic, impish aspect. Reggie Dunlop, foul-mouthed, adulterous, drunk, punchy, and filled with unsubstantiated, cockeyed hope, was the epitome of the type: this was truly an eternal boy-man.

But then came the death of Scott, and Newman began to behave as if he had learned that playing men to whom life, death, responsibility, and the feelings of others didn't matter might not be such a cool hand after all. The five films he made after losing his son—*Fort Apache the Bronx, Absence of Malice, The Verdict, Harry & Son,* and *The Color of Money*—found his film characters suddenly enmeshed in a number of realities to which they had previously been immune: the scourges of age, death, disloyalty, greed, sullied honor, soured blood. There was a commensurate leap in his skills. Previously, even when he was playing against his looks, as in, say, *The Life and Times of Judge Roy Bean,* the very act of attempting to look awful was a kind of joke. But now his characters had bags—and baggage—under their eyes. They had losses that they couldn't shake off with a beer or a brawl or by banging around with the boys or by bedding some girl. He played a cop for the first time in *Fort Apache,* and in that role he could be seen evolving from a fun-loving sort like Reggie Dunlop into the more haggard and rueful likes of Michael Gallagher, Frank Galvin, and the older, wiser, sour Eddie Felson.

The success of those roles—commercially and in the estimation of his peers and critics—was almost a bonus: he was so busy doing other things that his life's profession could sometimes seem an afterthought in his absurdly busy schedule. But he had finally achieved the confidence, the skill, and the self-awareness to be not the golden boy, not the eternal lad, not the smirking prodigal, but a battle horse, a ruin, a man whose handsome aspect was actually—when you took a good look at it—composed of scars. The Eddie Felson of *The Color of Money* never had to talk about what happened to him a quarter-century earlier: he wore it on his face just as he did the oversize tinted shades that both he and the actor who portrayed him had come to favor. His outbursts—like the scenes of anger in Newman's other mature films— were moments not of petulance or frustration but of weary familiarity with the way things happen and a righteous welling against the seemingly ceaseless tide of bad people, bad faith, and bad luck. These were tough old guys: wiry, clever, hard. You wouldn't bet against them in a fight—and you *really* wouldn't want to be the one they were fighting.

BUT SOON even fighting would appear unseemly. Into his sixties and after, Newman mellowed into another sort of role. The fractures were still there, the hard lessons, the failings, the wildness. But there would be a sense of comfortable acceptance of one's fate, in such films as *Blaze, Mr. & Mrs. Bridge, Nobody's Fool, Twilight, Where the Money Is, Road to Perdition, Empire Falls,* and even *Cars,* that had never been evident in him before. They would be slightly daft or soft, the characters he played in these films, even when clearly made of sterner stuff. They would have given up kicking at the world and moralizing about it and attempting to beat it or impose rules on it. They wouldn't be settled or compliant, not really, and they could still bare their teeth when they needed to. But they would be wise and chagrined and apt to amusement—especially when confronted by the spectacles of younger men filled with the spit and vinegar that they themselves used to carry around.

Inklings of that newfound indulgence of heart appear the very moment Eddie Felson hears Vincent Lauria smash apart a rack of billiard balls, and it carries through, in various guises, in the relationship of General Leslie Groves to Robert Oppenheimer in *Fat Man and Little Boy,* in the feckless Donald Sullivan's way of holding a town together in *Nobody's Fool,* in the familial duet that a gangster and a killer play on a piano in *Road to Perdition,* in the grudging acceptance an old race car affords an upstart one in *Cars,* and in the beatific but flinty attitude of the Stage Manager in a live production of *Our Town.*

He would, in short, spend the final decades of his career playing coots—but coots still capable of producing showers of wit and acid and pep and steel. And it would be hard to tell whether he enjoyed the role of the crusty old customer more on the screen or in life—because he reached a point, finally, when the two were almost inexorably intertwined. His life and his art had become synonymous. Lee Strasberg would have been amazed to see it.

Twenty-four

IN 1982 NEWMAN AND JOHN FRANKENHEIMER NEARLY MADE A movie about auto racing together, something to be called *Flat Out*. In fact, Newman had been looking for a chance to do another racing picture since *Winning* but hadn't found the right material or the right moment. Similarly, he had long wanted to make a movie about the atomic age, specifically the specter of fear and the burden of responsibility that had been born with the Hiroshima blast. But he never stumbled upon the right way to handle it.

In 1988, though, a fascinating opportunity came his way. Roland Joffé, the director of *The Mission* and *The Killing Fields*, had written a script about the birth of the atomic bomb at Los Alamos and, particularly, the struggles of ideology, power, and personality between J. Robert Oppenheimer, the so-called "father of the atomic bomb," and General Leslie Groves, who oversaw the construction of the Pentagon and was then given the task of supervising the Manhattan Project and providing the military with a functional nuclear bomb. Joffé envisioned the creation of the devastating weapon as the result of tensions between the two men's personalities and wills: the ramrod Groves with his urgent sense of a mission and the bohemian Oppenheimer, whose intellectual determination overwhelmed his fear of what might be unleashed if nuclear energy were weaponized.

Joffé had a deal at Paramount to make the film, named *Fat Man and Little Boy* after the bombs the United States dropped on Japan, and when he thought of Newman for the role of Groves, the studio agreed, even when they learned that it would cost them $7 million to get him for his first film since *The Color of Money.* "I wanted a bulky personality," Joffé said. "I wanted somebody who really counted." Newman relished the challenge, beefing up a bit and wearing some padding to fill the role and twisting himself subtly into a character with personal and political beliefs almost entirely opposite his own. "It's like a puritanical lady playing a whore," he told a reporter. "There's got to be something liberating about that."

For the role of Oppenheimer, Joffé had set his mind on an unlikely choice: Dwight Schultz, the longtime stage actor best known for his role as a comical sidekick on TV's *The A-Team.* Schultz looked a fair bit like Oppenheimer, though, and there was a certain poetic perversity in casting him, as it turned out that he was a political conservative. Joffé asked Newman to vet the actor, and one afternoon, sleepless from a red-eye flight from L.A. and nervous about auditioning for a screen icon, Schultz visited Newman's Upper East Side apartment. "I guess he's used to that reaction," Schultz recalled. "He allayed my fears simply by putting me to work—by asking questions about the script, by telling me what he thought, and showing me what he had changed and what he was going to say to Roland."

The film shot in the fall and winter in Tres Molinas, Mexico, about fifty miles from Durango, where a replica of Los Alamos was built. Joffé, who liked casting nonactors, had some actual prize-winning physicists playing members of Oppenheimer's team. And he had a couple of rising young stars as well, including Laura Dern and John Cusack. Also in the cast was the actor Todd Field, who had signed on to the film partly for the chance it would afford him to work with Newman.

Amid these youngsters and scientists, Newman was something of an outsider. He spent a lot of the downtime on the set riding a bike for exercise and sitting quietly with Michael Brockman, a buddy from the racing world who had become something of a factotum and companion for him when he traveled. Newman didn't joke around as he had on other shoots—his big gag was driving his rental car with a rubber chicken hanging out of the trunk. "He's not particularly warm," a crew member complained to a reporter. "Most of the time he kept to himself."

But Field found him a sensitive and gracious colleague. The two were talking one day about nothing in particular when Newman patted the younger man on the knee and called him "Scott." Hearing what he'd just said, he suddenly excused himself and walked away. Field turned to Brockman, who explained who Scott was and conjectured that Field reminded Newman of his son.

A few days later word got around that Field was needed on the set and would thus miss the first birthday of his baby girl, then his only child. Newman heard about it and invited Field to dinner at the house he was living in outside of Durango. "He cooked spaghetti and salad," Field remembered, "the famous dishes, just like you'd expect. And he had some really nice wine, but when he offered me a drink I asked him for a beer, and he gave me a Budweiser, but he gave me a look, too, because he rode a bike all day just so he could have those beers, and he didn't want to waste them on me."

Another dinner guest that evening was Schultz, who engaged in a vigorous but polite political debate with Newman, Field recalled. "It was just the opposite of their characters: Newman was the liberal and Schultz is very right-wing, exactly different from what they were doing in the film." Later still the company spent New Year's Eve together, and Newman told Field that it was the first time he'd marked the turning of the calendar apart from Joanne since they were married. "He had tears in his eyes while he was telling me," Field recalled.

PERHAPS IT was homesickness that made him dither about whether to accept another film job almost immediately after *Fat Man*. This time he was to play another larger-than-life historical character, Earl Long, the licentious, rascalish, and unapologetically outlandish governor of Louisiana who fell from political grace in the late 1950s in part because of his very public romance with the stripper Blaze Starr. Ron Shelton had written the script years before, and now that he had directed a hit film, the comic-romance-with-baseball *Bull Durham*, he had a chance to make it.

Shelton had worked on his script with the real Blaze Starr, who was still plying the ecdysiastic trade in Baltimore in her late fifties and who told him that she had always told Earl Long that he had Paul Newman's eyes. He got the script to Newman, and Newman took instantly to the part: a populist rogue and master political manipulator who championed civil rights and didn't care whose sensibilities he offended. He even appreciated the bawdy parts, such as Long explaining that he wore boots to bed with a lady so that he could "get traction" or Long and Starr eating watermelon during an explicit lovemaking scene. Indeed, simply as an inveterate teller of bad dirty jokes, Newman delighted in the opportunity to blurt out lines like "Ah got a weakness for tough-minded, iron-willed, independent women with big titties."

But when it came down to it, Shelton recalled, Newman was uncomfortable with the idea of himself paired with a younger woman. "He had a daughter the same age as the Blaze character," Shelton said, "and that made him uneasy." So even though the Hollywood trade papers had announced that he would play the role, he backed out. There was talk of offering the part to Gene Hackman. And then, Newman remembered, "I just woke up one morning and said, 'Screw it.'" He would make the film.

That, of course, left Shelton the problem of finding the right Blaze Starr. At one point, producer Dale Pollock claimed, the filmmakers had seen more than four hundred actresses for the part. With Newman attached, the pressure to get it right was heightened; rumors that Melanie Griffith or Nancy Travis would play the role bubbled up. In fact, recalled Shelton, neither was ever in the picture. "Those two were candidates," he said, "but we met with everybody in the world. The studio said, 'If you hold on to Paul, it doesn't matter if Blaze is played by an unknown.' So we had four or five candidates read with Paul. And one, who I won't name, looked too much like his daughter, and he said, 'I couldn't do that.'" Eventually Shelton had Newman read with a virtually unknown actress named Lolita Davidovich, "and she just blew him away. She got in his face and was funny and brave and guileless, and when she left, he looked at me and said 'What was that?!'"

The film, entitled *Blaze*, shot in Louisiana in the early months of 1989. Newman stayed in a home rented by the producers for him in the French Quarter, visited some of the best restaurants and clubs in the city, and was presented with a dog, a local hunting breed called a Catahoula Cur, by well-wishers.

Shelton found Newman an admirable collaborator. He reveled in the extra time that the director allowed him to rehearse scenes. "He loved the process of preparing more than the commitment to doing a take and picking it," Shelton said. "One time he said to me, 'I could just rehearse for a year!' And I said, 'That's great, Paul, but what do I tell the studio?'" There was one thing he didn't want to do, though— the final scene, in which Long lies dead in his coffin in the capital rotunda in Baton Rouge. "He hated that coffin," Shelton remembered. "He was really upset about being in it. He didn't like it at all. I told [cinematographer] Haskell Wexler, 'We're not gonna shoot any coverage on this. Just get him in and get him out.'"

It was the one balky moment on an otherwise wholly collegial project. "You don't know how shitty they can get in this business," Shelton told a visitor to the set. "Actors refuse to come out of their trailer for a scene because they haven't been stroked fifteen times that morning. But this guy Newman—you don't have to fuck around." And Newman was happy to tell anyone who asked how much fun he had shooting his sex scene: "I gave back four days of salary for that scene," he joked. "I gave back my per diem, too, my lunch money . . . We went through seven pairs of boots."

But in fact he was lonely. Perhaps it was the food or the Cajun accents, but Newman found himself, once again, pining for Joanne, whom he had openly courted on a Bayou State film set three decades prior. Joanne was, in fact, enrolled at Sarah Lawrence College during that spring term—she'd been attending on and off for more than a decade, hoping to finish the college degree she'd abandoned in Louisiana in the early 1950s. And then she got a pleading phone call from her husband. "He asked me to join him because he missed me," she remembered. "There's no academic degree in the world that can compare in importance to the fact that the person you've loved for thirty-one years is missing you." She put her educational plans on hold and went to join him on the film set.

AND AS he realized that he was happier with Joanne around, he agreed to make a third film in less than a year, this time with her. Joanne had discovered the project some years earlier—a spare, episodic novel named *Mrs. Bridge* published in 1959 by the writer Evan Connell. It told in discrete chunks the life story of India Bridge, a genteel, quiet, and depressingly ordinary upper-middle-class Kansas City housewife who raised three unhappy children with her husband, Walter, a stern and taciturn lawyer. The novel was joined a decade later by a counter-piece, *Mr. Bridge*, which focused more closely on Walter but shared the original's structure and resistance to overarching narrative. In the two books Connell told the story of his parents, himself, and his siblings in vivid, unsentimental, and precise fashion that played like a series of home movies or blackout tableaux. It was riveting.

In 1986, when she saw the glorious romance *A Room with a View*, Joanne met with its director, James Ivory, and his producing partner, Ismail Merchant, to explore the possibility of working together. She mentioned the *Bridge* novels, and they were able to acquire the option rights to them. Merchant and Ivory, as per their practice, gave the books to their longtime collaborator, Ruth Prawer Jhabvala, to adapt into a single script. When she finished, the Newmans had a look and agreed to play the title roles in what was now being called *Mr. & Mrs. Bridge*.

Newman, Merchant recalled, "said it was one of the best screen-plays he ever read." And indeed he responded not only to its depiction of a social and cultural milieu like the Shaker Heights of his youth but also to its strange, linear-but-nonlinear structure. "You could describe the story as being about absolutely nothing," Newman said. "But it really is about absolutely everything . . . It is accomplished by splashing essences of scenes, telling a story with a head-on impression followed by a glancing impression, and in the end coming away with a whole painting. More than anything else, that way of making a film appealed to me."

That said, Joanne always claimed that Walter Bridge was the nearest role Newman ever played to his own true self. Newman disagreed, but when he described the character he was, in fact, speaking in terms that he recognized deeply: "Walter Bridge is a man of extraordinary ethical and moral values. A patriot. He has great loyalties. He adores his wife, and he's disturbed by the fact that he isn't more outgoing and can't tell her how much he adores her."

They shot first in Paris, then in Kansas City, and then for a brief spell in Ottawa. And the Newmans were particularly keen on a project that so vividly recalled their own childhoods and backgrounds. Merchant and his production team were sticklers for period details to the point that they raided the homes of Connell and his sister for family heirlooms with which to decorate the sets. Ivory, who grew up comfortably in Klamath Falls, Oregon, spoke often with his stars of how much the setting and tone of Connell's story reminded them all of their own early lives. "It's the only film I've ever made that was about my own childhood and adolescence," he said. "When we talked about it, that seemed true of Paul and Joanne too."

The director didn't allow nostalgia to soften his demands when it came to work, however, insisting that his young script supervisor, Lisa Krueger, correct Newman when he kept swapping a *which* for a *that* in a particular line. Terrified, she did as she was told and made known to the actor about his mistake. ("It builds character," Ivory had assured her.) Newman gave her a look and replied that he would fix the mistake "if you're lucky"—and complied in all subsequent takes.

In fact, he was terrifically supportive of the film, as he proved when Merchant and Ivory ran into hassles with their distributors, Miramax, whose notoriously bullying boss, Harvey Weinstein, threatened to withhold payments for completion of the film unless they shortened it. As Ivory remembered, "We told Paul what was happening, and Paul got on the phone to Harvey and said, 'Lay off and pay 'em,' so they did."

THE RESPONSES to this spate of work varied. *Fat Man* was barely given a release by Paramount and was savaged by critics en route to one of the lowest box office returns of the year; *Blaze* was released amid a cloud of hullabaloo and fared slightly better with both audiences and critics, who once again found Newman's rascality fetching; *Bridge* achieved modest commercial success—it was never treated as anything more than a delicate art film—and was received with warmth, in the main, by critics; as a bonus, the film yielded an Oscar nomination for Joanne, her first in seventeen years. But even that little laurel didn't convince Newman to keep hanging around film sets: After *Bridge* he took another three-year hiatus from movie work.

Not that he missed the activity. In May he stood on a dais in Bronxville, New York, and gave a speech to the 286 graduating members of the Sarah Lawrence class of 1990, which included Clea and Joanne, who had finally finished her B.A. He shared some wise words and some jokes at his own expense. He had dreamed the night before, he said, of being scolded by a woman for "hanging on to the coattails of the accomplishments of your wife," and he made sure to leaven all his wisdom with the caveat that "actors tend to bathe in baloney." But he was a sincerely proud father and spouse and seemed not to mind being photographed in his mortarboard and academic robe. The school had become such a part of the family, in fact—Lissy had graduated two years earlier—that Newman presented a check the following year for $1 million to endow the Joanne Woodward Chair in Public Policy.

From there he jetted almost immediately to Indianapolis, where Michael Andretti, Mario's son, would be driving for Newman-Haas in the Indy 500. For all the races Newman and his teams had won over the years, he still hadn't drunk from the traditional bottle of milk in the winner's circle at Indy. In 1987 Michael Andretti was leading with a lap and a half to go when a valve spring snapped and his engine died. Two years later he had another engine blow out while he was leading the race. Newman didn't necessarily love the event itself—"The more people there are, the more difficult it is for me to get around," he told a journalist—but the atmosphere of the race was unequaled, as was the prestige of winning it. So he kept coming back.

He wasn't racing so much as he used to himself, in part because he was running into tight spots and little accidents more frequently than he had at any time since he first started. Indeed, he had gravitated toward another pursuit—backyard badminton, which he played with competitive relish, whether against one of his daughters or against such perennial nemeses as politicians Tom Downey, Marty Russo, and Charles Schumer and actor James Naughton. He was so cutthroat, in fact, that he demanded that the championship of the Hamptons summer season be played not in the open air, where wind currents could unfairly affect the outcome, but inside a high school gymnasium that he rented out for the purpose.

WHILE HE played and raced and sold food products and built camps and avoided the acting work that he'd pursued for nearly five decades, laurels came to him. In 1991 the Franklin and Eleanor Roosevelt Institute honored Newman and Joanne with one of its Four Freedoms Medals, citing their charitable endeavors in awarding them the Freedom from Want prize.

The following year the couple was granted an even splashier recognition by being among the recipients of Kennedy Center Honors, the nation's highest cultural award. Their peers in that fifteenth class of honorees were jazz musician and educator Lionel Hampton, dancer and actress Ginger Rogers, cellist and composer Mstislav Rostropovich, and dancer and choreographer Paul Taylor. In an end-of-the-year gala in Washington the Newmans sat with President George H. W. Bush and his wife in a box at the Kennedy Center as they were lauded from the stage by Sally Field and Robert Redford and serenaded by a group of children who had attended Hole in the Wall camps over the years. "It's so heady," Joanne admitted. "It's a little unreal." Newman, downplaying himself as ever, simply declared the evening "stylish and civilized."

Inside him still, though, was that Peck's Bad Boy just itching to get out. In the summer of 1993, when his fellow Westporter David Letterman moved his talk show from NBC and Rockefeller Center to CBS and the refurbished Ed Sullivan Theater off Times Square, Newman took part in a delicious prank. Hiding in the audience, he stood up during Letterman's introductory monologue and growled, as if confused, "Where the hell are the singing cats?" He pulled some tickets out of his jacket, announced he was in the wrong theater, and walked out of the place, while Letterman gazed on as if taken by surprise.*

That same spirit of anarchic fun seemed to govern his next choice of film project, an unlikely meeting of minds between him and the savantlike darlings of American independent filmmaking, Ethan and Joel Coen, whose cultish little hits would seem to have nothing to do with the high-gloss stuff Newman had been making since the 1950s. The Coens were following up their Cannes Film Festival–winning *Barton Fink* with *The Hudsucker Proxy*, another story about a schnook sucked into something bigger than himself. It was the tale of Norville Barnes, a gormless Indiana business school graduate who finds himself suddenly running a huge New York company after its managers have realized that they need a patsy figurehead as part of a convoluted scheme to manipulate the price of their stock. As Barnes, the Coens cast Tim Robbins, the lanky, curly-haired, bulb-nosed goofball from Ron Shelton's *Bull Durham*—and an outspoken political liberal whom Newman knew from the New York activist scene. Newman would play Sidney Mussburger, the ruthless, cigar-chomping Machiavel who's convinced he's found the perfect putz, only to watch helplessly as Barnes's idiotic moneymaking idea—a circular tube "for kids"—turns out, in fact, to be a moneymaker.

It was a juicy part filled with broad, gruff, angry comedy—unlike anything Newman had ever done before. And Newman, not quite clear how anyone had imagined him playing it, asked the Coens point-blank why they had thought of him. "We were stumped," the brothers admitted. (They have a way of finishing sentences for each other that makes transcribing interviews with them a bizarre sort of puzzle). "It's not that we've seen him in anything else close to this. There are certain ineffa-

---

* Newman and Letterman became genuine friends and would collaborate on many such pranks for the program. In November 1994, after the Republican Party, led by Newt Gingrich, crushed the Democrats in congressional elections, Newman stepped out onto the stage of the Letterman show as if spontaneously, and asked an indulgence of the audience. "Here's the gag," he told a reporter before the taping. "I come out on-stage and say, 'I was feeling kind of wretched, what with the election and the leaves being off the trees, and I just needed a little applause.' The audience claps and I say, 'Thanks, good-bye,' and I walk off."

ble qualities about actors that come to mind, and he responded immediately to the humor in the role. Maybe he was intrigued to be the bad guy." In fact, Newman said that he saw Mussburger in an altogether different light. "I think he's a hero," he said. "Every character every actor plays has to be the hero."

The film, budgeted at more than $25 million and produced for Warner Bros. by the action-movie meister Joel Silver, shot in the winter of 1992–93 in Wilmington, North Carolina, where the producer Dino De Laurentiis had built soundstages. The sets were enormous and stylized in a kind of fever dream version of Art Deco, evoking the era of screwball comedy epitomized by such directors as Preston Sturges, Howard Hawks, and Frank Capra. "Paul walked onto the set," Ethan Coen recalled, "and he said it was the biggest he'd seen since *The Silver Chalice*"—a joke that Newman could afford to make. It was neither his money nor his reputation on line with the film, after all. "What's the downside of this?" he asked rhetorically. "That I'm booted out of the Hollywood fraternity and [become] unhirable? So? And then what?"

In fact, he found that making the film was a blast. The Coens asked all sorts of physical stuff from him: hanging from gravity boots, breaking through windows, stripping to the waist for a massage, and so forth, and he rose to the challenges with glee—and, it has to be said, with a remarkably lean and sculpted physique for a man who had just celebrated his sixty-eighth birthday. Whatever it was the Coens had, he seemed to catch it and keep up with them stride for stride. "I don't know if I've ever worked with that original a bunch of guys," he marveled later on.

The film wasn't released for almost a year after it wrapped—the Coens hadn't made such a costly film before and had fights on their hands over the question of test screenings and edits to accommodate audience preferences. And as with many Coen films, the initial response was muted in part because there was no easy way to categorize the thing. It puzzled critics out of the box, and Warner Bros. had no idea how to market it; the $2.8 million gross—*$2.8 million!*—was the lowest for any film of Newman's since *Quintet*, although like so many other Coen brothers pictures, *Hudsucker* would acquire a larger audience over time.

O<small>N</small> <small>HIS</small> sixty-ninth birthday, January 25, 1994, the phone rang in Westport. It was Arthur Hiller, the film director and, at the time, president of the Academy of Motion Picture Arts and Sciences. He was calling to let Newman know that he had been selected by Academy officers to be honored with the Jean Hersholt Humanitarian Award, for "an individual in the motion picture industry whose humanitarian efforts have brought credit to the industry," at the Oscar ceremony in March. After decades of being overlooked or overtaken in Academy Award sweepstakes, he would be picking up his third statuette in nine years. And he would be doing so at a time when he was expanding the business that fed his charitable efforts *and* working on a film that would have Oscar voters thinking about him all over again.

As had been the case for decades, he was turning down more chances to make movies—some of which became quite successful for other actors—than he was actually appearing in. In the years between projects, he had passed on the chance to appear in Roman Polanski's *Death and the Maiden*, Ron Howard's *The Paper*, Steve Zaillian's *A Civil Action*, Sydney Pollack's *The Firm*, Richard Donner's *Maverick*, and Jocelyn Moorhouse's *A Thousand Acres*. Robert Redford wanted him to play the role of literary scholar Mark Van Doren in his film *Quiz Show*, but Newman demurred, explaining, "I would have been struggling with that patrician quality. You can take the kid out of Ohio, but you can't take Ohio out of the kid." (Paul Scofield eventually took the role and had no such problems.) He had talks with Merchant and Ivory about appearing in an adaptation of Junichiro Tanizaki's novel *Diary of a Mad Old Man* and with John Guare about starring in and directing a mystery entitled *Stark Truth*. And he was still pursuing *The Homesman*, his road-show western, with a new script by Naomi Foner, as well as the much-talked-of *Rachel, Rachel* sequel in collaboration with Stewart Stern.

But the picture that he actually made was one that came to him from Robert Benton, whom he'd come close to working with more than twenty years earlier on the unrealized film *The Tin Lizzie Troop*. Benton had been selected by producer Scott Rudin to write and direct a film version of *Nobody's Fool*, a homey, character-driven story by novelist Richard Russo about a small upstate New York town that's home to Donald Sullivan, a ne'er-do-well handyman offered a chance at personal redemption during a holiday visit from his estranged son, whose own career and marriage have sputtered into failure.

As Benton recalled, he was only thirty or so pages into the book when he called Rudin back and said, "This would be a perfect part for Paul Newman, and when I write it, I'm going to write it for him, and I'd like him to be the first person we go to see with it." But that idea caught Russo by surprise. Sully, as the main character was known, was in his view a seedier and slighter man than Newman. "My first thought," Russo remembered, "was that my Sully wasn't a great-looking guy. I thought of him as a Don Quixote—Don Sullivan. So when I heard it would be Paul Newman, my reaction was, 'Well, I can see why they're doing that to guarantee the success of the movie, but that's not my Sully.'"

Benton, though, had always been thinking of Newman. "I had Newman in mind for every line I wrote," he recalled. "I tailored it to him, and I don't know what I'd have done if he'd said no." As it happened, Newman's quick yes put the picture on the fast track, Russo remembered, and drew money and talent to the project.

Russo was called to New York to give Benton some assistance with the script, which necessarily had cut chunks out of the book. When he got there, he recalled, "[Newman] immediately pigeonholed me and started asking me questions: What kind of music did Sully like? And things like this. I must have disappointed him, because I had to confess that everything I knew about that man was in the book." The novelist stayed on to witness a bit of the shoot, and he was gratified to see that his initial impression of the casting of the central role had been mistaken. "I wasn't looking at the physical man anymore," he remembered. "He'd gotten inside the character. There's something going on in him that connects not just to my rogues but to messed-up human beings of many sorts. He understands them."

The picture filmed in several towns in the Hudson Valley in the winter of 1993–94, when so much snow fell that the crew not only had to return the snow-making equipment that had been rented as a safeguard but also had to come out daily and groom the locations to make the drifts on the streets resemble, as best they could, the way they'd looked before the previous night's accumulation. "The people who we'd hired to make snow wound up spending all their time removing it," Benton recalled. "Otherwise it would have looked like we had filmed it in Alaska."

Alongside Newman in a true ensemble cast were Melanie Griffith, Dylan Walsh, Pruitt Taylor Vince, Gene Saks, Philip Seymour Hoffman, and Jessica Tandy, who didn't let on to anyone involved in the production that she was battling cancer, a fight she would soon lose. ("She knew she was going into the hospital right after the film was over and gave no indication of that," Newman recalled. "She was just this extraordinary presence.") Also in the cast was Bruce Willis, who proudly revealed to Newman that they were actually working together for the second time: as a young extra, Willis had played a courtroom spectator in *The Verdict*. He was appearing in Benton's film without billing and, in fact, without even seeing the part he'd play. "Robert Benton called me and said, 'I'm doing this film with Newman,'" Willis remembered. "And I asked him, 'Do I have any scenes with him?' He said, 'All your scenes are with him. Want to read it?' I said, 'No, I'm in. I'll do it.'"

During filming Newman amused himself by playing Ping-Pong against his younger colleagues. "He took me out to dinner and challenged me to a game," Hoffman remembered. "He beat me three times in a row. I remember him wanting to beat me—he was so competitive, and it was so much fun." Newman laughed off the extreme weather—it was so cold, in fact, that a teardrop froze on Melanie Griffith's cheek during one shot—and relished the excesses of his character, a boozy rake who flirts with his boss's wife, delights in taunting the local cop, relies on an inept, one-legged drunken lawyer to fight his legal battles, and resolutely avoids anything like responsibility or emotional connection. "There's a lot of the character," he confessed, "that is closer to me than any role I've done . . . In his search for privacy, he starts putting up walls, and the unfortunate part of the process is at some point these walls break down. I've been there, and I know what it's like."

Newman gave credit to Benton for allowing him to build his performance delicately: "He allows things to develop. He just eavesdrops."

But Benton said that Newman's success was due to his innate empathy. "He has a real sympathy for people who get neglected," the director said.

Despite the weather problems the film was finished on time and then got stuck in a kind of limbo as the producers and the studio battled over when to release it. The first thought was for an autumn premiere, but as admiring word for the film and, especially, Newman's performance came back from early critics' screenings, they considered holding it until the Christmas season, when Oscar candidates are traditionally released. That, finally, was the decision they made, and it turned out to be an inspired one.

Nobody's Fool got the best reviews of any film of Newman's since *The Color of Money*—and maybe since *The Verdict*. Partly it was because the film was simply well made. "*Nobody's Fool* is so eloquently straightforward, it practically sings to the soul," wrote Deeson Howe in the *Washington Post*. The Internet-based critic James Berardinelli similarly stated, "*Nobody's Fool* is about as sublime a motion picture as is likely to come out of Hollywood." Newman, declared Edward Guthmann in the *San Francisco Chronicle*, was "an actor so masterful, so lacking in ostentation, that you barely notice he's acting." And Caryn James in the *New York Times* flat-out called Newman's performance "the single best of this year."

But partly, too, the affection for *Nobody's Fool* was based on the knowledge that it offered a summation of Newman's career that was unlikely to be equaled in another potential film. As Roger Ebert put it, casting his eye back to the 1950s, "Like Brando, Newman studied the Method. Like Brando, Newman looked good in an undershirt. Unlike Brando, Newman went on to study life, and so while Brando broke through and then wandered aimlessly in inexplicable roles . . . Newman continued to work on his craft. Having seen what he could put in, he went on to see what he could leave out. In *Nobody's Fool*, he has it just about figured out."

The film did nearly $40 million in business, and Newman reaped prizes to go with the praise: the best actor awards from the New York Film Critics Circle and the Berlin Film Festival and his ninth Oscar nomination as best actor. It looked like a reasonably competitive race, with Newman and Tom Hanks *(Forrest Gump)* reckoned as favorites over Morgan Freeman *(The Shawshank Redemption)*, Nigel Hawthorne *(The Madness of King George)*, and John Travolta *(Pulp Fiction).** But Newman didn't even bother attending the ceremony, spending Oscar night dining with family at the Russian Tea Room in New York while Hanks won the second of his back-to-back Academy Awards.

HIS MIND, in fact, was on newer and more exciting possibilities—an expansion of the Newman's Own empire, in fact.

For years after graduating from the College of the Atlantic in Bar Harbor, Maine, with a degree in human ecology, Nell worked on bird conservation issues in her home on the central coast of California. The bohemian lifestyle she grew up with in Westport stood her in good stead in towns like Santa Cruz, and her way of life gave her a business idea. She lobbied her dad about the virtues of organic food and the idea of establishing a line of organic foods under the Newman's Own label. But for years he had turned up his nose at her, declaring, "If it's organic, it tastes bad." Within the family Nell had taken up the duties of preparing holiday meals, and for Thanksgiving 1992 she had flown back east with her bags secretly stuffed with organic ingredients, including a free-range turkey. After they ate dinner, she asked Newman how he'd liked it. He allowed he'd liked it quite well, and then she told him that it had been entirely organic. He respected being hustled as much as he enjoyed the food, and he agreed to front her some seed money to see if there wasn't some merit in her proposal. But he insisted that she and her business partner, Peter Meehan, who used to clean the Newmans' pool, pay the investment back. "It's charity money that I would have given away," he reminded her.

Nell and Meehan took the loan—about $125,000—and researched the organic food field with an eye toward filling a hole in the market and complementing the existing line of Newman's Own products. They hit on pretzels—after popcorn, Newman's favorite snack food,

---

* Ironically, Paul Scofield was up for best supporting actor for his work in *Quiz Show.*

and a treat that was then enjoying a rise in popularity. Rather than produce some grainy health-food-store version, they came up with a
recipe that resembled familiar mainstream supermarket pretzels but
was made with organic ingredients. Newman approved of what they
did and allowed them to launch themselves as a subdivision: Newman's
Own Organics—The Second Generation, with the motto "Great-
tasting products that happen to be organic." (Nell's sister Lissy, then
working as an artist and a singer, helped design the company logo, in
which Newman and Nell posed in a parody of Grant Wood's *American
Gothic.*)

Newman presented only two stipulations. One was that Nell and
Peter do some real good with their organic philosophy. "I don't want
you to save just one wheat field in Kansas," he declared. "I want you to
make a real difference." The other was more in the way of a concession:
"You don't have to give the money to charity. You don't have the income
I do." Nell balked: "Great, then I'll be the only division of Newman's
Own keeping the money." She announced that she would not only make
donations of her profits but that she also would let her employees—the
chef who developed the pretzel recipe, the packagers and the drivers—
decide what to do with the profits. Newman was delighted.

The first line was a hit: within three years Newman's Own Organics held a 75 percent share of the organic pretzel market. Newman
bragged, "She's cornered the market, run everybody else out of business, which I like. I like the barracuda aspect of her business." They
followed with chocolate bars, microwave popcorn, and cookies. The
first cookies, Newman-O's—organic versions of Oreos—were another success. Then they had an idea for a fig cookie and the inspiration to call it Fig Newmans; that would, they figured, entail a battle
with Nabisco, whose Fig Newtons were obviously being invoked.
Newman launched a personal campaign to win the corporation's permission, writing directly to the president to explain why he thought
Newman's Own should be allowed to horn in on their trademark. "We
were all on pins and needles about the name," Nell remembered, "and
he calls me up like a ninth-grader and says, 'We got it!' "

The Fig Newman would, in fact, become one of the best sellers in
the Newman's Own Organics line, which went on to include produce,

olive oil, pet food, coffee—more than one hundred products in all. Nell ascribed the positive reception of Newman's Own Organics products to the company's trust of Paul Newman's own tastes: "Everything had to be something that my father, who was born in 1925, would look at and recognize and eat." (The mint-flavored Newman-O's were, she said, his personal favorite.) And like the parent company, Newman's Own Organics fulfilled multiple civic duties as it sold its wares: encouraging environmentally sensitive farming practices and supporting charities. In its first decade of existence it gave away close to $2 million.

The actual charitable arm of Newman's Own had given away much more than that—more than $60 million in total by 1995. And Newman and Hotchner had begun to use their unbelievably profitable little company to do good in other ways. In 1992 they began to endow a First Amendment Prize administered through the PEN American Center, an organization dedicated to protecting the rights of writers; they focused their assistance on school librarians, bookstore owners, high school teachers, and independent journalists.

The unlikely enterprise had gotten so big that it had become worthy of study. In 1995 the School of Business at Fairfield University in Connecticut began working with Newman's Own to teach the next generation of executives how to create and market new products and turn the profits into philanthropic donations. If the company actually took up any of the student proposals, it promised to turn whatever money was earned into scholarships for the school.

Somehow the little inspiration to start a company and give away the profits had become a model for others. Newman had, in effect, turned Newman's Luck into a course of study, a career arc, and a way of life.

Twenty-five

HUSBAND; FATHER; ACTOR; MOVIE STAR; SEX SYMBOL; ENTRE-preneur; philanthropist; film director; activist; champion driver; championship team owner; Oscar winner; national treasure: he had a lot of hats to choose among.

But one title had eluded him: grandpa.

That would change in the spring of 1996, when Lissy, the next-to-youngest of the five girls, gave birth to Peter Stewart Elkind and then, a couple of years later, another son, Henry. Lissy, the boys, and their father, schoolteacher Raphael Elkind, lived in the Newmans' original Westport house—just over the footbridge from the new one—where Lissy kept busy with art and singing projects, including providing the voice of an AT&T advertising campaign that featured Joanne as well.

It was a curiosity that a man with six children, some already in their forties, should have had to wait so long for grandkids, but there were actually very few marriages among the Newman daughters. Nell had been married once briefly in the 1990s and then more permanently to Gary Irving, a Welshman who operated a shop in Santa Cruz where she bought surfing gear. Clea had been engaged back at Sarah Lawrence to a classmate and fellow equestrian—Marshall Field VI, no less—but five weeks before the wedding, which had been announced in the *New York Times*, she called it off; she ultimately married, for the first time, in 2003. Susan and Stephanie hadn't married by the time Lissy had her boys.

Why not? All the girls were lovely, with their father's fine features complemented, in Joanne's daughters, by a pleasant softness around the cheeks and mouth and, in Jackie's, by oval-shaped faces and slender eyes that gave them an exotic air. They were almost all active in the sorts of outdoor pursuits that the family favored, and they were accomplished in a variety of areas—if not exactly careers, then such worthy avocations as political and environmental activism, charity work, the arts. Nell, for instance, had kept up her ornithological pursuits and been involved with saving falcons in California before starting the organics business; Clea worked for a foundation that used horse riding as therapy for special needs children and then at a school for the autistic. They were also, of course, due to inherit money; even though he gave away his Newman's Own profits and invested in race cars and racing teams, Newman had invested wisely—he would soon buy an interest in a Connecticut Volvo/Mazda dealership—and had become a wealthy man.

The girls were, in short, eligible. But they were unattached until strangely late in their lives. Perhaps potential suitors were simply cowed, as Scott seems to have been, by the prospect of measuring up to Newman. "It's hard on my boyfriends," Susan once said. "They feel compelled to live up to some sort of an image." In her case, she said, she tended to gravitate toward men who were distinctly unlike her father. Growing up seeing women behaving in the most foolish fashion in front of Newman, she said, steered her toward "doggy-looking guys." She explained, "I really don't want to walk into a room with my boyfriend and know that five hundred women are dying to jump on him." Hovering over it all, terribly, was the specter of Scott, the only boy among Newman's six children and the one who, by tradition, should have carried on the family name and the male genes; perhaps his absence was an aspect of his sisters' hesitancy toward marriage.

But whether they were being protective of their father or of themselves, or whether Newman made them feel that no man was quite good enough or Scott made them fear that no man could endure comparison with him, or maybe even whether the bohemian tenor of their upbringing made them feel that marriage and children were too traditional to bother with, they remained for long periods on their own. And Lissy's two boys would be the only children ever privileged to call Newman "Pop-Pop."

THEN AGAIN, there was nothing especially grandfatherly about him. The year before little Pete was born, for instance, Pop-Pop entered the history books as the oldest driver ever to win a sanctioned professional motor race. At the 24 Hours of Daytona, sharing the wheel with his Connecticut racing chum Michael Brockman, NASCAR veteran Mark Martin, and Trans-Am champ Tommy Kendall, Newman did approximately six hours of driving spread out over an entire day in a car that finished third overall and first in its class.* The Newman car, a Mustang, was plastered with an advertisement for *Nobody's Fool* on its side. He was an old-timer, and he didn't care who knew it.

As Jack Roush, who owned the car, remembered, when the drivers met for practice sessions, Newman seemed anxious about driving for a team that actually had a shot at winning such a prestigious race. "He was a little bit apprehensive," Roush said. "He wasn't on his game. From a race-car driver's point of view or a pilot's point of view, I think he was riding on the car instead of wearing it. To be really effective, you need to sense what's going to happen with a certain input, and that's when you start wearing it."

In fact, he had reason to be chary; it had been nearly four years since the last time he'd won, in an amateur club race at Lime Rock. In 1994 he'd had some really poor luck. "I had six races and five crashes," he said. "I think that somebody might be giving me a sign." But he nonetheless enjoyed testing himself, and according to Roush, he did what he had to do to win at Daytona.

After his first one-hour stint behind the wheel, he seemed relieved simply to have gotten his feet wet. With each session he drove, his confidence improved. During the night portion of the race, he called

---

* Like many endurance races, Daytona was essentially several races in one, with an overall championship at stake as well as races-within-the-race for each of several different classifications of vehicles.

into his crew from the car to suggest that he was losing pace, but they told him that he was exactly where he needed to be; reassured, he came in for gas and new tires and went back out to put in a double shift. With about ninety minutes left in the race, he got out of the car after what he believed was his last run. "He gave a big sigh of relief—'Wow, I've made it,' " Roush recalled. "He said, 'Man, I'm glad it's over.' And I said, 'It's not over, Paul. You're going to get in the car for the last forty-five minutes. You're gonna finish this thing.' He did, and he took that checkered flag."

He had driven in bursts all through the day and the night at speeds well over 150 miles per hour, in darkness, without proper sleep, against pros, and he had won.

At age seventy.

THAT SAME winter he became the owner of a new business, or rather the new owner of a venerable American business. *The Nation*, the progressive journal that had been published regularly since 1865, was being sold off by its publisher. Editor in chief Victor Navasky was seeking to round up a consortium of liberal sugar daddies who could buy the magazine—which, he admitted, had never been profitable in its history—and keep it afloat.

To that end, he requested a business dinner with Newman, and Newman—sensing, perhaps, that he was about to have the touch put on him—brought Joanne along. Navasky presented the situation, and Newman seemed to dig in his heels. He wanted to know why *The Nation* wasn't run as a nonprofit; Navasky explained that by taking nonprofit status, the magazine would forfeit the right to endorse elective candidates or lobby for legislation. One by one Newman's questions were parried and his doubts erased. And then came the question of money. Navasky outright asked Newman for $1 million. Newman was leery. "I don't know," he said. "That's pretty rich." And Joanne piped up with the perfect rejoinder: "Yes, but you're pretty rich, dear."

Newman joined in with such fellow investors as the novelist E. L.

Doctorow and the actor Michael Douglas. He asked just one indulgence of management: the right to be able to publish the occasional essay on this or that issue in the public eye. He took the opportunity initially in 1997, imagining a series of hypothetical questions he would like to have asked Senator Jesse Helms if the conservative lawmaker had ever appeared before a Senate committee for a confirmation hearing. The following month he wrote a parodic attack on Speaker of the House Newt Gingrich, who suggested that Hollywood liberals could come up with the $10 billion used to fund the National Endowment for the Arts by donating 1 percent of their gross income.

Those two pieces—"hiccups," as he described them—stood as his only contributions for a few years, until he started writing, again with tongue in cheek, about the political opinions of "my grandson, Pete," who he claimed "is about to overtake Leonardo da Vinci both in art and science." He even contributed little squigglelike cartoons over the years, with jokes about such topics as the impeachment of Bill Clinton. He saw it all in the spirit of playful public engagement, much like the humorous verse that his uncle Joe Newman had written about current events for Cleveland newspapers decades earlier. "If government is unable to give us government," he wrote in one of his columns, "it ought, at least, to give us a few laughs."

Briefly he almost allowed himself to be seduced by the idea of having a public platform. For more than a decade he had been in the habit of watching CNN while he did his morning exercise, and he gave some thought to becoming a commentator on the cable network. "I wrote a little essay about Star Wars or weapons systems or something, and I went down and taped it, and it was simply terrible. I was stiff and formal and unpersuasive. I looked at myself and I said, 'I would not buy a used car from that man.' "

But he continued to speak out, lending his name, his money, and sometimes his face, voice, and presence to such causes as the plight of Haitian refugees, the effort to put limits on handgun ownership, wetland conservancy, clean air and water, and, as always, nuclear disarmament. He would occasionally stump for a favored political candidate, a very short list that came to include his brother, Art, who had retired from the movie business, married a second time, and was running for a seat on the city council in Rancho Mirage, California.*

And he was happy to lead through his example as much as through his fame or fortune. Along with John F. Kennedy Jr.'s *George* magazine, Newman encouraged the sort of corporate philanthropy that his food businesses epitomized. The Newman's Own/*George* Award was an annual award for a corporation that practiced "innovative and significant philanthropy." The prize of $25,000, to be presented to the charity of the winner's choosing, was endowed by a $250,000 grant from Sony Electronics. The award was irresistible to the media, but it ceased after Kennedy's death and the shuttering of his magazine.

Newman also continued his efforts to turn corporations into more responsible public citizens with his Committee Encouraging Corporate Philanthropy, an informational group that showed businesspeople how their companies might follow in the shoes of Newman's Own. At the same time, he donated his time and image to Business Leaders for Sensible Priorities, a group formed by Ben & Jerry's ice cream cofounder Ben Cohen to lobby Congress for tighter budgetary control of military spending and the reassignment of excesses from the defense budget to schooling programs and health care for children.

THROUGHOUT IT all—the family changes, the racing, the political activity, the ongoing expansion of Newman's Own, the process of aging into his seventies—he was still a working actor.

Sometimes it was a lark, such as when Joanne appeared as Abby Brewster, one of the homicidal aunties in *Arsenic and Old Lace*, in a 1995 production at the Long Wharf Theater in New Haven. In an old tradition associated with the play, the curtain call on opening night was marked by a stagehand opening the door to the basement, where Abby and her sister, Martha, have buried the lonely men whom they've killed off with poisoned elderberry wine; a cast of a dozen ac-

---

* He would win his race; a decade later, also with Newman's backing, Art's second wife, Patricia, ran for election to the same body but lost.

tors, representing the corpses, would come out to take a bow. There among the dead men that night, to the audible delight of the sold-out audience, was Newman, wearing a Yale sweatshirt and a red baseball cap: his first appearance in a play in more than thirty years, and he got an ovation without even delivering a line.

But he was still looking for good films to make and, especially, good people to make them with. In 1997, having forsworn living in California ever again, he changed agents, leaving CAA (which Mike Ovitz had himself done two years earlier) and signing with Sam Cohn of International Creative Management's New York office. Ironically, when the deal was announced, Newman had just returned from making a film in Los Angeles, his first since *Nobody's Fool* and a reunion with Robert Benton, who again directed and cowrote with Richard Russo.

The picture, originally entitled *Magic Hour* but renamed *Twilight*, concerned an ex-cop working as a gofer and a fixer for a pair of movie stars (played by Susan Sarandon and Gene Hackman). There was a blackmail plot, a couple of dead bodies, and assorted nasty business. In some senses, it felt like a third Lew Harper film, with the old wise-cracker and shit-stirrer, named Harry Ross here, reduced to living over his friends' garage and running their errands, some of which rose to the level of carrying a gun around. Benton and Russo had written it specifically for Newman, and they made some pointed decisions. "We felt we needed him to be slightly older than he was in *Nobody's Fool*," Benton said. "I don't know that it was entirely conscious, but we definitely wrote it for the man we had come to know, and we dressed him to look a little older." A supporting cast that included James Garner, Stockard Channing, Liev Schreiber, John Spencer, and Reese Wither-spoon made it seem like an ensemble film when, truly, it was almost entirely Newman's.

Despite the fact that he had pushed past seventy, Newman did some of the stunts that the script called for. Schreiber learned of New-man's dedication to the material immediately upon working with him. "It was my first day on set," he recalled, "and they put the coat on me and they said, 'Okay, Liev, this is Paul. Paul, Liev.' 'How you doing?' 'Okay.' 'Now, kick him in the head.' Ugh. So I kicked him in the head. Of course, he's Paul Newman, and he goes, 'Harder! Kick me harder!'"

'I don't want to kick you harder.' 'Kick me harder!' It was terrible . . . I'd much rather have Paul Newman beat me up than the other way around." Having made his young costar nervous with his Methodish dedication to the film, Newman disarmed him even further one day when Joanne visited the set. "He put his arm around my shoulder," Schreiber recalled, "and said to me, 'Will you look at the ass on her?' "

He had similar fun with Channing. One of the ongoing jokes in the script was the scuttlebutt around the police department that Ross had been shot in the groin and could no longer fulfill his manly duties. Channing played a detective and potential love interest, a take-charge gal who flat-out sticks a hand down Ross's trousers to find out if the rumor is true. At first blush she wasn't keen on the scene. "I didn't go to Harvard to stick my hand down a man's pants," she complained to Benton. "Yes, but it's Paul Newman's pants," he replied. A trouper, she went ahead. "Paul didn't say a word," she recalled, "while Robert kept telling me to 'Reach deeper, deeper!' But finally [Paul] whispered in my ear, 'Let me know when you strike oil!' "

Despite a dream cast and the reunion of the creative minds behind *Nobody's Fool*, *Twilight* didn't capture that film's energy, charm, or level of easeful commitment. It was intended as an Oscar candidate for late 1997, but it stayed on the studio's shelf until the spring. The reviews were respectful but inevitably compared the film to *Fool*, and *Twilight* came out the worse. Neither the ticket sales nor the awards that greeted the earlier film were equaled.

Soon afterward Newman was in Canada shooting a story about small-time bank robbers entitled *Where the Money Is*. It was something of a head-scratcher. The director, Marek Kanievska, didn't have a terribly impressive résumé; the other actors, Linda Fiorentino and Dermot Mulroney, weren't stars. Newman had a juicy part—a bank robber who has sidestepped a lifetime prison sentence by pretending to have a stroke and being sent to an assisted living center, only to have his secret sussed out by a suspicious nurse who blackmails him back into the robbery game. And maybe that was enough for him at this stage. "Listen, if there was more stuff out there, I would work more," he confessed to an interviewer. "It's dry."

He had looked for other projects; director Jonathan Demme was working on one with him that never came to fruition. Demme remembered a script conference that Newman brought to a halt by taking off his glasses and asking his collaborators, "Fellas, are we perfecting this thing into a failure?" So perhaps he leaped into this picture simply because it had a roguish plot ("Larceny is always fun to play," he said), and it would afford him the challenge of portraying a man who has deteriorated physically. He went to a rehabilitation clinic in Connecticut and spent time studying poststroke paralysis with a doctor there, and he even looked into the possibility of getting Novocain injections to freeze the muscles in his face. That was nixed: "Considering how often I'd need them, the doctor was afraid there might be some damage." He considered using makeup: false, sunken cheeks, say. Again, not a good solution. Finally, Kanievska explained, "He realized he had to trust his own inner stillness."

That was in front of the cameras. On the set he was something of a dervish. There was a Ping-Pong table and a badminton net, and he delighted in suckering people into playing the old man for a couple of bucks, only to whip them. "You know, he really is a hustler," Fiorentino said. "One by one he methodically destroyed everyone on the picture."

What he couldn't do, though, was trick the producers into getting the film into theaters. Again, the film sat on the shelf—this time for almost two years, finally being released in the spring of 2000 without making a ripple, despite affection for Newman in virtually every review.

By the time *Where the Money Is* opened, Newman had already come and gone in another unlikely role, that of Kevin Costner's crusty, rakish dad in *Message in a Bottle*, based on the lugubrious best-selling romantic novel by Nicholas Sparks. In some ways the pairing of Newman and Costner was natural, if belated; there had been a time when Costner seemed a potential heir to Newman's throne as the screen's casually roguish superstar. But the younger man's career had waned precipitously after his late-1980s hits, and he hadn't aged with anything like the grace or beauty that Newman still possessed. His audience, which had once compared him to Newman, had thinned. That didn't matter, evidently, to Newman, who didn't see it as his job to carry the picture. Joking that he would play the titular bottle, he said, "I haven't done a lot of films where I didn't have to carry the film. And that was nice. That was a relief, to know that the whole thing wasn't completely on my shoulders."

Would that it had been. The picture was more or less reviled by critics, who, as with *Where the Money Is*, took special notice of Newman's work as an isolated bit of quality. "Paul Newman handles his role . . . with the relaxed confidence of Michael Jordan shooting free throws in your driveway," wrote Roger Ebert in a representative notice. The film actually grossed more than any Newman film since *The Color of Money*. But it didn't stop Costner's continued slide. And Newman clearly had involved himself for the pleasure of it, not for the potential reward.

Better by far was his brief, self-mocking turn in an episode of *The Simpsons*. His fleeting appearance came after housewife Marge Simpson makes her husband, Homer, jealous by revealing that she has a crush on the cartoon lumberjack pictured on a package of paper towels. That night Homer dreams of a romance of his own with a character from a logo. A bottle of Newman's Own salad dressing appears to him, and Newman's familiar face suddenly becomes animated, declaring, in the unmistakable gravel of his late-life voice, "Homer, I'll tell you what I told Redford: it ain't gonna happen."

WHEN HE had gone out of his way for the producers to do some publicity for *Where the Money Is*, he confessed to reporters, "I just get restless, and the best thing that happens to be around at that time, I've got to do it." He was thinking about retiring—"I'd like to find a film I could bow out on"—but none of the projects he had been making would seem to serve adequately as the final grace note to a career of such unprecedented length, breadth, and quality. Finally, in 2001, the right job presented itself.

Road to Perdition was a searingly violent graphic novel by Max Allan Collins and Richard Piers Rayner dealing with deceit and revenge among the members of a midwestern crime mob in the 1930s. It focused on Michael Sullivan, a paid killer whose life is imperiled when his young son stows away in the family car and witnesses him at his bloody work. Connor Rooney, the shiftless son of crime boss John

Rooney, decides that Sullivan and his boy must die, but he botches the job and inadvertently kills the boy's brother and mother instead. Sullivan then dedicates himself to avenging his slain wife and son while protecting the one boy he has left.

The story, adapted for the screen by the English director Sam Mendes, would shoot in Chicago in the winter and spring of 2001. Tom Hanks would play against type as Sullivan, Daniel Craig would play the unreliable Connor Rooney, Stanley Tucci took the role of Chicago gangster Frank Nitti, Jude Law was Maguire, a hit man on Sullivan's tail invented newly for the film, and Newman would play John Rooney in a part much expanded from the original.

Mendes had gone to Newman's apartment overlooking Central Park for a luncheon meeting to see if they could work together. "He shuffled about and made great play of the fact that he was becoming old and forgetful," the director recalled, "but I got the sense he was watching me like a hawk." After asking a lot of questions about the character's wardrobe, temperament, and background, Newman had one final query of Mendes: "You any good at holding hands?" Mendes said yes. "Then let's do it," Newman replied.

"There was something so comforting about getting on an airplane to come to Chicago to know that you're going to start shooting a film with people like this," Newman said later. "This guy Mendes has to be dealt with. He has a brilliant mind in terms of storytelling. You expect him to be good with actors, from his stage experience. But he has that artist's eye with the camera. Not only as an artist but as a storyteller."

Newman and Hanks had never met before—although Joanne had played Hanks's mother in *Philadelphia* and they had competed in the Oscar derby in the year of *Nobody's Fool* and *Forrest Gump*. Despite the thirty-plus-year difference in their ages and their distinct approaches to their work, they hit it off. Hanks admitted that he was initially awed by his costar. "Paul can do anything he wants," he said. "If he wants to call me 'kid' and never learn my name, fine. If he wants to do one take and walk away, fine. If he wants to come in with two little lapdogs and talk to them all day long, he could have done that too." He especially treasured homey memories of Newman on the set. "He had corned beef and cabbage on Saint Patrick's Day while watching a replay of the

Talladega 500," he recalled. He cherished the image of Newman calling Joanne between shots and the memory of Newman confessing to first-day jitters.

Speaking in tandem to a reporter, the two stars described their rapport in jocular but fond terms that actually revealed something about their joint process:

Newman: "We respected each other's isolation. We didn't do a lot of stuff before scenes."

Hanks: "It was like playing catch—but he was way over there."

Newman: "We respected each other's territory. He pissed on his tree, and I pissed on my tree, and then someone yelled 'action!' "

Hanks: "We were two dogs snarling at each other, and our chains only went so far."

Inevitably, Newman sported himself on the set: twice Mendes was shocked to find him walking on his hands to amuse the two boys who were cast as Hanks's sons. But he had done some homework for the role, asking the writer Frank McCourt to record his lines for him so that he could study an Irish accent and brushing up on his piano playing for a scene in which Rooney and Sullivan bond over the keyboard. (Originally the scene asked for the two actors to dance, but Newman told the filmmakers, "Go and look in my wife's closet and check her shoes, and you will know immediately that I can't dance.")

For all the joking, Newman was, Mendes remembered, still a very precise and analytical actor. "He wants to know, partly because he feels shaky now with lines sometimes, exactly what I want from him," he said. "He'll talk about the placing of a full stop or a comma." At one moment Newman was frustrated with his dialogue and asked Mendes if he could change the word *where* to the word *here*. "We changed one letter," according to Mendes, "and he was thrilled. He said, 'That's much better. What a relief. Now I can do something with it.' He's that particular."

In another scene, Mendes recalled, Newman was meant to chew out Craig, only to stop halfway through his tirade and hug him. Newman had a different idea: "Paul had this very clear image, a physical image, of what he wanted to do. He wanted to hit [Craig] so hard that he knocked him to the ground, then pick him up so he could hit him again, only to end up embracing him. The important things are the things that are not articulated, just dramatized."

The film was photographed by Conrad Hall, who had worked with Newman on *Harper, Cool Hand Luke,* and *Butch Cassidy and the Sundance Kid,* but not since. Hall found Newman to be "the same identical person" as he had been decades earlier. Except in one respect: Once, Mendes recalled, as they were preparing to shoot Newman, "I turned around to find that Conrad was crying as he lit the shot. I asked him what was wrong, and he just said, 'He was so beautiful.' And I said, 'Well, he's beautiful now.' And Conrad repeated, 'Yes, but he was so beautiful.' " Later, more composed, Hall observed that Newman "saves the best part of his performance for the close-up. As an actor and a director, he knows how important that part of the performance is for him. So he gives his all."*

NEWMAN SPENT only two weeks on the film—plus, to the studio's financial woe, a couple of days. A clause in his contract calling for an additional $250,000 for his time kicked in. "He made the studio pay for the extra two days and then gave it straight to his charity," Mendes recalled. When shooting finally ended in June 2001, the intention was for an Oscar-season release. But Mendes, making only his second film, hadn't yet arrived at a satisfactory cut. So it was pushed back to the summer of the following year, an unlikely release date for a film with such dark themes, no sex, no comedy, no special effects, and not even, given how many deaths it contained, much blood.

The decision to release it as a bit of counterprogramming to the summer's usual menu of fluff paid off in ticket sales—over $100 million, Newman's first such gate in three decades—and very positive reviews. "It's a genteel film with a gun in its pocket," wrote Michael

---

* Sadly, Hall may have given *his* all for *Road to Perdition.* The film was shot during long days in the terribly cold Chicago winter and early spring. Several of Hall's friends, including cinematographer Haskell Wexler, believed that the grueling schedule brought on a recurrence of Hall's cancer, which killed him not long after the film was released.

Wilmington in the *Chicago Tribune*, "but it's also a film with a universal chord of feeling that keeps welling up from the dark surfaces." In the *Los Angeles Times*, Kenneth Turan said, "Because it is so careful with its effects, this film's ability to create feeling sneaks up and surprises. This is a story with a will to move us and the ability to do whatever it takes to make that happen." Mick LaSalle in the *San Francisco Chronicle* added, "Not much is on the surface of Newman's performance, yet every moment is alive with what's underneath it—the weight of a misspent life, of guilt, of the certainty of damnation."

The following winter the film was indeed remembered by Oscar voters, chiefly for such so-called technical elements as cinematography, score, art direction, and sound—and also for Newman's work in a supporting role. His tenth Academy Award nomination found him for the first time in the best supporting actor category, running against the estimable quartet of Chris Cooper (*Adaptation*), Ed Harris (*The Hours*), John C. Reilly (*Chicago*), and Christopher Walken (*Catch Me If You Can*). Once again he had nothing to do with the ceremony or the hoopla leading up to it. If he tuned in to see Cooper's victory from his home or some other place, there was no record of it.

For prizes he still had racing: not his own, necessarily, but those of the Newman-Haas team, which had become one of the dominant outfits in all of motor sports. After Mario Andretti won the CART championship in 1984, it took the team until 1991 to win another title, when Michael Andretti repeated his father's feat. In 1993 Newman-Haas scored the immense coup of convincing Nigel Mansell, the Englishman who was then the reigning champ of Formula 1, the world's most prestigious racing circuit, to be its principal driver. Mansell, who oozed braggadocio and oily charm, was an oversize character after Newman's heart. "I kept telling him he should have been in films," Newman recalled. "First time he drove for us, it was on one of those oval tracks, and he swore the United States wasn't worth living in, that you could take these oval tracks and shove them. Fifteen laps later he'd knocked two-tenths off the lap record. Honestly, the guy

was the biggest hustler you ever saw. He'd hustle you for a nickel—
'Bet you a nickel that gumdrop tastes better than that gumdrop.' "
Mansell won the championship for Newman-Haas that year and then
went back to Europe. It would be another nine years before the team
won another title, in 2002, with the Brazilian Cristiano da Matta as its
top driver.

In that time, though, the conditions under which Newman-Haas
raced changed notably. In the mid-1990s, tensions broke out between
the managers of the open-wheel racing series in which the team competed and Tony George, the owner-operator of the Indianapolis
Motor Speedway. The result was a split of open-wheel racing into two
factions, the CART (later Champ Car) series, where Newman-Haas
stayed, and the Indy Racing League, or IRL, a new competition that
had exclusive rights to appear in the Indy 500, the jewel event of the
sport. There were angry voices on both sides of the divide, none more
bitter or frequently quoted than Newman's. He derided George as
greedy and extortionate and accused him of destroying not only open-
wheel racing but his own home city. "The damage Tony George has
done to the sport is unconscionable," he told a reporter for *Road &
Track* a decade into the battle. "I'd love to see an economic impact
study of the effects on the business of the city of Indianapolis for the
month of May and another one of the effects on the racing industry in
that town. I think the results of an economic impact study would shock
everybody." (At one point in his war with the IRL, Newman hired college students to count the number of seats at George's track to give
him statistical ammo in his propaganda battle.)

Given that sort of pugnacity, it was no wonder that Newman kept
on driving in races throughout his seventies. Indeed, he bragged about
his age, having it painted on his car each year in increasing numbers—
79 in 2004, 81 in 2006, and so forth—and tooling around the pad-
docks and pits on a scooter. His luck and his reflexes, however, weren't
what they had been. In January 2000 he injured his ribs in a wreck at
Daytona that could have been a lot worse: he was going upward of
180 miles per hour when he skidded into a barrier. And as ever, he
blamed himself for the accident: "I got overconfident on a fresh set of

tires. The tires weren't warm enough, and I slipped. I'm angry at myself. It was a stupid thing to do." Two years later he was driving a practice session at Watkins Glen with Kyle Petty in the passenger seat when he cracked up against a wall; he was unhurt, but he was shaken up.

His problems were age-related, and he knew it: "The teeth get longer. The hair gets thinner. The eyes and ears don't sense danger as quickly as they did before. You can't go as fast, so you try to go faster." But at the same time, he contended that the actual danger these incidents represented was blown out of proportion by the media. "Last time I totaled a car somewhere in Ohio," he joked, "one of the papers carried a headline: 'Paul Newman Almost Killed—But Uninjured.'"

In fact, he suffered his worst auto-related injury not on the track but on a road in Westport, when his souped-up Volvo station wagon, one of a series of such customized rides, was sideswiped by a driver who was coming in the opposite direction and crossed into Newman's lane. Newman skirted a truly bad accident—Joanne happened to be with him at the time—but he lost the driver's side-view mirror and his left hand was broken, requiring him to wear a cast for several weeks. Typically, he made light of it: "I wept more for my car than for my hand."

The excitement of driving and of being around racing, he claimed, was the most enjoyable part of his life and, in fact, the thing that kept him going. "My blood pressure is generally 117 over 76," he told a reporter, "and I went to the doctor for a checkup, and my blood pressure was 140 over 80 or something. So then we went down and ran the 24 Hours at Daytona and came back, and my blood pressure was 115 over 70. I recommend it to everybody."

Twenty-six

A ND FOR ALL THAT, IN CERTAIN CIRCLES AND IN A CERTAIN light, the most remarkable thing he'd done was to stay married to the same woman for forty years, as of 1998, and on into a new century. How in the world did a couple in their position manage that remarkable milestone and more? "Ultimately, I think we both delight in watching the progression," he told a journalist. "And we laugh a lot."

By accounts, he still acted around Joanne like he was hopelessly in love. He would light up when she entered a room, observers noticed, even if he'd been glowering or grumbling or cussing or complaining or sitting in one of his unreadable silences barely a minute before. He held her hand on walks or as they sat at the symphony or the ballet. He surprised her with phone calls, flowers, little gifts. ("He gave her his electrocardiogram for Christmas," Stewart Stern recalled.) He teased her with mocking little praises—"You have a great figure, and you make a hell of a hollandaise sauce," he told her in front of a reporter— but he needed her in an almost childlike way that he couldn't disguise. When he was making a film in the late 1990s, she visited the set; between shots, he beckoned her over to sit on his lap; as she did, he was overheard asking her, in a sweet voice, "Are you my broad?" When he talked about her, it was with a zeal that could frankly startle. "She's a mercurial lady," he once said. "I never know what I'm going to wake up with the next morning. That's made for some fascinating experiences, I can tell you." (An old-fashioned fellow, he demurred from offering an example.)

Predictably, Joanne was better able to articulate certain things about the marriage, which in her view they had been able to sustain because they saw it as an entity in and of itself. "There were times when Paul and I both had to hang in," she said, "when it felt that the marriage wouldn't last another day. We had to step outside ourselves and become aware that three things were operating—my ego, his ego, and *our* ego. For the relationship to survive, we had to put the his-and-hers on hold and go for the *our*."

And despite their famous differences—beer vs. sherry, race cars vs. ballet, popcorn vs. hollandaise—they had professional interests and passions in common. Their way of life in Connecticut was one, and another was the theater, which they attended together regularly. In 2000 they were able to combine the two in another of the selfless acts for which they had become revered in Westport.

For more than forty years Jim McKenzie had been the artistic director of the Westport Country Playhouse. But financing the operations of the theater, which ran on box office receipts, rental fees, and donations, had long been a year-to-year game of can-we-do-it? By the time McKenzie retired, after the 1999 season, the directors of the Playhouse had determined that they had to take significant steps to ensure the viability of the institution.

That was when the Newmans—Joanne especially—stepped in and put their stamp on the place. Joanne had long been a donor to the theater and had appeared in benefits—but never a proper play. She agreed to take over some of McKenzie's functions on a part-time, volunteer basis and to direct a play each season as she was able. Newman joined the artistic advisory council, which boasted Connecticut locals Christopher Plummer, Marlo Thomas, Gene Wilder, and Jane Powell in its ranks. The following year, with a new fund-raising campaign in progress and a successful season behind her, Joanne accepted a full-time appointment as artistic director.

At the start of her tenure, subscriptions and donations to the Playhouse rose appreciably. It helped that she was able to bring to the stage for the occasional staged reading or benefit the international movie star who shared her bedroom. During Valentine's Day week 2000 Newman joined her on the Playhouse stage for performances of A. R. Gurney's

Love Letters. Later that year he played alongside her in a production of Gurney's family drama *Ancestral Voices*, with Swoosie Kurtz, James Naughton, and Paul Rudd. (They reprised the roles in 2002 with Matthew Broderick, Tim Robbins, and Susan Sarandon.) The following year he appeared on the Playhouse stage in a fund-raiser for local families affected by September 11. In 2004 he headlined in *Trumbo*, a one-man show about the blacklisted screenwriter Dalton Trumbo, who, a lifetime ago, had written the script for *Exodus*. And in 2007 he stood onstage beside Joanne and read love poems in another Valentine's Day program entitled *Come Be My Love*.

But his biggest contribution to the health of the Playhouse came in 2002, when Woodward and her colleagues were thinking of ways they could respond artistically to the trauma of 9/11. On a personal level, Newman had already made a dramatic gesture. The night after the terrorist attacks, he and Joanne were dining at a restaurant near West-port when Newman, responding to the air of gloom hanging in the room, stood and began singing "The Star-Spangled Banner"; the entire house joined him.

A similar communitarian urge inspired a more organized artistic response to the trauma. Specifically, the Newmans got to thinking about *Our Town*, Thornton Wilder's 1938 chestnut about life, love, and death in a small American town. The sparseness of the show (performed traditionally on bare stages without sets or curtains), its vision of the consolation of the departed, its emphasis on home and simple pleasures and the human need to accept whatever life brings: all of this made it seem a natural curative for a wounded civic soul. And it had a history at the Playhouse: Wilder himself had performed the role of the Stage Manager—the narrator and presiding genius of the play—in a fondly remembered production mounted in 1946 amid the sense of loss associated with World War II. Joanne discussed the idea of putting on the show with Newman, and he so immediately grasped the aptness of the choice that he asked if he could play the Stage Manager, the role he'd played at the Woodstock Opera House more than forty years prior.

Suddenly the Playhouse had something big on its hands. James Naughton, another member of the artistic advisory council, would direct the show, and a number of actors with local connections—including Jayne Atkinson, Frank Converse, Jane Curtin, and Jeffrey DeMunn—joined the cast. When the production was announced, it sold out its entire two-and-a-half-week run almost immediately—a financial bonanza as well as a publicity coup.

The show opened on June 5 after only three weeks of rehearsals, and the *New York Times* deemed the production "rickety," adding that "the pace of the play is fitful; so are the New England accents of the players." But for Newman there was nothing but praise. Calling the role "a perfect fit," the *Times* declared, "It's his show; the rest of us are there in his honor . . . When he is still, he is commanding. His profile is stunning and fierce, and often, as he stands observing with other actors at center stage, you can feel your gaze drawn by the magnetic tug of his presence." Another writer for the *Times*, also dismissive of the production but not of the star, saw in the show the seeds of what Woodward and her colleagues had first intended. "If only this production," wrote Alvin Klein, "crossed the state line—a mere 50 miles or so—for a short stopover on Broadway, it could be a heady balm for a still-grieving city."

When *Our Town* closed in late June, Woodward and her fellow executives turned their heads to the question of whether there could be a bigger stage yet for it. The Playhouse hadn't exported a show to Broadway since *Butterflies Are Free* more than thirty years earlier; but it seemed possible that they could bring this one, with this star, anywhere. There was a hitch: the Roundabout Theater Company had already announced that it would be doing a production of *Our Town* on Broadway during the 2002–3 season. But that company decided to concentrate on works with smaller casts and canceled its plans. In September it was announced that the Playhouse would be bringing the show—at a cost of $1 million—to the Booth Theater, and that Newman would be making his first appearance on a New York stage in nearly forty years.

As he told a reporter at the time, the choice to come to Broadway was his alone. "I decided I would not go to my grave without coming back," he explained. "There is no second reason." But the Playhouse was also engaged in a $17 million fund-raising campaign intended to completely renovate itself, and a successful Broadway run of *Our Town* might result in a real windfall.

It did. The show was set to open on December 5 and run until January 26, Newman's seventy-eighth birthday, and every performance was sold out before the first reviews were published. As before, the play was shown no special love by the reviewers, but they could find nothing but superlatives for the star. Calling it "the most modest performance ever by a major American star on a Broadway stage," Ben Brantley of the *Times* wrote, "Mr. Newman has . . . the aura of someone figuring out things as he goes along, almost seeming to invent his lines on the spot and to marvel when they sound deep . . . He now knows that his living-legend status requires no special enhancement, and he's all the more resonant for not working at it." "He is the star here," wrote the *Washington Post*, "yet this is no star turn." And nodding to his evident age, *Entertainment Weekly* said, "Whatever he lacks in vocal strength these days, he more than makes up for in charisma (of course) and arrow-sharp, punctuated gestures." He was really superb, imparting a combination of homespun wisdom, Yankee cynicism, paternal affection, and wiseacre knowingness to his scenes, standing aside for most of the play while the real protagonists lived, loved, worked, played, died, and mourned as Wilder's script called for them to. If ever there was a valedictory performance, he had achieved it— and onstage, night after night, for weeks, at a time in life when most actors of his stature might be leery of filming a commercial for fear of shocking their public with the spectacle of age's toll. It was a remarkable coup.

On many nights during the play's short run, there was as much going on behind the scenes as onstage. Newman had been ensconced in a tiny dressing room upstairs from the stage area at the Booth, a space no bigger than the bathroom of an ordinary home, according to Randy Blair, who served as Newman's dresser for both productions. "People would see it and say, 'This is where Paul Newman is?' " he recalled. It was. Newman was visited by a firmament of stars from the worlds of acting, auto racing, and politics, including Secretary of State Madeleine Albright and actors Tom Hanks, Kate Winslet, John Travolta, Liam Neeson, Al Pacino, James Earl Jones, and Matt Damon.

Because there was no waiting area near the dressing room, Blair had Newman's guests gather downstairs and would bring them up, one by one, after announcing them to Newman, who never wanted to know who was in the house before he went on. Blair found too that if he told anyone in the show who the night's guests were, word would seep out and little scenes of chaos would result. "The rest of the cast and crew would come to me and say, 'Who are we going to get to see tonight?' " he remembered. "And I'd have to tell them, 'I'm not telling. I don't want him to hear it, because I'll get yelled at.' " His vigilance was tested one night when an unannounced visitor appeared. "His name wasn't on the list," Blair said, "but I mean, it's Robert Redford. I said, 'Okay, sneak him backstage so he doesn't get mobbed, and I'll tell Paul.' That was incredible, to see them together."

Before the show wrapped, on Newman's birthday, with the cast and crew greeting him with a cake and appropriate salutations, a performance was filmed over a couple of days to air on the Showtime cable network and, later, on PBS. In May, when the Tony nominations were announced, Newman's name alone among the people involved with *Our Town* appeared on the list as best actor in a play alongside Brian Bedford *(Tartuffe)*, Eddie Izzard *(A Day in the Death of Joe Egg)*, Stanley Tucci *(Frankie and Johnny in the Clair de Lune)*, and the eventual winner, Brian Dennehy *(Long Day's Journey into Night)*. Predictably, just as he had ignored the Oscar nomination he'd received for *Road to Perdition* earlier that year, he skipped the big night on Broadway. "I burned my tuxedo five years ago," he explained, "and with that comes a certain resolution . . . I promised myself that I wasn't going to attend any of those functions. I've never been very comfortable at them, and at my age a man is entitled to burn his tuxedo."

AT HIS age a man would also have been entitled to slow down, but he didn't, not really. He still considered various film scripts, he still supervised the rollout of new Newman's Own products, he still toured the various Hole in the Wall Camps to be among the kids, he still did private charity work such as putting in sweat equity hours for Connecticut chapters of Habitat for Humanity, he still showed up for fund-raising events, he still attended the theater, he still involved himself in his race team, he still drove the occasional race himself.

In September 2004 he appeared in a clown getup—red nose, bowler hat, baggy suit, big yellow shoes—and entertained three hundred kids as a part of Zippo's Circus, which was then performing under an old-fashioned traveling big top in London's Highbury Fields. Presented incognito to the audience as Butch Bolognese, he set about pouring plates of pasta down the pants of the other clowns. Later, in the company of his brother, Art, who'd made the trip with him, he laughed off the whole thing, declaring, "I'm just grateful I didn't get a pie in the face out there."

He was back in the States in time for the presidential election and spent a day in Ohio ringing doorbells in support of John Kerry. He made a special trip to Shaker Heights and, inevitably, 2983 Brighton Road, where, his eyes now and again brimming with tears, he introduced himself to the current owners and wandered through the rooms, pointing out to the people who accompanied him, among other highlights, the nook in the basement where he and his brother had hidden their cigarette butts from their mom.*

Not long before that he had spent a fair bit of the summer in Maine, making a movie. He had secured another role as another rascal in another adaptation of a Richard Russo novel, *Empire Falls*, for which he served as a producer as well as scene-stealing rogue Max Roby, the larcenous and unkempt father of the novel's beleaguered protagonist. As Russo recalled, Newman got his hands on the novel while it was still in galleys and phoned him excitedly about the prospect of adapting it not into a film but into a long-form project that would preserve its kaleidoscope of characters and scenes. "He was one

---

* Two years later, he took an active part in Ned Lamont's campaign to unseat Joe Lieberman as U.S. senator from Connecticut. He actually manned phone banks and cold-called voters, few of whom believed he was whom he claimed to be. "It's some quack pretending to be Paul Newman," one recipient yelled to his wife when she asked who was on the phone.

of the first people to call me after reading the book," Russo said, "and he was very kind about it, and the last thing he said before he hung up was, 'And you know: no one will be better as Max.' "

Russo drove from his Maine home to Westport to discuss the project with Newman and producer Marc Platt, and the plan was to have dinner together afterward. When they all stepped into the driveway, Newman's eye was caught by Russo's new Audi sedan, which was parked beyond the limousine that was waiting to take them to the restaurant. "Whose car is that?" Newman wondered aloud, and told it was Russo's, he asked if he could drive it to the restaurant and have the limo follow.

"Well," remembered Russo, "are you gonna tell Paul Newman he can't drive your car? So I give him the keys, and he starts to pull out onto the street with the limo behind us, and suddenly he stomps on the pedal, and my head whips back, and we go ass-out into the road, and we're gone. And he's testing the steering, going left-right, left-right. And now we're finally heading into Westport, and he slows down to about thirty-five, and he says, 'I like your car. It's a good car.' And he looks into the mirror and says, 'Where the hell are those guys?' "

The film shot in the summer of 2004 along the Maine coast with an impressive cast of stars—including Joanne, Ed Harris, Helen Hunt, Philip Seymour Hoffman, Estelle Parsons, Robin Wright Penn, Theresa Russell, and Aidan Quinn—under the direction of Fred Schepisi. When it aired in two parts the following spring, it received respectful but largely unenthusiastic reviews—comparisons to *Nobody's Fool* generally didn't favor it. But Newman, appearing in a mere handful of scenes, was universally lauded as a show-stealer. With a spotty beard (he never could get a truly robust one going, not really), tattered clothes, and a bony frame, he looked like the desiccated old uncle of Judge Roy Bean.

Newman, naturally, reveled in the role: "I'm playing this old goat who kidnaps a priest with Alzheimer's, steals a car and the church's money, leaves for the Florida Keys, and has no contact with anybody," he told a reporter. "When he finally calls his son back home, the first words out of his mouth are, 'Where's my Social Security check?' You get that character in one sentence."

He had pride in the film, but only to a point. He received not one, not two, but *three* nominations for his acting—an Emmy, a Golden Globe, and a Screen Actors Guild Award—and once again, he failed to show up for any of the prize ceremonies, even though he was named the winner all three times.

THAT IMPRESSIVE feat, though, paled in comparison to one he really relished. In 2003 the young French driver Sebastien Bourdais joined the Newman-Haas Champ Car team, which was then defending the title won the previous year by Cristiano da Matta. Bourdais, then only twenty-four years old, finished a respectable fourth place in the season's rankings. But the next year he burst out to win the championship, a feat he repeated for the next three years to claim a four-peat, 2004–7, the most dominant string ever in American open-wheel racing. Newman could be counted on to attend several races each season, buzzing around the pits and the paddock on his red scooter, having a beer and a burger and a laugh, and often showing up on the podium to have his photo taken with the victorious Bourdais. His enjoyment of racing weekends had increased as his face had become less famous and his presence less a cause for disruption and embarrassment. When Bourdais won the 2006 San Jose Grand Prix, Newman couldn't get past the security guards at the gate to the winner's circle and had to stand by as a number of young women in skimpy attire were admitted; rescued by the race's publicity director, he waved off an apology, nodding toward the girls and admitting, "They're better looking."

The smashing success of this team led Newman to invest in another, Newman-Wachs, part of Champ Car's Atlantic Series, which was, in effect, a minor-league circuit for the development of young drivers. In 2007 Newman and Carl Haas took on another partner, businessman and longtime racing sponsor Mike Lanigan. Newman also lent his name to a group that tried to get a racetrack built at Floyd Bennett Field, alongside Jamaica Bay in Brooklyn, a project that was ultimately scuttled on environmental grounds. That same year Newman-Haas-Lanigan, as the team was newly christened, sought to expand into NASCAR for the first time by forging a partnership with

Robert Yates, a veteran of the stock-car circuit that had become America's favorite form of racing in the years after the divisive split among open-wheel racers.

After lengthy negotiations that deal fell through, but stunning progress was made on another front: in early 2008 it was announced that the Champ Car series and the Indy Racing League had buried the hatchet and would reunite under the rubric of IndyCar. The Champ series would expire with that remarkable string of wins by Bourdais, who returned to Europe and Formula 1. And the path would be cleared for Newman to return to the Indy 500. As part of the reunification deal, he joined Roger Penske in penning an open letter asking fans of both series to reunite at the 500, and Tony George, his former nemesis, agreed to have the new league become a charitable partner of the Hole in the Wall Camps.

Even in the ultracompetitive world of auto racing, this was a true win-win. "When I heard about the reunification, I felt like I had died and gone to heaven," Newman said. "It was absolutely necessary for both groups. It's tragic that it didn't happen sooner . . . It's wonderful to be running against Roger Penske, Bobby Rahal, and Michael Andretti once again."

When he talked about running against those other teams, he was exaggerating only slightly. He still raced a couple of times a year, even into his eighties. "I'd like to assume the role of elder statesman," he said, "taking walks in the woods and going fishing, but here I am, forever strapping myself into these machines . . . And I will, with the blessing of my wife, continue until I embarrass myself." He rarely did; rather, he continued to have amazing adventures behind the wheel. In 2005 he ran a few practice laps in the runup to the 24 Hours of Daytona, having to flee his vehicle when it caught fire due to a faulty engine mechanism; he was unhurt. In 2006, visiting his Hole in the Wall affiliate camp in San Marcello Pistoiese, Italy, he stopped off in nearby Maranello to tour the Ferrari plant and try out the company's new high-end 599 GTB Fiorano on the practice track. In 2007—*at age eighty-two*—he ran in an SCCA amateur race at Watkins Glen, New York, despite the fact that his coolant suit (a kind of vest employed by racers to keep body temperature down) stopped functioning on the third lap; he needed a little oxygen afterward, but he needed no help on the track, finishing fourth. "I pulled alongside him, but he shut the door on me," said the fifth-place driver, William Rozmajzl. "He's a smart guy. He has a lot of experience."

Some of that experience, as Richard Russo's account would indicate, was earned off the racetrack. In 2003 Newman had acquired a car inspired by his Volkswagens with the Porsche engines in them. He had been driving V-6 Volvo station wagons and found a mechanic who was able to soup them up even further, sticking in Ford V-8 engines and turbo superchargers—"puffers"—that turned them into unassuming little suburban rocket ships. Newman knew that his Westport buddy David Letterman was fond of a fast car, and he offered him the chance to buy one while his own was being built. As Letterman remembered, Newman was all excited about the prospect: "This thing will turn about four hundred horsepower, so if you pop the clutch you're gonna tear up the rear end. I tell ya, from twenty to a hundred you can chew anybody's ass!" "And you know," Letterman said, "I'm thinking to myself, what circumstance would Paul find himself in driving around in a Volvo station wagon where he feels like he's gotta chew somebody's ass? But when Paul Newman offers you a puffer, I mean, you take it. You don't turn down Paul Newman."

In a way this forty-year obsession with cars and speed and racing had become the perfect balance to the acting craft that had similarly beguiled him and turned him into a lifelong devotee. But where acting's rewards were, in his view, spiritual, fleeting, and rare, racing's were verifiable, demonstrable, and concrete. "I'm a very competitive person," he said. "I always have been. And it's hard to be competitive about something as amorphous as acting. But you can be competitive on the track, because their rules are very simple and the declaration of the winner is very concise." As he put it another time, "It's right to a thousandth of a second. Your bumper is here. That guy's bumper is there. You win."

NONETHELESS, ACTING was still one of his true loves, and he was still searching for something he'd enjoy doing. He had long been looking for a film he could do with Joanne, or maybe one that could serve as a suitable farewell to the screen. "There's a lot of stuff floating around," he said in 2005, "but I don't like to talk about it until it's in cement. I think I'd like to make one more film and then take a powder. It's time Joanne and I spent quality time together."

As it happened, it wasn't Joanne but rather his grandsons, Pete and Henry, who were most likely to enjoy Pop-Pop's new movie. For the first time since *Winning* he would be playing a racer on-screen and not on a track. This time, though, he would be playing not the driver but *the vehicle.* He would provide the voice for a character in *Cars,* a digitally animated feature set in a world where cars were alive and written and directed by John Lasseter, the maker of the *Toy Story* films and chief creative officer for Pixar Animation Studios and Walt Disney Animation.

Lasseter had written a story about a cocky championship race car, Lightning McQueen, who found himself lost in the desert town of Radiator Springs, where he would learn some lessons about life, love, and racing from the locals, who included Doc Hudson, the town physician, judge, and—though nobody knew it—celebrity-in-hiding, the one-time racing champion of the world, Hudson Hornet. Newman's character would have blue eyes, a hint of a southern accent, a surly temper, and no lady friend: another crusty rogue from the gallery of late-period Newman portraits.

In late 2004 Lasseter came to Newman with a full package of incentives to be in the movie: it was a quality project, offered a good salary for a job that didn't require him to shave or wear wardrobe, and included a sponsorship deal between Disney and Newman-Haas in the upcoming 24 Hours of Daytona:* and a donation of $500,000 would go to the Association of Hole in the Wall Camps. The director was smart enough to bait the hook not with money or talk about Pixar's excellence but with the choice of car they had for his character: "It's a '51 Hudson Hornet," Lasseter explained, "which most people don't know about.

---

* It would be the last one Newman would run; his team came in fifty-first because of engine problems.

But those who do, know of its legendary nature. It was really way ahead of its time and dominated the stock car–style of racing back then and was the fastest production car of its day . . . Paul was very excited about that." Newman leaped in, sticking around after his recording sessions to talk details of cars and racing with Lasseter, conveying his passion for the sport so ardently that, as Lasseter said, "I gave him a 'racing consultant' credit because his working with me was so valuable."

For his part Newman delighted in being able to act without worrying about his appearance or any of the cumbersome machinery of live-action filmmaking. "The nice thing," he said, "is you don't even really have to account for yourself. All of the physical stuff that you work on as an actor you just throw away . . . You can have a line and you can say that it's wrong and you can just jump on it and do it sixty different ways back-to-back . . . You can just keep improvising and improving on it or making it completely different or changing words. You just have a lot more freedom."

The whole thing delighted him. In May 2006 he showed up with much of the rest of the cast of the film—Owen Wilson, Cheech Marin, Bonnie Hunt, and Pixar's house good-luck charm, John Ratzenberger—at the Loews Motor Speedway in Concord, North Carolina, where a publicity event for the film coincided with a NASCAR race. It was a big media to-do, with press conferences, an outdoor screening of *Cars*, and, to Newman's delight, a little bit of driving. Specifically, he had the chance to drive a Hudson Hornet chassis mounted on top of a racing-quality stock-car frame and engine. Other drivers got to run the car before he did, and as NASCAR champ Jimmie Johnson recalled, "The only man on pit road with a stopwatch was Paul Newman. He was timing the laps I was running, other guys were running. Then he got in that car, that had no business, with that body especially, going around that track at speed, and he was trying to break the lap times that we were running."

For all the movie stars at the track that weekend, it was Dale Earnhardt Jr., who had a small speaking part in the film, who got the biggest ovation on premiere night. And it was Richard Petty, the beloved outlaw king of NASCAR, and also a voice in the film, who had the most charming response to what he saw: "You sit there for a couple of minutes and say to yourself, 'How dumb can I be to sit here and watch cars talk to each other?' Then all of a sudden you're right dead in the middle of the movie, man, and you don't realize that they aren't really people"—a review any Method actor would be proud to have in his scrapbook.

BACK IN January 2000, when he turned seventy-five, there had been a nice party at the house in Westport that included a video greeting from Jimmy Carter. It would be tough to top that, but Joanne had some ideas.

One day a few years later Newman was using the men's room at a Broadway show, and a fellow beside him said, "I understand the Emerson String Quartet is playing for your eightieth birthday." "How do you know that?" Newman asked. "Because I play for the Emerson String Quartet," he replied. In fact, Joanne had made the arrangements two years before the big day, and when January 26, 2005, finally came, the Newmans celebrated at home once again with some seventy-five of their friends and family members.

AND STILL he refused to slow down, to stop moving forward. "I don't seem to be living up to my timetable" is how he put it.

In 2006, on the grounds of the newly renovated Westport Country Playhouse, he became a partner in the Dressing Room, a high-end organic restaurant that specialized in locally grown and raised food products and bore a certain casual elegance that Newman insisted upon. His partner was the successful young chef Michel Nischan, a ponytailed advocate of sustainable restaurant practices and, as it happened, a Westport resident. They were an unlikely pair—Nell Newman had actually introduced Nischan to her father in hopes that he would talk him *out* of his desire to get into the restaurant business. But they got along very well, each realizing after their initial meetings that they had the same vision in mind. "After I talked," Nischan recalled of his first proposal to Newman, "he got up and hugged me and said, 'That's what I want. Can you help us?' "

Each man invested $1.5 million, with Newman assuring an additional $500,000 to meet any overruns. They chose the menus together, with Newman insisting on his famous hamburger recipe and on pot roast made with brisket; Nischan instituted a strictly seasonal food-sourcing policy. Part of the profits from the Dressing Room would be funneled back into the Playhouse. But the opening of the restaurant was meant to revitalize downtown Westport as well. The parking lot would be the site of a regular farmers market, for instance, and Newman was looking into holding go-kart races there. "Main Street used to be filled with small, individually owned, resident-owned businesses," he said. "Now it's Cartier and the Gap, and they have no hook into this community. We're going to try and make this place a Main Street again."

He loved buzzing about the restaurant, kibitzing about the hamburger buns, banning steak from the menu, trying different desserts. ("It looks like a turd on the plate," he said of a chocolate soup, "but it's delicious.") And if the idea that they could see those famous blue eyes enjoying a meal enticed diners into the place, the very idea that the boss was a living legend could rattle the staff. "Not long ago," recalled Nischan, "one of the girls got so nervous that he went over and put his arm around her and said, 'You know, if you pinch me I say ouch.' "

IN FACT, he was ambivalent about the iconic stature that he had achieved and that could fluster a young waitress. On the one hand he was contemptuous because so much of it depended on the vagaries of fortune. "Living legend?" he sneered to an interviewer. "All right, then. But what do I have to do with that? The answer is 'very fucking little.' "

At the same time, he was genuinely concerned that the position he had reached, whether deserved or not, belonged to him and his heirs and his charities, to deploy and exploit and profit from, and to nobody else. He had seen the power of putting his face on a bottle of salad dressing, and he didn't want the fruits of such a brazen act to fall to anyone but the parties he chose. In 2006 and 2007 he appeared before the judiciary committee of the Connecticut state legislature to lobby for a law protecting the images of public figures as a kind of property,

a so-called "right of publicity." In particular, he and his fellow witnesses Christopher Plummer, Charles Grodin, and James Naughton
were concerned about the new technologies that gave anyone the ability to manipulate, duplicate, alter, or misrepresent the public images of
celebrities. "What I am talking about is ownership of self," Newman
said in his testimony. "To me, that is nothing less than theft."

But he was opposed in both legislative sessions by such filmmaking
interests as NBC Universal, Sony Entertainment, and the Motion Picture Association of America. Twice the bill died when the session
ended without its coming to a vote.

Which, of course, simply meant that, eternal terrier, he would have
to come back and give it another try.

Twenty-seven

J UST AS HE HAD ALWAYS ENJOYED PLAYING KNAVES AND HANGING with the boys and acting like it was an ordeal to present himself as anything more than scruffy or comfortable, so he enjoyed becoming a codger who was entitled to fuss and slough off decorum—within limits, of course.

In addition to burning his tuxedo, as he claimed, he had taken to wearing a pair of cheaters on a string around his neck (and not some fussy designer glasses, either, but cheap pairs of specs sometimes held together with tape), and among his favorite fashion accessories was a black ball cap with gold letters reading "Old Guys Rule." He cut such a dubious figure, in fact, that good friends could sometimes fail to recognize him. One evening in the summer of 2007 he was headed to the Manhattan celebrity watering hole Elaine's for a party celebrating A. E. Hotchner's upcoming nuptials, and he had some trouble opening the door to the place. Elaine Kaufman, the famously cantankerous owner, noticed a scraggly fellow trying to get inside her restaurant and braced for action. "I saw some guy fumbling with the door," she remembered. "I thought it was one of the Second Avenue drunks. I was about to tell him to hit the road, but it turned out to be Newman."

He loved moments like that, and he bragged about the effects of his advanced years, quoting Bette Davis's saw that "old age is no place for sissies." When a reporter inquired about his health, he responded with pride, "I go to the doctor once a year to have my face scraped. All the rough edges—it's sore as hell. It's what they call a precancerous growth.

One of those choice things that come with age." Another journalist was surprised to encounter him in tears. "My eyes have no tolerance for cold anymore," he explained. "I was just out on the terrace. People think I'm filled with poignant memories."

But in truth these were minor physical limitations in a vital and active man. He still walked or rode a stationary bike most days, and he still lifted weights. When he was in a hotel in a strange city (he preferred to check in under the alias Mr. Leonard), he could often be found getting his daily exercise by climbing the stairs. He liked to talk himself down—"I'm a dinosaur: antediluvian, antiquated. I mean, I'm on my last legs." But he still carried a great deal of force, decisiveness, and authority.

One thing that had changed, those close to him noticed, was that he didn't seem to feel so defensive about the space between the person who he considered himself to truly be and the person defined by his celebrity. "I'm more comfortable in my own skin," he admitted. "I don't scurry for cover these days." He even gave the occasional autograph with a smile and no complaint. He had mellowed. Some.

But he was realistic. He knew that he couldn't keep on as he had forever, perhaps not even for very long, and he made plans for when he would be unable to see to everything he wished to. He transferred his partnership stake in Newman's Own to the Newman's Own Foundation, effectively making a charitable donation of his portion of a thriving business. He did it in two installments: the first in 2004 was valued at $76.6 million; the second, the following year, was valued at $40.374 million. The foundation had already given away upward of $250 million in its first twenty-five years. When it eventually disbursed this infusion of $117 million, the sum would push close to $400 million.*

Some of the gifts he oversaw in this period were massive, such as the $10 million he donated to Kenyon College to establish a scholar-

---

* Not long before this, he and Joanne began the practice of sending Christmas cards to friends with a note that read "We have more than we need. Call this number and tell my assistant your favorite charity. I'll try not to embarrass you." Donations of $5,000 and $10,000 typically followed. This wasn't Newman's Own money, but, rather, Newman's *own* money.

ship fund for minorities and underrepresented groups. And some were equally staggering because they were so particular, personal, and unheralded. In July 2007 he sent a check for $5,000 to the drama club of Ypsilanti High School in Michigan in response to a letter of solicitation—one of thousands the Newman's Own offices received each year—for help raising funds so that the students could perform at the Fringe Festival in Edinburgh, Scotland. "The enclosed contribution is sent with every good wish for continued success in your worthy endeavors," a note accompanying the check read. It was no surprise at all that he was a charter member in 2007 when *BusinessWeek* magazine decided to select names for a Philanthropic Hall of Fame.

AND HE was still working, although only in the mode of *Cars*—with his voice rather than in person. He narrated *Dale*, a full-length documentary about stock-car legend Dale Earnhardt that proved to be the most-watched program ever in the history of Country Music Television, the cable network that produced it. He narrated *The Price of Sugar*, also a documentary, which advocated for fair trade practices in Caribbean agriculture. And he narrated *The Meerkats*, yet another documentary, about the little mongoosy critters that were a cult favorite at the time among children his grandsons' ages.

But real acting, that was another proposition. He'd been talking about a swan song—something with Joanne, perhaps, or more beguilingly, a reunion with Robert Redford. The latter would have been the holy grail of buddy movies, and there was no shortage of interest in seeing it happen—and indeed, in being the person who managed to pull it off. Richard Russo had an idea. "I came up with not quite ten pages of the first draft of a script," he said. "It had a couple of roguish characters and a very unique start. And I showed them to Robert Benton and I sent them to Paul. And he called me up and said he liked them but that he just didn't feel like he could give the work the level of quality that he would want to. And I spoke to Benton later, and we agreed that if he got his teeth into the right script he would be back in a flash. He just wasn't looking at the right stuff."

Screenwriter John Fusco also entered the sweepstakes with a script

called *The Highwaymen*, a western about a retired gunfighter drawn re-
luctantly by an old partner into one last job. Newman, Fusco recalled,
had a real feel for the character. "This guy just doesn't want to do it,"
Newman said at a script conference in his New York apartment.
"When Bob [Redford] comes looking for him, he runs the other way.
Maybe he locks himself in the shithouse and hides. He just *doesn't want
to do it.* But he's got a duty." There was genuine promise in the air, but
someone at the studio had the idea to rewrite the script that Newman
had read, and when he saw the new version, he pulled out.

In 2005 it felt like the reunion might finally happen. Redford
bought the rights to *A Walk in the Woods*, humorist Bill Bryson's account of a hiking trip taken in middle age in the company of a crusty
pal. The book deals with issues of mortality, environmentalism, and
friendship in a light and ironic fashion that seemed perfect for the pair.
Scripts were drafted; directors were approached. (Barry Levinson was
rumored to be on top of the short list.) But the process of development
didn't move quickly enough. In the summer of 2007, according to
Redford, this iteration of the project died. "It's not happening, sadly,"
he said in an interview. "We couldn't decide if we were too old to do it.
Then we decided, let's go for it. But time passed, and Paul's been getting older fast. I think things deteriorated for him. Finally, two months
ago, he called and said, 'I gotta retire.' The picture was written and
everything. It breaks my heart."

Soon after that phone call Newman let the world in on a secret.
Talking with ABC News about organic farming and the restaurant
business for a piece about the Dressing Room, he dropped a bomb-
shell: he was through with acting. "I'm not able to work anymore as an
actor at the level I would want to," he said. "You start to lose your
memory, your confidence, your invention. So that's pretty much a
closed book for me. I've been doing it for fifty years. That's enough."

Actually it was longer than that: sixty years after winning the role of
Hildy Johnson in a Kenyon College production of *The Front Page*, after
fifty-eight movies and five Broadway plays and ten Oscar nominations
and a score, perhaps, of indelible roles, he was done being an actor.

H<small>E</small> <small>MADE</small> his regular tours of Hole in the Wall Camps that summer, and he followed the fortunes of Newman-Haas-Lanigan, and he ran some races of his own, and he gave Barbara Walters a good scare by whipping her around Lime Rock as part of a TV special about aging in which he looked old but hale.

As autumn approached, though, he felt poorly, and he let Joanne and his daughters know about it. He saw doctors, and worrying reports about shortness of breath and limited mobility started to circulate among friends and in gossip columns. Newman, naturally, said nothing, but it was noted that he wasn't seen around Westport as often as previously.

In January, just as he and Joanne prepared to celebrate their fiftieth wedding anniversary, a supermarket tabloid reported that he had undergone cancer surgery—for lung cancer, specifically—and that his prognosis was poor. Warren Cowan, still fielding media queries for his longtime client and friend as he himself neared eighty-seven years of age, issued a denial of the story, in which Newman declared, "I'm being treated for athlete's foot and hair loss. Maybe the doctors know something I don't." That same month, another tabloid reported chatting with him as he left the Dressing Room after dinner one evening. "As you can see, I'm doing okay," he said when asked if the reports of his ill health were true. "It's all this good hometown food I eat that keeps me going."

On the twenty-sixth he reached his eighty-third birthday; on the twenty-ninth he and Joanne marked their golden anniversary. As ever, these were family events, although celebrated in a decidedly lower key than they had been in the past. Tenderly, Newman toasted Joanne before their children and their dearest friends. "I feel privileged to love that woman," he said. "That I am married to her is the joy of my life."

In February the Westport Country Playhouse announced its 2008 season, and among the shows in preparation was an adaptation of John Steinbeck's *Of Mice and Men* that would mark Newman's professional debut as a stage director. But the hopefulness of that prospect was undercut just a few weeks later when he was a no-show at a fundraising event for the Hole in the Wall Camps. This time Cowan's office claimed that he'd "been having trouble with his back." But reports were popping up in newspaper gossip columns that he had been seen in the waiting rooms of oncologists' offices in New York, looking frail, sporting a stringy beard, keeping quietly to himself. There was talk of a late-night ambulance trip from his Westport home. There was even a flurry of confusion one day when a number of journalists and private citizens began phoning Newman's Own and the Hole in the Wall Association to ask if he had, in fact, died.

In April Newman wrote a new will, cementing plans to leave the majority of his estate to Joanne. There were other details seen to: selling his race cars and airplane to add to a trust fund he'd created; forgiving personal loans to his daughters and to a family employee; adding his Oscars and theatrical awards to the assets of Newman's Own Foundation; and very carefully stipulating how Newman's Own, the Hole in the Wall Gang organization, his racing teams, and other entities could use his name and likeness in the future. He initialed each page and signed it with a strong hand (as he did a codicil he added in July).

In May he made himself visible publicly for the first time in many months, showing up at the qualifying stage of the Indy 500, rooting on his new drivers, Graham Rahal and Justin Wilson. His appearance was shocking—almost unrecognizable. His face had acquired a little bit of jowliness as he hit his late seventies, but now it was all gone, and beneath the wisps of beard his jaw jutted out almost starkly. His hands seemed too bony to support his wristwatch or the CART championship ring he always wore, a gift from Nigel Mansell. His sweater dangled from his shoulders as if from a hanger. His pant legs seemed to stand up on their own as if there were nothing inside of them. Hale and healthy and seemingly younger than his years for so long, he had become a frail old man—one who had done great things, yes, but frail and old still.

It was a disconcerting sight, and Newman's words didn't offer much reassurance. At Indy he told a small press conference, "One thing we're looking forward to is winning this race. There are other races, and God knows eight championships is nothing to be sneezed at, but we'll be there one of these days. I may be someplace else watching from above, but we're going to win this one way or the other."

It would have been hard to put a shiny spin on such words emanating from such a gaunt fellow. And unfortunately no one was in a position to do even that much. Cowan had himself been fighting cancer, and just as the worst fears for Newman's health seemed to be confirmed, no reassuring responses were coming from his office. Just one week after Newman spoke at Indy, Cowan died. A week after that the Westport Country Playhouse announced that Newman would be unable to direct *Of Mice and Men* in the fall. And in early June Newman was photographed once again, standing beside Martha Stewart at a charity function at her Westport home and looking as frail as he had in Indianapolis.

Now the mainstream press picked up the story. The Associated Press got A. E. Hotchner on the phone, and he confirmed that Newman was battling cancer and that it was a back-and-forth struggle. "He's doing all the right stuff," he said. "Paul is a fighter. He seems to be going through a good period right now. Everybody is hopeful. That's all we know." Two other close associates were contacted: James Naughton told the wire service, "I think he's feeling quite well," and Michael Brockman agreed: "I think he's doing better than he was. I think he looks great. I wish I looked that good." An official statement from Cowan's successor declared that Newman was "doing nicely"—a classic nondenial. The following day Hotchner tried to backpedal by denying he had used the word *cancer* when initially contacted. (The AP stood by its account.) But now the word was out, and no one doubted it: Newman was dying. It was just a matter of time.

He made calls to longtime friends and chatted, as if he had merely been curious about how they were doing and was taking a moment to check in. He was drinking milk shakes, trying to put on some weight. He was traveling back and forth between New York, where he was being treated by doctors, and Westport, where he was given ease. A very select few friends and associates came by to see him, including Robert Redford, who recalled, "He'd been in and out of the hospital. I knew what the deal was, and he knew what the deal was, and we didn't talk about it. We talked about what was on our minds: the election, politics, what needed to be done. Ours was a relationship that didn't need a lot of words."

In August he was photographed leaving Memorial Sloan-Kettering Cancer Center in Manhattan in a wheelchair, and word surfaced that he had told Joanne and his daughters and his doctors that he wanted no more chemotherapy, that he was prepared to go home to Westport and see out his illness and his life. On the thirteenth of that month Lime Rock Park was shut to the public for a few hours so that Newman could gun around it in the Corvette that his team had prepared for him that spring in hopes that he would be able to run a couple of races during the season. Joanne and the girls rode behind him in the Volvo station wagon with the V-8 under the hood.

Later that month he visited the original Hole in the Wall Camp in Ashford one last time. He and Joanne toured the grounds in a golf cart and then ate sandwiches at a table beside the pond. "All of a sudden," remembered Ray Lamontagne, the camp director, "Paul looked up with this look of joy on his face. He said, 'I can still hear the laughter of the children!' "

Back in Westport in the coming weeks, Joanne kept up her scheduled tasks with the Playhouse and the daily chores of the household. And in a crucial way, their lives together changed. He used to joke about being driven around by her—"When we start out together and I'm driving, she always says, 'Now, we're not in a hurry, are we?' When we start out together and she's driving, I always say, 'Now, we're not in a hurry.' They're for different reasons." But now she was the one driving him, and he would sit in the car while she ran errands around town or bought corn from a roadside vegetable stand. In September she attended a fund-raising gala at the Playhouse in the company of such notables as Angela Lansbury, Julia Roberts, James Earl Jones, and Bernadette Peters. A few days later she attended an antique-car show at a nearby country club. Newman had been meant to accompany her to both events, but he stayed home.

And it was at home, on the afternoon of Friday, September 26, that he died.

WORD TRICKLED out in the way it did in the age of instant media: in a bunch of disparate places seemingly at once and from no single source.

Awards Daily, an inside-showbiz blog, was first with an uncredited report stating simply, "Paul Newman has died," citing a confidential but supposedly reliable tipster; the notice was live on the site only for a few hours late Friday night before disappearing, as if it had been another false alarm. A few hours later the director of the Hole in the Wall camp in Italy declared to a staff meeting that he had received an e-mail telling him, "Paul Newman is no longer with us." News of these words was published on the websites of several Italian newspapers and then echoed similarly in Spain and France.

At approximately nine A.M. Connecticut time on Saturday morning, a press release was issued by Newman's Own Foundation; Newman's passing wasn't explicitly acknowledged, but he was referred to in the past tense. The notice declared, "Paul Newman's craft was acting. His passion was racing. His love was his family and friends. And his heart and soul were dedicated to helping make the world a better place for all."

Similar press releases from the Hole in the Wall Gang camps and the Westport Country Playhouse followed. Late in the day an official obituary was released. And then there was a statement from his five daughters, which said, in part, "Paul Newman played many unforgettable roles. But the ones for which he was proudest never had top billing on the marquee. Devoted husband. Loving father. Adoring grandfather. Dedicated philanthropist . . . He will be profoundly missed by those whose lives he touched, but he leaves us with extraordinary inspiration to draw upon."

The response was overwhelming. The many reports of his ill health meant that news agencies all over the world had prepared full obituaries in advance of the inevitable. Within twenty-four hours more than five thousand news stories about Newman appeared online in the English language alone. On Sunday's front pages almost every major newspaper in the United States marked his passing with a lengthy, biography-size account of his days and works. There were appreciations of his film and stage performances; there were reminiscences of his decades of racing; there were stories about his food businesses and the charitable largesse that flowed from them. The newspapers of little towns where Newman had made films or driven in races or helped build camps for ailing children seemed all to run articles filled with anecdotes about his visits. In the towns in which he'd lived—Cleveland,

New York, Los Angeles, Westport—neighbors spoke to newspapers of his desire to remain an ordinary man despite his extraordinary fame and deeds. State news agencies around the world, including those in such unlikely places as Iran and Cuba, marked his passing.

There was an official statement from Art Newman, who described himself and his wife as "devastated," adding "Paul was my loyal and supportive brother for the past eighty-three years. Although he was a year younger, for the time we were boys I always considered him my role model and mentor . . . He was just about the best human being I have ever known."

Tributes poured in from Hollywood. "Sometimes God makes perfect people, and Paul Newman was one of them," said Sally Field. "I loved that man with all my heart," declared Elizabeth Taylor. "Everything about Paul Newman was real," Gene Hackman said. "He was always a hero of mine both as an actor and as a man," offered Tim Robbins. And George Clooney suggested, "He set the bar too high for the rest of us. Not just actors, but all of us."

Throughout the world of auto racing, his teammates, colleagues, and competitors offered heartfelt condolences and fond memories. "His pure joy at winning a pole position or winning a race exemplified the spirit he brought to his life and to all those that knew him," said Carl Haas. "He was a man of class," remarked Bobby Rahal, "and he was also deservedly very highly regarded for his driving skills." "He could not only talk the talk on film," added Jack Roush, "but, more important, he could walk the walk as a private citizen."

A. E. Hotchner, who knew him longer and better than almost anybody, said, "Paul was an unadorned man. He was simple and direct and honest and off-center and mischievous and romantic and very handsome . . . He was the same man in 2008 that he was in 1956—unchanged, despite all the honors and the movie stardom." Tom Cruise wrote a tribute to his costar and mentor in an issue of *People* magazine that had Newman's face on its cover. Robert Redford did the same in an issue of *Time*.

In the pages of the *New York Times*, artistic and charitable organizations wishing to memorialize Newman bought so many classified obituaries that new ones appeared for four days. On the Internet

Newman-Haas-Lanigan, Newman's Own, the Hole in the Wall Camps Association, and Kenyon College all published memorials that included pictures, video clips, and official statements. (On the Kenyon campus itself flags were lowered to half-staff, and the chapel bells were rung forty-nine times in commemoration of the year of Newman's graduation.) National broadcast and cable networks prepared tributes, including expanded versions of a biographical documentary on the Biography Channel and an all-day festival of representative films on Turner Classic Movies. Video store shelves were emptied by renters eager to see *The Hustler, Cool Hand Luke, The Sting, Slap Shot, The Verdict,* and *Nobody's Fool* while the memory of their star was still vivid. Broadway theater owners made plans to dim their marquee lights for three minutes on an upcoming evening in Newman's memory. An auction was held on eBay for a special helmet worn during the summer by Graham Rahal, then racing for Newman-Haas; decorated with images of Newman's movie posters, it fetched $40,900 for one of the Hole in the Wall camps.

In Syracuse, New York, a minor-league hockey team made plans to retire the number 7 jersey of the fictional Reggie Dunlop, whom Newman had portrayed on the team's ice three decades earlier. In San Francisco a benefit performance for a Hole in the Wall Camp— passages of Ernest Hemingway read by the likes of Julia Roberts, Tom Hanks, Jack Nicholson, Sean Penn, and Warren Beatty—was turned into a memorial tribute. In Westport the production of *Of Mice and Men* that he was to have directed was dedicated to him, and the announcement of his name was greeted with standing ovations at each performance. At Lime Rock Park officials considered a monument in his honor, or perhaps naming a stretch of the track for him, although there was, one admitted, "no corner that he always went off of." In March 2009, the U.S. Congress passed a resolution honoring his "humanitarian works and incomparable talents."

On the day of his passing, as the news spread, members of the public wishing to pay respects left flowers on Newman's star on the Hollywood Walk of Fame, but people who tried to leave similar remembrances at the Westport Country Playhouse were met with a sign asking them to make donations to the Hole in the Wall Camps instead. Elsewhere in town a remembrance book—*Our Town Remembers Paul Newman*—was made available to Westporters who wished to inscribe their memories and good thoughts. Reporters gathered near the Newmans' house but kept a respectful distance; a pair of police cars stood by to keep order, needlessly.

Inside, the family made plans according with Newman's wishes: cremation and a private memorial service, followed by a gathering at the Dressing Room, and then eventually the scattering of ashes, perhaps on the pond at the first Hole in the Wall Camp. On Saturday afternoon Lissy Newman, wearing one of her father's "Old Guys Rule" caps, emerged to speak to TV cameras on what was her own forty-seventh birthday. "He was just incredible," she said of his final days. "We're really blessed and very, very lucky. We had awesome people helping us and—it was as beautiful as it could be." Like others, she summed up her father's life not by his film work or his racing career or his entrepreneurism but by his charitable deeds. "Just look out for each other," she said. "That's what he was all about . . . So many of his ideas were reaching out. I think that's what he'd like people to remember."

Lissy's call to charitable action underscored the overriding theme of the coverage of Newman's death. As much as they noted the passing of the gorgeous man, the devoted husband, the accomplished performer, the iconic movie star, the steely driver, and the puckish food entrepreneur, the obituaries took special note of the man of charity and philanthropy who had done so much for so many, particularly the ailing children who attended the Hole in the Wall camps.

At his passing the world stopped, despite a presidential election season and an economic crisis, to pay due homage to a fine and rare individual. The sheer volume of death notices, and their universal sentiment of respect and tribute, made it evident that the world had lost more than an actor. Indeed, the tone of reverence would surely have made Newman uncomfortable if he'd heard it.

During those long months of sickness, he had come, in fact, to see himself not as a major artist or a great man but rather as someone who had simply given back the least bit of what had been granted him. He believed that his legacy would not be found in films or photographs or racing trophies or salad dressings or even the stack of heartfelt obituaries and memorials. Rather, he felt, it was those camps, and the affirmation, comfort, hope, rebirth, and freedom they afforded all those endangered children, that were his greatest accomplishment. And for the opportunity to help those children he felt not so much pride as gratitude.

In helping others, he said, "I wanted, I think, to acknowledge Luck: the chance of it, the benevolence of it in my life, and the brutality of it in the lives of others: made especially savage for children because they may not be allowed the good fortune of a lifetime to correct it." And that, he was sure, would be the best reason for remembering him.

The entire string of his life—the remarkable eyes and metabolism, his comfortable home, the high caliber of his schooling, the fortune to survive a war, the career opportunities that fell to him, the serendipity to meet and wed a true life partner, the achievement of one-in-a-billion stardom, the high-speed realization of his athletic potential, the whimsical success of his business empire, the decades of good health— all of it, he reckoned, could be thought of merely as the fruit of a lucky streak of many decades.

He wouldn't have wanted all the fuss. But then he had learned before the end to be appreciative. Just days before he succumbed, sitting in the garden at Westport with his daughters, he spoke his last recorded words and revealed how he felt about it all.

For full effect, his thoughts would have to be spoken aloud in an early autumn light, in a verdant setting, among family, and in the husky notes of his voice as it sounded in those last years. Barring that, the words alone could carry all the precious weight he put into them: "It's been a privilege to be here."

Notes

Introduction

10: "He's probably" — Jim Murray, "Perfect for the Part," *Los Angeles Times*, November 24, 1976.

10: "I don't think" — Denise Worrell, *Icons: Intimate Portraits* (New York: Atlantic Monthly Press, 1989), p. 81.

10: "The toughest role" — Vernon Scott, "Paul Newman, Sex Symbol," *Cleveland Press*, April 16, 1971.

One

15: "a cloister" — Charles Hamblett, *Paul Newman* (Chicago: Henry Regnery, 1975), p. 6.

25: "My mother" — "Barbara Walters' Last Interview with Paul Newman," ABCNews.com.

26: "That didn't really take" — Hamblett, *Newman*, p. 2.

Two

28: "pooh-pooh" — Peter S. Greenberg, "*Playboy* Interview: Paul Newman," *Playboy*, April 1983.

28: "lakes and forests" — Charles Hamblett, *Paul Newman* (Chicago: Henry Regnery, 1975), p. 5.

29: "In high school" — Aaron Latham, "Paul Newman Takes the Stand," *Rolling Stone*, January 20, 1983.

29: "beautiful little boy . . . yodeled" — Julian Krawcheck, "In College Days and After, Paul Newman Sold Himself," *Cleveland Press*, June 4–6, 1959.

29:    "I didn't like it" — Lillian Ross and Helen Ross, *The Player: A Profile of an Art* (New York: Simon and Schuster, 1962), p. 239.

29:    "frustrated actress" — Edwin Miller, "What's Behind Those Beautiful Blue Eyes?," *Seventeen*, November 1970.

31:    "I don't know that we ever connected" — Jess Cagle, "Two for the Road," *Time*, July 8, 2002.

31:    "uncommunicative . . . undemonstrative" — Bob Thomas, "Paul Newman: His Life Story," *Good Housekeeping*, May 1979.

31:    "six days a week" — Greenberg, "*Playboy* Interview."

32:    "an informal way" — Hamblett, *Newman*, p. 5.

32:    "when I was a kid" — "In Newman's Own Words," *Good Housekeeping*, May 1995.

32:    "Judeo-Christian" — Hamblett, *Newman*, p. 2.

32:    "baseball glove" — Ibid., p. 3.

32:    "toss-up" — Krawcheck, "In College Days."

33:    "felt the pinch" — Thomas, "Life Story."

34:    "never heard my father" — Ibid.

35:    "stage-managed" — Ross and Ross, *Player*, p. 240.

36:    "quaff a few" — Joy Ream, "Stalking the Newman Legend," *Athens*, Spring 1973.

36:    "A date" — Greenberg, "*Playboy* Interview."

36:    "Gus" — Ream, "Stalking."

THREE

38:    "couldn't wait" — Lillian Ross and Helen Ross, *The Player: A Profile of an Art* (New York: Simon and Schuster, 1962), p. 240.

38:    "uniform" — Aaron Latham, "Paul Newman Takes the Stand," *Rolling Stone*, January 20, 1983.

39:    "errors in altimeters" — Dick Wells, "Interview: Paul Newman," *Motor Trend*, August 1970.

39:    "potshots" — Latham, "Takes the Stand."

40:    "a copy of Nietzsche" — Gore Vidal, *Palimpsest: A Memoir* (New York: Random House, 1995), p. 270.

41:    "There I was" — "Paul Newman's Getting More Beautiful As He Grows Older," *National Star*, October 14, 1975.

41:    "My father wrote" — John Skow, "Verdict on a Superstar," *Time*, December 6, 1982.

42:    "one of the worst" — Grover Lewis, "The Redoubtable Mr. Newman," *Rolling Stone*, July 5, 1973.

46:    "A bunch of us" — Ibid.

47:   "Almost everybody" — Dan Groberg, "Paul Newman '49," *Kenyon Collegian*, October 2, 2008.

47:   "The beer cost me" — Jane Wilson, "Paul Newman: 'What If My Eyes Turn Brown?' " *Saturday Evening Post*, February 24, 1968.

48:   "One day a stallion" — Peter S. Greenberg, "*Playboy* Interview: Paul Newman," *Playboy*, April 1983.

49:   "worst college actors" — Ross and Ross, *Player*, p. 241.

49:   "He took that stage" — Groberg, "Newman '49."

Four

53:   "a deal with his family" — Joe Morella and Edward Z. Epstein, *Paul and Joanne: A Biography of Paul Newman and Joanne Woodward* (New York: Delacorte Press, 1988), p. 8.

54:   "I grew up" — Charles Hamblett, "The Private World of Paul Newman," *Woman* [U.K.], 1972.

54:   "I wasn't 'searching' " — Paul Newman Oral History, Columbia University Oral History Research Collection, June 1959.

54:   "I think the only thing" — Ibid.

59:   "He treated me" — John Skow, "Verdict on a Superstar," *Time*, December 6, 1982.

60:   "Paul worked hard" — Julian Krawcheck, "In College Days and After, Paul Newman Sold Himself," *Cleveland Press*, June 4–6, 1959.

62:   "I had no stars" — Newman Oral History.

63:   "The machinery" — Ibid.

63:   "The muscles" — Peter S. Greenberg, "*Playboy* Interview: Paul Newman," *Playboy*, April 1983.

64:   "I was terrorized" — Skow, "Verdict."

64:   "If you talk" — Greenberg, "*Playboy* Interview."

64:   "I like to think" — Charles Hamblett, *Paul Newman* (Chicago: Henry Regnery, 1975), p. 24.

65:   "I was prepared" — Lillian Ross and Helen Ross, *The Player: A Profile of an Art* (New York: Simon and Schuster, 1962), p. 242.

Five

71:   "I had one decent suit" — Lillian Ross and Helen Ross, *The Player: A Profile of an Art* (New York: Simon and Schuster, 1962), p. 243.

71:   "For the strange" — Richard Christiansen, "Paul Newman: Down-to-Earth Superstar," *Youngstown Vindicator*, November 26, 1978.

72:   "Boy, there was work" — Nikki Finke, "Sentimental Favorites," *Los Angeles Times*, March 15, 1987.

72:   "I heard a lot" — Ross and Ross, *Player*, p. 242.

75:   "When I did my first scene" — Jane Wilson, "Paul Newman: 'What If My Eyes Turn Brown?' " *Saturday Evening Post*, February 24, 1968.

75:   "Lee can be destructive" — Paul Newman Oral History, Columbia University Oral History Research Collection, June 1959.

76:   "primarily a cerebral actor" — Ross and Ross, *Player*, p. 243.

77:   "Bill always had" — Joe Morella and Edward Z. Epstein, *Paul and Joanne: A Biography of Paul Newman and Joanne Woodward* (New York: Delacorte Press, 1988), p. 19.

78:   "I had it for about four days" — Gordon Gow, "Involvement," *Films and Filming*, March 1973.

Six

80:   "I had been making the rounds" and "Jeez" — Gene Shalit, "Joanne & Paul: Their Lives Together and Apart," *Ladies Home Journal*, July 1975.

81:   "My mother tells" — Joanne Woodward Oral History, Columbia University Oral History Research Collection, June 1959.

82:   "Sandy Meisner discovered" — Ibid.

82:   "For two years" — Joe Morella and Edward Z. Epstein, *Paul and Joanne: A Biography of Paul Newman and Joanne Woodward* (New York: Delacorte Press, 1988), p. 17.

83:   "twelve-year-old girl" — Woodward Oral History.

85:   "I could just as easily" — Louella O. Parsons, "The Paul Newmans: 'We Love Working Together,' " *Los Angeles Herald-Examiner*, February 3, 1963.

87:   "When I first saw him" — William Glover, "Paul Newmans Now Teamed on a Stage," *Newark Evening News*, April 12, 1964.

87:   "The fashion" — Morella and Epstein, *Paul and Joanne*, p. 17.

88:   "I can remember" — Bob Thomas, "Haunted by the Shadow of His Dad, Paul Newman," *New York Post*, March 29, 1982.

88:   "Jackie lost her interest" — Kirtley Baskette, "Joanne Woodward and Paul Newman," *Redbook*, February 1959.

88:   "From the beginning" — Alan Ebert, "The Private Woodward," *Lear's*, September 1989.

Seven

92:   "I had a lot of people" — Paul Newman Oral History, Columbia University Oral History Research Collection, June 1959.

93:   " 'Have you ever thought' " — Ibid.

94: "That was the last" — Lee Eisenberg, "Him with His Foot to the Floor," *Esquire*, June 1988.

95: "I was flailing" — Lillian Ross and Helen Ross, *The Player: A Profile of an Art* (New York: Simon and Schuster, 1962), p. 244.

95: "Three weeks after" — Richard Warren Lewis, "Waiting for a Horse: Paul Newman Makes a Western," *New York Times Sunday Magazine*, November 6, 1966.

98: "About 10 of us" — Roy Newquist, *"Playboy* Interview: Paul Newman," *Playboy*, July 1968.

98: "I was horrified" — Craig Modderno, "Paul Newman: An Exclusive Portrait," *Playgirl*, June 1980.

100: "I like to nail those guys" — Grover Lewis, "The Redoubtable Mr. Newman," *Rolling Stone*, July 5, 1973.

Eight

103: "Mr. Montgomery and I" — Paul Newman Oral History, Columbia University Oral History Research Collection, June 1959.

109: "He is the most aware" — Kent R. Brown, *The Screenwriter as Collaborator: The Career of Stewart Stern* (New York: Arno Press, 1980), p. 123.

110: "I'm still convinced" — Peter S. Greenberg, *"Playboy* Interview: Paul Newman," *Playboy*, April 1983.

111: "There were two things" — Newman Oral History.

115: "They say you can take" — Greenberg, "Playboy Interview."

116: "more of an ordeal" — Kirtley Baskette, "Joanne Woodward and Paul Newman," *Redbook*, February 1959.

Nine

120: "One time I remembered" — Roy Newquist, *"Playboy* Interview: Paul Newman," *Playboy*, July 1968.

121: "That was a painful experience" — Paul Newman Oral History, Columbia University Oral History Research Collection, June 1959.

121: "I had grave misgivings" — Newman Oral History.

122: "The house was full of people" — Gore Vidal, *Palimpsest: A Memoir* (New York: Random House, 1995), p. 296.

123: "He sees what he thinks" — Fred Kaplan, *Gore Vidal: A Biography* (New York: Doubleday, 1999), p. 417.

124: "The horse and I" — Richard Christiansen, "Paul Newman: Down-to-Earth Superstar," *Youngstown Vindicator,* November 26, 1978.

124: "I lived in a bunkhouse" — Graham Fuller, "The Outsider as Insider," *Interview*, March 1998.

124: "Somewhere along the line" — Newman Oral History.

125: "It helped me" — Peter S. Greenberg, *"Playboy* Interview: Paul Newman," *Playboy*, April 1983.

126: "She was tougher" — Gabriel Miller, ed., *Martin Ritt Interviews* (Jackson: University Press of Mississippi, 2002), p. 144.

126: "The newspaper editor" — Newman Oral History.

127: "I said to him one day" — Miller, *Ritt Interviews*, p. 166.

128: "Orson and I" — Newman Oral History.

128: "Three could sleep" — Newquist, *"Playboy* Interview."

131: "It wouldn't be fair" — Kirtley Baskette, "Joanne Woodward and Paul Newman," *Redbook*, February 1959.

131: "What happened to us" — Greenberg, *"Playboy* Interview."

Ten

133: "There were no tourists" — Charles Hamblett, *Paul Newman* (Chicago: Henry Regnery, 1975), p. 73.

134: "That very nice doctor" — Fred Kaplan, *Gore Vidal: A Biography* (New York: Doubleday, 1999), p. 439.

134: "I'm in my pajamas" — Kitty Hanson, "Stranger in Hollywood," *New York Daily News*, April 4, 5, 6, 1962.

135: "You son of a bitch" — George Stevens Jr., *Conversations with the Great Moviemakers of Hollywood's Golden Age* (New York: Alfred A. Knopf, 2006), p. 552.

136: "If I had an infinite" — Mason Wiley and Damien Bona, *Inside Oscar: The Unofficial History of the Academy Awards* (New York: Ballantine Books, 1987), p. 283.

136: "Acclaim is the false aspect" — John Skow, "Verdict on a Superstar," *Time*, December 6, 1982.

137: "In Hollywood" — Joanne Woodward Oral History, Columbia University Oral History Research Collection, June 1959.

137: "I was raised" — Alan Ebert, "The Private Woodward," *Lear's*, September 1989.

139: "Wasserman was a master" — Lynn Hirschberg, "Has Paul Newman Finally Grown Up?" *New York*, December 12, 1994.

140: "This was my first crack" — Paul Newman Oral History, Columbia University Oral History Research Office, June 1959.

141: "The mistake that you make" — Ibid.

142: "I was so amazed" — Ibid.

143: "Whenever he would give me" — Leonard Probst, "Talking with Paul Newman," *Atlantic*, November 1975.

145: "A baby was always" — Peer J. Oppenheimer, "The Paul Newmans Fight for Their Marriage," *Hollywood Citizen-News*, October 9, 1960.

146: "He waited" — Hirschberg, "Grown Up?"

146: "I have a recurring nightmare" — Erin James, "Paul Newman: At Home with Himself," *Saturday Evening Post*, October 1977.

147: "Paul hasn't had" — Sidney Blackmer Oral History, Columbia University Oral History Research Collection.

Eleven

149: "I'm two people" — Sidney Skolsky, "Tintyped: Paul Newman," *New York Post Magazine*, May 19, 1963.

153: "If he doesn't like something" — Muriel Davidson, "Joanne Woodward Tells All about Paul Newman," *Good Housekeeping*, February 1969.

154: "For me" — Lillian Ross and Helen Ross, *The Player: A Profile of an Art* (New York: Simon and Schuster, 1962), p. 240.

154: "If I were a dog" — Peter S. Greenberg, "*Playboy* Interview: Paul Newman," *Playboy*, April 1983.

154: "John Foreman" — Ibid.

154: "I know that I can function" — Donna Chernin, "Paul Newman," *Cleveland Plain Dealer*, July 4, 1976.

154: "I am beginning to get sick" — Roddy McDowall, *Double Exposure* (New York: William Morrow & Co., 1990), p. 190.

154: "It isn't" — Chernin, "Newman."

154: "I'm glad" — McDowall, *Double Exposure*, p. 188.

156: "In order to be an actor" — Greenberg, "*Playboy* Interview."

156: "There's nothing" — Fred A. Bernstein, "Paul Newman," *People*, March 19, 1984.

157: "I've seen fan-magazine" — Roy Newquist, "*Playboy* Interview: Paul Newman," *Playboy*, July 1968.

Twelve

162: "He's got the reputation" — Grover Lewis, "The Redoubtable Mr. Newman," *Rolling Stone*, July 5, 1973.

162: "came to me one morning" — Muriel Davidson, "Joanne Woodward Tells All about Paul Newman," *Good Housekeeping*, February 1969.

163: "I could have directed" — Foster Hirsch, *Otto Preminger: The Man Who Would Be King* (New York: Alfred A. Knopf, 2007), p. 332.

163: "Israelis are movie mad" — Ninette Lyon, "Joanne Woodward and Paul Newman: A Second Fame: Good Food," *Vogue*, August 1965.

163: "They stand in front" — Roddy McDowall, *Double Exposure* (New York: William Morrow & Co., 1990), p. 190.

164: "The day we left" — Louella O. Parsons, "Joanne Woodward and Paul Newman: A Parisian Idyll," *Los Angeles Examiner*, August 27, 1961.

164: "I suppose" — Gabriel Miller, *The Films of Martin Ritt* (Jackson: University Press of Mississippi, 1995), p. 51.

167: "I think Robert Rossen" — Graham Fuller, "The Outsider as Insider," *Interview*, March 1998.

168: "I spent the first thirty" — Kitty Hanson, "Stranger in Hollywood," *New York Daily News*, April 4, 5, 6, 1962.

168: "I told Rossen" — Lewis, "Redoubtable."

172: "My husband behaved" — Davidson, "Woodward Tells All."

179: "I have steak" — Roy Newquist, "*Playboy* Interview: Paul Newman," *Playboy*, July 1968.

179: "She's like a classy" — Maureen Dowd, "Testing Himself," *New York Times Magazine*, September 28, 1986.

179: "He's an oddity" — Davidson, "Woodward Tells All."

179: "Paul has a sense" — John Skow, "Verdict on a Superstar," *Time*, December 6, 1982.

179: "They're peculiar" — Hanson, "Stranger."

180: "We haven't had to be" — Newquist, "*Playboy* Interview."

180: "For quite a while" — Davidson, "Woodward Tells All."

THIRTEEN

181: "I love it" — Patrick Goldstein, "Mel Shavelson: Hollywood from a Front-Row Seat," *Los Angeles Times*, May 1, 2007.

181: "I read it" — Aaron Latham, "Paul Newman Takes the Stand," *Rolling Stone*, January 20, 1983.

184: "I got a lot of letters" — Gabriel Miller, ed., *Martin Ritt Interviews* (Jackson: University Press of Mississippi, 2002), p. 66.

186: "Because I am a motion picture personality" — "Newman 'Won't Abdicate' Citizen's 'Responsibility' to Safeguard Career," *Variety*, June 21, 1963.

186: "We would like to hope" — "Four Actors Rebuffed in Alabama Deny 'Rabble-Rousing' Charges," *New York Times*, August 24, 1963.

188: "Lee was so happy" — Foster Hirsch, *A Method to Their Madness: The History of the Actors Studio* (New York: Da Capo Press, 1984), p. 280.

188: "Paul bent over" — "Cool Hand Paul," *Time*, January 23, 1967.

191: "I tried brown" — Jeff Dawson, "Paul Newman Begins to See His Legacy," *Daily Breeze*, June 5, 1998.

192: "She threw her sable" — Tom Burke, "Paul Newman," *Cosmopolitan*, January 1983.

193: "I said, 'How are ya?'" — Roy Newquist, *"Playboy* Interview: Paul Newman," *Playboy*, July 1968.

195: "The first day of production" — Donald Spoto, *The Dark Side of Genius: The Life of Alfred Hitchcock* (New York: Little, Brown, 1983), p. 519.

196: "in a mood of quiet outrage" — Peter Bogdanovich, "Is That Ticking (Pause) a Bomb?" *New York Times*, April 11, 1999.

197: "He just lost his heart" — Spoto, *Dark Side*, p. 519.

197: "I always say" — Vincent Canby, "Hitchcock on Job Selling New Film," *New York Times*, July 7, 1966.

198: "We had to wait hours" — Newquist, *"Playboy* Interview."

Fourteen

200: "I seem to play" — Charles Champlin, "No Blinkers on This Private Eye," *Los Angeles Times*, August 18, 1965.

201: "My father, my uncle" — Bob Thomas, "Paul Newman: His Life Story," *Good Housekeeping*, May 1979.

201: "He got to be twenty-nine" — Robert Daley, "Paul Newman: How Turning 40 Changed His Marriage," *Coronet*, October 1971.

202: "He's forty-four" — *New York Times*, October 19, 1969.

205: "larger and more heavily built" — Jane Wilson, "Paul Newman: 'What If My Eyes Turn Brown?'" *Saturday Evening Post*, February 24, 1968.

207: "We needed a place" — "The Factory," *Time*, March 15, 1968.

208: "You can't really appreciate" — Amy Longsdorf, *Allentown Morning Call*, April 9, 2000.

208: "When Paul is angry" — Thomas, "Life Story."

209: "He is the most private" — John Skow, "Verdict on a Superstar," *Time*, December 6, 1982.

209: "If you have success" — Bob Ivry, "Making It Look Easy," *Bergen Record*, March 1, 1998.

209: "The thing I've never figured out" — Maureen Dowd, "Testing Himself," *New York Times Magazine*, September 28, 1986.

211: "I got involved in it" — Michael Billington, "The Thinking Man's Outdoor Hero," *Times* [London], August 2, 1969.

212: "because of difficulty" — Pat McGilligan, *Backstory 2: Interviews with Screenwriters of the 1940s and 1950s* (Berkeley: University of California Press, 1991), p. 301.

212: "I got total rejection" — Roger Ebert, "Newman's Complaint," *Esquire*, September 1969.

212: "I'm curious" — Wilson, "What If My Eyes."

212: "He's the only man" — Joan Barthel, "Paul Newman: How I Spent My Summer Vacation," *New York Times*, October 22, 1967.

213: "There was some talk" — Billington, "Outdoor Hero."

213: "I called them together" — Roy Newquist, *"Playboy* Interview: Paul Newman," *Playboy*, July 1968.

214: "He's sometimes stymied" — Wilson, "What If My Eyes."

214: "My motto" — David Castell, "Why Paul Newman Is Still Hollywood's Blue-Eyed Boy," *Films Illustrated*, December 1972.

214: "We have the same acting" — Abe Greenberg, "Paul Newman Tells About His New Career," *Hollywood Citizen-News*, November 4, 1967.

215: "Dede Allen" — McGilligan, *Backstory 2*, p. 301.

216: "Paul knew as much" — "George Kennedy (AKA Dragline) Dishes on Paul Newman in *Cool Hand Luke*," *Entertainment Weekly*, September 30, 2008.

FIFTEEN

219: "Hey Paul" — Bob Thomas, "Paul Newman: His Life Story," *Good Housekeeping*, May 1979.

220: "I've admired the man" — Roy Newquist, *"Playboy* Interview: Paul Newman," *Playboy*, July 1968.

220: "I am not a public speaker" — E. W. Kenworthy, "Paul Newman Drawing Crowds in McCarthy Indiana Campaign," *New York Times*, April 22, 1968.

221: "What did [the cop] think" — Roger Ebert, "Newman's Complaint," *Esquire*, September 1969.

223: "Now, listen, you queer" — Fred Kaplan, *Gore Vidal: A Biography* (New York: Doubleday, 1999), p. 602.

223: "I come wheeling" — Richard Weidman Oral History, Columbia University Oral History Research Collection.

224: "We blew the convention" — Ebert, "Complaint."

224: "I've got sort of a short" — Ibid.

224: "I can barely" — Peter S. Greenberg, *"Playboy* Interview: Paul Newman," *Playboy*, April 1983.

225: "He had a chance" — Thomas, "Life Story."

226: "I had so much" — Joseph Bell, "Paul Newman: Activist and Pessimist," *Rochester Democrat and Chronicle*, December 7, 1969.

226: "I hope it's successful" — Rex Reed, "The Doug and Mary of the Jet Age," *New York Times*, September 1, 1968.

226: "Four critics walked out" — Ebert, "Complaint."

226: "I couldn't have been" — Mason Wiley and Damien Bona, *Inside Oscar: The Unofficial History of the Academy Awards* (New York: Ballantine Books, 1987), p. 421.

233: "Suppose I liked it" — Tom Burke, "Redford: 'I Like Fighters,' " *New York Times*, October 26, 1969.

233: "Redford never intellectualizes" — Martha Weinman Lear, "Anatomy of a Sex Symbol," *New York Times*, July 7, 1974.

237: "It's a way to really" — Bell, "Activist and Pessimist."

Sixteen

240: "I finally said to myself" — All Nancy Bacon quotes are from Bacon, *Stars in My Eyes . . . Stars in My Bed* (New York: Pinnacle, 1975), and from an interview by the author.

245: "There aren't many" — Peter Bart, "Newman Fought for His Convictions," *Variety*, September 29, 2008.

248: " 'You need twenty setups' " — Leonard Probst, "Talking with Paul Newman," *Atlantic*, November 1975.

248: "I drank whiskey" — Peter S. Greenberg, "*Playboy* Interview: Paul Newman," *Playboy*, April 1983.

249: "Those schmucks" — Shaun Considine, "The Effect of 'Gamma Rays' on the Newmans," *After Dark*, March 1973.

250: "His face is so handsome" — Candice Bergen, "The Cool-Sex Boys," *Vogue*, October 1971.

252: "Joanne *never* brings" — Lee Eisenberg, "Him with His Foot to the Floor," *Esquire*, June 1988.

255: "My one great regret" — Bob Thomas, "Paul Newman: His Life Story," *Good Housekeeping*, May 1979.

256: "Children like" — "The Paul Newmans' Not-So-Perfect Marriage," *McCall's*, November 1980.

257: "I think that I experimented" — Gene Shalit, "Joanne & Paul: Their Lives Together and Apart," *Ladies Home Journal*, July 1975.

258: "For chrissakes" — Ibid.

Seventeen

261: "The name didn't register" — Jane Gross, "Paul Newman, Race Driver," *New York Times*, July 2, 1979.

262: "It is dangerous" — Earl Wilson, "Paul Newman Just Loves Racing Cars," *New York Post*, January 23, 1971.

263: "He drove it smoothly" — Sam Posey, "The Perils of Paul," *Sports Illustrated*, August 25, 1980.

265: "I'm not a professional" — Brock Yates, "Cool Hand Luke Meets Luigi," *Sports Illustrated*, October 7, 1974.

266: "There's an awful strong sense" — Shawn Courchesne, "Newman Found Grace, Accomplishment at Wheel," *Hartford Courant*, September 28, 2008.

269: "I always felt very" — Lawrence Grobel, *The Hustons: The Life and Times of a Hollywood Dynasty* (New York: Cooper Square Press, 2000), p. 643.

269: "among the gods" — John Huston, *An Open Book* (New York: Ballantine Books, 1981), p. 382.

269: "I was vaguely ashamed" — Grobel, *Hustons*, p. 662.

272: "I certainly don't feel" — Aaron Latham, "Paul Newman Takes the Stand," *Rolling Stone*, January 20, 1983.

273: "The trick was" — Jamie Malanowski, "Shaping Words into an Oscar: Six Writers Who Did," *New York Times*, March 18, 2001.

275: "It was just dumb" — Abe Greenberg, "Paul Newman Tells About His New Career," *Hollywood Citizen-News*, November 4, 1967.

Eighteen

281: "You go into the kitchen" — Leonard Probst, "Talking with Paul Newman," *Atlantic*, November 1975.

283: "*Towering Inferno* was" — Clarke Taylor, "Paul Newman: Star on Ice," *Cosmopolitan*, February 1977.

286: "he complains" — Marilyn Beck, *Cleveland Plain Dealer*, July 23, 1976.

291: "The thing that I'm concerned about" — Probst, "Talking."

291: "My teeth hurt" — Gene Shalit, "Joanne & Paul: Their Lives Together and Apart," *Ladies Home Journal*, July 1975.

292: "Neither of us" — Bob Thomas, "Paul Newman: His Life Story," *Good Housekeeping*, May 1979.

293: "Newman has something" — Sam Posey, "The Perils of Paul," *Sports Illustrated*, August 25, 1980.

295: "They were insufferable" — Gordon Kirby, "Paul Newman: Talking Racing with the Academy Award–Winning Actor," *Road & Track*, January 2005.

Nineteen

298: "Nell . . . also got into drugs"—"The Paul Newmans' Not-So-Perfect Marriage," *McCall's*, November 1980.

299: "The terrific part" — Clarke Taylor, "Paul Newman: Star on Ice," *Cosmopolitan*, February 1977.

300: "It was hard" — Vernon Scott, "For Paul Newman, It's the Public That's Tough," *Los Angeles Daily News,* June 22, 1976.

300: "Isn't the movie business" — Bob Thomas, "Paul Newman: His Life Story," *Good Housekeeping,* May 1979.

301: "It's interesting to watch" — Taylor, "Star on Ice."

301: "I'll tell you one thing" — Ibid.

310: "There are liabilities" — Maureen Dowd, "Testing Himself," *New York Times Magazine,* September 28, 1986.

311: "Scott was a big" — Dinitia Smith, "A Star in Twilight Turns Reflective," *New York Times,* March 1, 1998.

311: "Don't you know" — Kathy Cronkite, *On the Edge of the Spotlight: Celebrities' Children Speak About Their Lives* (New York: William Morrow & Co., 1981), p. 19.

311: "terrorized by the idea" — Bob Thomas, "Haunted by the Shadow of His Dad, Paul Newman," *New York Post,* March 29, 1982.

313: "In a way" — Peter S. Greenberg, "*Playboy* Interview: Paul Newman," *Playboy,* April 1983.

313: "You know, for someone" — Dennis Hamill, "Newman's Own 'Twilight,' " *Los Angeles Daily News,* March 1, 1998.

314: "I think Scott" — Nancy Spiller, "Brother's Death Inspires Susan Newman's Life Work," *Los Angeles Herald-Examiner,* October 9, 1986.

315: "I remember" — Cronkite, *Edge of Spotlight,* pp. 302–5.

TWENTY

317: "I've smoked grass" — Peter S. Greenberg, "*Playboy* Interview: Paul Newman," *Playboy,* April 1983.

318: "Maybe it would have been" — "The Paul Newmans' Not So Perfect Marriage," *McCall's,* November 1980.

318: "This may sound corny" — *Playboy,* April 1983.

319: "The biggest problem" — Timothy Carlson, "Paul Newman and Daughter Give USC Center $1.2 Million to Fight Drug Abuse," *Los Angeles Herald-Examiner,* April 2, 1985.

319: "Losing my virginity" — "Susan Newman Is Making It, in Spite, She Says, of Being Paul's Daughter," *People,* July 17, 1978.

319: "That predisposition" — Nancy Spiller, "Brother's Death Inspires Susan Newman's Life Work," *Los Angeles Herald-Examiner,* October 9, 1986.

320: "In the last year" — Aaron Latham, "Paul Newman Takes the Stand," *Rolling Stone,* January 20, 1983.

320: "We got together" — Robin Brantley, "The Uneasy Odyssey of 'The Shadow Box,' " *New York Times,* December 28, 1980.

321: "I'm an actress" — Aljean Harmetz, "A Rainy Day at Camp 'Shadow Box,' " *TV Guide*, July 19, 1980.

323: "You get two appraisals" — Charles Champlin, "Hot, Sexy and (Almost) 70," *Los Angeles Times*, November 18, 1994.

326: "It is not a racist" — Richard F. Shephard, "Newman Rebuts 'Apache' Bias Charge," *New York Times*, April 8, 1980.

329: "had to push" — Susan Wloszczyna, "A Legend with a Soft Heart and Sharp Wit," *USA Today*, March 27, 1995.

329: "The movie was a direct" — Latham, "Takes the Stand."

330: "I was always" — Maureen Dowd, "Testing Himself," *New York Times Magazine*, September 28, 1986.

Twenty-one

334: "He is an enthusiastic" — Sidney Skolsky, "Tintypes: Paul Newman," *Hollywood Citizen-News*, July 19, 1956.

334: "It was one" — John Skow, "Verdict on a Superstar," *Time*, December 6, 1982.

335: "He was off" — Ron Hogan, "*PW* Talks with A. E. Hotchner: It's Not Just for the Money," *Publishers Weekly*, October 13, 2000.

336: "If your dressing" — Paul Newman and A. E. Hotchner, *Shameless Exploitation in Pursuit of the Common Good* (New York: Doubleday, 2003), p. 36.

339: "We won't meet" — Carol Lawson, "Paul Newman the Philanthropist: A Real-Life Role," *New York Times*, January 25, 1985.

339: "I begin to understand" — Graham Fuller, "The Outsider as Insider," *342*, March 1998.

342: "Why are you making" — Ivor Davis, "Shifting Gears in Mid-Life," *Philadelphia Inquirer*, November 2, 1980.

344: " 'At least seventy-five' " — Bill Dwyre, "Racing Loses a Cool Hand in Paul Newman," *Los Angeles Times*, September 28, 2008.

345: "She says I was getting" — Peter S. Greenberg, "*Playboy* Interview: Paul Newman," *Playboy*, April 1983.

346: "It's a relief" — Charles Champlin, "The Verdict on Paul Newman," *Los Angeles Times*, November 21, 1982.

347: "I told him" — Sidney Lumet, *Making Movies* (New York: Vintage, 1995), p. 60.

348: "He personally" — Ralph Tyler, "A New Newman," *On Cable*, April 1983.

350: "I thought it was stageworthy" — Fred A. Bernstein, "Paul Newman," *People*, March 19, 1984.

351: "The name Scott Newman" — Ibid.

352: "Joanne was working" — David Ansen, "The Big Hustle," *Newsweek*, October 13, 1986.

353: "In the last, I don't know" — Bob Ivry, "Making It Look Easy," *Bergen Record*, March 1, 1998.

TWENTY-TWO

354: "Wherever I look" — Roy Newquist, *"Playboy* Interview: Paul Newman," *Playboy*, July 1968.

355: "We're sitting there" — David Ansen, "The Big Hustle," *Newsweek*, October 13, 1986.

356: "As I kept telling" — David Thompson and Ian Christie, *Scorsese on Scorsese* (London: Faber and Faber, 1989), p. 106.

356: "Sometimes Newman would say" — Myra Forsberg, " 'The Color of Money': Three Men and a Sequel," *New York Times*, October 19, 1986.

357: "Everything was comprehensively" — Mary Pat Kelly, *Martin Scorsese: A Journey* (New York: Thunder's Mouth Press, 1991), p. 196.

358: "I keep thinking" — Ansen, "Hustle."

358: "We were walking" — Dinitia Smith, "A Star in Twilight Turns Reflective," *New York Times*, March 1, 1998.

359: "This KGB agent" — Maureen Dowd, "Testing Himself," *New York Times Magazine*, September 28, 1986.

361: "For a time" — Susan Mulcahy, *My Lips Are Sealed: Confessions of a Gossip Columnist* (New York: Doubleday, 1988), p. 84.

365: "That camp was" — Colneth Smiley Jr., "Paul Newman and Me: A Hole in the Wall Kid Remembers," *Boston Herald*, September 27, 2008.

365: "Two of the kids" — Renee Graham, "The Last Movie Star," *Boston Globe*, March 1, 1998.

369: "We talked a bit" — "Paul Newman, No Longer a Loser, Finally Hustles Up That Oscar for 'The Color of Money,' " *People*, April 13, 1987.

TWENTY-FOUR

384: "It's like a puritanical" — Larry Rohter, "The Road to Critical Mass," *New York Times*, October 15, 1989.

387: "You don't know how shitty" — Robert Scheer, "The Further Adventures of Paul Newman," *Esquire*, October 1989.

388: "You could describe" — Larry Rohter, "Crossing the Bridges with the Newmans," *New York Times*, November 18, 1990.

389: "It's the only film" — Aljean Harmetz, "Partnerships Make a Movie," *New York Times*, February 18, 1990.

389: "We told Paul" — Peter Biskind, *Down and Dirty Pictures* (New York: Simon and Schuster, 2004), p. 89.

393: "I think he's a hero" — John Clark, "Strange Bedfellows," *Premiere*, April 1994.

394: "I would have been struggling" — Lynn Hirschberg, "Has Paul Newman Finally Grown Up?" *New York*, December 12, 1994.

396: "Robert Benton called me" — *USA Today*, October 12, 1999.

399: "You don't have to give" — Peggy R. Townsend, "The Newmans' Own," *Santa Cruz County Sentinel*, May 30, 1999.

399: "She's cornered" — Douglas J. Rowe, "Paul Newman, the Actor, Talks Business," *Cleveland Plain Dealer*, February 21, 1999.

399: "We were all on pins" — Kim Severson, "Newman Grown," *San Francisco Chronicle*, October 21, 2001.

400: "Everything had to be" — Kim Severson, "And Then There Was the Food," *New York Times*, October 1, 2008.

Twenty-five

402: "I really don't want" — "On Being Susan Newman: A Daughter's Perspective," *Us Weekly*, January 23, 1979.

405: "I wrote a little" — Robert Scheer, "The Further Adventures of Paul Newman," *Esquire*, October 1989.

408: "He put his arm" — "Schreiber Admires Newman's Marriage," *PR Newswire*, January 9, 2007.

408: "I didn't go to Harvard" — Dan Hulbert, "New Man at 73," *Atlanta Journal and Constitution*, March 1, 1998.

409: "He realized" — Amy Longsdorf, "After 55 Movies, Paul Newman Is Still in His Salad Days," *Allentown Morning Call*, April 9, 2000.

409: "You know, he really is" — Rick Lyman, "Newman's New Buddy," *New York Times*, April 14, 2000.

411: "He shuffled about" — Sam Mendes, "He Was at Peace with Death. He Knew How Fortunate He'd Been," *Guardian* [U.K.], October 4, 2008.

411: "There's something so comforting" — Rick Lyman, "No Goons in Spats, No Rat-a-Tat-Tat Dialogue," *New York Times*, July 14, 2002.

411: "This guy Mendes" — *CNN Sunday Morning*, July 14, 2002.

411: "Paul can do" — Jess Cagle, "Two for the Road," *Time*, July 8, 2002.

412: "We respected" — Ibid.

412: "He wants to know" — Duane Dudek, "Paul Newman," *Milwaukie Sentinel-Journal* (reprinted), September 27, 2008.

412: "Paul had this very clear" — Lyman, "No Goons."

413: "I turned around" — Mendes, "At Peace with Death."

415: "The damage" — Gordon Kirby, "Paul Newman: Talking Racing with the Academy Award–Winning Actor," *Road & Track*, January 2005.

416: "My blood pressure" — Luaine Lee, "Newman Still Racing, Acting at 74," *Cleveland Plain Dealer*, April 18, 2000.

Twenty-six

417: "He gave her" — Dinitia Smith, "A Star in Twilight Turns Reflective," *New York Times*, March 1, 1998.

418: "There were times" — Alan Ebert, "The Private Woodward," *Lear's*, September 1989.

421: "People would see it" — Michael Smith, "Hanging with Paul Newman," *Tulsa World*, December 14, 2003.

427: "I'm a very competitive" — Peter Howell, "What Drives Paul?" *Toronto Star*, May 26, 2006.

427: "It's right" — Jess Cagle, "Two for the Road," *Time*, July 8, 2002.

428: "It's a '51" — Rob Driscoll, "Taking the Road to Success," *Western Mail* [U.K.], July 28, 2006.

429: "The nice thing" — Jeff Otto, "Interview: Paul Newman," movies.ign.com, June 9, 2006.

429: "You sit there" — Daniel Fienberg, " 'Cars' Voices Toot Their Horns," zap2it.com, June 8, 2006.

431: "Main Street" — Jason Zinoman, "Paul Newman's Next Act," *Food and Drink*, March 2007.

431: "Not long ago" — Bryan Miller, "Inside the Newmans' New Dressing Room," *New York Observer*, October 9, 2006.

431: "All right, then" — Jeff Jensen, "Killer Instinct," *Entertainment Weekly*, July 19, 2002.

Twenty-seven

433: "I saw some guy" — *New York Post*, July 29, 2007.

433: "I go to the doctor" — Scott Raab, "The Graceful Exit," *Esquire*, May 2000.

434: "My eyes" — Cal Fussman, "The Conversation: Paul Newman and Ed Harris," *Esquire*, June 2005.

436: "It's not happening" — *New York Post*, October 6, 2007.

440: "When we start out" — Jeff Chu, "Q&A Paul Newman," *Time*, June 12, 2006.

Bibliography

Newman Biographies and Memoirs

Godfrey, Lionel. *Paul Newman: Superstar.* New York: St. Martin's Press, 1978.

Hamblett, Charles. *Paul Newman.* Chicago: Henry Regnery, 1975.

Landry, J. C. *Paul Newman: An Illustrated Biography.* New York: McGraw-Hill, 1983.

Lax, Eric. *Paul Newman: A Biography.* Atlanta: Turner Books, 1996.

Morella, Joe, and Edward Z. Epstein. *Paul and Joanne: A Biography of Paul Newman and Joanne Woodward.* New York: Delacorte Press, 1988.

Netter, Susan. *Paul Newman and Joanne Woodward.* Toronto: Paperjacks, 1989.

Newman, Paul, and A. E. Hotchner. *Shameless Exploitation in Pursuit of the Common Good.* New York: Doubleday, 2003.

———. *Newman's Own Cookbook.* New York: Simon and Schuster, 1998.

O'Brien, Daniel. *Paul Newman.* London: Faber and Faber, 2004.

Oumano, Elena. *Paul Newman.* New York: St. Martin's Press, 1989.

Quirk, Lawrence J. *The Films of Paul Newman.* Secaucus, N.J.: Citadel Press, 1980.

———. *Paul Newman.* Dallas: Taylor, 1996.

Stern, Stewart. *No Tricks in My Pocket: Paul Newman Directs.* New York: Grove Weidenfeld, 1989.

Assorted Bibliography

Abramowitz, Rachel. *Is That a Gun in Your Pocket? Women's Experience of Power in Hollywood.* New York: Random House, 2000.

Bacon, Nancy. *Stars in My Eyes . . . Stars in My Bed.* New York: Pinnacle, 1975.

Biskind, Peter. *Easy Riders, Raging Bulls.* New York: Simon and Schuster, 1998.

———. *Down and Dirty Pictures.* New York: Simon and Schuster, 2004.

Buford, Kate. *Burt Lancaster: An American Life.* New York: Alfred A. Knopf, 2000.

Chandler, Charlotte. *I, Fellini.* New York: Random House, 1995.

Cronkite, Kathy. *On the Edge of the Spotlight: Celebrities' Children Speak About Their Lives.* New York: William Morrow & Co., 1981.

Dunne, Dominick. *The Way We Lived Then.* New York: Crown, 1999.

Farber, Stephen, and Mark Green. *Hollywood on the Couch: A Candid Look at the Overheated Love Affair Between Psychiatrists and Moviemakers.* New York: William Morrow & Co., 1993.

Garfield, David. *A Player's Place: The Story of the Actors Studio.* New York: Macmillan, 1980.

Gartner, Lloyd P. *History of the Jews of Cleveland.* Cleveland: Western Reserve Historical Society, 1978.

Goldman, William. *Adventures in the Screen Trade: A Personal View of Hollywood and Screenwriting.* New York: Warner Books, 1983.

Graham, Sheila. *Confessions of a Hollywood Columnist.* New York: William Morrow & Co., 1969.

Greenslade, Thomas B., Jr. *A Short History of Kenyon College.* Gambier, Ohio: Kenyon, 1997.

Grobel, Lawrence. *The Hustons: The Life and Times of a Hollywood Dynasty.* New York: Cooper Square Press, 2000.

Harwood, Herbert H., Jr. *Invisible Giants: The Empires of Cleveland's Van Swearingen Brothers.* Bloomington: Indiana University Press, 2003.

Henry, William A., III. *The Great One: The Life and Legend of Jackie Gleason.* New York: Doubleday, 1992.

Hethmon, Robert H., ed. *Strasberg at the Actors Studio.* New York: Viking Press, 1965.

Hirsch, Foster. *A Method to Their Madness: The History of the Actors Studio.* New York: Da Capo Press, 1984.

Horton, Andrew. *The Films of George Roy Hill*, rev. ed. Jefferson, N.C.: McFarland, 2005.

Huston, John. *An Open Book.* New York: Ballantine Books, 1981.

Jackson, Carlton. *Picking Up the Tab: The Life and Movies of Martin Ritt.* Bowling Green, Ohio: Bowling Green State University Popular Press, 1994.

Jones, Gerard. *Men of Tomorrow: Geeks, Gangsters and the Birth of the Comic Book.* New York: Basic Books, 2004.

Kaplan, Fred. *Gore Vidal: A Biography.* New York: Doubleday, 1999.

Kelly, Mary Pat. *Martin Scorsese: A Journey.* New York: Thunder's Mouth Press, 1991.

Lambert, Gavin. *Natalie Wood: A Life.* New York: Alfred A. Knopf, 2004.

Levy, Donald. *Report on the Location of Ethnic Groups in Cleveland.* Cleveland: Institute of Urban Studies, Cleveland State University, 1972.

Lumet, Sidney. *Making Movies.* New York: Vintage, 1995.

Macdonald, Dwight. *On Movies.* Englewood Cliffs, N.J.: Prentice Hall, 1969.

Manso, Peter. *Brando: The Biography.* New York: Hyperion, 1994.

Marshall, Bruce T. *Shaker Heights. Images of America.* Chicago: Arcadia Press, 2006.

McDougal, Dennis. *The Last Mogul: Lew Wasserman, MCA, and the Hidden History of Hollywood.* New York: Crown, 1998.

McDowall, Roddy. *Double Exposure.* New York: William Morrow & Co., 1990.

McGilligan, Pat. *Backstory 2: Interviews with Screenwriters of the 1940s and 1950s.* Berkeley: University of California Press, 1991.

McMurtry, Larry. *In a Narrow Grave: Essays on Texas.* Albuquerque: University of New Mexico Press, 1983.

Miller, Carol Poh, and Robert A. Wheeler. *Cleveland: A Concise History, 1796–1996.* Bloomington: Indiana University Press, 1997.

Miller, Gabriel. *The Films of Martin Ritt.* Jackson: University Press of Mississippi, 1995.

———, ed. *Martin Ritt Interviews.* Jackson: University Press of Mississippi, 2002.

Mordden, Ethan. *Medium Cool: The Movies of the 1960s.* New York: Alfred A. Knopf, 1990.

Mulcahy, Susan. *My Lips Are Sealed: Confessions of a Gossip Columnist.* New York: Doubleday, 1988.

My Hero Project. *My Hero: Extraordinary People on the Heroes Who Inspired Them.* New York: Free Press, 2005.

Oldenburg, Chloe Warner. *Leaps of Faith: History of the Cleveland Play House, 1915–85.* Cleveland: Cleveland Play House and the George Gund Foundation, 1985.

Papp, Susan. *Hungarian Americans and Their Communities of Cleveland.* Cleveland: Cleveland State University, 1981.

Phillips, Julia. *You'll Never Eat Lunch in This Town Again.* New York: Random House, 1991.

Reed, Rex. *People Here Are Crazy.* New York: Dell, 1974.

Rose, William Ganson. *Cleveland: The Making of a City.* New York: World, 1950.

Ross, Lillian, and Helen Ross. *The Player: A Profile of an Art.* New York: Simon and Schuster, 1962.

Rubenstein, Judah. *Merging Traditions: Jewish Life in Cleveland.* Kent, Ohio: Kent State University Press, 2004.

Sahl, Mort. *Heartland.* New York: Harcourt Brace Jovanovich, 1976.

Schickel, Richard. *Elia Kazan: A Biography.* New York: HarperCollins, 2005.

Shores, Edward. *George Roy Hill.* Boston: Twayne, 1983.

Somerset-Ward, Richard. *An American Theater: The Story of Westport Country Playhouse.* New Haven: Yale University Press, 2005.

Spada, James. *Peter Lawford: The Man Who Kept the Secrets.* New York: Bantam, 1991.

Spoto, Donald. *The Dark Side of Genius: The Life of Alfred Hitchcock.* New York: Little, Brown, 1983.

Strasberg, Lee. *A Dream of Passion: The Development of the Method.* New York: Plume, 1987.

Stevens, George, Jr. *Conversations with the Great Moviemakers of Hollywood's Golden Age.* New York: Alfred A. Knopf, 2006.

Thompson, David, and Ian Christie. *Scorsese on Scorsese.* London: Faber and Faber, 1989.

Truffaut, François. *Hitchcock/Truffaut,* rev. ed. New York: Simon and Schuster, 1984.

———. *Correspondence, 1945–1984.* New York: Noonday Press, 1988.

Vidal, Gore. *Palimpsest: A Memoir.* New York: Random House, 1995.

———. *Point to Point Navigation: A Memoir, 1964–2006.* New York: Doubleday, 2006.

Vigil, Vicki Blum. *Finding Your Family History in Northeast Ohio.* Cleveland: Gray, 2003.

Vincent, Sidney Z., and Judah Rubenstein. *Merging Traditions: Jewish Life in Cleveland.* Cleveland: Western Reserve Historical Society, 1978.

Vineberg, Steve. *Method Actors: Three Generations of an American Acting Style.* New York: Schirmer Books, 1991.

Wiesenfeld, Leon. *Jewish Life in Cleveland in the 1920s and 1930s: The Memoirs of a Jewish Journalist.* Cleveland: Jewish Voice, 1965.

Wiley, Mason, and Damien Bona. *Inside Oscar: The Unofficial History of the Academy Awards.* New York: Ballantine Books, 1987.

Wise, James E., Jr., and Anne Collier Rehill, *Stars in Blue: Movie Actors in America's Sea Services.* Annapolis, Md.: Naval Institute Press, 1997.

Worrell, Denise. *Icons: Intimate Portraits.* New York: Atlantic Monthly Press, 1989.

Major Interviews

Ansen, David. "The Big Hustle." *Newsweek,* October 13, 1986.

———. "Newman's Own." *Newsweek,* December 19, 1994.

Baskette, Kirtley. "Joanne Woodward and Paul Newman." *Redbook,* February 1959.

Bean, Robin. "Success Begins at Forty." *Films and Filming,* January 1966.

Bell, Joseph. "Paul Newman: Activist and Pessimist." *Rochester Democrat and Chronicle,* December 7, 1969.

Billington, Michael. "The Thinking Man's Outdoor Hero." *Times* [London], August 2, 1969.

Cagle, Jess. "Two for the Road." *Time,* July 8, 2002.

Castell, David. "Why Paul Newman Is Still Hollywood's Blue-Eyed Boy." *Films Illustrated,* December 1972.

Champlin, Charles. "Hot, Sexy and (Almost) 70." *Los Angeles Times*, November 18, 1994.

Chernin, Donna. "Paul Newman." *Cleveland Plain Dealer*, July 4, 1976.

Christiansen, Richard. "Paul Newman: Down-to-Earth Superstar." *Youngstown Vindicator*, November 26, 1978.

Considine, Shaun. "The Effect of 'Gamma Rays' on the Newmans." *After Dark*, March 1973.

Davidson, Muriel. "Joanne Woodward Tells All About Paul Newman." *Good Housekeeping*, February 1969.

Davis, Ivor. "Shifting Gears in Mid-Life." *Philadelphia Inquirer Magazine*, November 2, 1980.

Dowd, Maureen. "Testing Himself." *New York Times Magazine*, September 28, 1986.

Ebert, Roger. "Newman's Complaint." *Esquire*, September 1969.

Eisenberg, Lee. "Him with His Foot to the Floor." *Esquire*, June 1988.

Gow, Gordon. "Involvement." *Films and Filming*, March 1973.

Greenberg, Peter S. *"Playboy* Interview: Paul Newman." *Playboy*, April 1983.

Hanson, Kitty. "Stranger in Hollywood." *New York Daily News*, April 4, 5, 6, 1962.

Hendrickson, Paul. "The Newmans: Fast Eddie and Eve in Paradise." *Washington Post*, December 6, 1992.

Hickey, Neil. *Cleveland Plain Dealer*, November 22, 1959.

Higham, Charles. "Paul Newman Gets High on Speed." *New York Times*, April 18, 1971.

Hirschberg, Lynn. "Has Paul Newman Finally Grown Up?" *New York*, December 12, 1994.

Hopper, Hedda. Unpublished draft interview, August 12, 1956.

———. Unpublished draft interview, January 4, 1959.

Kirby, Gordon. "Paul Newman." *Road & Track*, January 2005.

Kitman, Jamie Lincoln. "Blue Eyes on the Set, Blue Streak at the Wheel." *New York Times*, November 13, 1998.

Krawcheck, Julian. "In College Days and After, Paul Newman Sold Himself." *Cleveland Press*, June 6, 1959.

———. *Cleveland Press*, June 4, 1959.

Latham, Aaron. "Paul Newman Takes the Stand." *Rolling Stone*, January 20, 1983.

Lawson, Carol. "Paul Newman the Philanthropist: A Real-Life Role." *New York Times*, January 25, 1985.

Lewis, Grover. "The Redoubtable Mr. Newman." *Rolling Stone*, July 5, 1973.

Lewis, Richard Warren. "Waiting for a Horse: Paul Newman Makes a Western." *New York Times Sunday Magazine*, November 6, 1966.

Morgan, Al. "New Breed of Screen Lover." *Show Biz Illustrated*, February 1962.

Newquist, Roy. *"Playboy* Interview: Paul Newman." *Playboy,* July 1968.

Newman, Paul. Oral History. Oral History Research Office, Columbia University, June 1959.

Probst, Leonard. "Talking with Paul Newman." *Atlantic,* November 1975.

Rader, Dotson. "Why Paul Newman Came Back Home." *Parade,* October 28, 1990.

Richmond, Peter. "The Man Behind the Curtain." *GQ,* January 1995.

Shalit, Gene. "Joanne & Paul: Their Lives Together and Apart." *Ladies Home Journal,* July 1975.

Sheraton, Mimi. "Newman's Salad Dressing: Oil, Vinegar and Ballyhoo." *New York Times,* September 15, 1982.

Skow, John. "Verdict on a Superstar." *Time,* December 6, 1982.

Smith, Dinitia. "A Star in Twilight Turns Reflective." *New York Times,* March 1, 1998.

Taylor, Clark. "Paul Newman: Star on Ice." *Cosmopolitan,* February 1977.

"TW Interviews Paul Newman." *This Week,* April 13, 1969.

Thomas, Bob. "Paul Newman: His Life Story." *Good Housekeeping,* May 1979.

Tyler, Ralph. "A New Newman." *On Cable,* April 1983.

Wilson, Earl. "Paul Newman: Beer, Popcorn and Perception." *Los Angeles Mirror News,* May 9, 1959.

Wilson, Jane. "Paul Newman: 'What if My Eyes Turn Brown?' " *Saturday Evening Post,* February 24, 1968.

Woodward, Joanne. Oral History. Oral History Research Office, Columbia University, June 1959.

Zeithin, Arnold. "Clevelander Paul Newman Revels in His Return to the Broadway Stage." *Cleveland Plain Dealer,* April 13, 1959.

Acknowledgments

I never spoke with Paul Newman.

I wanted to; I tried.

I first got the idea to write this biography in late 2005 and was given a green light from Harmony Books the following spring. Not long after that I contacted Warren Cowan, who was still representing the Newmans in a public-relations capacity from his Los Angeles office. I introduced myself, told him what my project was about, and forwarded him a copy of the book proposal that I'd written for Harmony, describing my attitude toward Newman and his life. Warren thanked me for contacting him and being open about my project, and he informed me that he was "99 percent certain" that the Newmans would not be interested in participating. In fact, he asked his assistant to read the following statement to me, a bit of boilerplate the Newmans had prepared to deal with requests of the sort I was making:

> On January 26, 1995, which was my 70th birthday, Joanne and I resolved not to accept any more honors. Not, you understand, out of arrogance, just a mellow belief that we had been honored in gracious sufficiency and that more would constitute excess. As the daughter says in Thornton Wilder's *Our Town*, "Momma, am I pretty?" Momma replies, "You're pretty enough for all normal purposes." Joanne and I have been fortunate to be honored enough for all normal purposes.

As a matter of course, I called Cowan again about three weeks later and was told the Newmans were, in fact, not interested in assisting my book project. And then, just to be sure, I called back one last time, in about July 2007; once again I was told the door to Newman was closed. And then I began to hear that he was ill, and I determined to respect his privacy.

By that time I had done a lot of research: talking to colleagues, acquaintances, collaborators; sorting through previously published biographies of Newman and people he had known or worked with; reading histories of his hometown, his colleges, the Actors Studio, the Hollywood system; gathering and absorbing literally thousands of articles, interviews, archived papers, transcripts, letters, memos, and legal documents; watching films and TV shows and listening to audio recordings. I traveled to New York and Los Angeles and Cleveland and Gambier, Ohio, and added even more material about his days and deeds to my file cabinets, of which three full drawers were eventually filled with Newmaniana.

I kept up the hope that I would someday be able to speak with the man himself—if only to nail down some wobbly details that continually beguiled me. But I always suspected I'd never have the chance. So I did the next best thing: I assembled a massive interview with Newman out of the things he had told other interviewers. Starting with his family origins, continuing through his childhood and schooling, tracing his acting career from the start to the end, and touching on his marriages, his children, his homes, his habits, his racing career, his businesses, his politics, his philanthropy, and his health: his life, in his words, in chronological order, with the added benefit that he was often talking about things quite soon after experiencing or doing them. It was, in effect, the sort of soup-to-nuts interview that an authorized biographer might have gotten out of him: nearly forty thousand words' worth. True, I was relying on the work of previous writers—and on their accuracy, their ears, their instincts, and their interests—but barring access to the man himself, it seemed the next best thing.

Throughout the writing of this book, I used that massive collection of Newman's raw words as a road map and a tuning fork. I came to hear in those words his voice, as it were, quite vividly: repetitions, variations, inflections, confessions, lapses, elisions, evasions, favorite words, favorite stories. I developed a sense for when he was being open and when he was just doing the work of being interviewed. It wasn't the same as actually asking him questions, but it gave me a real feel for him.

I also spoke with about fifty people who knew Newman, if only briefly. Of course, without the blessing of the Newmans, there were many folks who weren't willing to talk to even the most respectful and best-intentioned author. For example, through mutual acquaintances I was granted an introduction to Stewart Stern, Newman's best man at his wedding to Joanne and a lifelong friend. He promptly and graciously told me that he wouldn't dream of participating in a project that his old friend hadn't authorized; but he pointed me toward some valuable resources, and I thank him for that.

Other friends and associates of Newman's were willing to talk to me only if they weren't cited or acknowledged, and I hereby thank them by respecting their wishes for anonymity. Among the interviewees and sources whom I'm free to name, I am obliged to Bob Ames, Nancy Bacon, Peggy Behrens, Pete Belov, Robert Benton, John Cohan, Brad Coley, John Considine, Jonathan Demme, Bill Demora, Todd Field, Barbara Fyfe, Jack Garfein, Joel Grey, Todd Haynes, Sally Kirkland, Hugh Leslie, Ted Mahar, John Malkovich, Peter McAlevey, Karin McPhail, Don Mitchell, Don Peasley, Arthur Penn, Richard Russo, Ron Shelton, Bill Tammeus, and Ted Walch.

Two folks I spoke with were especially helpful in supplying me with information and images: Sue Bronson and Kurt Wanieck. I was given valuable materials (or told how to get them) by Rosemary Acena, Roger Friedman, and Jon Ward. And I was led to specific interview sources by Laura Bobovski, Charlie Haddad, Gabriel Mendoza, Marc Mohan, Russ Smith, Janet Wainwright, and Mark Wigginton.

I'm especially grateful to Clint O'Connor of the *Cleveland Plain Dealer* for help in researching Newman's early years—and particularly for connecting me to childhood acquaintances of Newman's who still call northeastern Ohio their home. I'd also like to thank a few friends who passed along ideas, materials, tips on sources, or generally helpful vibes, including Doug Holm, Ray Pride, David Row, Mike Russell, Tom Sutpen, Willy Vlautin, and Jeffrey Wells.

I worked on this book using a number of archives and libraries, including the Multnomah County Library (especially its interlibrary loan service and the quiet rooms at its Hillsdale branch), the Margaret Herrick Library of the Motion Picture Academy of Arts and Sciences, the UCLA Film and Television Archive, the Humanities and Social Sciences Library of the New York Public Library, the Billy Rose Theater Division of the New York Public Library for the Performing Arts, the Oral History Research Office of Columbia University, the Cleveland Public Library, the Special Collections Department of the Cleveland State University Library, the Reference Department of the Western Reserve Historical Society, and the Special Collections and Archives Department of Kenyon College's Library and Information Services. I used any number of online archives, including Ancestry.com, the Encyclopedia of Cleveland History, Genealogy.com, Google News, the Internet Movie Database, LexisNexis, Rootsweb, and Wikipedia.

In Portland I was able to use three resources of the sort that make it the best city I can imagine in which to be a working writer: Powell's Books, which is bigger than a lot of libraries—and has better hours; Movie Madness, which had virtually every film Newman made on its shelves, along with some real rarities; and ActivSpace, where I was able to work cozily away in just about the perfect writer's garret.

Also in Portland I got access to some resources through my work at the *Oregonian,* and I have a great many people to thank there. The management of the newspaper were generous in allowing me to arrange my schedule to work on the book; I thank Fred Stickel, Sandra Rowe, Peter Bahtia, and Tom Whitehouse for their support. My editors were, as ever, exemplary: I thank Shawn Vitt, Grant Butler, and Jolene Krawczak for their unflagging patience and collegiality. And I haven't anything near the means to thank Barry Johnson for his peerless editorship, his long-lasting friendship, and especially his careful reading of the first third of the manuscript of this book—and his subsequent assurance that I would not be out of my mind to continue writing it.

As good a friend is Richard Pine, an exemplary sounding board, headshrinker, and businessman—just the qualities you want in an agent; thanks, too, to his colleagues at Inkwell Management.

I didn't know John Glusman when he commissioned the book from me, and he was patient, keen-eyed, and sure as an editor; I'm lucky to have gotten to work with him. Thanks as well to Anne Berry, Kate Kennedy, and the many other people at Harmony whom I've gotten to know only in the final weeks of my work, especially copy editor Janet Biehl, a great eye. I feel in very good hands.

My chief thanks go to my family. The kids—Vince, Anthony, and Paula—have always been cheerful and inspiring despite the mania that settles on their dad when he gets to work. And their mother, Mary Bartholemy, has demonstrated the most remarkable strength, loyalty, insight, patience, and care. I can't begin to compensate her for all she's done for me, taught me, and shared with me. All I can say is that without her I couldn't have created a page of this.

Index